Poindexter Monique

II				III			IV	V	VI
Physical 4	Cognitive 5	Communication 6	Creative 7	Self 8	Social 9	Guidance 10	Families 11	Program Management 12	Professionalism 13

Monique Poindexter

Essentials of Child Care and Early Education

Linda S. Estes

St. Charles Community College

PEARSON

Boston   New York   San Francisco
Mexico City   Montreal   Toronto   London   Madrid   Munich   Paris
Hong Kong   Singapore   Tokyo   Cape Town   Sydney

Series Editor: Traci Mueller
Series Editorial Assistant: Krista E. Price
Marketing Manager: Elizabeth Fogarty
Senior Production Editor: Annette Pagliaro
Editorial-Production Service: Trinity Publishers Services
Composition Buyer: Linda Cox
Manufacturing Buyer: Andrew Turso
Cover Administrator: Linda Knowles
Text Design: Denise Hoffman
Photo Research: PoYee Oster/Photoquick Research
Text Composition: Omegatype Typography, Inc.

For related titles and support materials, visit our online catalog at www.ablongman.com.

Between the time Web site information is gathered and then published, it is not unusual for some sites to have closed. Also, the transcription of URLs can result in unintended typographical errors. The publisher would appreciate notification where these errors occur so that they may be corrected in subsequent editions.

Library of Congress Cataloging-in-Publication Data

Estes, Linda S.
    Essentials of child care and early education / Linda S. Estes.
       p. cm.
    Includes bibliographical references and index.
    ISBN 0-205-34852-1 (pbk.)
    1. Child care. 2. Child development. 3. Early childhood education. 4. Early childhood teachers. 5. Home and school. I. Title.

HQ778.5.E85 2004
372.21—dc22

    2003054453

Printed in the United States of America

10 9 8 7 6 5 4 3 2 1   RRD-IN   08 07 06 05 04 03

Dedicated to the memory of my father,
Paul Joseph Allen (1928–2000).

I miss you, Dad.

Brief Contents

Contents

CHAPTER 3   The Cognitive Domain   42

CHAPTER 4   The Affective Domain   74

MODULE 2
Teachers in Early Childhood Education   101

CHAPTER 5   View of the Early Childhood Teacher   102

CHAPTER 6   Historical Foundations of Child Care and Early Education   122

CHAPTER 7   Contemporary Models of Early Care and Education   146

CHAPTER 8   Roles of Early Childhood Teachers   178

MODULE 3
The Emerging Learning Environment   199

CHAPTER 9   Developing Curriculum for Young Children   200

CHAPTER 10   Preparing the Climate of Early Care and Education Classrooms   222

CHAPTER 11   Safety, Health, and Nutrition for Young Children   240

MODULE 4
Connecting with Families and Communities   261

CHAPTER 12   Connecting with Families   262

Preface

This book, *Essentials of Child Care and Early Education,* provides a broad overview of the field of early care and education by focusing on four major areas of knowledge: child development, professional growth of teachers, early care and learning environments, and home-school-community connections. Taken together, these four modules provide a comprehensive education and training program for individuals who plan to work with children from birth to age 6.

Chapter content is based on current research and the recommendations of well-respected professional organizations such as the National Association for the Education of Young Children (NAEYC) and the Council for Exceptional Children/Division of Early Childhood (CEC/DEC). Additionally, chapter content reflects teacher competencies identified by the Council for Professional Recognition, the organization responsible for awarding the national Child Development Associate (CDA) credential. Within each chapter, CDA margin icons are used to identify specific competency goals and functional areas covered in each major section. The inside front cover of the book provides a CDA scope-and-sequence chart, which allows you to quickly and easily view the location of information pertaining to particular functional areas. At the end of the book, Appendix A provides a description of all of the CDA competency goals and their related functional areas. The NAEYC's position statement on linguistic and cultural diversity is provided as Appendix B.

Throughout the book, a number of pedagogical features are used to facilitate your success as a learner as you increase your awareness and level of knowledge about early care and education. For example, each chapter begins with a list of learning outcomes to focus your reading on key concepts and terms. Additionally, specialized terms are highlighted in bold print, and the definitions are provided in a glossary at the end of the book. Throughout the book, headings, tables, and figures are used to help you locate and review particular topics of information quickly. Bulleted chapter summaries help you review key concepts and terms before moving on to following chapters.

Other pedagogical features help you connect theory to practice and provide you with opportunities to reflect on significant issues in early childhood education. Throughout each chapter, quotations from philosophers, educators, social scientists, and other key individuals are provided to encourage discussion and critical thinking. Vignettes that explore practical, true-to-life examples of concepts and situations occur regularly throughout chapters to illustrate concepts and to prompt reflection on issues central to the care and education of young children. The Learning Activities feature at the end of each chapter is designed to encourage group discourse and active exploration of target concepts and skills.

Many chapter features offer the opportunity for self-directed learning so that you may personalize your studies and extend your pursuit of knowledge about early childhood education to the broader professional community. The Portfolio Artifacts feature suggests ways for you to document and reflect on your professional development as you broaden your awareness of contemporary child care and early education practices. End-of-chapter resources are included in the Professional Connections and Web Links and Suggestions for Further Reading features. These features provide many opportunities for pursuing special interests and networking with other professionals in the field. Reference sections at the end of each chapter supply other relevant sources.

It is my hope that this book will not only affirm your decision to become part of the child care and early education profession, but also strengthen your resolve to make a difference in the lives of young children and their families.

Acknowledgments

Many individuals have contributed to the production of this book. I would first like to acknowledge my family, especially my husband, daughter, and granddaughter, as well as my colleagues at St. Charles Community College, who were called to serve as amateur reviewers, editors, and sometimes typists. Additional thanks go to the students in my child care and early education courses, who participated in many of the activities included in the book.

My friend and research assistant, Amanda Landwehr, deserves special recognition for the many hours she spent churning out references and proofing seemingly endless pages of text. I would also like to acknowledge the contributions of Traci Mueller, editor at Allyn and Bacon, and Linda Bieze, the developmental editor, for their valuable feedback and steady encouragement as this book emerged.

In addition, I would like to extend thanks to the individuals who served as reviewers for sharing their expertise with me at various stages of the book's development. The reviewers were: Carolyn A. Beal, Southwestern Illinois College; Janie H. Humphries, Louisiana Tech University; Celeste Miller, Winona State University; Gayle Mindes, De Paul University; Linda Pickett, University of North Florida; and Carrie Whaley, Union University.

Author Biography

Linda Estes is a professor of child care and early education and has been actively engaged in the education of children for more than two decades, first as a classroom teacher, then as a program director, and most recently as a teacher educator. Over the years, she has continued to be both learner and teacher through her participation in preservice and inservice educational experiences with future generations of teachers who, likewise, dedicate themselves to the care and education of young children.

The Developing Child

*T*he trusting innocence of a sleeping infant, the playful antics of an active toddler, and the wide-eyed wonder of the young child are images that evoke a myriad of responses from adults. Infants and young children somehow hold inexplicable fascination for us. Perhaps it is the seeming perfection of the tiny fingers and toes of the newborn, or the charming, but toothless, grin of a four-month-old that reaches out and captures our fancy. Whatever the cause, adults have responded with enthusiasm to the arrival of each new generation.

Childhood is a journey, not a race.

—Anonymous

As a soon-to-be teacher, you may be fascinated with young children, and this may translate into an abiding curiosity about the developing child. Every encounter with children adds to your expanding knowledge of child development. Each experience contributes to your overall view of young children. Module One: The Developing Child provides you with information and opportunities to broaden your knowledge of the multifaceted field of child development.

The opening chapter provides an overview of the developing child and establishes a framework for understanding how the components of child growth and development fit together to portray the whole child. This chapter also examines how teachers use their knowledge of child development to provide quality care and education for young children. Subsequent chapters in the module explore multiple perspectives of human development. The chapters profile the sequential, interrelated nature of growth and development and discuss factors that influence development. In addition to providing in-depth information about child development, these chapters illustrate through vignettes that each child's development is unique.

Taken together, the four chapters of this module help you build personal understanding of the fascinatingly complex processes at work within the developing child. For it is through our greater understanding of child development that the essence of childhood can best be supported and appreciated.

View of the Whole Child

Fourteen-month-old Samantha stands with her feet slightly apart as she intently watches the antics of a small, striped kitten playfully batting a ball of yarn with its paw. Suddenly, the kitten pounces on the ball of yarn and then darts across the room and into the hallway. Samantha claps her hands together, giggles aloud, and takes a few tentative steps toward the hallway where the kitten disappeared.

This momentary glimpse of Samantha gives us information about several facets of her development. Physically, Samantha is able to visually focus on the kitten, clap her hands together, and walk. By following the kitten's path into the hallway Samantha demonstrates that she understands that the kitten still exists even when she cannot see it. We also get a hint at her stable emotional development when she shows enjoyment and fearlessly follows the kitten's path. By viewing the many facets of Samantha's development collectively, rather than separately, we obtain a realistic impression of her overall growth and development.

 he first years of life, including birth to age 5, encompass a remarkable period of growth and development in the lives of children. During the period of **early childhood**, defined as birth to age 8, children master important behaviors that they will use for the rest of their lives. This chapter explores the interrelationships among various components of development and offers a holistic view of young children. The process of human development occurs simultaneously, and each area of development, in turn, affects other areas of development. These interactions among areas of development contribute to the uniqueness of individuals. An amazing number of factors combine to produce a distinctly different timetable of development for each individual.

If we gather together a group of children of the same age we would observe similarities in their appearances, abilities, and interests; but no two children would be exactly alike. Although they would share the commonality of age, their development has not been determined by age alone, but by many overlapping factors resulting in a group of unique individuals. When development is portrayed holistically, a more realistic picture of the vibrancy of childhood is created.

Meeting the Needs of the Whole Child

A holistic view of children recognizes that the components of development overlap as they occur simultaneously and reciprocally (Bredekamp & Copple, 1997). For example, when infants observe interesting objects, they reach out and grasp the objects. The infants coordinate their muscle movements with information obtained through their senses in order to investigate their surroundings and build understandings of themselves, others, and their environments. When others respond to their explorations, infants experience social interactions and communication. Infants are holistically involved in playing, interacting, and exploring. Their naturally integrated activity serves to support their total development.

CDA

COMPETENCY GOAL II
• Functional Areas 4–7

For ease of study, psychologists and child development specialists group related areas of development into broader categories referred to as domains. Benjamin Bloom and other psychologists (Bloom & Krathwohl, 1956) spent a number of years labeling, defining, and organizing these diverse areas of growth and development into three **developmental domains.** Physical growth and maturation, as well as nervous system development, are part of the **psychomotor domain** (Harrow, 1972), while development of intellect and language are the **cognitive domain** (Bloom & Krathwohl, 1956). The third domain, which includes emotional, social, and moral development, is the **affective domain** (Krathwohl, Bloom, & Masia, 1964). Taken together, these domains include many of the factors that contribute to human growth and development. Exploring each of the developmental domains separately provides an organized method

> *Development in one domain influences and is influenced by development in other domains.*
>
> —Editors Sue Bredekamp and Carol Copple,
> *Developmentally Appropriate Practice in Early Childhood Programs* (1997, p. 12)

The interplay of biological and environmental influences contributes to developmental differences observed among children of the same age.

for learning about, observing, and understanding the complex process of human development. Later chapters in this module will provide in-depth explanations of each of the developmental domains as well as opportunities to investigate specialized theories of child development. However, even as we teachers of young children study the many factors that contribute to development, we must continually reconcile these factors with our holistic view of child development. The field of early care and education often uses the phrase "the **whole child**" to describe the ideal that children's development across the domains is both simultaneous and overlapping.

Knowing the typical sequence of development within each domain is essential for providing experiences for young children that are appropriate for their ages. However, knowing a child's age gives you only some of the information you need to determine appropriateness, because rates of development vary widely from one child to another. Many child development theorists attribute these variations in growth rate to the interplay of biological and environmental influences (Berk & Winsler, 1995; Forman & Kuscher, 1983; Gesell & Ames, 1956). They call effects of biological influences on development **maturation**; effects of environmental influences are called **experience**. Whether maturation or experience has more influence over development remains an ongoing discussion among biologists, psychologists, and educators. Sometimes called the **nature-nurture controversy**, the debate about the relative roles of maturation and experience in human development has been a topic of child development research for decades (Shonkoff & Phillips, 2000).

For early childhood practitioners, the nature-nurture discussion helps to explain how the dual influences of maturation and experience contribute to differences in development among individual children of the same age. When planning play and learning experiences for children, effective teachers consider chronological age (nature), as well as individual developmental levels (nature and nurture) (Bredekamp & Copple, 1997). Culture, which is influenced by both nature and nurture, is a third factor to consider when determining appropriateness of children's experiences. Broadly defined, **culture** refers to race, ethnicity, language, religion, gender, family structures, and value systems. Teachers can collect information about children's specific cultural influences from direct observation as well as other sources, such as family members who can provide relevant personal information (Bredekamp & Copple, 1997). Caregivers' knowledge of child development theories, combined with what they observe and learn from children's families, provides a comprehensive basis for determining developmental appropriateness.

Supporting Play among Children

Although children's rates of development and many other characteristics differ, children also share much in common. One common characteristic is that all children are active learners. Many psychologists and child development specialists agree that children actively build understandings of themselves, others, and their environments as they engage in active explorations (Piaget, 1962; Vygotsky, 1934/1984). Children are always busy investigating as they try to absorb new information and ideas. Each time they encounter pieces of the puzzle, they try either to fit them in with their existing frameworks of knowledge or to build other frameworks to hold the newly acquired puzzle pieces.

COMPETENCY GOAL II
• Functional Areas 4–7

COMPETENCY GOAL III
• Functional Areas 8–9

How do young children naturally go about the process of learning? The answer to this question highlights another common characteristic of children. Children often learn through freely chosen, self-satisfying activities commonly known as **play.** Play is a universal characteristic of childhood; playful encounters with objects and individuals broaden children's conceptual understanding of their world.

Early childhood educators who understand the concept of the whole child take steps to provide natural learning environments that maintain focus on the total development of children. Teachers build opportu-

*P*lay . . . is a way of learning by trial and error to cope with the actual world.
—Lawrence Frank, American educator and writer

nities to explore, play, and interact around cues taken from children's behavior. They observe children's current levels of development and use this information, along with their knowledge of child development, to provide materials and experiences that promote positive development across all of the developmental domains. Play and learning are not segmented into developmental domains, but knowing the sequence of development within each domain can aid teachers to anticipate and guide play and learning.

Social Play among Young Children

When these playful encounters include social elements, children reap additional benefits. The ways in which children engage in social play follow a developmental pattern;

for example, children younger than three years old tend to play in smaller groups and are more likely to play alone or beside others with limited interaction (Howes, 1997). As children mature, their participation in play with others expands and becomes increasingly social.

Mildred Parten (1932) researched social participation among preschool-age children during self-directed, or **free play**, episodes by observing and recording their play behaviors related to selection of toys and activities, choice of playmates, and group sizes. Parten grouped the degree of social participation into six categories ranging from least to most social participation. (See Table 1.1.) The first category, **unoccupied behavior**, included no social participation and represented times when children were idle without involvement with objects or others. **Solitary play**, Parten's second category of social play, represented times when children were playing alone without interaction with others and was most commonly observed in two- and three-year-old children. The term **onlooker behavior** was used to describe children's noninvolvement in play accompanied with di-

Table 1.1   Parten's Categories of Social Play

Age of Onset	Category of Social Play	Characteristics
Infancy and toddlerhood	Unoccupied behavior	• No sustained activity • No sustained observation of play of others
Infancy and toddlerhood	Solitary play	• No social interaction • No indication of awareness of play of others
Infancy and toddlerhood	Onlooker behavior	• Social interaction by proximity • No direct participation • Participation by asking questions or offering suggestions
Infancy and toddlerhood	Parallel play	• Social interaction by proximity • No real acknowledgment of play of others • May involve shared materials
Early preschool years	Associative play	• Earliest form of group play • Some sharing of play space and/or materials • Some social change (turn taking, sharing) • Usually separate play dialogue and scenario • No common goals or rules
Later preschool years	Cooperative play	• Group play by design • Social interaction through shared materials, play space, and dialogue • Sustained dialogue about play scenario and usage of collective language (our, we, us) • Commitment to the same play scenario • Some mutually agreed-on but flexible rules

rect observation of the play of others. Parten identified painting as an activity that is likely to draw onlookers. **Parallel play**, Parten's next category of social play, marks the onset of social participation during play episodes. During parallel play, children play near each other, sometimes with the same toys or materials, but with minimal social interaction; their focus is generally on the play objects. For children under age 4, typical parallel play activities included playing in the sand and manipulating beads, small blocks, clay, and scissors. Because unoccupied behavior, solitary play, onlooker behavior, and parallel play are most often observed in children under four years of age, teachers who work in child-care settings with infants, toddlers, and preschoolers are more likely to see these categories of social play than kindergarten or primary-grade teachers.

Parten's last two categories of social play, **associative play** and **cooperative play**, occur when children play in groups and involve the highest level of social participation. Associative and cooperative play occur among older preschool children and frequently involve larger groups than parallel play. During associative play, children organize into groups and play with the same materials. They acknowledge each other's play behaviors and maintain conversations for functional purposes, such as sharing supplies, but may not all have the same goal for their play. Parten observed the highest occurrences of associative play when children were building with large blocks, riding in wheeled vehicles, or swinging in swings on the playground. These activities require that children share the same space and equipment but do not necessitate the level of social interaction required for cooperative play. The major difference between associative play and cooperative play is that during cooperative play, the children in the group have the same play goals and mutually accepted rules. Cooperative play occurred most often when children engaged in play episodes where they used their imaginations and assumed roles, such as when playing "house." Early childhood teachers will observe frequent episodes of associative and cooperative play when children engage in self-directed play in classroom areas that are set up to accommodate small groups, such as dramatic play, blocks, and puppets.

As Parten (1932) noted, as children mature, their tendency to play in larger groups gradually increases. Accordingly, their social participation with peers also increases with age. Carollee Howes (1997) extended Parten's research and investigated social participation during cooperative group play experiences. She concluded that children become more adept at sustaining social play as they spend more time in play experiences with peers. Howes and Matheson (1992) divided cooperative play into categories to distinguish *competent forms of play with peers* from forms of play that were interactive but not necessarily reciprocal. For example, a group of five preschool-age children using blocks and other building materials from the block area and plastic models of animals from the science area are engaged in cooperative play as they work toward their mutual goal of constructing a pretend zoo. However, as the play episode unfolds, one of the children, Laura, demands that the other children build the zoo the right way or she will just build her own zoo. Initially, the other children in the group attempt to include Laura's ideas in their play, but when she still refuses to compromise, the other children in the group ignore her. After a few minutes, Laura angrily picks up several of the plastic animals and goes to another section of the room, where she begins to build her own zoo. In this situation, the cooperative play is not reciprocal, because Laura's contributions are not accepted by the other children, and Laura is unwilling to accommodate her contributions to the group's play goal. In this example, Laura's behavior is less socially competent than that of her peers; therefore, she is unable to sustain her role in their play episode.

In addition to identifying competent forms of peer play, Howes and Matheson (1992) also examined how adult caregivers influence children's social competence during play and concluded that children benefit most when they have positive social interactions with both peers and adults. Additional aspects of competence during children's social play are discussed in Chapters 4 and 9.

Pretend Play and Development of the Whole Child

Sharing play and learning experiences with more able children or adults challenges children to extend learning beyond the boundaries of what they could accomplish alone (Berk & Winsler, 1995). Children's interactions with each other and with the significant adults in their lives not only promote social development but also reinforce the development of language. Lev Vygotsky, a Russian psychologist, described how knowledge was socially constructed though interaction and shared conversations or dialogues (Berk & Winsler, 1995; Vygotsky, 1934/1984). Gradually, these **collaborative dialogues** become part of children's thinking. One of the best vehicles for collaborative dialogues is play, particularly play that involves make-believe scenarios.

Play that involves use of the imagination and make-believe elements is commonly referred to as **pretend play.** Pretend play gives young children many opportunities to explore, talk to each other, and solve problems (Berk & Winsler, 1995). Pretend play also serves as an outlet for young children's creativity and imagination; it runs the gamut from relatively simple episodes with make-believe objects to complex scenarios involving elaborate role play with a variety of props (Garvey, 1990; Smilansky & Shefatya, 1990).

When children take on imaginary roles, their pretend play evolves into **dramatic play.** Dramatic play involving other children within the role-play scenario is called **sociodramatic play.** Sociodramatic play supports development of the whole child because it demands participation of the mind as well as the body (Smilansky & Shefatya, 1990). In all types of pretend play, children use their imaginations to develop complex make-believe scenarios. At the same time, they use their social skills and language to engage others in their play, and they use their bodies to actively make the pretend play come alive (Piaget, 1926).

*F*our-year-olds Desmond, Rickie, and Lea rush to the window in their preschool classroom as soon as they hear the fire truck sirens. They watch and listen intently as the fire truck races past with its lights flashing and sirens blaring. Desmond, whose father is a fire fighter, eagerly explains to his classmates about the hoses and ladders that are attached to the truck. Rickie and Lea ask Desmond questions about the boots, hats, and coats they saw on the fire fighters riding on the truck. Rickie and Lea, who have never viewed fire trucks up close before, compare the real fire truck to the trucks pictured in their storybooks. Once the sirens of the fire truck can no longer be heard, Lea suggests that they pretend that they are fire fighters.

Pretend play provides a natural avenue to support the psychomotor, cognitive, and affective development of children.

Together, the children go to the block area and build a fire truck with large wooden blocks. As they build their truck, they talk about what else they need to finish their truck. They decide to use the long paper tubes from the art center as the hoses and some of the dress-up hats from the dramatic play center as the fire fighters' hats. As they gather their materials, they practice making siren noises with their voices. Desmond announces he should be the driver since he knows the most about fire trucks, and Lea and Rickie agree. All three children put on their hats, grab their hoses, and climb onto the back of their newly constructed fire truck and pretend to hold on tight as the imaginary fire truck races to the scene of the fire.

During the dramatic play episode described in this vignette, Desmond, Rickie, and Lea are totally engrossed in their play. Pretend play provides a natural way to support the development of the whole child, because all three of the developmental domains are represented in one or more segments of the play. Review this vignette and identify how the play episode positively supports development in the psychomotor, cognitive, and affective domains.

How does learning take place during the pretend play like that described in this vignette? The catalyst for that episode of pretend play was the speeding fire truck. First, the sound of the siren caught the children's attention and alerted them to look for the fire truck; then the sight of the fire truck sparked dialogue that generated ideas for the children's play scenario. Finally, dramatizing the scene completed the play episode.

Pretend play often employs three modes of learning, each using a particular type of sensory input: **auditory**, **visual**, or **kinesthetic** (Bloom & Krathwohl, 1956; Harrow, 1972). The different sensory channels that learners use to take in information are called **learning modalities.** All typically developing children are able to use all three sensory modes at the same time, but for some individuals, one mode may be more dominant than the others.

Hearing is the primary input source for the auditory mode. Young children who are dominantly auditory learners enjoy listening to stories, making sounds, and asking questions. Although they like to receive information (listening), they also like to deliver information (talking). Sight is the main source of input for the visual mode. Young children who are dominantly visual learners look intently at pictures in storybooks; they are observant and notice details in pictures and events. They sometimes focus so intently on how something looks that they may not attend to the sounds around them. Touch and movement provide input for the kinesthetic mode. Young children who are dominantly kinesthetic learners touch the pages in storybooks or act out the motions of the characters. They also like to handle objects to feel their texture and other properties. Kinesthetic learners are often active and prefer movement to stillness; they may wiggle around while doing activities in which they are engrossed. Kinesthetic learners often demonstrate well-developed abilities to control their body movements.

Through meaningful experience the learner improves his perceptual abilities, which in turn facilitates his development in the psychomotor, cognitive, and affective domains.

—Anita J. Harrow, *A Taxonomy of the Psychomotor Domain: A Guide for Developing Behavioral Objectives* (1972, p. 185).

Children who embody each of the learning modalities in various combinations of dominance make up the typical early childhood classroom. Effective teachers of young children understand the different ways that children perceive input and provide appropriate learning environments for all children. Rather than restricting children's learning options to their dominant learning modalities, early care and education teachers and learning environments provide a multitude of materials, interactions, and experiences that integrate and stimulate all three modalities. For example, when reading a storybook aloud to a small group of young children, teachers also share the book's colorful illustrations with them. Those children in the group who are primarily auditory learners could probably follow the story based only on what they hear, but the opportunity of using their visual modality by seeing the illustrations enriches their overall story experience. The teacher could also enlist the kinesthetic modality by encouraging hand motions or body movements to complement actions in the story. Activities and learning experiences that simultaneously support all three modalities facilitate learning for all children regardless of preferred learning modality. Such experiences spontaneously encourage development of the whole child. The following vignette is another example of a classroom activity that provides multiple opportunities for children to use all of their learning modalities.

For the past two weeks, the children in Mr. Johnson's kindergarten class have been learning about versions of familiar fairy tales from around the world. The children are so interested in the fairy tales that they have been role-playing the characters during recess.

Mr. Johnson asks whether the children would be interested in making puppets of their favorite fairy tale characters.

The children are enthusiastic about the idea, so they begin collecting materials from around the classroom to use in making their puppets. Mr. Johnson provides small paper bags and paper plates as options to use for the puppets' bodies or heads as the children assemble crayons, markers, glue, scissors, construction paper, and bits of yarn and material from the scrap box. Stacia, Marty, and Ling race to get the fairy tale books from the literacy center and pore over the pictures until they find just the right image to serve as inspiration for their puppets. Nathan and Ambrose ask Mr. Johnson to reread a detailed description of a troll they remember from one of the stories. Some children jump right into the construction of the puppets, testing out various materials for the hair and clothes. Although the children are conversing and moving about the classroom, they are engaged in the process of creating. Within an hour, most of the puppets are constructed and ready for play. Each puppet is unique, just as each puppet's creator is unique.

In this vignette, Mr. Johnson demonstrates his knowledge of the different ways in which young children learn by providing materials and resources to support each of the learning modalities. The visual learners sought out illustrations from storybooks; the auditory learners asked to have descriptive passages reread to them; and the kinesthetic learners immediately began manipulating available materials. In short, Mr. Johnson orchestrated this puppet-making project to support the whole child.

When Mr. Johnson developed the puppet-making project, he did not focus on a single outcome for the children, such as having them all create green troll puppets using construction paper and crayons. Rather, after selecting their own materials, the children could construct their puppets as simply or elaborately as they desired. More able children could add detail and props or use more complex techniques to assemble their

Open-ended activities, such as making puppets, allow young children to selectively employ the auditory, visual, and kinesthetic learning modalities.

puppets. Children with less interest, ability, or experience could construct their puppets within their own levels of development and still feel competent and successful. Play and learning experiences that allow for a variety of learning processes and successful outcomes are referred to as **open-ended activities.**

Young Children with Special Needs

COMPETENCY GOAL II
• Functional Areas 4–6

COMPETENCY GOAL III
• Functional Areas 8–9

COMPETENCY GOAL IV
• Functional Area 11

The concept of the whole child extends beyond overlapping developmental domains, universal aspects of childhood, and learning preferences; it also includes aspects of development that are associated with special needs. In education, the term **special needs** describes any type of difference in learning ability or style that requires significant adaptation of the learning situation. Special needs refers to **disabilities** that may restrict children's abilities to learn or engage in learning activities as well as to *enhanced abilities* that may exceed the abilities of same-age peers. Most early childhood educators recognize that all children have special needs, but they also know that some children's needs are exceptional.

Out of respect for the children, educators use **person-first language** when discussing children with special needs. In other words, the individual is mentioned before the disability because the individual is more significant than the disability. Also, the language focuses on what children are able to do rather than what they are unable to do. For example, the expression "children with visual impairments" is preferred to the expression "visually impaired children" or "blind children."

Educators are also cautious about using labels or disability categories when discussing young children with special needs. The Division for Early Childhood of the Council for Exceptional Children (DEC/CEC) advocates use of an inclusive category, such as **developmental delay,** to designate children under the age of nine years who have special needs (DEC/CEC, 2000). DEC/CEC defines developmental delay as "a condition that significantly delays the process of development" (DEC/CEC, 1991, p. 1). Because the category of developmental delay is broadly defined, younger children might be eligible for special education services that are often restricted to specific disabilities in older children. Additionally, DEC/CEC and NAEYC (National Association for the Education of Young Children) contend that the developmental delay category allows for consideration of the whole child rather than limiting intervention strategies to a portion of the child identified as disabled (DEC/CEC, 2000; NAEYC, 1998).

For example, this chapter's recurring theme of the whole child applies to children with special needs as well as to typically developing children. Maintaining the focus of early intervention on the whole child, rather than on the disability, impacts the ways in which early care and education communities serve the needs of those young children with special needs for which they are responsible.

Many early childhood educators, and most early childhood professional organizations, view **inclusion** as the best model for serving most young children with special needs. Inclusion means that young children with special needs are fully integrated into early childhood education programs along with typically developing peers. Inclusion is guided by the assumption that all children, whether they are identified with special needs or as typically developing, differ in abilities, interests, and needs. Therefore, providing integrated learning environments for all children is often the most reasonable option.

Public Law 105-17, the Individuals with Disabilities Education Act (IDEA), as amended in 1997, safeguards the educational rights of persons with disabilities by asserting that individuals identified with special needs have the same rights to free public education as their nondisabled peers. This mandate further stipulates that such education should take place in learning environments that do not unduly limit children's educational experiences. For example, a child restricted to a wheelchair could participate in many of the activities in which other preschoolers engage if classroom aisles were wide enough and free from obstacles. In the language of the law, the terms **free appropriate public education (FAPE)** and **least restrictive environment (LRE)** are used to describe these provisions (U.S. Department of Education, 1999). Although the range of disabilities varies widely from child to child, learning environments that place the fewest restrictions on children with special needs are often inclusive settings.

For example, whenever possible, special education services for children are integrated into the typical school day. Special education interventions might include (but are not limited to) speech and language services, physical and occupational therapy, and medical support. A variety of qualified specialists—such as psychologists, speech and language therapists, early childhood special education teachers, medical personnel, and paraprofessionals—provide special education services. Positive relationships between the early childhood teacher and special education service providers are crucial to successful implementation of inclusion.

The 1997 amendments to IDEA stipulate that whenever possible, intervention services for young children occur in the **natural environment** of the children. For most children, the natural environment would be their homes and whatever community education settings the children would attend if they were typically developing (Dunst, Herter, Shields, & Bennis, 2001; Warger, 1999). Within the natural environment, the interventions themselves should intrude as little as possible on the children's daily routines. Instead, interventions should follow the lead of the children and build on daily routines and activities (Warger, 1999). For example, children who need intervention to strengthen the small muscles of the hands and fingers could receive those services while participating with peers in typical preschool activities such as squeezing modeling dough, manipulating objects in the sand and water table, and stringing beads. This type of transparent intervention in early childhood classrooms is most successful when classroom teachers and special education service providers work collaboratively.

A collaborative team approach to early intervention and inclusion maintains focus on the holistic needs of the children. Involving all significant individuals, or key *stakeholders,* throughout planning and implementation is essential in order to provide appropriate and cohesive interventions (DEC/CEC, 1993). No one individual stands out as the expert dispensing advice to the others. Classroom teachers, service providers, and family members work together to form a collaborative team. The team assesses, plans, and implements the **individualized family service plan (IFSP)** or **individualized education plan (IEP)** (Cook, Tessier, & Klein, 2000), based on the particular abilities, disabilities, and needs of the children. The IFSP or IEP identifies the target child's present level of functioning and states expected outcomes. The plan also outlines early intervention strategies and services necessary to reach the outcomes.

Particularly in inclusive settings, part of the intervention strategy may be to modify classroom environments to enable children with special needs to participate as much as possible with their peers. Many modifications within classrooms relate to children's abilities to reach and use equipment or areas that their nondisabled peers can access. If individuals with special needs cannot use typically available facilities or services (such as tables, computers, or bathrooms) solely because of their disabilities, the facilities or services are considered inaccessible. Adapting facilities or services so individuals with disabilities can use them without undue assistance establishes **accessibility.**

Within early childhood classrooms, some modifications for accessibility may be relatively simple. Sometimes the height of tables or shelves needs to be adjusted so children who use wheelchairs for mobility can reach items independently. Other times, minor rearrangements of furniture to widen aisles or reduce congestion enable children with motor or visual disabilities to navigate around the classroom with little or no assistance. Certain classroom materials (such as crayons, scissors, or paintbrushes) may require modifications before children with cerebral palsy or other disabilities affecting fine motor skills can manipulate them. (Refer to Professional Connections and Web Links at the end of the chapter for a Web site that suggests toys and accessories for young children with special needs.) Every classroom adaptation that enables children with special needs to participate with their typically developing peers is one step closer to an inclusive environment that is appropriate for all children.

Developmentally Appropriate Practice

In an effort to provide guidelines for identifying teaching and learning processes that effectively meet the developmental needs of all children, the National Association for the Education of Young Children (NAEYC) published a position statement outlining practices that take into account the developmental needs of children (Bredekamp, 1987). The NAEYC coined the term **developmentally appropriate practice (DAP)** to describe the wide range of factors that impact the care and education of young children. These factors include, but are not limited to, teaching methods, room arrangement, care-giving behaviors, child-teacher interactions, and equipment and materials.

According to the NAEYC, educators should consider three categories of information when determining developmentally appropriate practice. First, decide whether a suggested teaching or learning practice is appropriate to the ages of the children in the group; in other words, would the behavior in question be a reasonable expectation for a group of typically developing children of this age? If so, then the practice is considered **age appropriate.** For example, it would be unreasonable (not age appropriate) to expect two-year-old children to sit at a table and put together puzzles with twenty pieces. However, it would be reasonable (age appropriate) to invite them to place one larger puzzle piece, like a circle, into a cut-out frame. Second, decide whether the behavior in question

CDA

COMPETENCY GOAL II
· Functional Areas 4–7

COMPETENCY GOAL III
· Functional Areas 8–10

COMPETENCY GOAL IV
· Functional Area 11

is appropriate for each specific child. Educators' knowledge of age appropriateness, combined with information about specific children derived from various sources (such as observations by classroom teachers and information provided by family members), provides specific factors relevant to individual children. If so, then the practice is **individually appropriate.** The third area to consider when determining developmentally appropriate practice was not part of the NAEYC's original position statement on DAP, but it is included in the second edition of the statement and is based on feedback received in response to the first publication (Bredekamp & Copple, 1997). Knowledge about children's families and communities provides input for practice that is **culturally appropriate.** Culturally appropriate practice relates to elements of diversity, such as language, religion, ethnicity, and gender. In sum, developmentally appropriate practice incorporates knowledge and consideration of age, individual, and cultural characteristics.

The NAEYC's second edition of *Developmentally Appropriate Practice in Early Childhood Programs* (Bredekamp & Copple, 1997) also lists principles about how children develop and learn. These principles serve as the foundation for developmentally appropriate practice and support the concept of the whole child (discussed throughout this chapter). Developmentally appropriate practice is based on the following principles:

- The developmental domains are *interrelated.*
- Development follows a *sequence,* or pattern.
- *Rates* of development *vary* among children.
- Early experiences have both *cumulative* and *delayed* effects.
- Development proceeds in a predictable direction *toward* greater *complexity.*
- Multiple factors, including *social* and *cultural,* affect development.
- Children are *active learners.*
- Children learn through *interacting* with their environments.
- *Play* is a vital part of the development process.
- Development advances through *practice* and *challenges.*
- Children learn through *auditory, visual,* and tactile (*kinesthetic*) modes.
- Children learn best within the context of a *community* where they feel safe and secure. (adapted from Bredekamp & Copple, 1997)

Over time, the concept of developmentally appropriate practice has broadened to include most facets of early care and education. DAP is not limited to teaching and learning practices; it also encompasses practices that make up the total play and learning environment, including organizing learning environments, selecting equipment and materials, planning and implementing curriculum, communicating with and involving families, and observing behaviors and assessing development. The central challenge of developmentally appropriate practice is to meet the needs of all of children as well as the diverse needs of individual children.

A developmentally appropriate curriculum relies on knowledge of child development theory while at the same time considering information about specific children. Teachers play vital roles in the development and implementation of curriculum that is developmentally appropriate by orchestrating learning experiences based on the children's interests, needs, and abilities. As they observe children to glean information about curriculum, teachers are simultaneously and systematically observing and recording children's behaviors. The focus of the observations is to document and collect evidence of children's current levels of functioning. The gathered data are used to organize learning environments, plan and implement curriculum, and communicate with family members about their children.

Summary

- Early childhood is the period of development from birth to age 8.

Meeting the Needs of the Whole Child

- The psychomotor, cognitive, and affective developmental domains overlap.
- The concept of the whole child advocates a holistic view of child development.
- Rates of development vary among children.

Supporting Play among Young Children

- Children are active learners.
- Play is a vital part of the learning process for young children.
- Children's social play and interactions in their environments facilitate learning.
- During pretend play, learning occurs through auditory, visual, and kinesthetic modalities.

Young Children with Special Needs

- Some young children have special needs, such as developmental delays.
- Inclusion places children with special needs in learning environments with typically developing peers whenever possible.
- Learning environments and practices can often be adapted to accommodate young children with special needs.

Developmentally Appropriate Practice

- Developmentally appropriate practice is age appropriate, individually appropriate, and culturally appropriate.
- Developmentally appropriate practice influences learning environments, curriculum, family involvement, and assessment.

LEARNING ACTIVITIES

1 Simulation: Learning Modalities. In small groups, brainstorm several open-ended activities (similar to the puppet-making activity described in the vignette on pp. 10–11) that would give children opportunities to employ the auditory, visual, and kinesthetic modes of learning. Select one of the activities and analyze how it would stimulate the learning modalities. Record your analyses in a three-column chart representing each of the modalities.

2 Activity: Room Arrangement/Developmentally Appropriate Practice. Working in a small group, se-lect one of these developmental levels: infants and toddlers (birth–3) or preschoolers (ages 3–5). Briefly sketch a floor plan and room arrangement that would facilitate developmentally appropriate practice. Write captions around the edges of your sketch, describing aspects of the floor plan and room arrangement that facilitate play and active learning. Contrast your design with early care and education environments that are developmentally inappropriate. To extend the activity, write five tips for early childhood educators to consider when arranging developmentally appropriate classroom spaces and share your group's ideas with the class.

PORTFOLIO ARTIFACTS

1 Observation: Social Play. Visit a local preschool or child-care center during free play time and observe children in two different age groups to compare their levels of social interaction. Record, in chronological order, the behaviors you observe. Later, analyze your observations and identify examples of social play according to the categories identified by Parten. (Refer to Table 1.1., p. 6.) Take a moment to reflect on the observations and describe your impressions of the children's social play behaviors. Consider how the children's levels of social play relate to their ages and developmental levels.

2 Interview: Early Childhood Teacher on Inclusion. Make arrangements to interview one or more early childhood educators who teach in inclusive settings. Prior to the interview, prepare at least four open-ended questions to encourage the teachers to describe and reflect on their experiences with inclusion from multiple points of view (teachers, family members, typically developing children, children with special needs, etc.).

3 Application: Books about Young Children with Special Needs. Visit the Web site and read the annotations for several of the children's books listed in the resource collection Children's Books about Disabilities from ERIC Clearinghouse on Disabilities and Gifted Education (see p. 18). Select two or three book titles appropriate for an age group of your choice and visit the children's section of your local library to read the complete text of the book(s). After reading the books, contemplate how your level of awareness of young children with special needs has changed. In your portfolio, record bibliographic information, a short summary of the books, your reflections, and your suggestions for using the books with children.

4 Activity: Modifying a Learning Activity. Look through teacher resource books to locate an activity appropriate for young children. Read through the list of materials and procedures for the activity. On a copy of the activity, make suggestions to improve the developmental appropriateness of the activity by modifying the materials and/or procedures. As you describe the modifications, identify whether the modifications are related to age appropriateness, individual appropriateness, or cultural appropriateness.

Professional Connections and Web Links

Division for Early Childhood of the Council
for Exceptional Children (DEC/CEC)
1110 North Glebe Road, Suite 300
Arlington, VA 22201-5704
888-232-7733
http://www.cec.sped.org/
http://www.dec-sped.org/

The Division for Early Childhood of the Council for Exceptional Children (DEC/CEC), founded in 1973, is a nonprofit professional organization supporting the rights of young children (birth through age 8) with special needs and their families. DEC/CEC informs educators, families, and the public about policies and teaching and intervention practices that support the full development of young children. The organization holds meetings and conferences and publishes two journals, *Young Exceptional Children* and *Journal of Early Intervention*. In addition to information about the organization and its publications, DEC's Web site provides access to their position statements and links to related sites, including CEC and a site devoted to IDEA (Individuals with Disabilities Education Act).

National Association for the Education
of Young Children (NAEYC)
1509 16th Street NW
Washington, DC 20036-1426
800-424-2460
http://www.naeyc.org/

With over 100,000 members, the National Association for the Education of Young Children (NAEYC), which was founded in the early 1900s, is the largest professional organization in the United States devoted to early childhood education and educators. Their position statement, *Developmentally Appropriate Practice in Early Childhood*

Programs, Revised Edition (1997), provides detailed information about recommended teaching and learning practices for young children from birth to age 8. In addition, NAEYC hosts periodic local, state, and regional conferences as well as an annual international conference each fall that draws thousands of participants from its diverse membership of students, teachers, parent educators, administrators, and family members. Their Web site provides access to the organization's position statements and related research and a searchable index for their journal, *Young Children*. NAEYC also sponsors the Week of the Young Child, a public awareness and advocacy celebration each spring.

ERIC Clearinghouse on Disabilities and Gifted Education
1110 North Glebe Road
Arlington, VA 22201-5704
800-328-0272
http://ericec.org

ERIC (Educational Resources Information Center) sponsors several clearinghouses for dissemination of specialized information on educational practices, research, and policies, including the Clearinghouse on Disabilities and Gifted Education. The Web site provides a bibliography of articles, position statements, and documents related to special education. In addition, the Web site offers several resource collections, including:

> Toys and Accessories for Children with Disabilities
> http://ericec.org/fact/toys.html
>
> Children's Books about Disabilities
> http://ericec.org/fact/kidbooks.html

U.S. Office of Special Education Programs (OSEP)
http://www.ed.gov/offices/OSERS/OSEP.html

The U.S. Office of Special Education Programs (OSEP) administers the 1997 amendments of PL 105-17, Individuals with Disabilities Education Act (IDEA), and is responsible for evaluating, monitoring, and reporting implementation of special education policies for children and youth with disabilities from birth through age 21. OSEP's Web site provides access to national studies, related statistics, and information and resources about implementation of IDEA in the United States.

Suggestions for Further Reading

Bredekamp, Sue, & Copple, Carol. (Eds). (1997). *Developmentally appropriate practice in early childhood programs* (rev. ed.). Washington, DC: National Association for the Education of Young Children.

- The revised edition of NAEYC's handbook for developmentally appropriate practice (DAP) in programs serving children from birth to age 8 identifies twelve principles of child development that support the concept of the whole child. The book also defines the three components of DAP, cites related research, and offers examples of effective and ineffective practice. One of the unique features of the book is its two-column approach; practice that is developmentally appropriate is described in one column, and practice that is developmentally inappropriate is described in the other column so that readers can compare caregiving and teaching behaviors.

Chandler, Phyllis A. (1994). *A place for me: Including children with special needs in early care and education settings*. Washington, DC: National Association for the Education of Young Children.

- Chandler's book focuses on the role of early childhood educators in providing positive environments for typically developing children as well as those with special needs. She clearly addresses basic issues, such as maintaining positive attitudes towards inclusion, adapting physical environments, building strong relationships with families, and collaborating with families and community agencies to provide optimum experiences for all involved. The book also includes a list of organizations, publications, and other resources for further study.

Odom, Samuel L. (2002). *Widening the circle: Including children with disabilities in preschool programs*. New York: Teachers College Press.

- This book presents a selection of well-written, research-based essays on a variety of critical topics related to inclusion of young children with special needs into classrooms and communities. The result of a five-year research project orchestrated by the Early Childhood Research Institute on Inclusion (ECRII), this book models the concept of collaboration among stakeholders to provide quality inclusive early care and education experiences for young children.

References

Berk, Laura, & Winsler, Adam. (1995). *Scaffolding children's learning: Vygotsky and early childhood education.* Washington, DC: National Association for the Education of Young Children.

Bloom, Benjamin S., & Krathwohl, David R. (1956). *Taxonomy of educational objectives: The classification of educational goals. Handbook I: Cognitive domain.* New York: Longmans, Green.

Bredekamp, Sue. (Ed.). (1987). *Developmentally appropriate practice in early childhood programs serving children from birth to age 8.* Washington, DC: National Association for the Education of Young Children.

Bredekamp, Sue, & Copple, Carol. (Eds.). (1997). *Developmentally appropriate practice in early childhood programs* (rev. ed.). Washington, DC: National Association for the Education of Young Children.

Cook, Ruth E., Tessier, Annette, & Klein, M. Diane. (2000). *Adapting early childhood curricula for children in inclusive settings.* Upper Saddle River, NJ: Merrill/Prentice Hall.

Division for Early Childhood of the Council for Exceptional Children (DEC/CEC). (1991). *Concept paper on developmental delay as an eligibility category.* Arlington, VA: Council for Exceptional Children.

Division for Early Childhood of the Council for Exceptional Children (DEC/CEC). (1993). *Position statement: Position on inclusion.* Arlington, VA: Council for Exceptional Children.

Division for Early Childhood of the Council for Exceptional Children (DEC/CEC). (2000). *Position statement: Developmental delay as an eligibility category.* Arlington, VA: Council for Exceptional Children.

Dunst, Carl J., Herter, Serena, Shields, Holly, & Bennis, Leslie. (2001). Mapping community-based natural learning opportunities. *Young Exceptional Children, 4*(4), 16–24.

Forman, George E., & Kuscher, David S. (1983). *The child's construction of knowledge: Piaget for teaching children.* Washington, DC: National Association for the Education of Young Children.

Froebel, Friedrich W. (1826). *The education of man.* New York: Lovell.

Garvey, C. (1990). *Play.* Cambridge, MA: Harvard University Press.

Gesell, Arnold, & Ames, L. B. (1956). *Youth: The years from ten to sixteen.* New York: Harper and Row.

Harrow, Anita J. (1972). *A taxonomy of the psychomotor domain: A guide for developing behavioral objectives.* New York: Longman.

Howes, Carollee. (1997). Teacher sensitivity, children's attachment and play with peers. *Early Education and Development, 8*(1), 41–49.

Howes, Carollee, & Matheson, C. (1992). Sequences in the development of competent play with peers: Social and social pretend play. *Developmental Psychology, 28,* 961–974.

Krathwohl, David R., Bloom, Benjamin S., & Masia, B. (1964). *Taxonomy of educational objectives. Handbook II: Affective domain.* New York: David McKay.

National Association for the Education of Young Children (NAEYC). (1998). *Position statement: Inclusion in early childhood education.* Washington, DC: National Association for the Education of Young Children.

Parten, Mildred. (1932). Social play among preschool approach. *Journal of Abnormal and Social Psychology, 28,* 136–147.

Piaget, Jean. (1926). *The language and thought of the child.* New York: Harcourt, Brace, & World.

Piaget, Jean. (1962). *Play, dreams, and imitation.* New York: Norton.

Shonkoff, Jack P., & Phillips, Deborah, A. (Eds.). (2000). *From neurons to neighborhoods: The science of early childhood development.* Washington, DC: National Academy Press.

Smilansky, Sara, & Shefatya, Leah. (1990). *Facilitating play: A medium for promoting cognitive, socio-emotional, and academic development in young children.* Gaithersburg, MD: Psychosocial and Educational Publications.

U.S. Department of Education/Office for Civil Rights (DOE/OCR). (1999, July). *Free appropriate education for students with disabilities: Requirements under Section 504 of the Rehabilitation Act of 1973.* Washington, DC: U.S. DOE/OCR.

Vygotsky, Lev S. (1934/1984). *Thought and language.* Trans. Alex Kozulin. Cambridge, MA: MIT Press.

Warger, Cynthia. (1999). Early childhood instruction in the natural environment. *ERIC Digest, E591.*

The Psychomotor Domain

After reading this chapter and completing the related activities, you should be able to

- Define the psychomotor domain
- Give examples of early sensory abilities
- Identify some of the reflex behaviors of newborn infants
- Describe two patterns of physical development
- Describe the sequence and milestones of psychomotor development
- Give examples of gross motor, fine motor, and perceptual-motor skills
- Identify the stages of drawing
- Explain how children use motor skills to explore their environments
- Suggest experiences and teaching practices that support development in the psychomotor domain
- Describe how play supports psychomotor development

Six-week-old Oliver lies on his back in his crib, staring fixedly at the slowly rotating mobile hanging above his head. Each time one of the brightly colored butterflies on the mobile flutters its wings, Oliver renews his visual exploration of the butterflies. When his father winds the music box connected to the mobile, Oliver shows excitement by waving his arms and looking toward the source of the sounds. Oliver's father detaches one of the plush butterflies from the mobile and holds it within reach of the infant. Oliver fixes his gaze on the butterfly held in his father's hand and brings both arms forward, reaching toward it. As his father gently places the butterfly against his hand, Oliver opens his hand and grasps it, waving his arm to and fro as if to show off his captured prize.

mazingly, within the first seconds of life, infants begin to explore their surroundings via their senses; they peer at the images closest to them and grasp objects that touch their hands. The sights, sounds, and textures around them introduce infants to the physical world. Initially, their explorations are accidental rather than deliberate, but within a few weeks infants seek out new sources for exploration. As children grow and develop, their ability to use complex exploratory physical movements increases, and they spend countless hours throughout childhood gathering information with their senses and fueling their curiosity for more experiences.

Oliver's antics in the chapter opening vignette demonstrate many aspects of physical development encompassed within the *psychomotor domain*. As discussed in

CHAPTER 2

Chapter 1, the psychomotor domain includes the components of development related to neurological (that is, brain and nervous system) and physical growth and maturation. When Oliver uses his senses of sight, hearing, and touch to observe and gain information about the butterfly mobile, he is coordinating the muscles in his eyes to stare at the mobile and the muscles in his neck to turn toward the sources of the sound. Oliver also employs the muscles in his arms and hands to reach for and grasp the butterfly. In so doing, Oliver uses three specific aspects of the psychomotor domain: **gross motor, fine motor,** and **perceptual-motor** behavior. Gross motor behavior uses the large muscles in the torso, neck, arms, and legs (reaching with his arms). Fine motor behavior refers to the use of the small muscles of the hands and fingers, feet and toes, and face (grasping the butterfly in his fist). Perceptual-motor behavior coordinates sensory input with motor, or muscle, movements (looking toward the mobile in response to the sights and sounds). This chapter explores the development and use of psychomotor abilities from infancy throughout early childhood.

Early Sensory Abilities

Most sensory abilities begin to develop prior to birth within the **prenatal** environment, where the unborn child initially experiences sensory sensations. As soon as infants leave the womb, they begin to employ their senses and motor skills to explore their new surroundings. Infants receive a variety of stimuli through the five senses of vision, hearing, taste, smell, and touch. At birth, all of the senses are functional to some degree.

The vision of newborn infants is not as sharp as the vision of adults, because the parts of the brain that process visual information are not yet fully developed at the time of birth. Although **visual acuity** is not as well developed as it is in adults, infants are still able to take in enormous amounts of visual information (Gesell, 1949). Within a few minutes of birth, infants are able to gaze fixedly at faces or objects within eight to ten inches from their faces (Klaus & Klaus, 1998). For approximately the first six weeks of infants' lives, objects outside of this optimal field of vision are somewhat blurry, but by the time infants are six months old, their visual acuity is very similar to that of adults.

Newborn infants also demonstrate another visual ability shortly after birth: they are able to follow slowly moving objects, within their field of vision, with their

> *O*ne of the newborn's first responses is to move into a quiet but alert state; the baby is still; her body molds to yours; her hands touch your skin; her eyes are bright and shiny. She looks directly at you.
>
> Marshall H. Klaus and Phyllis H. Klaus, *Your Amazing Newborn* (1998, p. 22)

eyes. This skill is known as **visual tracking.** Visual-tracking abilities have been documented with infants who are only hours old.

Research has also indicated that very young infants can recognize and distinguish patterns (Klaus & Klaus, 1998). Klaus and Klaus have also documented that infants are able to remember some of what they see and, further, that they have definite visual preferences. Though prenatal environments are dark and infants' optic nerves have had little exposure to light, the first months of life provide thousands of visual experiences for their optic nerves. As the brain processes these images, they become part of the **visual memory.** Because humans tend to show heightened interest when presented with new images or objects, researchers designed an experiment, using specialized cameras and other devices, to observe and record the amount of time infants gazed fixedly at a variety of images. They recorded decreases in visual interest (less gazing time) if infants were repeatedly shown the same images and temporary increases (more gazing time) in visual interest when new images were presented, indicating that infants *remembered* images they had previously viewed (Fantz, 1963). Additionally, based on the premise that the longer infants gazed at a particular image the more they preferred it, researchers concluded that infants prefer patterns such as circles or stripes to plain surfaces and also that they prefer visual contrasts such as dark colors against light colors (Fantz, 1961). To see how many toys feature contrast and patterns (such as black-and-white stripes or circles) that appeal to infants, stroll down the aisle of infant toys at a local toy

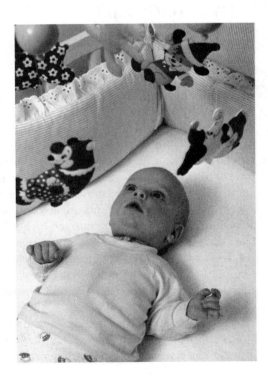

Research indicates that young infants show visual preferences for patterns and contrasts.

store. (Learning Activity 1, at the end of this chapter, suggests additional ways to explore the visual abilities of young infants.)

Another avenue through which infants explore their worlds is the sense of hearing. Because some sound travels through the womb, the hearing abilities of newborn infants are more developed at birth than is their vision. In fact, their hearing is nearly as well developed as the hearing of adults. Once again, research has documented that infants have preferences for particular stimuli. They prefer to hear the sounds of human voices. They also prefer higher-pitched voices to deeper ones (Klaus & Klaus, 1998). If you have had experience with young infants, you may have noticed that adults sense this preference and tend to speak to them using higher-pitched, rhythmic voices. This practice, called speaking **parentese**, has been observed in many cultures around the world and appears to be universal. Studies have also documented that newborn infants prefer familiar voices to unfamiliar voices.

Other senses that are developed well at birth are those of taste and smell. The sense of taste is strongly connected to the sense of smell; thus, changes in taste preferences that occur during the first two years of life are connected to changes in abilities to distinguish odors. For example, newborn infants show preferences for sweet tastes, like sugar water and some sweetened fruit juices, and displeasure for sour, salty, or bitter tastes. However, by the time most infants reach their second birthdays, the smell receptors in the nose interact with the taste receptors on the tongue and in the throat to produce the sensation of flavors. Just as newborn infants can distinguish between pleasant tastes (sweet) and unpleasant tastes (sour, salty, or bitter), so they can also distinguish between pleasant and unpleasant smells. Newborn infants indicate their smelling preferences by turning toward pleasant odors and away from unpleasant odors.

The fifth sensory channel through which individuals collect information about their surroundings is the sense of touch, which is activated by stimulation to the skin. Skin serves as the primary sensory organ for touch and is by far the largest sensory receptor. Experiences involving the sense of touch are called **tactile**. Tactile experiences begin inside the womb, where skin is touched by warm amniotic fluid. Unborn infants also touch their faces and other body parts with their hands. Ultrasound x-rays, administered during pregnancy, have even documented fetuses sucking their thumbs. After birth, newborn infants continue to seek close physical contact by nestling against others; they are often comforted by soft touches, such as stroking or patting. Other components of the sense of touch include responses to texture, temperature, and pain. Touch, or one of the other senses, often serves as the stimulus for involuntary muscular responses of newborn infants.

Reflex Behaviors

Many of the early muscular, or motor, movements of infants are responses to external stimuli rather than deliberate motor movements; these involuntary movements are called **reflexes**. For the most part, reflexes are triggered by the senses. For example, infants often startle in reaction to loud sounds. When startled, young infants arch their

COMPETENCY GOAL II
· Functional Area 4

backs and quickly fling out their arms. This reaction is called the startle reflex, or **moro reflex.** Infants do not make deliberate decisions to arch their backs and fling out their arms; rather, their nervous systems react automatically to threatening situations and enact the appropriate reflex. While the moro reflex is usually triggered by sound (auditory stimuli), many other reflexes that infants exhibit are triggered by the sense of touch (tactile stimuli).

When something touches infants' palms, they automatically grasp the object by curling their fingers around it. This reflex is called the **palmer grasp reflex.** Although during early infancy the palmer grasp is a protective reflex that enables infants to hang on tightly to things in their grasp, it later becomes a deliberate motor action, where the whole hand is used to pick up or hold objects. Similar to the palmer grasp reflex, when something touches infants' soles, they respond by turning their feet inward and spreading out their toes while pulling their legs toward their bodies and away from the object. This reflex is called the **Babinski reflex.** Both the moro and Babinski reflexes, which also serve as protective reactions to potentially threatening situations, gradually fade away during the first year of life. Another reflex that serves a protective function occurs when infants quickly close and then reopen their eyes when they sense anything near them. This reflex is referred to as the **blinking reflex.**

Some reflexes relate to basic survival rather then protection. For example, both the **rooting reflex** and the **sucking reflex** enable infants to obtain nourishment. The rooting reflex is stimulated when something strokes infants' cheeks; they respond by turning toward the object and opening their mouths, preparing to suck. The sucking reflex occurs when something touches infants' mouths; they respond by sucking rhythmically in search of nourishment. Within a few months of birth, the rooting reflex disappears, and the sucking behavior becomes voluntary rather than reflexive. Most reflexes fade away by the end of the first year of life. One reflex, previously described, remains throughout the life span. Can you identify this lifelong reflex? Don't blink or you may miss it!

Newborn infants display involuntary muscular movements, such as the Babinski reflex, in response to external sensory stimuli.

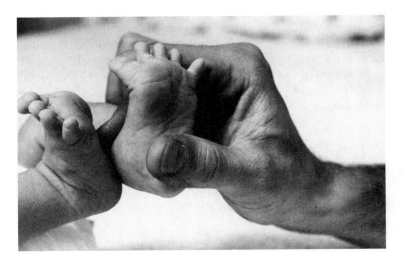

Gross Motor Development

In addition to involuntary motor movements, infants demonstrate a myriad of voluntary motor behaviors. Beginning during prenatal development and continuing throughout childhood and adolescence, motor skills are influenced by two patterns of physical development. One pattern of growth and development proceeds from head (cephalo) to tail (caudal)—a top-down pattern that is referred to as the **cephalocaudal pattern.** This pattern is easily observed by examining the changes in body proportions illustrated in Figure 2.1.

During the first trimester of pregnancy, the head of the fetus comprises about one-half of total body length. As the fetus continues to develop, the torso, arms, and legs become more defined. At birth, the head accounts for about one-fourth of total body length. This cephalocaudal pattern continues throughout changes in body proportion, shape, and size during early childhood. As the torso elongates, the arms and legs also lengthen; this increase in height alters the head-to-body ratio so that the heads of preschool-age children represent a considerably smaller proportion of total body length than the 1 to 4 head-to-body ratio of infants. Body proportions continue to change during middle childhood as the torso continues to elongate and the arms and legs increase in length. As a result of this growth pattern, the head is now only about one-tenth of the total body length. This proportion remains stable from middle childhood through

CDA

COMPETENCY GOAL II
· Functional Area 4

Figure 2.1   **Changes in Body Proportions during Development**

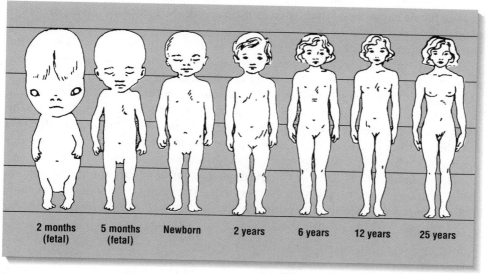

| 2 months (fetal) | 5 months (fetal) | Newborn | 2 years | 6 years | 12 years | 25 years |

Source: From J. A. Schickedanz, P. D. Forsyth, and G. A. Forsyth (1988), *Understanding Children and Adolescents,* 3rd ed. (Boston: Allyn and Bacon). Copyright 1988 by Pearson Education. Reprinted by permission of the publisher.

adulthood. (Learning Activity 3 describes an opportunity to gain a more in-depth hands-on look at the changes in body proportions from prenatal development through childhood.)

The sequence of gross motor development gives other evidence of the influence of the cephalocaudal pattern of development during the first year of life. First, the large muscles of the neck and torso develop to enable infants to support the weight of their heads without external assistance. Gradually, over the next several months, infants' muscular control increases, and they master several gross motor behaviors, such as holding their backs upright, rolling over, sitting up, crawling, pulling to standing positions, and perhaps standing unassisted. Notice the top-down progression of this physical development. First, infants exercise control over the neck and back muscles (holding their backs upright), then the upper torso (rolling over and sitting), and finally the lower body (crawling, pulling up, and standing). The sequence of development of these significant gross motor behaviors depicts the cephalocaudal pattern.

At the same time the cephalocaudal pattern is influencing motor development, another pattern of development is also operating. This pattern of development proceeds from the center of the body and outward and is referred to as the **proximodistal pattern.** The term derives from the root words *proximo,* meaning near, and *distal,* meaning far, and represents the pattern of development that begins near the center of the body and proceeds outward to the extremities. Examine the illustrations in Figure 2.2, showing the sequence of prenatal development during the first trimester when the embryo's torso and heart are evident before arm buds or leg buds emerge. As pregnancy continues, the arm and leg buds elongate before the hands and fingers and feet and toes are formed.

Just as the cephalocaudal pattern continues to influence physical development after birth, so does the proximodistal pattern. During the first few months of life, infants use their whole hands when attempting to grasp objects. Several months will pass before infants refine their small muscle movements enough to master the fine motor skill of picking up small objects using the thumb and forefinger. This behavior, known as the **pincer grasp,** marks a significant step in development. Mastery of the pincer grasp represents a major achievement in fine motor development, because it is the precursor to other important fine motor behaviors such as holding eating utensils, buttoning and unbuttoning, and drawing and writing. Notice the sequence of development; first, the arm, which is nearest the center of the body; then, the hand; and finally, the fingers, which are most distant from the center of the body. The proximodistal pattern of development is clearly evident in the transition from the whole-hand grasp to the pincer grasp.

These simultaneous patterns of development that dominate the predictable sequence of emerging motor skills are most evident during early childhood but continue to influence physical development through adolescence.

Psychomotor Developmental Milestones

During the first years of life, children's development is punctuated by a series of behaviors and skills that emerge sequentially and thus somewhat predictably; these noteworthy achievements are referred to as **developmental milestones** (Gesell, 1952;

Figure 2.2   Sequence of Physical Development during the Prenatal Stage

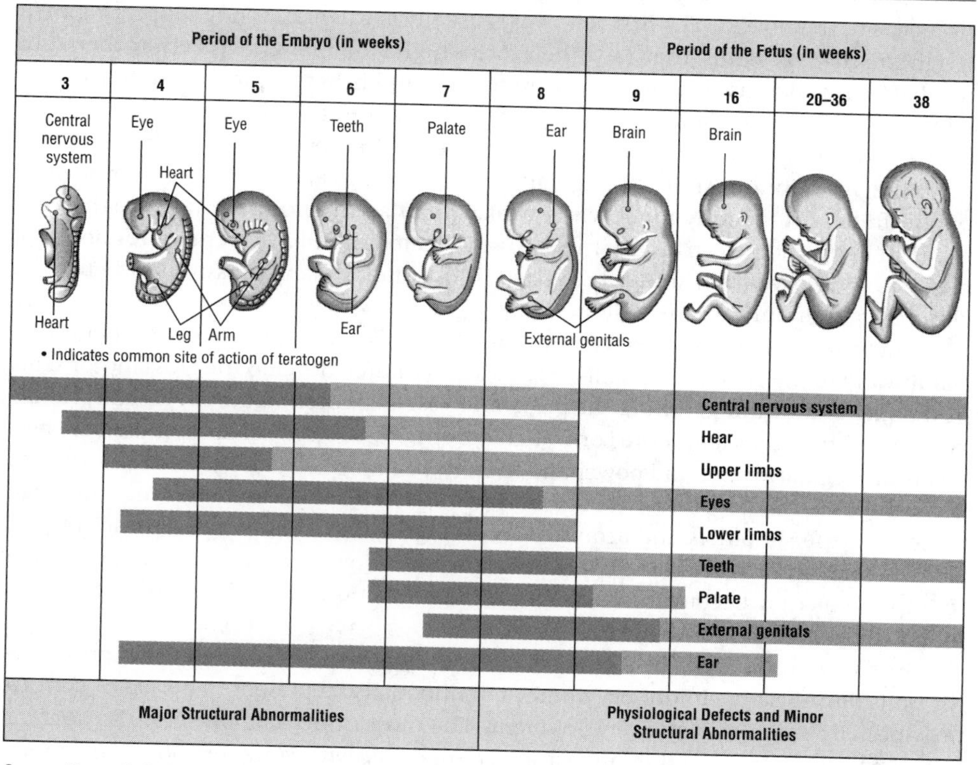

Period of the Embryo (in weeks)						Period of the Fetus (in weeks)			
3	4	5	6	7	8	9	16	20–36	38
Central nervous system	Eye	Eye	Teeth	Palate	Ear	Brain	Brain		

Heart   Leg | Arm   Ear   External genitals

• Indicates common site of action of teratogen

Central nervous system
Hear
Upper limbs
Eyes
Lower limbs
Teeth
Palate
External genitals
Ear

Major Structural Abnormalities	Physiological Defects and Minor Structural Abnormalities

Source: From J. A. Schickedanz, P. D. Forsyth, and G. A. Forsyth (1988), *Understanding Children and Adolescents*, 3rd ed. (Boston: Allyn and Bacon). Copyright 1988 by Pearson Education. Reprinted by permission of the publisher.

Harrow, 1972). These milestones represent key points in the process of growth and maturation in all of the developmental domains. Developmental milestones in the area of psychomotor development are usually the easiest milestones to document, because the behaviors are overt, or observable. As with other areas of development, psychomotor milestones follow a predictable sequence, although the exact age at which children first demonstrate these behaviors may vary, depending on biological and environmental influences. Many psychomotor milestones occur during the first year of life.

By the second month of life, typically developing infants support their upper bodies on their forearms when lying on their stomachs, sometimes raising their heads, shoulders, and upper chests a few inches and turning their heads from side to side at will or in response to interesting sights or sounds. Initially, infants maintain this position for only a few seconds, but over several weeks, the large muscles strengthen and balance improves so that they can remain in this position for several minutes. At some point, usually between the third and sixth months of life, infants roll over from their stomachs to their backs. The first roll-over is usually accidental. While supporting their weight on their forearms, they raise their torsos higher on one side than the other, thus overbalancing. Because infants' heads are so large and heavy in proportion to their total body size, this imbalance gently flips the infants onto their backs. As long as there is plenty of space for rolling over, the infants are not injured. In fact, other than being surprised, most infants smile or laugh at the feeling they get from rolling over. If given opportunities for "tummy time" while awake, infants will informally practice this new motor skill until they can voluntarily control this milestone in psychomotor development. Rolling over from stomach to back is just one of many gross motor behaviors children master during early childhood.

The proximodistal pattern of development is also evident as preschool children acquire and refine gross motor skills. As toddlers, children develop the gross motor skills of walking and running; during the preschool years, children refine these skills, resulting in smoother gaits and more controlled movements. Preschool-age children are better able to regulate speed and power and to negotiate more accurately through space. At the same time the large muscles in the upper body and torso are maturing, the large muscles in the shoulders and arms are becoming stronger. Children's abilities to perform movements involving the upper body, such as throwing a ball overhand, continue to improve as they become more adept, through practice, at regulating the speed and power exerted by their muscles (Gallahue, 1998).

Just as children make great strides in the development and refinement of gross motor skills during early childhood, middle childhood also represents a period of continued specialization for motor development. The most noticeable physical changes for school-age children lie in their increasing competence with complex motor behaviors. Throughout childhood, actual attainment of motor skills depends on factors within the individual, the task, and the environment, although the sequence of psychomotor development is similar among cultures (Gallahue, 1995). (See Figure 2.3.)

Much of the information about the developmental sequence of milestone behaviors during the first six years of life comes from the research of physician Arnold Lucius Gesell (1880–1961). Gesell and his Yale University colleagues documented the development of hundreds of young children and recorded when key behaviors (milestones) first emerged. Statistical analysis of Gesell's data identified not only the predictable sequence of these milestone behaviors, but also an age range during which typically developing children might be expected to exhibit such skills (Ilg, Ames, & Baker, 1992). The accumulated data were organized into tables and graphs illustrating the typical, or "normal," age range at which certain developmental milestones are mastered, and this information became known as **developmental norms.** Gesell contended that development is most strongly determined by neurological readiness, or maturation, rather than by environmental factors, although he did not completely exclude the effect of environment on development (Gesell, Halverson, Thompson, Ilg, Castner, Ames, & Amatruda, 1940).

Figure 2.3   Typical Developmental Sequence of Locomotor Skills

8 months
Stand with help
(7–9 months)

8 months
Stand holding furniture
(5–9 months)

8 months
Pull to stand
(6–9 months)

10 months
Creep on hands and knees
(9–11 months)

11 months
Climb stairs
(10–12 months)

11 months
Walk when led
(10–13 months)

11 months
Stand alone
(10–13 months)

12 months
Walk alone
(11–13½ months)

Source: From J. A. Schickedanz, P. D. Forsyth, and G. A. Forsyth (1988), *Understanding Children and Adolescents*, 3rd ed. (Boston: Allyn and Bacon). Copyright 1988 by Pearson Education. Reprinted by permission of the publisher.

One of the areas of development for which Gesell established norms was the progression of gross motor behaviors that involve a change in location of the body. Gross motor behaviors (such as crawling, creeping, walking, running, and skipping) that move the body from one location to another are referred to as **locomotor skills.** Locomotor skills begin to emerge during infancy, and most are mastered before the third birthday (Ilg, Ames, & Baker, 1992).

Between ages 6 and 12, children become increasingly proficient at complex gross motor tasks that require balance, coordination, strength, endurance, and flexibility. While most school-age children are already proficient walkers and runners, they are still developing their abilities to coordinate upper-body movements with lower-body movements into complex patterns of movement. Take a moment to think of some of the large muscle activities, games, and sports popular with children between ages 6 and 12. Your list might include jumping rope, climbing on jungle gyms, riding bicycles, swimming, rollerblading, and playing kickball, soccer, and baseball. Each of these activities involves specific gross motor skills, including some, or all, of the complex skills.

Why are school-age children better able to perform these complex motor tasks than preschool children? Part of the answer lies in the realm of growth, or physical maturation. Rates of growth fluctuate widely during childhood; annual increases in height and weight vary from one period of development to another. For example, before their first birthdays, most infants triple their birth weights and add several inches to their heights, whereas preschool-age children increase in weight about four pounds and in height about three inches per year. Moderate rates of growth continue throughout middle childhood, with weight increases of three to six pounds and height increases of two to three inches annually.

Increases in overall height and corresponding increases in body strength, along with decreases in head-to-body proportions, contribute to a shift in the point at which the body's weight is equally balanced above and below. This point is referred to as the **center of gravity.** Before middle childhood, the center of gravity is located high above the waist, near the shoulders, and causes a top-heavy condition that influences the balance and coordination of infants, toddlers, and preschool-age children. During the school-age years, the center of gravity shifts lower, to the area around the navel, provid-

Throughout childhood, children become increasingly proficient at complex motor tasks that require balance, coordination, and precision.

ing more stability and balance and enabling children to better coordinate upper- and lower-body movements and exert more deliberate control over the degree of strength employed for specific tasks (Gallahue, 1982). In other words, in early childhood children have less experience with motor skills and still have to develop proficiency at performing complex motor tasks that require not only balance and coordination but also precision and accuracy.

Fine Motor Development

Precision and accuracy are also necessary for the dozens of fine motor, or small muscle, skills that emerge during the preschool years. Many of these skills are physical behaviors that enable children to attend to some of their personal needs for eating, dressing, toileting, and grooming. Fine motor behaviors that fit under this category are called **self-help skills.** Older toddlers master self-help skills associated with nourishment, such as drinking from cups and holding spoons or forks, with enough efficiency that they get much of the food into their mouths. Over the next three years, most preschool children master the use of eating utensils and become adept at feeding themselves independently. Other self-help skills involve dressing and undressing. If you have been around

CDA

COMPETENCY GOAL II
• Functional Areas 4–7

COMPETENCY GOAL III
• Functional Area 8

Self-help skills, such as buttoning, provide many natural opportunities for young children to practice fine motor skills.

young children very often, then you may have noticed that they master undressing first! Pulling off socks, unbuttoning buttons, and untying their shoelaces are some of the first dressing, or undressing, skills they demonstrate. As small muscle movements refine according to the proximodistal pattern of development, preschool children master fine motor skills such as buttoning, snapping, zipping, and untying that require precision and coordination, enabling them to become less dependent on adults for assistance with their dressing and undressing routines.

Advances with self-help skills also enable children to be more independent at toileting. Toileting requires children to combine the fine motor self-help skills with gross motor skills to successfully remove and replace clothing when using the bathroom. Basic grooming tasks, such as washing hands and combing hair, also combine gross motor and fine motor behaviors.

Any motor behaviors that use the small muscles of the face, hands and fingers, or feet and toes are considered fine motor behaviors. Other tasks involving the small muscles of the hands and fingers include drawing, coloring, writing, painting, cutting, and manipulating modeling dough. Many of these tasks begin as gross motor behaviors during infancy and toddlerhood and refine into fine motor behaviors during the preschool years. Throughout early childhood, children gradually develop specialization and control over the small muscles of the hands and fingers. This increased **manual dexterity** enables them to manipulate objects and tools, like cutlery and drawing implements, with greater precision.

The emergence of drawing skills is one of the more obvious examples of their increasing manual dexterity. For example, when toddlers color or draw, they grasp the crayons or other writing utensils in their fists (whole-hand grasp) and move their whole arms, sometimes their whole bodies, when making marks on paper. Over the next several months, the way toddlers hold onto crayons will shift from whole-hand grasp to a pincer grasp, where the thumb and index finger hold the crayon in place as it rests on the middle finger. This motor refinement allows preschool-age children to have more control over their drawing, coloring, painting, and sculpting behaviors.

Drawing Behaviors during Early Childhood

There is a long history of interest in children's drawings and other artistic renderings as guideposts to children's psychomotor, cognitive, and affective development. Over the decades, child psychologists and other researchers have examined children's drawings to gather information about a variety of developmental issues, including progression of fine motor abilities, emergence of cognitive perspective taking, and stability of emotional health.

One of the more ambitious studies of children's drawings was undertaken by Rhoda Kellogg (1969), who collected and analyzed thousands of drawings from children in many parts of the world. From her research, Kellogg identified four stages of drawing through which children progress. As toddlers, children make random marks on paper with little deliberate thought and minimal control over results; their main satisfaction comes from the physical process of drawing and their results hold little

Table 2.1   Kellogg's Stages of Drawing

Age of Onset	Stage of Drawing	Characteristics
2 years old	Scribble	• Less developed fine motor skills • Demonstrate whole-hand grasp
3 years old	Basic forms	• Purposefully draw repetitive renderings using shapes and lines
3–4 years old	Placement	• Create patterns with well-defined borders
4–5 years old	Pictorial	• Think about what they intend to draw before they begin drawing • Use symbols to represent real objects and ideas

interest for them. These first efforts at drawing occur during the **scribble stage,** when children's fine motor skills are less developed and they still use the whole-hand grasp for drawing implements. Through her analysis of drawing during the scribble stage, Kellogg identified twenty basic forms of scribble that form the basis for other drawings.

Sometime before their third birthdays, as children begin to use pincer grasps on drawing utensils, they display some deliberation and control over placement and intensity of drawing. Children's scribbles produce some noticeable basic forms that occur spontaneously as they draw; as they notice these recurring forms, they attempt to reproduce them. These behaviors indicate that children have entered the second stage of drawing, the **basic forms stage.** During this stage of drawing, children purposefully draw repetitive renderings, using shapes and lines; this demonstrates their increasing visual awareness. During the third stage of drawing, the **placement stage,** children extend their deliberate use of shapes and lines to create patterns with well-defined borders, indicating their improved eye-hand coordination. The outcomes of their drawings begin to gain importance, although the psychomotor satisfaction remains primary.

One signal that children are emerging from the first three stages of drawing occurs when they look at their picture after they finish drawing and, with some surprise, say, "Look, I drawed a doggy!" This newfound awareness precedes Kellogg's (1969) fourth, and final, stage of drawing—the **pictorial stage.** Howard Gardner (1980) calls the phenomenon of drawing with no particular intent and then labeling the drawing **romancing.** The pictorial stage represents not only the progression of children's fine motor skills but also a shift in their intellectual, or cognitive, development (Gardner, 1980). During the pictorial stage, which continues beyond early childhood, children capitalize on their previously mastered drawing abilities, but now they think about what they intend to draw before they begin drawing. This cognitive shift is a result of children's abilities to use symbols to represent real objects and ideas. (Chapter 3 offers

Figure 2.4   **Samples of Children's Drawings**

Source: From Richard Fabes and Carol Lynn Martin (2000), *Exploring Child Development: Transactions and Transformations* (Boston: Allyn and Bacon). Copyright 2000 by Pearson Education. Reprinted by permission of the publisher.

a more in-depth exploration of cognitive abilities.) With practice and maturation, children continue to add detail and perspective to their drawings, which provides information about their increasingly precise fine motor behaviors and their emerging perspective-taking abilities.

As indicated by Gardner (1980), the degree of sophistication in children's drawings represents children's cognitive abilities as well as their psychomotor abilities. In fact, children's drawings of people have been used to measure their intelligence. Florence Goodenough (1926) collected and analyzed thousands of children's spontaneous and prompted drawings of people to get an indication of their level of intelligence. Goodenough's original purpose was to develop a nonverbal way to measure the intelligence of children with hearing impairments and those who were non-English speakers. Based on her analysis, Goodenough developed a measurement scale for her draw-a-man test that calculated an intelligence score based on children's ages and the number of details included in their drawings of people. For example, Gretchen, who is three years old, represents a person by drawing a single circle (for the body), with two straight lines sticking out at the bottom (for the legs). Christopher, who is also three years old, draws a person using a small circle (for the head) atop a larger circle (for the body), with two straight lines at the sides (for the arms) and two straight lines at the bottom (for the legs). Analysis of these drawings would indicate that Christopher's drawing indicates a higher level of intelligence than Gretchen's drawing because he included more body parts, which demonstrates more developed perspective-taking abilities. Goodenough's draw-a-man test was later revised and extended to include a draw-a-woman test (Harris, 1963).

Perceptual-Motor Development

CDA

COMPETENCY GOAL II
· Functional Area 4

Newborn infants require external assistance to support their heads, because their neck muscles are immature; however, within a few days infants are able to turn their heads from side to side when lying on their backs or when held with their heads and necks supported. Infants use these emerging motor skills to respond to the sights and sounds around them. Within a few weeks, infants hold their heads in upright positions when they are awake and their backs are supported. The upright position provides infants with a greater range of motion. Gradually, infants deliberately coordinate their movements to sensory stimuli to gain information and interact with others. For example, infants turn toward familiar voices and open their eyes more widely when the speakers are within view, which indicates the infants' interest and desire to interact. As mentioned earlier in this chapter, the coordination of muscles and movement to sensory stimuli is called perceptual-motor development. As with other areas of psychomotor development, perceptual-motor abilities are evident during the first weeks of life and improve rapidly through early childhood due to influences of maturation and experience.

For example, by age 3 or 4, most children are able to coordinate their senses and motor movements well enough to target objects with increasing accuracy. Activities such as throwing beanbags into baskets or jumping into chalk circles drawn on the sidewalk present preschool-age children with opportunities to use their visual and motor skills together. Following the proximodistal pattern of development, children first control their torsos and large muscles of the arms and legs, which are muscles closer to the center of the body. Gradually, preschool-age children develop more control over the smaller muscles that are further away from the center of the body, such as those in the hands and fingers and feet and toes.

In addition to refining small muscle control, which advances fine motor skills, preschool-age children increase their abilities to interpret sensory information, thus allowing them to more accurately coordinate body movements to their sensory perceptions (Williams, 1983). This aspect of perceptual-motor development is referred to as **body awareness**, or **spatial awareness**, and relates directly to children's consciousness of where their bodies and body parts are in relationship to objects and others. Spatial awareness enables children to sense the position of their bodies as they engage in motor activities and to coordinate movements to sensory stimuli. For example, **visual-motor coordination** involves matching muscle responses to visual input, such as in the beanbag activity described previously. Visual-motor coordination may involve coordinating visual input to movement of the hands or feet; these particular cases of visual-motor coordination are called **eye-hand coordination** and **eye-foot coordination**, respectively.

During early childhood, children have not yet developed specialization, accuracy, and speed in visual-motor coordination. Their brains are not yet efficiently sending messages between the hemispheres, which eventually enables children to process complex perceptual information with increasing accuracy and speed. Therefore, many children under age 6 do not yet have fine motor skills for tasks such as sewing, drawing, handwriting, and assembling models, which require precise levels of **visual discrimination** in conjunction with small muscle control. Visual discrimination, the ability to use sight to compare appearances of symbols and objects, is an essential skill for many of the fine motor tasks previously listed and for many of the skills connected with reading and writing.

Promoting Development within the Psychomotor Domain

COMPETENCY GOAL II
• Functional Areas
  4–7

During the first five years of life, many of the milestones of psychomotor development are accomplished. As discussed throughout this chapter, the periods of infancy and toddlerhood are ripe with milestones of gross motor development, while the preschool years are filled with achievements in the areas of fine motor and perceptual-motor development. Later, during middle childhood, children will refine and become more efficient at gross, fine, and perceptual-motor skills. Fortunately, quality early childhood classrooms and playgrounds abound with materials, equipment, routines, and activities that enhance psychomotor development.

The psychomotor domain is particularly well suited to active learning approaches. Chapter 1 introduced the concept of children as active learners who learn about themselves and their environments by observing and interacting with others as well as by manipulating objects and directly participating in play and learning experiences. Young children eagerly explore and handle things to expand their knowledge of objects and their properties. Manipulating objects engages all of the senses and also involves the small muscles of the hands and fingers, further supporting fine motor development.

Many of the activities in which young children engage provide naturalistic opportunities to practice fine motor skills. Sensory play experiences—such as digging in the sand, splashing in the water, and squeezing modeling dough—provide spontaneous practice for the small muscles of the hands and fingers. Some fine motor activities—such as coloring with crayons or markers, cutting with scissors, and constructing with snap-together blocks—develop coordination of the left and right hands, as one hand serves as the helper and the other hand performs the primary task. Other fine motor activities—such as manipulating toy vehicles, dressing dolls, and putting on dress-up clothes—require not only precise movements of the hands and fingers but also coordination of those movements within confined spaces.

As with other facets of development, the areas of the psychomotor domain overlap, allowing one activity or experience to satisfy many psychomotor needs simultaneously. For example, putting on dress-up clothes supports fine motor development because of the buttoning, zipping, lacing, and tying involved, even as the activity enhances gross motor development when children use their large muscles to pull on garments over their heads and torsos. Perceptual-motor development is likewise stimulated as children push buttons through buttonholes, arms through armholes, and belts through buckles and belt loops.

Creative activities provide another avenue for rich psychomotor experiences. For instance, creating collages involves many fine motor skills such as tearing, cutting, pasting, and manipulating materials for placement. Additionally, children use perceptual motor behaviors as they arrange and rearrange items in the collages to achieve desired aesthetic effects. Music and movement activities that involve handling rhythm instruments or using finger, hand, or body motions in response to music also stimulate overall motor development.

Even self-help routines such as dressing, toileting, washing hands, and eating give children opportunities to use and extend their psychomotor abilities. Typical daily routines related to arrival and departure—such as removing and putting on jackets, unzipping and zipping backpacks, and gathering and returning items on shelves—also facilitate use of psychomotor behaviors. Teachers who observe children as they engage in these daily behaviors gain information about children's current abilities related to gross, fine, and perceptual-motor development.

Outdoor experiences also facilitate development within the psychomotor domain. Outdoor play spaces abound with various opportunities to explore and strengthen psychomotor skills and abilities. Climbing structures support development of the large muscles of the arms, legs, and torso, thus facilitating gross motor development. Additionally, many of the games children play outdoors involve running, throwing, catching, kicking, or batting, all of which use the large muscles. Each of these activities requires some degree of balance, strength, agility, and endurance, thereby enhancing children's overall physical development. As mentioned previously, the areas of development within the psychomotor domain overlap; therefore, activities that support one area of psychomotor development are likely to support other areas as well. For example, the games listed earlier in this paragraph not only require use of the large muscles, but also require coordination of those muscles with perceptual information. To accurately catch balls, children first have to see the balls and then time their muscle movements to the appropriate speed and path of the balls. Many outdoor games make a natural connection between gross motor movements and perceptual-motor abilities.

By encouraging young children to openly explore and interact with each other and their play and learning environments, teachers support development throughout the psychomotor domain. Following the cues of children, teachers can further enhance play and learning environments by selecting developmentally appropriate materials, equipment, and activities to assist gross, fine, and perceptual-motor development.

Summary

- The psychomotor domain encompasses every aspect of physical development including sensory, gross motor, fine motor, and perceptual-motor abilities.

Early Sensory Abilities

- By six months of age, the visual acuity of infants is very similar to that of an adult.
- At birth, infants' abilities to hear, taste, smell, and touch are very similar to adults'.

Reflex Behaviors

- Many of the infant's first movements are involuntary reflexes.

Gross Motor Development

- Development follows both the cephalocaudal and proximodistal patterns.
- Psychomotor abilities develop in a somewhat predictable sequence.
- Several psychomotor milestones are achieved during early childhood.
- Gross motor behaviors include sitting, standing, walking, and running.

Fine Motor Development

- Fine motor behaviors include self-help skills related to dressing, eating, and hygiene.
- Fine motor behaviors, such as manipulating objects, become increasingly precise through maturation and practice.

- Children's drawings provide information not only about their psychomotor development, but also about their cognitive and affective development.

Perceptual-Motor Development

- Perceptual-motor behaviors include eye-hand and eye-foot coordination.
- Children use their senses and motor skills to explore their environments.

Promoting Development within the Psychomotor Domain

- Activities that involve manipulation of objects allow children to gain practice using their fine motor skills.
- Sensory experiences with water, sand, and modeling dough support psychomotor development as children play.
- Creative experiences such as drawing, painting, and making collages encourage children to use their fine motor skills.
- Activities associated with music and movement can provide many opportunities for young children to explore their psychomotor abilities.
- Outdoor experiences—such as running, jumping, climbing, and swinging—enhance gross motor development.

LEARNING ACTIVITIES

1 Simulation: Visual Acuity. To roughly simulate the visual acuity of newborn infants, stand close to another person so that your face is within eight to ten inches of the other person's face. Hold a thin sheet of waxed paper over your eyes. How well can you see the other person's face? Now step backward about two feet. How well can you see the person's face, now that you have moved outside the infant's visual range? Devise additional simulations to experience other visual characteristics of young infants, such as their preferences for black-and-white contrast and their abilities to visually track the movement of objects. If time permits, brainstorm ideas for simulations related to other areas of sensory development.

2 Application: Developmentally Appropriate Materials for Sensory Exploration. Visit a toy store (or view a toy catalog) with a wide array of infant toys. Using your knowledge of the sensory capabilities of infants, design an infant or toddler toy that promotes sensory exploration. On posterboard, draw an enlarged illustration of your design. Share the illustration of your toy with one or more classmates and point out the developmentally appropriate features that support development within the psychomotor domain.

3 Demonstration: Body Proportions. (Refer to Figure 2.1, p. 25.) Cut a piece of string the length of your height. Fold the string in half, to represent 50 percent of your body length. Hold the folded string so that it extends from the top of your head halfway down your body. If you were a nine-week fetus, your head would comprise approximately one-half of your total length. Using the information from your text and Figure 2.1, continue folding your string to demonstrate the dramatic changes in body proportions that occur from prenatal development to adulthood. Which pattern of physical development is demonstrated by these changes in body proportion?

PORTFOLIO ARTIFACTS

1 Interview: Locomotor Milestones. (Refer to Figure 2.3, p. 29.) Interview one or more family members of preschool-age children to determine the ages (to the nearest month) when their children first demonstrated some of the locomotor skills. Compare their children's developmental timelines to the developmental milestones in Figure 2.3. What similarities and differences did you identify? How could a caregiver use knowledge of developmental norms when planning activities for young children?

2 Sample: Children's Drawings. (Refer to Table 2.1, p. 33, and Figure 2.4, p. 34.) Collect samples of young children's spontaneous drawings. Record the ages of the children to the nearest month. Analyze the drawings according to Kellogg's stages of drawing. Do the drawings of children of similar ages represent the same stage? What can you learn about children's psychomotor development from watching them draw and/or analyzing their drawings? What clues about children's cognitive development can you find by analyzing their drawings?

3 Activity: Fine Motor. Using common household items—such as plastic milk caps or small cardboard boxes—devise a fine motor, manipulative activity for children between ages 2 and 5. Describe how the activity supports children's developing fine motor skills. What specific fine motor behaviors would children employ while engaging in the activity? If possible, let one or more children try out the activity and record what happens. Did the outcome of the activity meet your expectations? Elaborate on your response.

Professional Connections and Web Links

I Am Your Child Campaign and Foundation
335 N. Maple Drive, Suite 135
Beverly Hills, CA 90210
310-285-2385
1325 Sixth Avenue, 39th floor
New York, NY 10019
212-636-5030
http://www.iamyourchild.org

Rob Reiner's "I Am Your Child" Campaign and Foundation sponsor this worthwhile Web site designed to raise public awareness of the importance of the early years. The site is directed toward parents and provides basic information on development, from the prenatal stage through age 3 in the Ages and Stages topic section. Other topics include Brain Facts and Quality Child Care. The site also lists resources, including several videos on child development that are available for only the cost of postage.

Association for Childhood
Education International (ACEI)
11501 Georgia Avenue, Suite 315
Wheaton, MD 20902
800-423-3563
http://www.acei.org

The Association for Childhood Education International (ACEI), an international association founded in 1892, provides a global view of childhood education, from infancy through adolescence. In addition to publishing the journal *Childhood Education,* the ACEI also publishes quarterly newsletters focusing on specific developmental levels as well as position statements and books on key topics related to child development and childhood education. The ACEI sponsors an international conference annually that provides workshops and networking opportunities.

Suggestions for Further Reading

Gardner, Howard. (1980). *Artful scribbles: The significance of children's drawings.* New York: Basic Books.

- Gardner provides an extensive and informative description of how children's drawing abilities emerge and provides dozens of examples from their first scribbles to the detailed renderings of adolescents. He discusses several significant theories about children's drawings and presents his own views about the connections between their drawings and psychomotor, cognitive, and affective development.

Klaus, Marshall H., & Klaus, Phyllis H. (1998). *Your amazing newborn.* Reading, MA: Perseus Books.

- Klaus and Klaus present a black-and-white photographic diary of the first hours of life, along with descriptions of the newborn's abilities, which are documented from various research projects.

Miller, Karen. (2000). *Ages and stages: Developmental descriptions and activities, birth through eight years.* Glen Burnie, MD: Telshare.

- Miller provides a brief, easy-to-read outline of the developmental stages of the whole child, from birth through age 8. Simple activities for many areas of development are described for each developmental level.

References

Fantz, R. L. (1961). The origin of form and perception. *Scientific American, 204,* 66–72.

Fantz, R. L. (1963). Pattern vision in newborn infants. *Science, 140,* 296–297.

Gallahue, D. H. (1982). *Developmental motor experiences for children.* New York: Wiley.

Gallahue, D. H. (1995). *Understanding motor development: Infants, children, adolescents, and adults.* Dubuque, IA: Brown & Benchmark.

Gallahue, D. H., & Ozmun, J. C. (1998). *Understanding motor development: Infants, children, adolescents, and adults* (4th ed.). New York: McGraw-Hill.

Gardner, Howard (1980). *Artful scribbles: The significance of children's drawings.* New York: Basic Books.

Gesell, Arnold. (1949). The developmental aspect of child vision. *Journal of Pediatrics, 35*(3), 310–316.

Gesell, Arnold. (1952). *Infant development: The embryology of early behavior.* New York: Harper.

Gesell, Arnold, Halverson, H. M., Thompson, H., Ilg, Francis L., Castner, B. M., Ames, Louise B., & Amatruda, C. S. (1940). *The first five years of life: A guide to the pre-school child.* New York: Harper.

Goodenough, Florence L. (1926). *Measurement of intelligence by drawings.* Yonkers-on-Hudson, NY: World Book.

Harris, Dale B. (1963). *Children's drawings as measures of intellectual maturity: A revision and extension of the Goodenough draw-a-man test.* New York: Harcourt, Brace and World.

Harrow, Anita J. (1972). *A taxonomy of the psychomotor domain: A guide for developing behavioral objectives.* New York: Longman.

Ilg, Francis L., Ames, Louise, B., & Baker, Sidney M. (1992). *Child behavior: The classic child care manual from the Gesell Institute of Human Development.* New York: Harper Perennial Library.

Kellogg, Rhoda. (1969). *Analyzing children's art.* Palo Alto, CA: National Press Books.

Klaus, Marshall H., & Klaus, Phyllis H. (1998). *Your amazing newborn.* Reading, MA: Perseus Books.

Williams, H. G. (1983). *Perceptual motor development.* Englewood Cliffs, NJ: Prentice Hall.

The Cognitive Domain

After reading this chapter and completing the related activities, you should be able to

- Describe research findings related to early brain development
- Define the cognitive domain
- Explain how maturation and experience influence cognitive development
- Outline Piaget's stages of cognitive development
- Give examples of characteristics of children's reasoning at each developmental stage
- State Vygotsky's view of cognitive development
- Explain the relationship between cognition and language
- Describe the sequence and give examples of language development
- Suggest teaching practices that support development in the cognitive domain

When asked to explain why the sun doesn't shine at night, four-year-old Tomas replies, "The sun gets tired and goes to sleep at night." From an adult standpoint, Tomas's response may seem illogical, because the sun is not alive and thus does not sleep. For the moment, consider the question from the child's perspective. As Tomas elaborates: "I play outside when it's sunny, but have to come inside when the sun goes in and it gets dark. At dark time [nighttime], I go to bed, and when I wake up the sun is up, too." Notice how Tomas uses information from his experiences to explain why the sun doesn't shine at night.

hildren and adults reason in distinctly different ways. Children's reasoning is strongly influenced by direct experiences and perceptions. While most adults can reason based on facts that are not always in evidence, children rely on what they see, hear, and experience to explain objects and events in their world. Exploring why children reason the way they do involves understanding both the physical development of the brain and the psychological development of the mind.

CHAPTER 3

Early Brain Development

While brain development is a component of psychomotor development and was briefly mentioned in Chapter 2, it is so closely linked to the psychological development of the mind that both topics will be discussed within this chapter. Recent research findings from studies of early brain development support the belief that both biological and environmental factors impact the physical development of the brain. Implications from these research findings have influenced the way many educators view child care and early learning experiences.

CDA

COMPETENCY GOAL II
• Functional Areas 4–5

Brain development begins during the prenatal stage; in fact, the brain and spinal column are among the first body systems to form. Even before the sixteenth week of pregnancy, the fetus's tiny brain is sending signals to the rest of its body. At birth, the newborn's brain is roughly one-fourth the size of an adult's brain but already performs many life-sustaining functions (Eliot, 1999). As shown in Figure 3.1 (p. 44), the brain experiences a growth spurt during the last three months of pregnancy. This growth spurt continues through the first eighteen months of life. In fact, by baby's first birthday, the brain will have grown to three-fourths of its adult size (Tanner, 1990).

Another facet of brain growth and development that takes place during the prenatal stage is biological programming that predisposes certain areas of the brain to be responsible for specific functions. For example, most higher-level thought processes and language operations originate in an area of the brain located in its outer layer, or **cerebral cortex**, in a region behind the forehead identified as the **frontal lobe.** (Refer to Figure 3.2, p. 45.) The cerebral cortex is the largest part of the brain and the least developed at birth (Eliot, 1999).

Recent research has added insights into how the brain develops and operates. Once researchers considered the brain to be fully formed neurologically at birth, but neuroscientists now believe that the brain continues to develop outside the womb. In fact, many areas of the brain remain malleable, or able to be shaped, for the first decade of life (Eliot, 1999). Some neuroscientists use the term **plasticity** to describe this adaptability of the brain.

During infancy, the brain's plasticity is at its most malleable state. Earlier in this chapter, we learned that certain areas of the brain are preprogrammed, or **soft-wired**, during prenatal development to perform specific functions. Soft-wiring of the brain prepares its many billions of brain cells, or **neurons**, to form the interconnections necessary for the intricate operations the brain will perform throughout a person's lifetime. This soft-wiring allows individuals' experiences to influence how the brain will use its billions of brain cells. Young children's experiences and interactions cause interconnections to develop between the neurons until millions of elaborate neural pathways

Figure 3.1 Prenatal Brain Development

Source: From J. A. Schickedanz, P. D. Forsyth, and G. A. Forsyth (1988), *Understanding Children and Adolescents,* 3rd ed. (Boston: Allyn and Bacon). Copyright 1988 by Pearson Education. Reprinted by permission of the publisher.

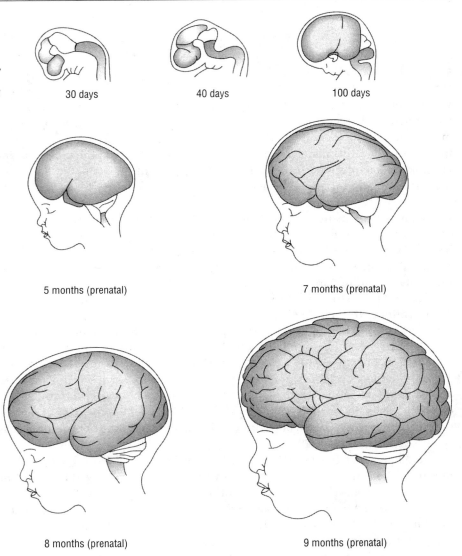

30 days   40 days   100 days

5 months (prenatal)   7 months (prenatal)

8 months (prenatal)   9 months (prenatal)

are formed. These neural pathways, or networks, enable neurons to transmit messages to each other. As shown in Figure 3.3, actual physical changes take place in the brain's structure as a result of experiences and interactions (Eliot, 1999).

One of the physical changes in the brain is the development of message-transmitting fibers designed to receive or send input. These fibers, developed by neurons, are called **dendrites** and **axons**. (See Figure 3.4, p. 46.) Neuroscientist Lise Eliot (1999) likens neurons to trees. The dendrites serve as the root systems, receiving input from other neurons.

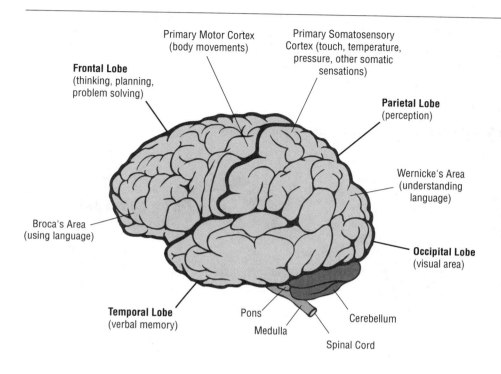

Frontal Lobe
(thinking, planning,
problem solving)

Primary Motor Cortex
(body movements)

Primary Somatosensory
Cortex (touch, temperature,
pressure, other somatic
sensations)

Parietal Lobe
(perception)

Broca's Area
(using language)

Wernicke's Area
(understanding
language)

Occipital Lobe
(visual area)

Temporal Lobe
(verbal memory)

Pons

Medulla

Cerebellum

Spinal Cord

Figure 3.2 Map
of the Brain

Source: From
Richard Fabes and
Carol Lynn Martin
(2000), *Exploring
Child Development:
Transactions and
Transformations*
(Boston: Allyn and
Bacon). Copyright
2000 by Pearson Ed-
ucation. Reprinted
by permission of the
publisher.

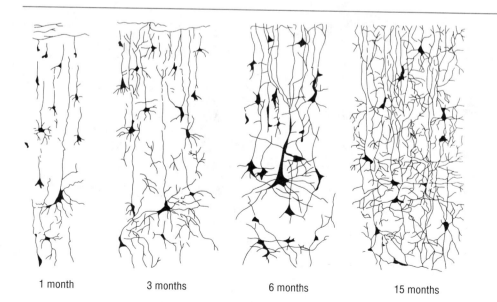

1 month   3 months   6 months   15 months

Figure 3.3
**Development of
Neural Networks**

Source: From J. A.
Schickedanz, P. D.
Forsyth, and G. A.
Forsyth (1988), *Un-
derstanding Children
and Adolescents,* 3rd
ed. (Boston: Allyn
and Bacon). Copy-
right 1988 by
Pearson Education.
Reprinted by
permission of the
publisher.

A young child's environment directly and permanently influences the structure and eventual function of his or her brain.

—Lise Eliot, *What's Going On in There? How the Brain and Mind Develop in the First Five Years of Life* (1999, p. 32)

The axons form the limbs of the trees, branching out to relay messages to the next neuron. The messages, or **impulses**, are electrically or chemically transmitted across a gap between neurons called a **synapse**, thus sparking more neural interconnections. The type and amount of stimulation infants encounter will influence how their neural connections form and thus how their brains develop.

Figure 3.4   Neurons with Dendrites and Axons

Source: From Richard Fabes and Carol Lynn Martin (2000), *Exploring Child Development: Transactions and Transformations* (Boston: Allyn and Bacon). Copyright 2000 by Pearson Education. Reprinted by permission of the publisher.

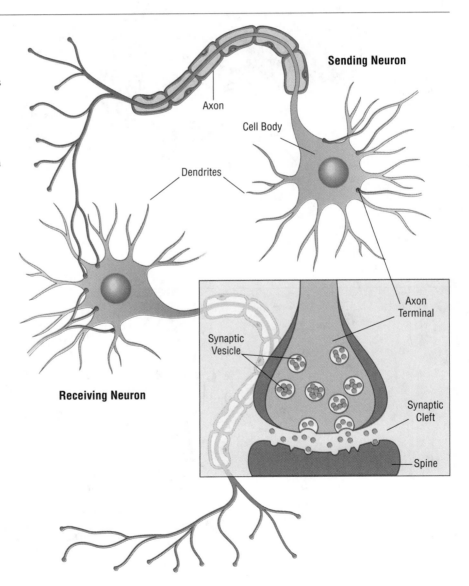

During early infancy, the brain's ability to transmit messages between neurons is relatively slow and inefficient. As the neural networks within the brain continue to develop and extend, efficient transmission of impulses becomes increasingly important. A process that improves the speed and efficiency with which nerve impulses are transmitted within the brain involves insulating the nerve cells with a fatty protein substance (myelin). This sheathing process is referred to as **myelination.** Although myelination begins during prenatal development, the process is not complete for several years.

During the first three years of life, the brain develops quite rapidly. Between ages 3 and 10, brain development is generally steady, although each half, or **hemisphere**, of the brain develops at a different rate. The left hemisphere undergoes a moderate growth spurt between ages 3 and 6, whereas the right hemisphere experiences a mild growth spurt between ages 8 and 10. By age 10, the brain reaches 90 percent of its adult size, and most of the myelination process is complete. Increases in both brain size and function can be partly attributed to myelination of the neurons. Improved brain function due to this increased insulation of nerve cells affects transmission of nerve impulses within each brain hemisphere as well as between the hemispheres.

Each hemisphere of the brain has areas that are preprogrammed to perform specific cognitive functions. Cognitive functions are performed by one hemisphere of the brain or the other; this specialization is called **lateralization.** Lateralization, in combination with myelination, contributes to the speed and efficiency of brain function. As children continue to grow and develop, areas of their brains become more highly specialized and therefore more efficient.

In order to transmit messages between the hemispheres, nerve impulses must travel across a large bundle of fibers connecting the two hemispheres. This large bundle of fibers, the **corpus collosum**, acts as a bridge between the right and left hemispheres of the brain. The brain's increased ability to send messages between the hemispheres contributes to the rapid increase in language ability evident during the later part of early childhood (ages 5 through 8). In fact, many abilities and skills developed during childhood involve both the left and right hemispheres of the brain.

The ability to read is one skill developed during childhood that uses both hemispheres of the brain simultaneously. For example, most, but not all, language processes are located in the left hemisphere of the brain. Figure 3.2 identifies several areas in the left hemisphere of the brain that are connected to processing language. The right hemisphere of the brain is the dominant side for visual spatial ability. The ability to read fluently requires both language skills and visual-spatial skills; therefore, neurons must be able to efficiently transmit messages across the corpus collosum to engage both the left and right hemispheres of the brain.

Understanding how the brain develops during early childhood highlights the crucial role of early experiences in shaping the brain; however, development of the brain is only one factor in the development of cognition, or mental functions. To fully appreciate the complex nature of cognitive development, one must also understand the developing mind.

Cognitive Development

CDA

COMPETENCY GOAL II
• Functional Areas 5–6

Development of the mind falls within the broader developmental classification of the *cognitive domain*. As discussed in Chapter 1, the cognitive domain encompasses many overlapping components, including development of reasoning, concepts, memory, and language. Although each aspect of cognitive development has specific characteristics and patterns, looking at the development of the whole cognitive domain more accurately portrays the dynamics behind the developing mind. Contemporary cognitive development theorists generally acknowledge that cognitive development is influenced by both biological and environmental factors. *Maturation* (as discussed in Chapter 1) is the sequence of development that is strongly influenced by biological factors, or heredity. However, maturation alone cannot explain all of the variations in cognitive development one might observe among a group of typically developing children.

For example, identical twins, by definition, share identical biological factors. These biological factors should cause their maturation to unfold along the same timetable. However, identical twins sometimes progress through cognitive development at different rates because of other factors, as the following vignette shows. What other factors influence cognitive development? The answer lies within children's environments. As discussed in Chapter 1, *experience* is the set of environmental factors that influence development. As children explore objects and events and engage in social interactions with people within their environments, they gain experience. It is the intricate interaction of maturation and experience that uniquely shapes the cognitive development of each child.

Sarah and Beth are identical twins who were adopted at six weeks of age by different families. Sarah's adoptive parents also have two preschool-age boys. Though Sarah's mother and father work outside the home, evenings provide many opportunities for the family to be together. Sarah's parents are comfortable interacting with her and her brothers and make many opportunities for touching, talking, and playing.

On the other hand, Beth's mother and father are first-time parents with little experience with infants and no extended family living nearby. Their interactions with Beth, though loving, are hesitant and inconsistent. Additionally, Beth's parents have demanding jobs that require long hours and frequent travel. They have hired an elderly neighbor to care for Beth during the day. The elderly neighbor carefully provides for Beth's physical needs but believes infants should not be held all of the time and frequently places Beth in the infant swing or playpen when she is awake. The caregiver's interactions with Beth are limited to providing for her physical needs. Beth's parents juggle their schedules so that one of them is with Beth in the evenings, and although Beth's parents enjoy playing with her, they follow the advice of their elderly neighbor and try not to hold her too often so that she will learn to entertain herself.

As identical twins, the infants in this vignette share biological traits that strongly influence their maturation. However, because their home environments differ, the infants have significantly different experiences. The physical needs of both infants are

Since identical twins share identical biological factors, differences in development are generally attributed to environmental influences.

being met, but one infant experiences more consistent nurturing as well as more frequent opportunities to interact and play with others. How might their cognitive development be affected? Could differences between their cognitive development be attributed mainly to environmental influences?

Piaget's Theory of Cognitive Development

Noted Swiss biologist and psychologist Jean Piaget (1896–1980) was a cognitive development theorist who believed that experiences within the environment are key factors influencing the developing mind. He sought a biological explanation for the connection between the developing mind and the developing brain but also believed that environment played a vital role throughout the course of cognitive development. As a biologist, Piaget was keenly aware that genetic factors strongly influence growth and development. As a psychologist, he searched for ways to explain how biological and environmental factors interact to construct knowledge.

Piaget theorized that cognitive development follows a predictable pattern of maturation, as determined by biological factors. He went on to propose that although the cognitive development of all children proceeds through the same sequence of development, the rate at which each child develops cognitively is determined by the interaction of biological and environmental factors. Piaget believed that children build, or construct, their own knowledge as they gain experience through active exploration and interaction (Piaget, 1936/1963).

Children construct knowledge as they encounter new experiences and attempt to mentally reconcile existing knowledge, or **schemas**, with new information and experiences. This mental process of reconciling existing and new information, or **adaptation**, can follow either of two possible avenues, as depicted in Figure 3.5 (p. 50). If the new information or experience can be incorporated within an existing schema, then the

Figure 3.5   **Constructing and Reconstructing Knowledge: Piaget's Cognitive Adaptive Process**

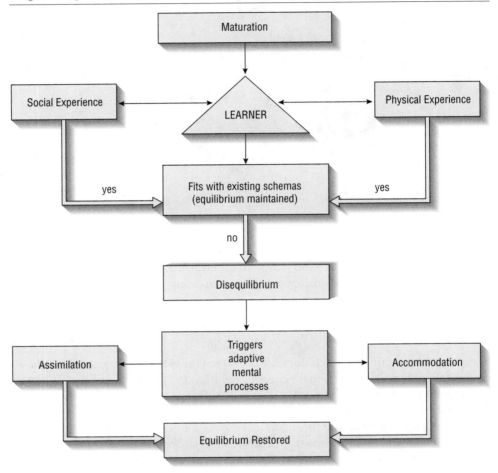

mental process of **assimilation** occurs. If, however, the new experience is contrary to an existing schema or if there is no existing schema into which the new experience fits, the learner uses the mental process of **accommodation.** Piaget believed that assimilation and accommodation, though lifelong processes, are not deliberate mental processes. Rather, these adaptive mental processes occur spontaneously and continuously to help individuals make sense of the world.

If assimilation and accommodation are not deliberate mental processes, what triggers human minds to engage in them? Piaget maintained that humans have an innate need to understand the world around them. Therefore, each new experience or encounter causes a momentary mental imbalance, or **disequilibrium**, that triggers the adaptive mental processes of assimilation and accommodation. Once the new experience or encounter has been assimilated into an existing schema or accommodated into a new schema, a state of mental balance, or **equilibrium**, is restored. The restoration of equilibrium indicates that the knowledge base has been reconstructed and that the new experience is now part of the person's unique knowledge base.

Six-month-old Jamal contentedly sucks on the nipple of his bottle until it runs out of formula. He begins to squirm and fuss, so, for the first time, his father places a pacifier in Jamal's mouth. Jamal immediately calms down and sucks on the pacifier's nipple. After a few seconds, Jamal's sucking becomes more intense. Then he suddenly pushes the pacifier out of his mouth with his tongue and begins to squirm and fuss with renewed vigor.

When Jamal sucked on the nipple of his bottle and received formula, he experienced equilibrium, because his sucking efforts met his expectations based on his prior experiences of sucking on the nipple of a bottle. When Jamal's father placed the nipple of the pacifier in his mouth for the first time, Jamal expected to receive formula when he sucked; however, when no formula was forthcoming despite increased sucking efforts, Jamal experienced disequilibrium. This new experience, sucking on a pacifier, did not fit within Jamal's existing schema of sucking on the nipple of a bottle. Without conscious thought, Jamal's adaptive mental processes of assimilation and accommodation are triggered. When the "sucking on a pacifier's nipple" experience cannot be assimilated into related prior experiences of "sucking on a bottle's nipple," Jamal's mind constructs a new schema through accommodation. Now, Jamal's knowledge base includes two schemas about nipples: one schema in which sucking on the nipple of a bottle supplies formula, and another schema in which sucking on the nipple of a pacifier provides comfort but no formula. As Jamal becomes accustomed to the pacifier, his mental equilibrium is restored, and his knowledge base is reconstructed to include knowledge of pacifiers.

Repeated encounters with objects like the pacifier in this vignette enable infants to add more detail to existing schemas. However, their understandings of objects are somewhat oversimplified, because they perceive things only in the present time, due to their limited understanding of time and space. Regardless of these perceptual limitations, young children's understandings of objects adapt as new experiences are interwoven with existing knowledge through assimilation or are placed into new schemas through accommodation. (These adaptive processes are illustrated in this vignette.)

Piaget's Three Categories of Knowledge As young children widen their active explorations of their environments, they extend their learning beyond the category of objects and their properties to a second category of the relationships among objects and events, and further still to a third category of the systems of behavior within their cultures. Piaget labeled these three categories of knowledge **physical knowledge**, **logico-mathematical knowledge**, and **socioconventional knowledge**, respectively. He contended that all knowledge fits within these three categories and, further, that all knowledge is constructed by means of the physical and mental actions of learners (Forman & Kuschner, 1983).

In the case of physical knowledge, learners manipulate objects and explore them with their senses. The objects themselves give learners feedback about their characteristics; in turn, learners construct mental representations, or schemas, that incorporate all of the sensory information they gathered by acting on—that is, manipulating and exploring—the objects. In the preceding vignette, the infant Jamal acts on the pacifier and, in so doing, constructs a schema that adds to his personal storehouse of physical knowledge. According to Piaget, the nature of objects serves as a catalyst for explorations, but it is the actions of the learners that cause the construction of knowledge to take place. The sensation of the pacifier triggers Jamal's interest, but his sucking on it and spitting it out cause him to learn about it.

As with physical knowledge, logico-mathematical knowledge comes from physical or mental actions with objects or events and through interactions with others. Logico-mathematical knowledge develops from physical knowledge when learners think about their experiences with objects, events, or people and mentally or physically act on their experiences. Logico-mathematical knowledge involves the mental construction of relationships among objects, events, and others (Piaget, 1967).

For example, when preschool-age children play with the pieces of a puzzle, they initially explore the individual pieces, noticing the colors, sizes, shapes, and textures of each piece. By acting on the puzzle pieces in this way, the children construct physical knowledge and build schemas. Discovering that the puzzle pieces interconnect and form a complete picture, the children can identify a relationship between the puzzle pieces and the whole puzzle. By physically acting on (manipulating) the puzzles pieces and thinking about the ways to fit the pieces together, the children have constructed logico-mathematical knowledge.

As children become more experienced at mentally representing ideas, they accumulate Piaget's third type of knowledge—socioconventional knowledge. As they do with physical knowledge and logico-mathematical knowledge, learners actively construct socioconventional knowledge. However, socioconventional knowledge is more dependent on interacting with others rather than acting on objects. Socioconventional knowledge includes knowledge of the customs, laws, values, and language systems of social or cultural groups. Socioconventional knowledge includes such behaviors as saying "please" and "thank you" at the appropriate times and looking both ways before crossing a street. Specific socioconventional knowledge varies among individuals, depending on their families, communities, and cultures.

Piaget's Four Stages of Cognitive Development   For all three types of knowledge, how the actions, events, and interactions are mentally represented will vary depending on the developmental level of the learners. Piaget explained how children's reasoning processes differ from the reasoning processes of adults and, at the same time, emphasized that children are not less intelligent than adults; they simply use qualitatively different cognitive processes (Forman & Kuschner, 1983). Throughout cognitive development, children's perceptions and reasoning abilities influence how they construct their knowledge. Based on detailed observational studies, Piaget drew distinctions between the ways children at various developmental levels perceive their experiences.

As shown in Table 3.1, Piaget's theory of cognitive development identifies four discrete stages from infancy through adolescence. Each stage is characterized by the ways in which children perceive their experiences and how they use mental processes to construct their knowledge. Development from one stage to the next is influenced by two interacting factors—maturation and experience. Maturation, the biological aspect of development, determines the sequence of development; that is, all children develop through the stages in order. Maturation also strongly influences approximate ages for the onset of each stage, while experience, the environmental aspect of development, strongly influences the amount of time individual children remain in each stage. Each discrete stage of cognitive development has distinct characteristics that are dependent on learners' perceptions and abilities to construct mental representations.

Table 3.1   **Piaget's Stages of Cognitive Development**

Approximate Age	Stage of Cognitive Development	Characteristics
Birth to age 2 years	Sensorimotor	• Use senses and motor skills to explore environment • Learn through trial and error • Imitate behaviors of others • Develop object permanence • Demonstrate deferred imitation • Develop symbolic representation
Ages 2 to 7 years	Preoperational	• Employ symbolic representation • Demonstrate egocentrism • Employ static reasoning • Demonstrate irreversibility • Demonstrate lack of conservation
Ages 7 to 11 years	Concrete operational	• Demonstrate less egocentrism • Demonstrate reversibility • Demonstrate emerging understanding of conservation • Employ inductive reasoning • Employ basic problem solving • Base ideas on concrete evidence or direct experience
Ages 11 to 15 years Continues into adulthood	Formal operational	• Understand conservation • Employ deductive reasoning • Engage in hypothetical (abstract) reasoning

Sensorimotor Stage Piaget's first stage of cognitive development, the **sensorimotor stage,** focuses on how infants respond to new experiences in their environments. According to Piaget, from birth to approximately age 2, infants use their senses and motor behaviors, or movements, to interact with and gain information from their environments. As they use their senses to investigate their surroundings, they employ their motor skills to increase opportunities for exploration. When infants feel objects touch their lips (sensory exploration), they immediately begin to mouth the objects (motor behavior). By sucking on the objects, they use their mouths to gather information about the taste, texture, size, and temperature of the objects; additionally, infants use their hands to hold, feel, and manipulate objects. These complementary sensory and motor behaviors contribute additional information to their developing schemas of objects. As infants have repeated trial-and-error opportunities to explore objects, they continue to add detail to existing schemas and construct more complete understanding of objects and their properties, thus adding to their physical knowledge base. Having many opportunities to explore and interact with their environments enables infants to add onto their existing schemas and construct new schemas to incorporate newly acquired knowledge, thereby broadening their physical knowledge base (Piaget, 1967). For example, a toddler who has a toy that plays a favorite tune whenever the big yellow button is pushed is likely to expect the same response from any toy with a big yellow button. Then he gets a new toy that also has a big yellow button, but instead of causing a tune to play when it is pressed, the yellow button causes a little clown to pop out of a door. The toddler has to adjust his schema for big yellow buttons to include actions other than playing a tune. With each new encounter with big yellow buttons, the toddler gains additional information and makes corresponding adaptations to his existing schema.

During infancy, what children perceive heavily influences how they interpret and understand objects, events, and others. For example, young infants are not aware that objects continue to exist even when they are not within view or hearing range; in other words, they lack a sense of **object permanence.** Lack of this sense of object permanence explains why very young infants (under six months) do not visually track the path of a falling object or cry out for a toy that has been moved outside their view. To them, the object ceases to exist when it is no longer visible.

People in infants' environments also seem to lack object permanence. For the first few months of life, most infants will not react negatively when familiar individuals leave or when unfamiliar individuals approach. However, around seven to nine months of age, many infants begin to exhibit anxiety by fussing or crying when these events occur. As infants in the sensorimotor stage gradually develop understanding of object permanence, they perceive the comings and goings of others differently, because they now understand that others exist even when they cannot be seen or heard. Since infants generally prefer the company of familiar caregivers, they may react with distress to the departure of familiar faces or the arrival of unfamiliar

> *T*he discoveries we make in infancy are
> implicitly used in all our subsequent
> discoveries.
> —George E. Forman and David S. Kuschner, *The Child's
> Construction of Knowledge: Piaget for Teaching Children*
> (1983, p. 9)

ones. (Chapter 4 provides more information about the distress exhibited by some infants in these situations.) The development of a sense of object permanence represents a milestone in the cognitive development of infants.

Throughout the sensorimotor stage, infants and toddlers often mimic the behaviors of others, such as covering their eyes to play peek-a-boo; these actions are referred to as **imitation.** Through imitation, infants and toddlers act on the behaviors of others with whom they interact. Toward the latter half of the sensorimotor stage, toddlers demonstrate abilities to imitate actions after a lapse in time rather than while they are observing the behaviors. The ability to imitate behaviors after they have been observed is called **deferred imitation.** Deferred imitation marks a shift in children's cognitive abilities, because being able to imitate behaviors after a lapse in time indicates not only emerging memory skills but also the ability to exhibit mental representations externally. For example, toddlers playing in the sandbox may repeatedly pour sand from one container to another because they have observed older children engaging in these same behaviors. These toddlers have constructed mental representations of playing in the sand based on their observations of the older children; however, their imitation of the behavior was deferred until they had access to the sandbox a few days later. Once children are able to mentally represent objects and actions, they are passing from the sensorimotor stage to the second stage of cognitive development.

Preoperational Stage Piaget labeled the second stage of cognitive development the **preoperational stage.** This stage begins around two years of age and, for most typically developing children, ends around seven years of age. As with all of Piaget's stages of cognitive development, the exact time of onset and duration varies from child to child, depending on the interaction of maturation and experience. Children entering the preoperational stage of cognitive development demonstrate abilities to act on their mental representations of objects and actions. Deferred imitation, which begins during the sensorimotor stage, enables them to act out behaviors from mental representations constructed from their prior experiences with objects, events, and interactions. Their imitative actions symbolize their mental representations. For instance, a toddler who sees her grandfather use a spoon to stir the tea in his teacup during supper might use her spoon the next morning to stir the milk in her cereal bowl. The toddler remembers the grandfather's actions and imitates them several hours later.

Related to deferred imitation is the ability to pretend that objects or actions represent other objects or actions. This ability is called **symbolic representation** and stands as one of the cornerstones of cognitive development. Symbolic representation serves as a gateway into the preoperational stage of cognitive development (Forman & Kuschner, 1983) as well as the foundation of language and imagination. Symbolic representation literally means representing objects, actions, and ideas with symbols. For example, the word *apple* is a language symbol used to represent the actual fruit. A photograph or illustration of an apple is a visual symbol used to represent the real apple. Symbolic representation can also mean using one object or action to represent another object or action. For example, preschool children might pretend to eat apples by holding small red blocks to their mouths and making biting and chewing motions as they "eat their apples." These symbolic behaviors represent the cognitive ability of preschool children to manipulate visual images in their minds. In addition to having the ability to use symbolic representation, children in the preoperational stage demonstrate several other cognitive characteristics.

One characteristic of all preoperational children is their tendency to view all objects and events from only their own perspectives and to assume that others also perceive objects and events exactly as they do (Piaget & Inhelder, 1958). Piaget labeled this cognitive characteristic **egocentrism.** This single-sided view creates some interesting interpretations of objects, events, and social interactions—especially when you consider that all of the other preoperational children are also viewing life from their own egocentric perspectives. The vignette below gives an example of such single-sided views among young children.

Preoperational children perceive each experience through the filter of egocentrism. That is, they build, or construct, their own knowledge within the limits of their personal experiences and understandings. As mentioned earlier, children use the dual mental processes of assimilation and accommodation to adapt their mental schemas as they encounter new experiences. However, preoperational children's perceptions of new experiences are limited by egocentrism to a single perspective.

Three-year-old preschool classmates Samuel and Carmen are visiting the zoo for the first time. Both children are viewing the zebra exhibit. Samuel, who lives on a farm, points to the zebra and says, "Look at that striped horsey!" Samuel is using the adaptive mental process of assimilation to include new experience (seeing the zebra) with an earlier experience (seeing a horse). Because both animals share similar features, Samuel reaches the cognitive conclusion that both are horses. On the other hand, Carmen, who lives in the city in an apartment, has never seen a real horse. Since Carmen does not have any existing schemas that fit with her new experience of seeing the zebra, she begins to build a new schema for the zebra. Carmen is using the mental process of accommodation to relieve the disequilibrium she experiences when she encounters a type of animal she has not seen before. Though Samuel and Carmen are sharing the same experience (seeing a zebra for the first time) and are spontaneously employing adaptive mental processes to adjust their schemas, they reach different conclusions. Their construction, or reconstruction, of knowledge is being influenced by their egocentrism, because both children view the zebra through the filter of their personal experiences. Additionally, due to egocentrism, both Samuel and Carmen will assume that the teachers and other children perceive the zebra just as they do!

Egocentrism contributes to many of the other cognitive characteristics exhibited by preoperational children. Because preoperational children rely on perception rather than logical reasoning, they tend to draw conclusions that focus on the most obvious attribute of an object, event, or interaction. The cognitive tendency to mentally focus on the single, most obvious feature of an object or event is called **centration.** For example, if you ask a group of four-year-old children on the playground to point out the

The egocentrism of preoperational children influences their assimilation and accommodation processes.

oldest child, they will most likely point to the tallest child. The most obvious physical difference between the children on the playground is height; therefore, they focus, or centrate, on that trait and reason that the child who is tallest is oldest, because one gets taller as one gets older.

Such conclusions are the result of **precausal reasoning.** In other words, children tend to believe that one event causes another just because they occur together. Preoperational children tend to use precausal reasoning because their logic is based on perception rather than deduction—and their perceptions are restricted by their egocentrism.

The cognitive abilities of preoperational children are qualitatively different from those of older children or adults, who can suspend the influence of perception in favor of logical reasoning. These cognitive limitations often cause preoperational children to misinterpret physical changes. When the physical nature of objects changes, the objects have undergone **transformation.** Transformations are the result of physical processes that change the appearances of the objects.

For example, when bread goes into the toaster, it may be white. When it comes out of the toaster, it is brown. The heating process within the toaster causes this change of appearance. However, preoperational children, whose egocentrism causes them to rely on perception rather than logic, centrate on the most obvious physical attribute—in this case, color. Therefore, preoperational children explain the change in the bread's color based on what they see or perceive. Since the bread was white when it was placed in the toaster and brown when it was removed from the toaster, the toaster itself caused the bread to become brown. Preoperational children do not consider the heating process that occurred inside the toaster to be related to the changes they observed in the bread. Instead, they base their conclusions on what they see at the beginning and what they see at the end of the process; their reasoning focuses on the outcome of the transformation rather than the process of the transformation. This type of reasoning is called **static reasoning.** Egocentric children are unable to mentally reverse the complete transformation process; instead, they connect the end result to the beginning without considering any intermediary events. The inability to mentally reverse a process or series of events is called **irreversibility.**

Using static reasoning, preoperational children may also attempt to explain the change in the bread's appearance by attributing lifelike qualities to the object involved. They may say that the toaster "wanted" the bread to be brown so it colored the bread while it was inside the toaster. Based on their life experiences, objects change color when they are colored with crayons, markers, or paint. Therefore, the toaster must have colored the bread brown. Attributing lifelike qualities to inanimate objects is called **animism.**

Yet another cognitive characteristic related to egocentrism and demonstrated by preoperational thinkers is concluding that thinking about something or wishing for something can make it happen. This characteristic of preoperational thought is called **magical thinking.** The following vignette provides an example of how preoperational children employ magical thinking.

> *Ling, who is five, wants her big brother Lee to watch a video with her. Lee tells her that he cannot watch a video with her because he has a basketball game in a little while. Ling is not happy when her brother refuses to play with her and says, "I wish you didn't have to play dumb old basketball anyway." A few minutes later, Lee's coach telephones to say that today's basketball game has been cancelled due to a scheduling conflict. Ling uses magical thinking when she concludes that the reason that her brother's game was cancelled was because she wished he did not have a basketball game today; therefore, the game was magically cancelled. Ling's egocentrism does not allow her to consider that the game may have been cancelled for reasons completely unconnected to her wish.*

Concrete Operational Stage   As preoperational children interact with others and gain experience, they will continue to adapt their mental schemas. The adaptations continue to be tempered by egocentrism and reliance on perception rather than logical reasoning. Sometime between ages 5 and 7, children's cognitive abilities gradually begin to shift away from egocentrism and therefore become less reliant on perceptions to explain objects and events. As children develop cognitive abilities that allow them to consider perspectives other than their own they are moving into Piaget's third stage of cognitive development, the **concrete operational stage.**

For most children, the concrete operational stage begins around age 7 and extends to approximately age 11. Concrete operational children rely more on logical reasoning and less on perception—at least when concrete objects or situations are involved (Forman & Kuschner, 1983). This move away from egocentrism allows concrete operational children to engage in rudimentary problem solving as long as they can relate the object, event, or interaction to their own experience.

Seven-year-old Jasmine overhears her grandfather say that he "can't see" why the neigh-bors haven't cut their grass yet. Jasmine interprets the statement literally and runs into the kitchen to grab Grandpa's glasses so he can see the neighbor's yard more clearly. Jasmine has applied the cognitive skill of problem solving. She identified the problem—Grandpa cannot "see" whether the neighbor's grass has been mowed. Jasmine has also determined a solution to the problem—Grandpa sees better when he is wearing his glasses. Therefore, Grandpa needs to wear his glasses in order to see the neighbor's grass more clearly. Jas-mine is clearly less egocentric than a preoperational child, because she can consider what Grandpa needs in order to see clearly, even though she can see the neighbor's yard clearly without glasses. However, she still tends to interpret what she sees and hears within the framework of her own experience.

In this vignette, Jasmine demonstrates the ability to reason by associating a specific example (Grandpa cannot see) with a generalization (glasses help people see). Putting the two concepts together, Jasmine applies the basic tenets of problem solving, relying more on logic than perception. This type of reasoning is called **inductive reasoning.** Inductive reasoning enables concrete operational children to reason by associating ex-amples with general rules or principles. For example, if children know that birds are an-imals that fly and have feathers, then when they encounter a previously unknown animal that flies and has feathers, they will logically reason that the new animal is also a bird. Piaget devised several tasks that demonstrate the ability or inability to reason in-ductively. These tasks deal with the ability to mentally reason beyond physical changes in appearance.

Piaget uses the term **conservation** to describe the ability to use logical reasoning, rather than perception, to draw conclusions about changes in the appearance of ob-jects. Children at the concrete operational stage demonstrate the ability to conserve, or mentally "save," what they know about the **identity** of an object or event, and they rea-son based on logic even when presented with conflicting visual evidence. Concrete op-erational children are able to mentally manipulate the processes that caused the changes and **compensate** for changes in appearance.

Piaget's classic conservation task is to present two identical balls of clay and ask if the balls have the same amount of clay. Both preoperational and concrete operational learners will confirm that both balls have the same amount of clay. Next, while the children watch, one of the balls of clay is rolled into a snake. Then the question is re-peated: Does each piece of clay have the same amount, or does one piece have more? Preoperational children usually respond that the snake has more clay because it is longer than the ball of clay. They are unable to mentally *compensate* for the changes in appearance of the clay by logically reasoning that nothing was added to or taken from either piece of clay. Preoperational children lack the ability to conserve; therefore, they centrate on physical appearances of the clay and "perceive" that one piece of clay is longer and has more clay. Concrete operational children are able to **decentrate** from the physical appearance and draw their conclusions based on logic rather than percep-tion, reasoning that the identities of the pieces of clay remain the same and therefore

Figure 3.6   Development of Conservation

Types of Conservation	Dimension	Change in Physical Appearance	Average Age at Which Invariance Is Grasped
Number	Number of elements in a collection 	Rearranging or dislocating elements 	5–7
Substance (mass) (continuous quantity)	Amount of a malleable substance (e.g., clay or liquid) 	Altering shape 	6–8
Length	Length of a line or object 	Altering shape or configuration 	6–8
Area	Amount of surface covered by a set of plane figures 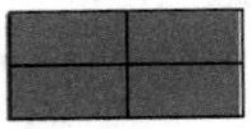	Rearranging the figures 	7–9
Weight	Weight of an object 	Altering its shape 	8–10
Volume	Volume of an object (in terms of water displacement) 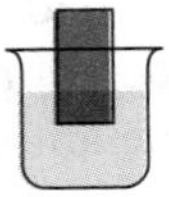	Altering its shape 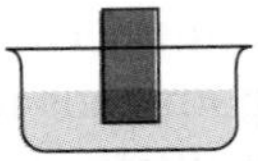	10–14

Source: From J. A. Schickedanz, P. D. Forsyth, and G. A. Forsyth (1988), *Understanding Children and Adolescents,* 3rd ed. (Boston: Allyn and Bacon). Copyright 1988 by Pearson Education. Reprinted by permission of the publisher.

that they still contain the same amount. Concrete operational children demonstrate abilities to mentally reverse the processes associated with transformations rather than focusing on outcomes. The cognitive ability of **reversibility** enables concrete operational learners to employ logical reasoning. Piaget identified several levels of conservation ability that emerge gradually throughout the concrete operational stage of cognitive development and some that continue to develop into the next stage.

Formal Operational Stage The last stage of cognitive development identified by Piaget is the **formal operational stage.** During this stage, which usually begins between ages 11 and 15 and continues throughout adulthood, individuals are capable of sophisticated thought processes that rely on logic rather than perception. The ability to engage in formal operational reasoning means that individuals are capable of considering abstract concepts, such as "justice" or "freedom," without relying on concrete experiences or examples. Their ability to use **abstract thinking** allows them to discuss complex ideas and beliefs in terms of what might be rather than what is. The ability to reason about abstract possibilities is called **hypothetico-deductive reasoning.** Hypothetico-deductive reasoning enables individuals to consider multiple possibilities or outcomes in a systematic manner. For example, a group of adolescents could systematically discuss the potential consequences of a decision or situation (such as dropping out of school) without having to try out each of the alternatives. Piaget's ideas about the formal operational stage have received some criticism, because not all adults with normal intelligence are capable of using abstract thinking in all situations.

Piaget's theory of cognitive development has many implications for early childhood education and continues to strongly influence curriculum and practices with young children. Another psychologist whose ideas about children's cognitive development have had far-reaching influence is Lev Vygotsky.

Vygotsky's Sociocultural Theory

Lev Vygotsky (1896–1934), a Russian psychologist, viewed infants and toddlers as **sociocentric** rather than egocentric. Vygotsky's **sociocultural theory** asserts that infants and toddlers are engulfed in families and culture and that their intelligence results from a combination of social experience and maturation. From birth to approximately eighteen months, according to Vygotsky (1934/1984), intelligence is primarily nonverbal. Adults, literally, speak for babies.

During toddlerhood, approximately eighteen to thirty-six months, language remains socially based. However, toddlers begin to mimic words and short phrases that their parents use. Adults, in turn, elaborate and extend the short phrases. Gradually, as their oral language abilities develop, toddlers acquire the tools for mental representation. The ability to attach names, or labels, to objects and processes is called **verbal mediation** (Bredekamp & Copple, 1997). Thinking and speech continue to be co-constructed between children and adults, and eventually toddlers are able to "think out loud" (Vygotsky, 1987).

According to Vygotsky, maturation alone cannot account for children's new language and thinking abilities. Indeed, it is children's continued social and cultural interactions, combined with maturation, that foster cognitive development. Vygotsky (1978) contends that learning is continually mediated by adults or more able peers. Children need mental challenges in order to progress developmentally in their language and cognitive abilities. Vygotsky described the level of optimal challenge as the **zone of proximal development (ZPD).** The ZPD describes the area of performance that is just beyond the child's current capabilities if attempted alone but is achievable if assisted by an adult or more able peer. This process of assistance is called **scaffolding.**

Vygotsky supported the premise that interactions with significant others are instrumental in cognitive and language development. He surmised that sometime before age 3, language merges with thinking, and children become able to wield the symbols and tools of culture—language. Vygotsky (1978) viewed social interaction, especially dialogue, as the primary vehicle for learning. Oral language provides the tools for mentally representing ideas, and social interaction transmitts not only language but also culture. Thought and language become intertwined as children gain knowledge and develop complex thinking through shared experiences with adults and peers.

According to Vygotsky (1934/1984), preschool children possess enough mastery of language that they are no longer completely reliant on adults or more able peers to speak for them. During infancy and toddlerhood, children are dependent on social interchanges with more able persons to represent thoughts through language. Children begin life sociocentric and dependent on others to communicate. As language emerges and children are able to use their own language to communicate, they become more egocentric. In other words, children's language and thought become internalized. Although children still need social interactions and scaffolding from adults or more able peers to continue to develop cognitively, they are now capable of using their own language for self-direction.

Three- to five-year-olds literally "think out loud." Vygotsky (1934/1984) used the term **private speech** to describe the self-talk behavior often demonstrated by preschool children. Young children use private speech, or self-talk, to control their own behavior, solve problems, and cope with emotions. Private speech represents children's verbalization of their thought processes. Private speech is not intended for an audience; it is simply the externalization of thought. Children's oral language becomes a tool to represent mental operations.

This process continues during the middle years, as children continue to internalize knowledge through social and cultural interactions. These interactions, or shared experiences, help children gain knowledge and skills. Cooperative dialogues between children and adults or more able peers serve as the primary means of transmitting language and culture (Vygotsky, 1934/1984). Cooperative dialogues and play experiences provide opportunities for children to explore and solve problems. When these dialogues and play experiences include adults or more able peers, children can be challenged to extend their current abilities.

Mixed-age groups support peer collaboration, and peer collaboration leads to assisted discovery and learning. Vygotsky's theory (Berk & Winsler, 1995) suggests that learning leads development. When children have opportunities to dialogue and play with more able persons, they are stimulated to step into their zone of proximal, or potential, development. Vygotsky believed that most learning takes place within the ZPD, where children's construction of knowledge can be scaffolded by more experienced individuals.

Comparisons between the Theories of Piaget and Vygotsky

Both Piaget and Vygotsky acknowledged the dual influences of nature and nurture, or heredity and environment, on the development of cognition. They highlighted the importance of interaction with objects and individuals as key to the process of cognitive development. However, where Piaget characterized young children as egocentric and developing beyond egocentrism, Vygotsky characterized them as sociocentric at a younger age and moving toward egocentrism as they become individuals and separate.

Both Piaget and Vygotsky acknowledged the link between cognitive development and the emergence of language, concluding that language represents the cognitive ability to symbolically represent objects, actions, and ideas. For example, a typically developing two-year-old child understands the word *cookie* before he can say the word. Once he is able to say the word *cookie,* he uses the word to mean the actual object (cookie) and also to represent the action "give me a cookie." Because of his limited language abilities, the child may use the word to represent any kind of sweet snack food rather than restricting its use to one type of sweet food. As he gains more experience with cookies, he will use his emerging language skills to make his specific ideas known, such as "I want a chocolate cookie, not a cracker."

Language Development

Minutes after birth, healthy newborns can maintain eye contact with someone within their range of vision. This fledgling attempt to interact marks the beginning of a lifetime of communication. A newborn's first vocalizations are more instinctive than deliberate. At birth, infants engage in **undifferentiated crying;** that is, a listener cannot distinguish between cries to communicate pain and cries to communicate loneliness. Undifferentiated crying sounds the same, no matter what the cause. However, within days, the cries of a newborn become distinguishable from one another. For example, **differentiated crying** allows familiar caregivers to discriminate between cries of pain or discomfort and cries for companionship or less urgent needs.

Not all of infants' communications are meant to indicate discontent; in addition to crying, young infants use other types of **prelinguistic speech.** Prelinguistic speech consists of vocalizations, or voiced sounds, to which the speaker has not assigned meaning. For example, **cooing** and **babbling** are early vocalizations that infants use to communicate contentment or interest. Cooing is the making of soft, repetitive vowel sounds, like "ooh" and "aah," that infants make during the first months of life. Babbling is repetitive consonant-vowel sounds like "da-da-da" or "ma-ma-ma." Babbling

CDA

COMPETENCY GOAL II
· Functional Areas 5–6

generally begins around six months of age and continues for several months. When babbling infants utter the sound "da-da," they are not calling for daddy; they are exploring the sounds of language. Adults often connect the repetitive syllables of babbling to real objects or people and reinforce infants' babbling efforts by repeating sounds back to them. The infants have yet to assign meaning to the sounds but happily participate in the give-and-take interaction with adults or older children.

As infants continue to receive favorable feedback for their vocalization attempts, they begin to imitate and repeat the sounds of frequently heard words. This prelinguistic behavior is called **echolalia**, or **echo speech**. Echo speech is still considered prelinguistic, because infants have not assigned meaning to speech sounds; they are simply playfully imitating frequently heard sounds. Echo speech begins around ten

Table 3.2   Emergence of Oral Language

Prelinguistic Speech	Description
Undifferentiated crying	At birth, infants signal their needs through this reflexive form of communication.
Differentiated crying	After one month, infants' crying is more precise, with different patterns, intonations, intensities, and pitches reflecting different emotional states.
Cooing	By 6 weeks, chance utterances of vowel sounds occur as part of infants' expressions of contentment.
Babbling	At about 3 to 4 months, infants playfully repeat simple consonant and vowel sounds (ma-ma-ma, ba-ba-ba, etc.). Babbling is also a sign of contentment.
Echolalia (echo speech)	By about 9 to 10 months, infants consciously imitate sounds of others, but without understanding of word meaning.
Linguistic Speech	
Holophrases	At about 12 months, infants use single words to express thoughts. Average one-year-olds have 5-word vocabularies (10-word vocabulary at about 15 months and 50-word vocabulary by 19 months).
Telegraphic speech	At about 24 months, children string 2 or 3 words together to form sentences, using only essential nouns and verbs approximately.
Grammatically correct speech	By 3 years, children may have vocabularies of some 900 words. They use longer sentences containing all parts of speech and apply many grammatical principles, although their sentence constructions tend to follow the rules too closely.

months of age and continues past the first birthday. Echo speech often serves as a bridge between prelinguistic and **linguistic speech.**

Linguistic speech occurs when meaning is consistently attached to a particular speech sound. Sometime around their first birthday, infants begin to assign meaning to units of sound. This behavior marks infants' entry into linguistic speech. For example, when repeated utterances of the same speech sound, such as "ba-ba," are consistently met with the same object or action (bottle), infants begin to connect the speech sound (word) with the object or action. Therefore, *ba-ba* becomes the word for bottle; the word is understood by both speaker (infant) and listener (caregiver).

These one-word sentences, or **holophrases,** may have multiple meanings and represent children's first form of linguistic speech. Holophrases generally represent familiar objects or actions. Often, infants and toddlers will overextend the meanings of holophrases, as illustrated in the following vignette.

Fourteen-month-old LaTasha turns to her caregiver, Mrs. Duffy, and says "juice." LaTasha may just be showing Mrs. Duffy that she has juice in her cup, or she may be trying to tell her that the cup is empty and she wants more juice. Mrs. Duffy thinks she knows what LaTasha means, because by looking in the cup she sees it is empty. Mrs. Duffy opens the refrigerator, grabs the apple juice, and begins to pour it into the cup. LaTasha yanks the cup away and repeats the holophrase "juice" loudly several times. Obviously, apple juice is not what LaTasha wants. Now Mrs. Duffy offers a variety of beverages to LaTasha one at a time, until she hits on the "right" juice, which in this case isn't juice at all, but milk! The toddler has overgeneralized the holophrase "juice" to mean any beverage. So, although LaTasha is using language, her meaning is nonspecific.

Adults often guide the language learning of infants and toddlers by extending or elaborating their statements (Berk & Winsler, 1995). In this vignette, Mrs. Duffy might have extended LaTasha's original demand, "juice," by filling in additional words to make the toddler's meaning more specific. She might have said, "Oh, you want more juice in your cup." Adults often model a more complete language statement to clarify a toddler's holophrase. In subsequent attempts to get the cup filled with a beverage, the toddler may imitate the language modeled, or demonstrated, by the caregiver. The next time the toddler may say "More juice." This truncated version of a sentence is called a **telegraphic sentence.** Telegraphic sentences are shortened sentences that include two or three key words but omit less important details.

Examples of typical telegraphic sentences are "Go bye-bye" and "Want ball." The action and the object are included in the telegraphic sentence, but the details are omitted. Overgeneralization is still common in telegraphic sentences. For example, "Go bye-bye '' could mean the child wants to go "bye-bye," someone else just went "bye-bye," or the child wants you to go "bye-bye." Once the caregiver determines what the child means, she may elaborate on the child's original statement by adding details.

Through modeling, extension, and elaboration, adults and more able children support the emerging language of infants and toddlers. As young children learn more words to symbolically represent objects, actions, and ideas, their language gradually becomes more complex and specific.

Children have been bombarded by the sounds of speech since before birth. Their ability to understand speech precedes their ability to produce understandable speech. As noted previously in this chapter, infants and toddlers explore the sounds of speech for several months before they say their first meaningful word. The emergence of language is a gradual process that is rooted in cognitive development but is also dependent on social interactions. Children's abilities to use words as symbols for objects and actions represent the beginnings of oral language.

By age 4, most children around the world have learned, without any direct training, to understand and speak their native language. What causes the acquisition of language to follow universal patterns? Neurobiologist Lise Eliot (1999) looks to the brain for explanation. Eliot maintains that the "act of learning language is what directs the specialization of the linguistic brain" (p. 353). In other words, as the brain is inundated with language, it actually lays out the neural connections necessary to support language learning.

Language is a social tool, complete with complicated rules and symbols (Owens, 1996). In order for children to become competent users of language, they have to demonstrate proficiency in four domains of language: phonemes, semantics, syntax, and pragmatics (Gleason, 1993). **Phonemes** are the sounds and patterns of speech. **Semantics** refers to the meaning of language. Semantics also includes receptive vocabulary and expressive vocabulary. *Receptive vocabulary* consists of words one understands. *Expressive vocabulary* consists of words one understands and uses to express meaning; hence, receptive vocabulary is much larger than expressive vocabulary. Expressive vocabulary is part of oral language. Typically, eighteen-month-old children have expressive vocabularies of approximately fifty words. By the time children are three years old, their expressive vocabularies will increase to more than 600 words. Vocabulary development continues to increase rapidly throughout the preschool years. **Syntax**, the third domain of language, refers to word order and the ability to arrange words in a sentence to convey the intended meaning. During the preschool years, children acquire grammatical skills through language encounters with more competent language users. **Pragmatics**, the fourth domain of language, deals with the use of language in social contexts and includes verbal and nonverbal aspects. Considering the complex nature of language, it is amazing to think that most five-year-old children have learned the basic components of language without any formal training.

During the middle years, children continue to increase their receptive and expressive vocabularies at an impressive pace. This increase in vocabulary can be partly attributed to their emerging abilities to distinguish between shades of meaning and to understand nonliteral word usage. One signpost of children's increasing capacity to understand words with multiple meanings is their frequent use of jokes and riddles with word puns. Children's word play with pronunciation and meaning enhances the growth of their vocabulary. During middle childhood, the estimated number of words in children's vocabularies ranges from 16,500 at age 6 to more than 40,000 by age 11.

As children's vocabularies and language skills continue to develop, they become more and more capable of expressing their ideas clearly and with elaborate detail. At the same time, they begin to understand more of the subtleties of language and show increased interest in many facets of spoken language, including storytelling and dramatization, paying close attention to the sounds and meanings of language.

Promoting Development within the Cognitive Domain

CDA

COMPETENCY GOAL II
• Functional Areas 4–7

Early child-care and education settings abound with opportunities to support children's language development and other cognitive abilities. With infants under one year of age, their emerging awareness of object permanence presents a variety of opportunities for interaction that can help provide them with a variety of stimulating developmental experiences. For example, the tried-and-true games adults play with young infants—such as peek-a-boo or hiding an object under a blanket and then "finding" it—give children opportunities to gain experience with objects and individuals, thereby supporting the development of object permanence and building children's physical knowledge of objects and their properties.

Many popular toys designed for infants and toddlers reflect children's gradual development of object permanence. For example, no matter how many times infants see Jack jump out of the box, they still laugh and act surprised; this is because they really are surprised! After all, to children in the sensorimotor stage, Jack ceases to exist whenever he enters the box, yet he magically reappears a few seconds later.

Infant and toddler toys are also linked to children's inquisitive natures and the ways they use their senses to explore their surroundings. Toys such as rattles and chime balls appeal not only to infants' sense of hearing, but also their senses of sight and touch. Still other toys, such as activity quilts and boxes, stimulate all of the senses by providing a variety of things to see, hear, touch, taste, and even smell.

In addition to experiences with objects and toys, children need interactions with adult caregivers and other children. These interpersonal experiences stimulate children's curiosity and engage their emerging language abilities. According to Vygotsky, these opportunities for shared communication are the foundation of sociocultural knowledge and language learning. Caregivers who respond to infants' cues make themselves available to participate in children's play whenever possible.

These experiences and interactions are essential for children's overall cognitive development, because the construction of knowledge and language occurs as a result of both maturation and experience. Because maturation is determined biologically, caregivers have little control over its unfolding. However, in the area of experience and interaction, family members, teachers, and caregivers definitely have an impact on cognitive development.

Because young children construct their understanding of concepts through their experiences, they require active learning environments where they can use their senses to indulge their curiosity. Additionally, since young children mature and develop at different rates, they benefit most from activities that are process oriented. Open-ended activities, such as block play, provide opportunities for successful experiences in a range of developmental abilities. Children can explore and construct knowledge and language at their own paces.

Our ability to observe young children's behaviors and reasonably interpret their stage of development enables us to plan, anticipate, and provide developmentally appropriate experiences and interactions throughout early childhood. For example, what types of behavior would toddlers demonstrate that would indicate that they are beginning to use symbolic representation—the foundation of pretend play? If you mentioned imitating familiar actions such as driving a car or making sounds for a toy dog, then you have demonstrated your understanding of symbolic representation and the role it plays in cognitive development. When we understand children's play from a cognitive perspective, we are able to provide developmentally appropriate play and learning experiences for them.

> *In play the child always behaves beyond his average age, above his daily behavior; in play it is as though he were a head taller than himself.*
> —Lev Semenovich Vygotsky, *Mind in Society: The Development of Higher Psychological Processes* (1978, p. 102)

Cognitive Categories of Play

Many psychologists—such as Piaget, Vygotsky, and other researchers—have developed theories about the characteristics and development of play and its relationship to children's overall development. Sara Smilansky (1968) used Piaget's ideas about cognitive development as the basis for her studies about children's play. Through a series of structured observations, Smilansky identified four categories of play that have cognitive overtones.

During infancy, children's play is made up of repetitive motions as they explore what objects are like and what they can do with objects. This category of cognitive play is called **functional play.** Through functional play, infants build their understandings of physical objects and their properties. When presented with new objects, such as a bright yellow rattle, infants show increased interest as they use their senses and motor skills to experiment with the object.

Sometime during toddlerhood, children begin to use more sophisticated exploratory behaviors in their play. Not only do they determine what the object does and what they can do with the object, they also use the object in some purposeful way. This category of cognitive play is called **constructive play.** Constructive play involves some type of problem-solving behavior as children attempt to figure out how things work. For example, a two-year-old who is given an empty purse will spend a large amount of time trying to figure out how to open and close the clasps and zippers. Once he masters those behaviors, he may fill the purse with a variety of small objects and repeatedly empty and refill each of the sections of the purse, practicing his newly learned behaviors for opening and closing clasps and zipping and unzipping zippers. His play has a purpose and requires him to think about and plan his actions. Constructive play may also involve actual construction of objects, such as putting together or taking apart snap-together blocks, although, in this case, the term *constructive play* actually refers to the construction of understandings, not objects. Play and learning materials that have many possible outcomes (or products)—such as large wooden building blocks or sand and water tables—firmly support constructive play, because each time children engage in their playful process with the materials, new possibilities arise.

> *The brain is what we have; the mind is what it does. In other words, the "mind" is not a thing, it is a process.*
>
> —Eric Jensen, *Teaching with the Brain in Mind* (1998, p. 15)

Another avenue of possibilities opens for children sometime before their third birthday—that is, pretend play. The concept of pretend play was introduced in Chapter 1 in relationship to social play, but it is also a function of cognitive play, because it involves the ability to use symbolic representation and substitute one object for another. Smilansky (1968) identified the third category of cognitive play as *dramatic play*. Dramatic play involves use of imagination in two ways. First, imagination allows children to pretend that a wooden block, or other object, is actually a racecar or a sandwich or any number of other things. Second, children use their imaginations to assume roles and act as if they are someone or something else. Preschool-age children typically use role-play to portray persons with whom they have direct contact, such as family members and schoolmates. Dramatic play combines reality and imagination as children develop play scenarios and try out roles and create new outcomes for real-life events (Smilansky & Shefatya, 1990). For example, a preschool-age child who recently got a new puppy might dramatize what happened at the veterinarian's by gathering up a collection of stuffed animals to represent pets and then pretending to be the doggy doctor, acting out some of the things he witnessed in reality.

The stuffed animals serve as **props** for the child's pretend play scenario; he substitutes the stuffed animals for his real pet puppy. Younger children need props that closely resemble the real items for which they are substituting, but older preschool-age children are able to let their imaginations fill in the details for the substituted items. Props that can be used in more than one way are very effective with preschool-age children as they use problem-solving skills to arrange their play scenarios. For instance, a large empty cardboard box can become a car, a cave, or a spaceship, whereas a large plastic car remains a car. Unstructured props like boxes, paper tubes, and squares of cloth provide nearly infinite possibilities for the imaginative minds of young children. Trying new ways to use props in play scenarios supports children's cognitive development (Jensen, 1998).

Older preschoolers and kindergarten-age children sometimes build elaborate play episodes that involve many characters for role-playing. When dramatic play takes on social dimensions by engaging two or more children in cooperative play episodes, it is called *sociodramatic play*. Smilansky (1968) describes sociodramatic play as a higher level of cognitive play than dramatic play, because children have to

Table 3.3   Smilansky's Categories of Cognitive Play

Category of Cognitive Play	Characteristics
Functional play	• Begins during infancy • Consists of repetitive motor play • Involves exploration of what objects are like • Involves exploration of what can be done with objects
Constructive play	• Begins during toddlerhood • Involves creating something with objects • Sometimes involves purposeful activity • Involves some problem solving
Dramatic play	• Begins during preschool years • Involves symbolic representation • Involves use of imagination as well as reality • Rules evolve from play scenario • Sometimes involves other children in the scenario (sociodramatic) • Supports development of language
Games with rules	• Begins in later preschool years or early primary years • Involves accepted, prearranged rules • Usually involves two or more children • Includes both sportlike games and table games

Source: Adapted from S. Smilansky (1968), *The Effects of Play on Disadvantaged Preschool Children* (New York: Wiley).

use problem-solving and negotiation skills to agree on "rules" that evolve as the play episode unfolds.

Smilansky's (1968) fourth category of cognitive play is **games with rules,** when two or more children planning to play a game understand and accept the rules prior to participating in the game. Games like hopscotch, tag, and marbles have some basic traditional rules but also may have added or altered rules according to specific regions or cultures. Children begin playing games with rules in the later preschool years and continue into the early primary years. Generally, the games of older children have more elaborate rule structures than the games of younger children. Many board games, such as checkers, have intricate levels of rules requiring children to consider many options and consequences before making decisions in the game.

Teachers who are aware of the cognitive categories of play use observations of play to gather information about children's development, particularly their cognitive and language development. As a result of these observations, the teachers gain insight into children's overall development, which aids them in providing developmentally appropriate play and learning experiences for young children.

Summary

Early Brain Development

- The brain is soft-wired at birth and maintains its plasticity for several years after birth. Early experiences cause changes to the physical structure of the brain.

Cognitive Development

- The cognitive domain includes components of development related to reasoning, concept development, memory, and language.
- Maturation and experience interact to affect cognitive development.
- Piaget's theory identifies four discrete stages of cognitive development between infancy and adolescence.

- Social interactions are vital to the development of thinking and speech.

Language Development

- Language acquisition follows a universally predictable sequence.
- There are critical periods for language development.

Promoting Development within the Cognitive Domain

- Smilansky identified four categories of cognitive play (functional, constructive, dramatic, and games with rules).
- Teachers gain information about children's cognitive development by observing their play.

LEARNING ACTIVITIES

1 Demonstration: Physical Knowledge. Bring an interesting but unusual object to class. Let other students examine the object. How do they construct their physical knowledge of the object? What do they learn about the object and its properties? Compare how preoperational and concrete operational children might explore the same object. What similarities and differences might occur?

2 Role-Play: Early Linguistic Speech. (Refer to Table 3.2, p. 64.) Work with a partner to develop a mock dialogue between a very young child (twelve months to thirty months) and an older child (age 4 or above) or adult. Role-play the dialogue, emphasizing how the adult or older child extends or elaborates the child's early forms of linguistic speech.

PORTFOLIO ARTIFACTS

1 Sample: Characteristics of Preoperational and Concrete Operational Thought. Collect three or four comic strips in which the characters demonstrate preoperational or concrete operational thought. Analyze each comic strip by pointing out the preoperational and/or concrete operational characteristics portrayed.

2 Activity: Scaffolding Learning. Design an open-ended activity for a young child that offers a

range of difficulty. If possible, observe a young child engaging in the activity. Once you have a sense of the child's abilities, attempt to extend the child's learning to the zone of proximal development by scaffolding her play. What strategies did you use to challenge the child? How did the child respond?

Professional Connections and Web Links

Parents as Teachers (PAT)
Parents as Teachers National Center, Inc.
10176 Corporate Square Drive, Suite 230
St. Louis, MO 63132
314-432-4330
http://www.patnc.org

Parents as Teachers (PAT), a nonprofit parent education and family support organization that focuses on the care and education of young children from the prenatal stage through kindergarten, utilizes a neuroscience-based curriculum and video series that incorporates findings from recent brain research. The Born to Learn curriculum is available through PAT programs in the United States, several U.S. territories, England, Australia, and New Zealand. PAT programs include home visits by specially trained parent educators who help family members understand child development and suggest and model ways to promote children's positive development. PAT also sponsors an annual Born to Learn conference for parent educators and other persons interested in how young children learn. Contact the PAT national center to obtain more information about the Born to Learn curriculum, PAT programs in your area, and educational qualifications for parent educators.

Zero to Three
2000 M Street NW, Suite 200
Washington, DC 20036-3307
202-638-1144
http://www.zerotothree.org

Zero to Three, a national nonprofit organization, maintains a research-based information center about the development of infants and toddlers. Zero to Three produces an array of publications and informational videos for families with young children and those individuals who work with young children and their families. In addition, Zero to Three has a Web site that caters to parents and teachers with specialized features such as Parenting A-Z, Professional Topics A-Z, Brainwonders, and Magic of Everyday Moments. Brainwonders provides information about early brain development as well as suggestions for adults to support children's development during the first three years of life. Six times per year, the organization publishes the journal *Zero to Three,* which addresses special topics in infant development, such as the impact of adult relationships on early development and music in the lives of babies.

Suggestions for Further Reading

Kotulak, Ronald. (1997). *Inside the brain: Revolutionary discoveries of how the mind works.* Kansas City, MO: Andrews McMeel.

- Kotulak describes recent research on brain development and functioning, including how brains get "built" and the brain's amazing ability to repair itself. He also discusses the importance of experience and language during the early years and the effect of stress and violence on children's brains.

Shore, Rima. (1997). *Rethinking the brain: New insights into early development.* New York: Families and Work Institute.

- This book draws connections between new findings on how the brain works and what caregivers can do to support brain development during the first five years of life.

References

Berk, L., & Winsler A. (1995). *Scaffolding children's learning: Vygotsky and early childhood education.* Washington, DC: National Association for the Education of Young Children.

Bredekamp, Sue, & Copple, Carol. (Eds.). (1997). *Developmentally appropriate practice in early childhood programs* (rev. ed.). Washington, DC: National Association for the Education of Young Children.

Eliot, Lise. (1999). *What's going on in there? How the brain and mind develop in the first five years of life.* New York: Bantam Books.

Forman, George E., & Kuschner, David S. (1983). *The child's construction of knowledge: Piaget for teaching children.* Washington, DC: National Association for the Education of Young Children.

Gleason, J. B. (1993). *The development of language.* New York: Macmillan.

Jensen, Eric. (1998). *Teaching with the brain in mind.* Alexandria, VA: Association for Supervision and Curriculum Development.

Kotulak, Ronald. (1997). *Inside the brain: Revolutionary discoveries of how the mind works.* Kansas City, MO: Andrews McMeel.

Owens, R. E. (1996). *Language development: An introduction.* Boston: Allyn and Bacon.

Piaget, Jean. (1962). *Play, dreams, and imitation in childhood.* New York: Norton.

Piaget, Jean. (1963). *The origins of intelligence in children.* (M. Cook, trans.) New York: Norton. (Original work published in 1936.)

Piaget, Jean. (1967). *Six psychological studies.* New York: Random House.

Piaget, Jean. (1969). *Science of education and the psychology of the child.* New York: Basic Books.

Piaget, Jean, & Inhelder, B. (1958). *The growth of logical thinking from childhood to adolescence.* New York: Basic Books.

Shore, Rima. (1997). *Rethinking the brain: New insights into early development.* New York: Families and Work Institute.

Smilansky, Sara. (1968). *The effects of play on disadvantaged preschool children.* New York: Wiley.

Smilansky, Sara, & Shefatya, Leah. (1990). *Facilitating play: A medium for promoting cognitive, socio-emotional, and academic development in young children.* Gaithersberg, MD: Psychosocial and Educational Publications.

Tanner, J. M. (1990). *Foetus into man* (2nd ed.). Cambridge, MA: Harvard University Press.

Vygotsky, Lev. (1978). *Mind in society: The development of higher psychological processes.* Cambridge, MA: Harvard University Press.

Vygotsky, Lev. (1984). *Thought and language.* (Alex Kozulin, trans.) Cambridge, MA: MIT Press. (Original work published 1934.)

Vygotsky, Lev. (1987). *Thinking and speech.* (N. Minick, trans.) New York: Plenum Press.

The Affective Domain

After reading this chapter and completing the related activities, you should be able to

- Define the affective domain
- Describe characteristics of temperament
- Describe the emergence of emotions and self-conscious emotions
- Describe the emergence of self
- Identify secure and insecure attachment behaviors
- Identify the stages of psychosocial development
- Describe the role of friendship during early childhood
- Identify the stages of moral reasoning and gender-related issues
- Suggest teaching practices that support development in the affective domain

Eight-month-old twins Kayla and Kari look around the colorful room with wide eyes as their mother, Krista Banks, pushes their double stroller through the lobby and into the corridor. At the director's invitation, Krista and her daughters are at the Discovery Child Care Center for their preenrollment visit. Krista and her husband, Doug, had visited four centers together before deciding to enroll their children at this center. Their main concern was that the girls be in a safe, healthy place with people who understood babies and cared about their feelings. Though Kayla and Kari are twins, their personalities are markedly different. Kayla is more outgoing and acts as though everyone is there to entertain her; Kari is more wary of people she does not recognize.

After releasing the girls from the stroller, Krista and the center director, Matt Walker, carries them into the infant/toddler room. Of the infant/toddler classrooms Krista and her husband had visited, this classroom is her favorite. The teachers are friendly and approachable and seem genuinely happy to be there with the children. This morning it is the same. As soon as they enter the classroom, one of the teachers, Ms. Louise, welcomes them with a cheery hello and invites Krista and the babies to come and play with her and two other babies who are crawling around on a large colorful mat on the floor. Still holding Kari, Krista sits down on the mat near the teacher as the director places Kayla on the mat a few inches away. In less than a minute, Kayla has crawled over to the teacher and is investigating a bright red ball she is holding. Kari has turned her face into Krista's shoulder, occasionally peeking at her sister's antics.

Still playing with Kayla, Louise asks Krista if she has any questions. Krista looks down at Kari and asks, "What do you do about babies who are shy?" Louise smiles and answers, "We let them be shy. We stay close and encourage them to play but give them the chance to warm up to us on their own. We want the babies to feel safe with us, and we just follow their cues. Don't worry; Kari will let us know when she wants to cuddle or play. In the meantime, she seems content just watching." Krista nods; that is exactly how she handles Kari's initial shyness. Once she gets comfortable, Kari becomes as curious and active as Kayla. Krista is happy they have chosen this program and taken advantage of the preenrollment visit. Even though the twins will only be attending the child care center four hours per day, she needs to know that they are in a nurturing place where they can be themselves.

ne of the more fascinating aspects of human diversity is the wide array of individual personalities. As with other aspects of development, even as children differ in personality, they also share common traits. Development within the *affective domain* is somewhat more difficult to assess because of the complex nature of emotional, social, and moral development. Behaviors in the affective domain often have to be inferred rather than directly observed. As this chapter will describe, emotional development includes topics such as temperament, the emergence of emotions, and self-esteem, while social development encompasses children's interactions with others and the role of play. The third major aspect of the affective domain is moral development, specifically moral reasoning and behavior. This chapter explores the emergence and interplay of emotional, social, and moral development from infancy through childhood.

Emotional Development

The emergence of emotions is a gradual process that reveals layers of personality along the way. Although infants demonstrate some emotions within the first weeks of life, it takes approximately a year before they routinely display the myriad of emotions that define humankind; and it takes much longer before they can accurately gauge emotions displayed by familiar others.

COMPETENCY GOAL III
• Functional Area 8

Temperament

One early indicator of personality, which infants begin to display shortly after birth, is their style of emotional response. Styles of emotional response vary in intensity and persistence; for example, some infants respond easily to attempts to be comforted, while others withdraw or are slower to accept comfort. When these individual patterns of emotional response become stable over time, they are called **temperament.** According to researchers Thomas and Chess (1977), infants demonstrate consistent temperaments within the first few months of life and frequently maintain these patterns throughout childhood.

Nine distinct traits linked to patterns of emotional response serve as indicators of temperament (Thomas, Chess, & Birch, 1970). These traits, or **dimensions of temperament,** represent ranges of behaviors along a continuum. For example, the dimension of *activity level* classifies infant behaviors from active to inactive, and the dimension of *quality of mood* rates infant behaviors from friendly to unfriendly. Table 4.1 identifies all nine dimensions and their characteristics. Each dimension represents a pattern of emotional response that is stable over time.

Thomas and Chess (1977) found that ratings in these nine dimensions of temperament tended to cluster into three general **categories of temperament,** as outlined in Table 4.2. The categories are not ranked one above the other, but simply describe the overall aspect of temperament, based on behavior observed across the nine temperament dimensions. The three categories of temperament are *easy, difficult,* and *slow-to-warm-up.*

Infants with easy temperaments are generally cheerful, develop regular routines during infancy, and tend to adapt easily to change. Infants with difficult temperaments often have irregular routines, are slow to accept new situations, and react intensely and negatively to change. Infants in the third category, with slow-to-warm-up temperament, are frequently inactive, exhibit mild reactions, adjust slowly to changes in their environments, and display negative quality of mood.

Of the 141 infants studied by Thomas and Chess (1977), 40 percent were in the easy temperament category, 10 percent were in the difficult temperament category, and

Table 4.1   Dimensions of Temperament

Dimension of Temperament	Characteristics
Rhythmicity	• Regularity of basic functions, such as sleep
Activity level	• Intensity and frequency of motor movements
Approach-withdrawal	• Degree to which a child accepts or rejects new people, objects, or situations
Persistence	• Amount of time a child devotes to an activity
Adaptability	• How quickly and easily a child adjusts to change
Quality of mood	• Extent to which a child expresses positive or negative emotions
Distractibility	• Degree to which stimuli in the environment alter a child's behavior
Threshold of responsiveness	• Intensity of stimulation needed to elicit a response
Intensity of reaction	• Energy level of a child's response

Table 4.2   Categories of Temperament

Category of Temperament	Characteristics
Easy	• Cheerful • Develop regular routines • Adapt easily to change
Difficult	• Have irregular routines • Slow to accept new situations • React intensely and negatively to change
Slow-to-warm-up	• Frequently inactive • Exhibit mild reactions • Adjust slowly to changes in environments • Display negative quality of mood

15 percent were in the slow-to-warm-up category. The remaining 35 percent of the infants in the study did not fit clearly into any of the categories and instead displayed a mixture of behaviors across the nine dimensions of temperament.

Although temperament has biological roots and is stable over time, Thomas and Chess (1977) stress that temperament is not fixed and unchangeable and that one type of temperament is not better than another type. Understanding the characteristics of different temperaments helps caregivers use practices that complement a child's temperament, whatever the category. Thomas and Chess suggest that **goodness of fit** between caregiver practice and child temperament can positively modify children's emotional responses to situations. Of course, the reverse would also apply; caregiving practices that are at odds with children's temperaments can have negative repercussions on children's emotional responses. Temperament is only one facet of emotional development to consider when determining the most individually appropriate methods of caring for infants and young children.

Emergence of Emotions

Another aspect of emotional development to consider relates to the developmental sequence of emotions. Research indicates that at birth infants display a few basic emotions, such as interest and sadness. Gradually, throughout the first year of life, infants add disgust, joy, surprise, fear, and anger to their repertoire of emotions. Because young infants are primarily nonverbal, caregivers must infer their emotional states from overt behaviors such as body movements, facial expressions, and vocalizations. These observable behaviors give caregivers cues to the emotional states of infants (Dettore, 2002).

One expression of emotion that has received much scrutiny is the smile. Infants only a few minutes old sometimes smile, but what do the smiles indicate? Are the infants smiling because they are content or happy, or are the smiles merely muscular responses?

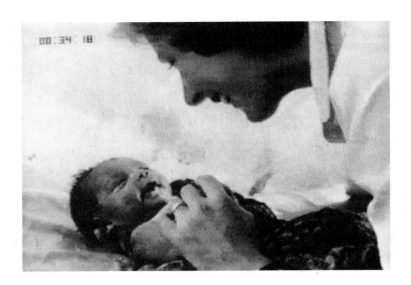

Social smiles are designed to engage others.

Most researchers agree that smiles that occur before six weeks of age are simply muscular responses to nervous system activity or external stimuli. Around six weeks of age, infants' smiles are triggered by social stimuli such as familiar voices or faces (Brazelton, 1992). **Social smiles** are emotional expressions of joy and interest and are designed to socially engage others. By the time infants are three or four months old, they add laughter to their collection of ways to express joy, surprise, or interest.

Young infants also display negative emotions such as anger and fear; however, until infants are about six months old, their expressions of anger are momentary. Between six months and one year of age, infants begin to express anger at a wider variety of situations and maintain expressions of anger for longer periods of time. Fear remains a fleeting emotion until about six months of age, when infants develop longer visual memories. Along with longer visual memories, infants develop cognitive awareness of the permanence of objects. These areas of development, discussed in Chapters 2 and 3, contribute directly to the fearful emotional response that some infants display when confronted with strangers. Most infants develop **stranger anxiety**, an expression of fear at the appearance of unfamiliar persons, between six and nine months of age, although some infants do not demonstrate fear of strangers regularly. Infants' reactions to strangers are influenced not only by their visual memories, which allow them to distinguish between familiar and unfamiliar faces, but also by past experiences with strangers. The situations under which infants meet strangers also contribute to their emotional responses. If the settings are familiar and trusted adults are available, infants may express minimal anxiety or fear at the appearance of strangers.

When infants visually or physically seek out trusted adults and base their emotional responses to situations on the reactions exhibited by these adults, they are demonstrating the process of **social referencing.** Social referencing generally emerges around ten months of age and is considered to be an indicator of **social competence**, the ability to effectively engage in social behaviors that are age appropriate and that enhance interpersonal relationships. Social competence, which is a strong indicator of children's overall abilities to adapt to social situations and form stable relationships, also impacts their emerging identity (McClellan & Katz, 1993).

> *Babies can use other people to figure out the world.*
>
> —Alison Gopnik, Andrew Meltzoff, and Patricia Kuhl, *The Scientist in the Crib: Minds, Brains, and How Children Learn* (1999, p. 181)

Emergence of Self

At some point in their development, usually around eight to ten months, infants begin to understand that expressions of emotion affect the ways others respond to their behaviors. For example, they smile to engage the interest of someone whose attention they want, or they cry out in anger to let someone know that something is not to their liking. Though still limited in their verbal abilities, infants effectively use a variety of body movements, facial expressions, and vocalizations to indicate their emotional states and to achieve desired results.

The classic example of young children expressing their emotions to achieve desired results is the **temper tantrum.** Initially, temper tantrums are merely age-appropriate displays of frustration and anger by young children, who are inexperienced in dealing with negative emotions and have limited capacity for language. The appropriate response of caregivers is to help children find more acceptable ways to express their displeasure and thus relieve their frustration or anger. Because temper tantrums are loud and often quite dramatic, they draw a lot of attention from other children and adults. If children like the attention they receive during their tantrums, then they may selectively use tantrums to garner attention and reactions from others. Although it is often difficult to distinguish children's age-appropriate temper tantrums from tantrums orchestrated to gain attention and achieve specific outcomes, children exhibiting the latter type generally show a greater awareness of how others are responding to them.

Once children are aware that they are individuals, distinct from others, they may demonstrate other emotional behaviors besides tantrums that reflect their growing consciousness of the emotions and expectations of others. Display of emotions such as pride, shame, embarrassment, and guilt are indicators that young children understand that there are expectations or standards that one must meet. **Self-conscious emotions** signal young children's budding sense of self.

Toddlers as young as eighteen months of age exhibit self-conscious emotions when they sense that their behaviors do not meet standards set by others. For example, three-year-old Jeremy bursts into tears when he spills his milk at the kitchen table. Though Jeremy's mother hastens to assure him that everyone spills milk sometimes, he is still embarrassed by his lack of skill and feels guilty for not being more careful with his cup; therefore, he cries. Jeremy has determined that he has not met the standard or expectation of drinking from a cup without spilling. Once children link their behaviors to expectations or rules, they sometimes feel responsibility for meeting the standards. As children develop emotional identities separate from others, they begin to seek opportunities to express their individuality.

Attachment

At the same time that children attempt to view themselves as individuals, they also seek to maintain strong emotional bonds with the significant adults in their lives. The process of forming strong positive emotional bonds with others is called **attachment.** Infants typically form attachments to familiar caregivers. Early theories of attachment linked the formation of emotional bonds between mothers and infants to the physiological need for nourishment; later theories examined the qualities of mother-infant interactions. John Bowlby (1980) suggested that attachment was linked to survival behaviors of infants and that infant-caregiver bonds are sets of inborn behaviors that infants use to draw caregivers to their sides. Bowlby focused on the role of infants in bonding rather than on the role of mothers or other familiar caregivers.

Bowlby (1980) identifies four **phases of attachment.** (See Table 4.3.) From birth to six weeks, infants use behaviors, or signals, to get close to caregivers. The signals they use during this **preattachment** phase include gazing, crying, smiling, and grasping. The second phase, **attachment in the making**, begins around six weeks of age and lasts until eight months of age. During this phase, infants begin to recognize familiar caregivers and respond differently to them than to strangers. Infants trust familiar caregivers to respond to their signals, and they take comfort from face-to-face interactions with caregivers, although infants may still respond positively to strangers. The third phase of attachment, **clear-cut attachment**, begins around six to eight months and lasts until infants are eighteen to twenty-four months of age. Infants' attachment to familiar caregivers is more obvious during this phase because they display distress on separation

Table 4.3   **Phases of Attachment**

Age of Onset	Phase of Attachment	Characteristics
Birth–6 weeks	Preattachment	• Use behaviors or signals to get close to caregivers (gazing, crying, smiling, and grasping)
6 weeks–8 months	Attachment in the making	• Begin to recognize familiar caregivers • Respond differently to strangers
6 to 8 months–18 to 24 months	Clear-cut attachment	• Display distress on separation from familiar caregivers • Demonstrate stranger anxiety
18 months to 2 years–throughout childhood	Formation of reciprocal relationships	• Learn to negotiate with familiar caregivers • Are willing to participate in give-and-take relationships

from familiar caregivers. They may also demonstrate stranger anxiety. Infants will take deliberate actions to keep familiar caregivers close by, frequently using the familiar person as a secure base from which to explore. They may move away from the familiar person but frequently glance at the person or return to within touching distance. The fourth phase of attachment, **formation of reciprocal relationships,** begins around eighteen months to two years and continues throughout childhood. During the formation of reciprocal relationships, toddlers learn to negotiate with familiar caregivers and are willing to participate in give-and-take relationships.

Attachments formed between infants and familiar caregivers serve as models for future close relationships. Mary Ainsworth and colleagues (Ainsworth, Biehar, Waters, & Wall, 1978) examined infant-caregiver bonds and identified four **categories of attachment,** which are illustrated in Table 4.4. **Secure attachment** describes patterns in which infants are distressed on the departure of familiar caregivers but are easily comforted on their return. The other three categories represent patterns of insecure attachment. In **avoidant attachment,** infants are distressed on the departure of familiar caregivers but avoid the caregivers on their return. **Resistant attachment** occurs when infants stay close to familiar caregivers before their departure and display angry behavior toward the caregivers when they return. In the last pattern of insecure attachment, infants appear confused or disoriented on the return of familiar caregivers. This pattern is called **disorganized/disoriented attachment.** These infants may not resist the familiar caregivers but may display contradictory behaviors such as walking slowly toward or turning away from caregivers.

Many factors influence attachment, including the opportunities infants have to form close, stable relationships with at least one familiar caregiver. Additionally, caregivers need to be sensitive and responsive to the cues of infants and need to reciprocate in the attachment relationship. Attachments formed during infancy serve as guides for all future social relationships.

Table 4.4　**Categories of Attachment**

Category of Attachment	Characteristics
Secure attachment	• Are distressed on the departure of familiar caregivers but easily comforted on their return
Avoidant attachment	• Are distressed on departure of familiar caregivers but avoid the caregivers on their return
Resistant attachment	• Stay close to familiar caregivers before their departure and display angry behavior toward caregivers when they return
Disorganized/disoriented attachment	• May not resist familiar caregivers but may display contradictory behaviors, such as walking slowly toward or turning away from caregivers

Social Development

Interpersonal or social relationships form between individuals when they have opportunities to interact. As discussed in the previous section of this chapter, the earliest relationships emerge from the strong emotional bonds of attachment between infants and their significant family members and caregivers (Honig, 2002). Using these attachment relationships as guides, infants expand their social worlds as they encounter others outside their circles of primary caregivers. Emotional development continues to play a key role in social development throughout the life span (Sroufe, 1996).

Erikson's Stages of Psychosocial Development

Erik Erikson (1902–1994), a German psychologist, developed the theory that both emotional and social development begin in infancy and continue throughout the life span. Erikson's **theory of psychosocial development** divides the life span into a series of eight stages, with each stage representing a different emotional-social crisis that individuals resolve either positively or negatively, depending on their current and previous emotional and social experiences (Erikson, 1950, 1968). These crises, or conflicts, depicted in Table 4.5, serve as the foundation of healthy emotional and social development.

According to Erikson (1950), each stage of psychosocial development presents a different critical struggle between opposing emotional-social outcomes for which individuals reach primary resolution during a critical stage of development. However, the struggle for resolution continues beyond the designated stage. For individuals to achieve and maintain healthy, well-balanced emotional and social development, resolutions to these crises need to be more positive than negative. Because of the cumulative effect of the resolutions, Erikson's theory reinforces the concept that experiences during early childhood continue to influence the emotional-social development of individuals throughout their lives.

During the first stage of psychosocial development, which begins at birth and continues throughout infancy and toddlerhood (until approximately eighteen months), children face the crisis of **trust versus mistrust.** What children learn to trust and mistrust in their environments depends on their experiences during infancy and toddlerhood. Children whose basic physiological, emotional, and social needs are generally met will end the trust versus mistrust stage with positive resolution (trust); therefore, these toddlers will enter the next stage of psychosocial development with healthy emotional-social identities. On the other hand, children whose basic needs are not met or who suffer from neglect or abuse resolve the trust versus mistrust crisis negatively on the side of mistrust. These toddlers enter the second stage of psychosocial development with a mistrustful outlook and are less well adjusted emotionally and socially than children whose needs are met with relative consistency.

Resolution of psychosocial crises is rarely dependent on a single incident; rather, it is a collection of experiences that determines the positive or negative outcome at each stage. Erikson's (1950) second stage of psychosocial development is the crisis of **auton-**

Table 4.5   Erikson's Stages of Psychosocial Development

Approximate Age of Onset	Psychosocial Stage	Characteristics
Birth–18 months	Trust versus mistrust	• Begin to learn what to trust and mistrust in their environments, depending on the types of experiences in infancy and toddlerhood
18 months–3 years	Autonomy versus shame and doubt	• Attempt to make some of their own choices • Demonstrate their independence
3–6 years	Initiative versus guilt	• Begin to try out their own ideas and actions
6–12 years	Industry versus inferiority	• Demonstrate what they can do • Compare what they can do with what others can do
Adolescence	Identity versus role confusion	• Struggle with questions about who they are and who they are going to be
Young adulthood	Intimacy versus isolation	• Seek stable reciprocal relationships with others
Middle adulthood	Generativity versus stagnation	• Reflect on their contributions to others • Redefine their goals • Make decisions related to these goals
Older adulthood	Integrity versus despair	• Attempt to share their accumulated knowledge and insight with members of newer generations

omy versus shame and doubt. This stage begins around eighteen months and lasts until approximately three years of age. During the stage of autonomy versus shame and doubt, children attempt to make some of their own choices and demonstrate their independence. **Autonomy** is the ability to make decisions and act independently. If their attempts at autonomy are frequently unsuccessful or met with ridicule, children begin to doubt their abilities and feel shame at their perceived ineffectiveness.

Two-year-old Pedro sits at the lunch table happily munching on French fries and applesauce when his teacher, Ms. Lana Woods, who is sitting beside him, casually mentions that there are still some green beans on his plate that he could finish eating. Pedro drops his spoon, looks into his teacher's face, stands up quickly (knocking over his chair in the process), and takes off running across the classroom shouting "no" along the way. Ms. Woods calmly walks toward Pedro, telling him that eating the green beans is his choice, and invites him back to the lunch table to finish his French fries and applesauce. Pedro takes his teacher's extended hand, smiles, and returns to the lunch table, where he picks up his chair and resumes eating.

In this vignette, Pedro demonstrates his desire to be autonomous and make his own choices. When toddlers make decisions that differ from what they are being asked to do, their actions do not always follow socially acceptable avenues. Negative verbal responses, such as Pedro's resounding "no," often signal that children are practicing or testing their autonomy and independence. Young children also display negative physical responses—such as running away from adults or throwing themselves on the floor and crying loudly—as cues that what they want to do is contrary to what they are being asked to do. Because toddlers and two-year-olds have limited language abilities, they often act out their frustration, anger, and desire for autonomy with body movements, facial expressions, and vocalizations. These behaviors are manifestations of children's psychosocial struggle for autonomy. If all of their attempts at autonomy are met with strong negative responses from their caregivers, children begin to doubt their abilities and experience the self-conscious emotion of shame. In the vignette, Ms. Woods responds positively to Pedro's attempts at autonomy, thereby encouraging him to make choices.

Of course, toddlers and two-year-olds are new at decision making, and therefore they tend to make some inappropriate choices; but family members and caregivers can provide opportunities for successful decision making by giving children a limited number of reasonable choices. Instead of asking two-year-olds, "What would you like to wear today?" ask, "Would you like to wear the red shirt or the blue-striped shirt?" In this way, either choice the child makes is successful, thereby supporting her fledgling attempts at independence. The first type of open-ended question presents too many potentially unacceptable responses and sometimes leads to a struggle for power between adults and children, whereas the fixed choices offered in the second question support children's autonomy and encourage their confidence in decision making.

Making decisions and demonstrating independence continue to be integral behaviors during the third stage of psychosocial development, **initiative versus guilt**,

Young children whose language is still somewhat limited often use body movements and facial expressions to demonstrate their attempts at autonomy.

when children begin to try out their own ideas and actions. During the stage of initiative versus guilt, children like to use their own ideas to solve problems, although they still seek guidance from other individuals at times. Children show pleasure or pride for their accomplishments and disappointment, guilt, frustration, or anger at their unsuccessful attempts. Sometimes younger children have difficulty distinguishing one strong emotion from another and may need someone more experienced to help them express their feelings in socially acceptable ways.

Mr. Ron Issacs, four-year-old Megan's teacher, reminds her to place the building blocks back on the shelf when she is finished constructing. However, Megan decides that the blocks should be placed on the shelf "standing up" instead of "lying down." When Mr. Issacs looks over to see how Megan is doing, he finds only a few blocks on the shelf and the rest scattered around on the floor as Megan struggles to keep the upright blocks she has placed on the shelf from falling over.

Mr. Issacs moves to the block center and kneels beside Megan, quietly asking her to explain how she is stacking the blocks. He responds positively to Megan's ideas for rearranging the blocks on the shelf, offers Megan a couple of suggestions for keeping the blocks from falling over, and then moves away from the block center. Megan tries both of Mr. Issacs's suggestions and decides that the first suggestion works best.

By offering suggestions or alternatives rather than telling Megan exactly what to do or forcing her to follow rigid rules for stacking blocks, Mr. Issacs has shown that he values Megan's initiative and respects her ideas. In this vignette, thanks to Mr. Issacs's emotionally sensitive teaching, Megan has resolved this conflict positively and reaffirmed her sense of initiative rather than experiencing guilt. When adults encourage children to complete tasks in their own ways, children feel confident about their abilities and are more willing to demonstrate initiative in future endeavors. Conversely, if children's attempts at initiative are consistently met with disdain, they experience feelings of guilt because they perceive themselves as lacking and unable to meet adult expectations.

As with all of Erikson's stages, no single experience determines whether children resolve the crisis of initiative versus guilt positively or negatively; instead, it is the accumulation of experiences that determines overall resolution of the crisis at this stage. This stage lasts for approximately three years, during which time children have many opportunities for experiences with initiative.

Around age 6, children enter the fourth stage of psychosocial development, **industry versus inferiority**. This stage lasts about six years and spans the end of early childhood and all of middle childhood. *Industry* refers to children's need to feel competent and equal in ability to their peers. During this stage, children like to demonstrate what they can do and compare what they can do with what others can do. Sometimes these comparisons can become quite competitive. The scope of abilities ranges from the cognitive domain (knowledge and skills) to the psychomotor domain (physical abilities and features) to the affective domain (emotional profile, social competence, and morality). Children at this stage who feel competent and industrious are eager to try new experiences, learn new skills, and then demonstrate those skills for others, whereas children who feel inferior and incompetent are less likely to take risks and try new things because they fear failure.

Children who attend before-and-after-school child care programs or who are in the primary grades are typically in the stage of industry versus inferiority and, as such, prefer activities that are challenging but achievable. Their skill levels, talents, and interests vary widely and are subject to frequent changes as they encounter new information, ideas, and individuals. Due to their need to feel industrious rather than inferior, they often create competitive situations and display enjoyment over winning and disappointment or anger over losing. Teachers of children between ages 6 and 12 who understand this group's need to feel competent provide play and learning situations that encourage group cooperation rather than competition and plan challenging activities that have many avenues to success.

With the onset of adolescence, children develop into Erikson's fifth stage of psychosocial development, **identity versus role confusion**, which spans all of adolescence—approximately ages 13 to 19. During this stage, individuals struggle with questions about who they are and who they are going to be. The struggle to move toward adulthood and away from childhood creates contentious situations between adolescents and adult authority figures, which adolescents perceive as obstacles to adulthood. In their quest for identity, adolescents often form strong bonds with their peers, who are likely to experience similar doubts and confusion as they attempt to sort out their roles and move toward a secure sense of self-identity as they enter adulthood.

Unlike many human development theorists, Erikson does not see adolescence as the completion of development; rather, his theory covers the entire life span. Erikson identifies three additional stages of psychosocial development that occur after adolescence. Young adulthood deals with the psychosocial conflict of **intimacy versus isolation** as individuals seek stable reciprocal relationships with others. Middle adulthood confronts the crisis of **generativity versus stagnation**, in which individuals reflect on their contributions to others, redefine goals, and make decisions related to those goals. The eighth, and final, stage of Erikson's theory of psychosocial development occurs during older adulthood, when individuals reflect on prior contributions, achievements, and failures. During this stage of **integrity versus despair**, individuals often attempt to share their accumulated knowledge and insight with members of newer generations. (Table 4.5, p. 83, provides a brief description of all eight stages of psychosocial development.)

Understanding the stages of psychosocial development is important to early childhood educators, because the ways in which educators respond to children's attempts at trust, autonomy, initiative, industry, and identity influence children's emotional and social stability and formation of healthy identity. Fortunately, single events rarely determine positive or negative resolutions to psychosocial crises at any stage; rather, the collection of experiences over time impacts emotional-social development (Sroufe, 1996). Although Erikson identified a particular emotional-social focus at each stage of psychosocial development, he also acknowledged that emotional-social issues reemerge throughout life. Because positive and negative emotional and social experiences are on-

going throughout life, subsequent experiences continue to influence the ultimate resolution of identity.

*Eight-year-old Jordon blows out the candles on his birthday cake as his parents snap pic-
tures and sing "Happy Birthday" to him. Jordon's mother offers to slice cake for everyone,
but Jordon objects, saying he is old enough to use a knife now that he is eight. His mother
laughs and says she is glad she has such a grown-up son to take care of the cake slicing.
Jordon carefully takes the cake knife and begins to slice the cake into squares as he has
seen his mother do before. Jordon offers the first slice to his mother and the second to his
father before he serves himself. As the family sits around the table and eats their birthday
cake, Jordon remarks that he is a pretty good cake cutter. Both his mother and father smile
and nod in agreement.*

*Eight-year-old Jordon is quite different from the Jordon who was found abandoned at
the city bus depot five years ago; that Jordon was at times timid and insecure and at times
angry and explosive. After nearly two years in the foster care system, Jordon was adopted
by Glen and Mary. At his fifth birthday party, a few months after his adoption, Jordon
was so afraid of doing something wrong that he cried for nearly an hour when he accidentally dropped his piece of cake on the floor. Glen, Mary, and Jordon spent many months
getting to know each other before Jordon began to trust that he was in their family to stay,
even if he sometimes made mistakes or got angry. Since that realization, Jordon has blos-
somed into the confident eight-year-old described in the opening scene.*

Jordan's psychosocial turnabout in this vignette illustrates the possibilities for
reresolution that unfold as current experience impacts on emotional and social crises
that were resolved at earlier stages of psychosocial development. Reresolution offers
both positive and negative potential effects on children's cumulative emotional and social development.

Effects of Abuse and Neglect on Children's Emotional-Social Development

One important implication of Erikson's theory of psychosocial development is that
children's experiences during their early years play major roles in shaping their adult
personalities. Sometimes the consequences of early life experiences can have devastating effects on the developing personalities of young children. Such is often the case
with **child abuse.** Child abuse is the illegal mistreatment of children either through action or lack of action. Child abuse assumes four basic forms: **physical abuse, emotional
abuse, sexual abuse,** and **neglect.**

Physical abuse causes harm to children through excessive force or restraint, such as
hitting, shaking, kicking, throwing, burning, or other forms of physical punishment.
Children who have been subjected to physical abuse often have bruises, cuts, sores,
burns, fractures, or broken bones. If excessive forms of restraint have been used, children
may have bruises or sores on their wrists, ankles, or necks where restraints such as ropes,

tape, leashes, or cords have been wrapped tightly around their torsos or limbs. Physical abuse is usually easier to document than other forms of abuse because of the physical evidence, such as bruises, left on children's bodies.

Emotional abuse, which is just as devastating to children's developing personalities as physical abuse, does not leave the same types of physical evidence; therefore, it is more difficult to document and prosecute. Emotional abuse usually consists of derogatory verbal comments intended to intimidate, threaten, or humiliate children. Often, emotional abuse precedes or occurs simultaneously with physical abuse and is designed to frighten children with possible physical repercussions such as beatings or abandonment. Children who are consistently subjected to emotional abuse often display lack of confidence and withdrawal or highly aggressive verbal and physical behaviors.

Sexual abuse, which can be physical or emotional in nature, has sexual overtones such as showing children pornographic material, forcing children to pose for pornographic photographs or videos, or coercing children to engage in sex acts with other children or adults. Sexual abuse also includes any form of fondling of children's bodies or molestation. When sexual molestation involves a member of children's immediate families, it is referred to as **incest.** Because the physical forms of sexual abuse involve parts of children's bodies that are commonly covered by clothing, signs of such abuse often go undetected once children are able to use the toilet independently.

Neglect is a form of child abuse that results from inaction rather than action. Neglect is failure to provide children with appropriate nourishment, protection, shelter, medical care, or supervision. Children who have been neglected have limited opportunities to develop trust in their environments or primary caregivers. Sometimes neglect is deliberately used as a form of punishment, such as withholding food because of children's misbehavior. At other times, neglect results from lack of concern for children's welfare, such as leaving children home alone or in parked cars without supervision. At other times, neglect may be a consequence of poverty that leaves families without financial means to purchase food, shelter, child care, or medical care.

Teachers of young children have not only moral obligations but also legal obligations to safeguard the lives of children. In the United States, teachers, child care staff, social workers, counselors, doctors, police officers, and others who interact with children on a regular basis as part of their employment are considered **mandatory reporters of child abuse** and are required to report any suspicion of child abuse to the proper authorities. Failure to do so can result in legal consequences for the mandatory reporter. The "proper authority" varies from state to state, but is usually the police, the department of health or social services, or the child abuse hotline. Schools often designate internal procedures for documenting and reporting suspected cases of child abuse; however, reporting such incidents to internal supervisors who do not follow through to the proper authorities does not relieve primary mandatory reporters from responsibility under the law. Children and family members may view early childhood teachers as "safe havens" and disclose situations of child abuse or other forms of family violence to them (Austin, 2000). Child abuse adversely effects children's abilities to form secure trusting relationships with family members, teachers, and other adults. It may also impede their relationships with other children.

Peer Relationships during Early Childhood

During early childhood, children form relationships with other children as they play together, but these relationships are based on the same criteria that older children and adults use to select friends. Friendship is an aspect of social development that emerges as children mature and gain experience interacting with their peers (McClellan & Katz, 1993). Peer relationships differ from child-caregiver relationships, because peer relationships are chosen freely by children. Early friendships are initially influenced by convenience, such as accessibility, but ultimately develop because of common interests and attitudes. The friendships of preschool-age children are often temporary and changeable, although most preschool children can distinguish between a friend and a playmate. In later childhood, friendships become more reciprocal because they build feelings of loyalty and are more long lasting. Throughout early childhood, friendships are usually mutually satisfying; that is, each child gains from the relationship. The ability to form successful relationships with peers is an indication of social competence, and children with high levels of social competence demonstrate more awareness of situation-specific behaviors (McClellan & Katz, 1993), which enables them to make decisions based on multiple factors.

Moral Development

The ability to reason and make decisions in social situations is related to another facet of affective development called **moral development.** Human development theorists often explore moral development and moral reasoning within the context of cognitive development, because the ways in which individuals perceive and understand situations affects their interpretation of morality. However, morality is also an important part of the emotional-social aspect of personality, or *moral character.* Moral character is the stable pattern of moral reasoning and decision making and is intricately connected to both emotional and social development. Interpretations of morality are also sensitive to the influence of culture; that is, behaviors that are considered socially or morally acceptable in one culture may be considered less than acceptable in another culture (McClellan & Katz, 1993). From infancy, children develop concepts of moral behavior from their relationships with others; however, interpretation of those concepts is tied to their level of cognitive development.

COMPETENCY GOAL II
• Functional Area 5

COMPETENCY GOAL III
• Functional Areas 8–10

Infants and young toddlers have limited ability to interpret right from wrong because their cognitive abilities only allow them to consider events in the present tense. At some point during late toddlerhood, as children develop the cognitive and language abilities to represent ideas symbolically, they gain awareness that some actions are right and other actions are wrong, partly depending on the circumstances under which they occur (Harlow & Cummings, 2000). This awareness

> *The little world of childhood with its familiar surroundings is a model of the greater world. The more intensely the family has stamped its character upon the child, the more it will tend to feel and see its earlier miniature world again in the bigger world of adult life.*
>
> —Carl Jung, *Theory of Psychoanalysis* (1913)

marks the beginning of moral reasoning. Several theories attempt to explain the complexities of moral reasoning.

Piaget's Stages of Moral Development

In his explanations of the development of morality, Piaget connected children's moral reasoning abilities to their level of cognitive development, implying that children's socio-conventional knowledge and moral reasoning reflect their perceptions and logical operations. (Chapter 3 provides descriptions of Piaget's stages of cognitive development.) Children in the sensorimotor and preoperational stages of cognitive development, who rely on perception rather than logic to build their understandings of the world, are in the **premoral stage** of moral development. During the premoral stage, children construct initial awareness of morality and make decisions about moral behavior through the filter of egocentrism (Piaget, 1932/1965). Therefore, children decide whether something is right or wrong based on how it will directly affect them rather than considering reasons behind rules or intentions of others. Due to their egocentrism, children in the premoral stage make moral decisions that will keep them from being punished or that will gain them rewards rather than basing moral decisions on any consistent sense of appropriate or inappropriate behavior. For example, a three-year-old picks up his toys when asked in order to avoid receiving a reprimand from the parent or to gain the parent's praise for his cooperative behavior. His reasons for picking up the toys are not from a moral belief that picking up toys is the right thing to do.

According to Piaget, around age 6, children move into the **heteronomous morality stage** of moral development. Although children in this stage are less egocentric than those in the premoral stage, their perspectives are still dependent on concrete experiences, so they continue to make decisions about morality based on positive or negative consequences rather than on intentions. They align moral behaviors according to the degree of potential punishment and view rules and consequences as absolute and inflexible (DeVries, 1998). During the heteronomous morality stage, children expect all misdeeds to be punished and react with dismay when wrongdoers are not caught and punished according to the rules in place. They demonstrate limited understanding that rules may apply differently in certain situations, and they make moral decisions within the constraint of externally developed rules (Piaget, 1932/1965).

After age 10, children are in the **autonomous morality stage** of moral development and understand that rules are social decisions subject to revision through the cooperation of interested parties (Piaget, 1932/1965). Children in the autonomous morality stage are able to consider the intentions of individuals as well as their misdeeds and believe punishment should be relative to both the misdeed and the intentions. For example, they understand that individuals who deliberately damage property or hurt others should be subject to stronger punishments than individuals who accidentally damage property or hurt others. Children in the autonomous morality stage also recognize that rules that are potentially harmful to individuals may be violated for the greater good of individuals (DeVries, 1998). Piaget's ideas about children's moral development evolved from his theory of cognitive development. Another theory of moral development that draws from Piaget's theory of cognitive development is Kohlberg's theory of moral reasoning.

Kohlberg's Theory of Moral Reasoning

Kohlberg's **levels of moral reasoning** are frequently used to explain how children view morality. Lawrence Kohlberg (1927–1987), an American psychologist, proposed a theory of moral reasoning based, in part, on Piaget's stages of cognitive development. Kohlberg identified six progressive stages that he categorized into three sequential levels: **preconventional moral reasoning, conventional moral reasoning,** and **postconventional moral reasoning** (Kohlberg, 1969).

Preconventional Level   Within the preconventional level of moral reasoning, individuals determine right and wrong based on personal wants and needs. During stage 1, individuals reason about morality based on an *obedience-and-punishment orientation* (Kohlberg, 1969), with the goal being to avoid punishment. During stage 2, individuals operate with an *instrumental exchange orientation* (Barger, 2000). Individuals base their moral reasoning on gaining personal advantage or reward. Children at this level make two types of decisions. They decide whether an action is right or wrong, and they decide whether to act morally (do the right thing) or immorally (do the wrong thing). Because preschool children view events and actions only from their own perspectives, they often make the choice that helps them avoid punishment or brings them personal reward. Developmentally, young children are unable to view situations from other points of view. Children between ages 4 and 10 often function at the preconventional level of moral development (Gill & Magee, 1998). Their inability to view situations from

Table 4.6   Kohlberg's Levels of Moral Reasoning

Level of Moral Reasoning	Stage of Moral Reasoning	Characteristics
Preconventional level	1. Obedience-punishment orientation	• Goal is to avoid punishment
	2. Instrumental exchange orientation	• Base their moral reasoning on gaining personal advantage or reward
Conventional level	3. Good-boy-or-girl orientation	• Make decisions about morality based on the expectations and approval of others
	4. Law-and-order orientation	• Feel an obligation or duty to follow the rules
Postconventional level	5. Social contract orientation	• Consider the larger needs of society over personal needs
	6. Universal-ethical orientation	• Consider universal principles and personal conscience

another's point of view can lead to some interesting interpretations of morality, such as those described in the following vignette.

Matthew, who is 4, wants to ride Miguel's tricycle. Matthew knows the rule is to take turns, but he believes his turn should begin when he wants the tricycle. After making sure their teacher is looking elsewhere, Matthew walks over to Miguel and pushes him off the tricycle saying, "It's my turn now." Miguel tumbles to the ground and begins to cry. Mr. Tonner, their teacher, squats beside Miguel, making sure he is not injured before asking him to tell what happened. Miguel stands up and points angrily toward Matthew. Mr. Tonner asks Miguel to wait and walks over to Matthew, who is happily pedaling the tricycle around the play area while making "vroom-vroom" sounds. When Matthew sees Mr. Tonner standing next to him, he blurts out, "Miguel wouldn't give me a turn." Mr. Tonner tells Matthew to park the tricycle and motions to Miguel to join them. Mr. Tonner calmly instructs the boys to go to the bench with him. When both boys are seated, Mr. Tonner squats down in front of them and calmly says, "Matthew and Miguel, you have a problem: there are two boys and one tricycle. Please talk to each other and decide what are you going to do to solve this problem. I'll let you two talk for a couple of minutes, and then I will be back and you can tell me what you have decided to do so you both can go back to playing." At first Matthew and Miguel look at the ground rather than each other, but in a minute they are talking and nodding and looking toward their teacher, signaling that they have a plan.

In this vignette, Matthew used preconventional moral reasoning, concluding that since he wants the tricycle (his reward), his turn should begin now; therefore, it is okay to make Miguel give him his turn now. Matthew is unable to take into consideration that Miguel also wants to ride the tricycle. Of course, as an adult you can see that Matthew's interpretation of this moral situation respects only one viewpoint—his! In fact, yesterday, when the situation was reversed, Matthew maintained that Miguel acted inappropriately by pushing him off the tricycle before his turn was over. Matthew has forgotten how he felt yesterday, when he was on the tricycle and Miguel pushed him off! But Matthew's cognitive abilities do not yet enable him to simultaneously consider multiple points of view.

If Matthew had decided to wait until Miguel got off the tricycle before taking his turn, what level and stage of moral reasoning would Matthew be employing? Since it is unlikely that Matthew would have reasoned that waiting was "the right thing to do," it is more likely that Matthew did not want to get into trouble for pushing Miguel, so he waited until Miguel dismounted in order to avoid punishment such as a reprimand from a caregiver. When you think about moral reasoning, consider not only the moral (or immoral) action but also the reasoning behind the action in order to determine the level and stage of moral reasoning being employed.

Conventional Level Kohlberg's second level of moral development suggests that individuals act morally because they are expected to act so (Kohlberg, 1969). The conventional level is also divided into two stages. Stage 3, the *good-boy-or-girl orientation,*

The cognitive inability of young children to view situations from perspectives other than their own influences their moral reasoning.

involves making decisions about morality based on the expectations and approval of others. Children do what they think "good" boys or girls should do. In order to operate at stage 3 of Kohlberg's theory, individuals must be able to consider someone else's perspective. Stage 4 of moral reasoning represents a *law-and-order orientation*, whereby the rule, or law, is unchangeable and of utmost importance. Rules and their consequences are often interpreted literally, without consideration of extenuating circumstances. Individuals feel an obligation or duty to follow the rules. Older preschool children and most school-age children are able to function at the conventional level of moral development.

Children reasoning at the conventional level of moral development interpret events through their understanding of someone else's interpretation of right and wrong. Consider the following examples. In the first case, Kyle, who is helping his mother with the dishes, accidentally drops and breaks three glasses. In the second case, Kenny wants to take some lemonade outside, but he cannot find a paper cup; he takes a glass outside, even though he knows it is against the rules. On his way outside Kenny drops and breaks the glass. Which child acted more immorally, Kyle or Kenny? As an adult you may take into consideration the intent of each child when the glasses were broken and decide that Kenny, who broke one glass on his way outside, performed a more immoral act than did Kyle, who broke three glasses, because Kenny's rule breaking was intentional, whereas Kyle's rule breaking was accidental and his intention was helpful, not harmful. However, a child operating at stage 4, the law-and-order orientation, might interpret the situation differently. If the rule is "Don't break the glasses," then Kyle, who broke three glasses, broke the rule three times; thus he acted more immorally than Kenny, who broke the rule only one time. The child's intent is not considered because the rule is viewed as fixed, and not dependent on the situation. Children at this level of moral reasoning often feel an obligation to let rule makers know when a rule, or law, has been broken.

Postconventional Level Kohlberg's highest level of moral development is the postconventional level. Adolescents and adults may be capable of moral reasoning at this level, although Kohlberg suggests that most individuals do not reach this level (Kohlberg, 1969). Postconventional moral reasoning is motivated by concern and respect for others, even if the others are not individuals one personally knows. In stage 5, the *social contract orientation,* moral reasoning considers the larger needs of society over personal needs. Respect for social order and the welfare of others is evident. Stage 6, the *universal ethical orientation,* employs moral reasoning that considers universal principles and personal conscience (Barger, 2000).

Although Kohlberg's ideas about the development of moral reasoning are widely cited, the theory has received some criticism. Some critics indicate that two few individuals achieve stages 5 and 6, indicating that the postconventional level may not be a universal characteristic of development. In fact, in 1978, Kohlberg addressed these concerns and combined stages 5 and 6 into one stage. Other critics suggest that Kohlberg failed to consider the influence of culture on moral reasoning, pointing out that the stages of moral reasoning appear to favor Western cultures over Eastern cultures, which have different social conventions (Crosser, 2002). Another potential limitation of Kohlberg's theory, according to one of his former students and research assistants, is that Kohlberg's stages are biased toward the male gender (Gilligan, 1977).

Gilligan's Views on Moral Reasoning

Carol Gilligan (b. 1936), an American psychologist and researcher who was a research assistant for Kohlberg, suggests that Kohlberg's stages of moral development fail to recognize the female perspective when analyzing moral reasoning. Gilligan (1982) explains that males use a **morality of justice** oriented toward individual rights and responsibilities, while females base their reasoning on a **morality of caring**, focusing more on responsibilities to relationships than individual rights. In her book, *In a Different Voice* (1982), Gilligan describes some of her research interviews with women who were faced with making important moral decisions in their lives and presents a stage theory describing the development of moral reasoning from a female perspective.

Regardless of their different views about the development of moral reasoning, Piaget, Kohlberg, and Gilligan all agree that moral reasoning occurs within the context of cognitive development. That is, at each of the stages of cognitive development, individuals reason about morality in different ways according to their cognitive characteristics. For example, preschool-age children, who are still egocentric, view moral situations from only their own perspective (Crosser, 2002), while older chil-

The aim of education is the knowledge not of fact, but of values.
—Dean William R. Inge

dren may consider moral issues from more than one perspective, but only if they have had concrete experiences that help them understand both sides of a situation.

Children's understandings of right and wrong develop gradually, based on maturation and experience, just as do other facets of development. From ages 1 to 3, children engage in behaviors with little consideration for whether those behaviors are considered right or wrong by others. Around the second birthday, children begin to display some self-conscious emotions—such as guilt, shame, and disappointment—that indicate they are beginning to judge their own moral behaviors on the basis of feedback from others. For example, two-year-old Annie may look toward her caregiver before grabbing an extra cookie, waiting for some type of signal from the caregiver to let her know if taking another cookie is all right. Even if the caregiver shakes her head to indicate that it is not all right, Annie may still take the cookie, but her behavior does show that she is using the caregiver as a social reference before deciding what to do.

By age 3, many children have developed awareness of socially acceptable and unacceptable behaviors, but may have difficulty consistently controlling unacceptable behaviors due to their egocentric perspectives (Buzzelli, 1992). Their moral reasoning is linked more to their perception of events than to logic. For example, three-year-old Jamie may not understand why his ten-year-old brother can stay up later than he can, even though his parents patiently explain that his brother is a lot older so, logically, he should be able to stay up later. All Jamie sees is that his brother gets to do something that he is not allowed to do and that this is "just not fair." When dealing with young children, caregivers need to consider children's moral reasoning in light of their overall development rather than viewing their moral decision making from adult perspectives.

Promoting Development within the Affective Domain

The first five years have profound influence on the affective development of young children. During these crucial years, children build the foundation of their emotional health, social competence, and moral character. Teachers of young children are presented with many opportunities to promote positive development within the affective domain as they interact with infants, toddlers, and young children and their families in early care and education settings.

Caregivers help children build strong relationships when they are responsive to children's individual temperaments and fit their nurturing and teaching to each child's special needs, allowing them to explore their environments and interact with others. Through these experiences and interactions, children develop a sense of self that adds to their abilities to form and maintain strong relationships.

Stable relationships and responsive interactions create play and learning environments where children can freely discover their emotions and social natures. They need

CDA

COMPETENCY GOAL II
• Functional Areas 5–6

COMPETENCY GOAL III
• Functional Areas 8–10

COMPETENCY GOAL IV
• Functional Area 11

many outlets for interaction with other children and adults. Teachers can serve as guides as they help children express their emotions in socially acceptable ways and increase awareness of social and cultural expectations.

Early care and learning environments provide many outlets for investigation of self and social and cultural expectations. Caregivers can acknowledge children's emotions and help them recognize these emotions by building on naturally occurring interactions among children. Role-play, dramatization, and puppetry give children opportunities to safely try out a variety of emotional responses and actions. In addition, culturally sensitive children's storybooks and some fairy tales provide opportunities for discussions about feelings and friendship and dozens of other topics related to affective development. (See the end-of-the-chapter Learning Activity 2 for another way to use children's books to promote positive development.)

Children should also be encouraged to express their feelings and individualism through other means such as art, music, and movement. For example, invite children into a large open space and provide them with some ribbons or streamers while you play a recording of some lively instrumental music. Encourage children to "feel" the music and move in ways to show how they are feeling. Give them enough time to experiment with movement and build more awareness of their bodies. After a while, change the music to something that conveys a different emotion and repeat the process. Throughout the activity, listen to the children as they talk about their feelings about the music.

Both large-group activities, like "move to the music," and small-group activities, like sharing storybooks or making puppets, support children's emerging social skills as they interact with other children through the course of the activity. Children also need opportunities for one-on-one attention with caring adults. Teachers need to balance classroom schedules so that one-on-one interactions occur on a regular basis, but teachers are not the only adults who can provide children with personal attention. Teachers can invite family members and community volunteers, such as high school students taking child development courses, into the classroom. These visitors broaden the cultural boundaries of the classroom and give children more ways to explore their feelings, practice their social skills, and gain understanding of their moral character.

Summary

- The affective domain includes aspects of emotional, social, and moral development.

Emotional Development

- From birth, infants display their own styles of emotional response or temperament.

- By the end of the first year of life, infants are able to express basic emotions such as interest, joy, sadness, disgust, surprise, fear, and anger.
- Self-conscious emotions—such as shame, guilt, and embarrassment—indicate that children are beginning to view their behaviors in relationship to expectations.

- Infants form strong emotional bonds, or attachments, to familiar caregivers.

Social Development

- Psychosocial development progresses in stages and involves both emotional and social factors.
- Play provides opportunities to develop social competence and form peer relationships.

Moral Development

- Moral reasoning occurs within the context of cognitive development.
- Culture and gender influence views of morality.

Promoting Development within the Affective Domain

- Young children and their caregivers need to form stable, responsive relationships.
- Children need opportunities to recognize, label, and express emotions.
- Many play and learning experiences provide opportunities for children to explore emotions and to practice social skills.
- Interaction with other children and adults helps children gain awareness of social and moral expectations within the context of culture.

LEARNING ACTIVITIES

1 Role-Play: Psychosocial Development. (Refer to Table 4.5, p. 83.) Get together with a small group of classmates and develop a skit showing a child in a situation in which the child will have to resolve a psychosocial conflict. Perform the skit for the rest of the class and let them determine the stage of psychosocial development being portrayed and whether the conflict has a positive or negative outcome for the child.

2 Discussion: Moral Reasoning. (Refer to Table 4.6, p. 91.) Locate a book that is written for young children and includes a moral dilemma, such as whether to tell a lie or to take something that does not belong to you, as part of the plot. Share the book in class. Identify the character's moral dilemma and the character's solution to the situation. Discuss the character's moral reasoning and moral behavior. What stage of moral development did the character demonstrate? Justify your conclusion.

PORTFOLIO ARTIFACTS

1 Survey: Temperament. (Refer to Table 4.1, p. 76, and Table 4.2, p. 77.) Conduct an informal survey of family members or friends who have children under age 3. Ask them questions about their children's patterns of behavior before their first birthday. Focus your questions on the nine dimensions of temperament. From the responses you receive, can you classify the temperament of any of the infants into the categories of temperament—easy, difficult, or slow-to-warm-up?

2 Observation: Attachment. (Refer to Table 4.4, p. 81.) Observe toddlers or two-year-olds as they arrive at a local child care center or preschool. Focus on the children's reactions to the departure of family members. Do the children show signs of distress? Are they easily comforted? What does the children's behavior tell you about the security or insecurity of their attachment? If possible, visit the same site when the children are picked up for the day. What other information about their attachment can you infer from their reactions to the arrival of family members?

Professional Connections and Web Links

Southern Early Childhood Association (SECA)
P.O. Box 55930
Little Rock, AR 72215-5930
800-305-7322
http://www.southernearlychildhood.org

The Southern Early Childhood Association (SECA), which was established in 1948, is a professional organization of about 16,000 preschool, kindergarten, and primary teachers as well as other individuals who work with young children and their families. SECA hosts local, state, and regional meetings and publishes a quarterly journal, *Dimensions of Early Childhood*. SECA has also published position statements on issues related to the well-being of young children, such as "Quality Child Care." These statements and other information about the organization's mission can be accessed through their Web site. Membership to SECA is open to individuals within and outside the southern region.

National Clearinghouse on
Child Abuse and Neglect
330 C Street, SW
Washington, DC 20447
703-385-7565
800-394-3366
http://www.calib.com/nccanch/

This site serves as the information source for the National Clearinghouse on Child Abuse and Neglect. It is a resource for individuals looking for information on child abuse, neglect, and child welfare. In addition to providing statistics and state statutes about abuse and neglect, the site offers a comprehensive catalog of resources and publications. Many of the publications can be downloaded. There are specific publications for caregivers of young children.

Suggestions for Further Reading

Brazelton, T. Berry (1992). *Touchpoints: Your child's emotional and behavioral development*. Reading, MA: Addison-Wesley.

- Brazelton provides a comprehensive look at development from the prenatal stage through the first three years of life. The book is directed toward helping parents and caregivers understand the accomplishments and challenges facing young children and the people who care for them.

Greenspan, Stanley, & Greenspan, Nancy T. (1985). *First feelings: Milestones in the emotional development of your baby and child*. New York: Viking.

- Greenspan and Greenspan provide an overview of the six stages of emotional growth during early childhood. The emphasis is on understanding feelings and the emotional relationships among young children and their families.

References

Ainsworth, M. D. S., Biehar, M. C., Waters, E., & Wall, S. (1978). *Patterns of attachment*. Hillsdale, NJ: Erlbaum.

Austin, Sue. (2000). When a child discloses sexual abuse: Immediate and appropriate teacher responses. *Childhood Education, 77*(1), 2–5.

Barger, Robert N. (2000). *A summary of Lawrence Kohlberg's stages of moral development*. Retrieved on April 12, 2001, from University of Notre Dame Web site: http://www.nd.edu/rbarger/kohlberg.html.

Berk, Laura E., & Winsler, Adam. (1995). *Scaffolding children's learning: Vygotsky and early childhood education*. Washington, DC: National Association for the Education of Young Children.

Bowlby, John. (1980). *Attachment and loss*: Vol. 3, *Attachment*. New York: Basic Books.

Brazelton, T. Berry. (1992). *Touchpoints: Your child's emotional and behavioral development*. Reading, MA: Addison-Wesley.

Buzzelli, Cary A. (1992). Young children's moral understanding: Learning about right and wrong. *Young Children, 47*(6), 47–53.

Crosser, Sandra. (2002). What's the difference between right and wrong: Understanding how children think. *Early Childhood News, 14*(3), 16–22.

Dettore, Ernie. (2002). Children's emotional growth: Adults' role as emotional archaeologists. *Childhood Education, 78*(5), 278–281.

DeVries, Rheta. (1998). Implications of Piaget's constructivist theory for character education. *Action in Teacher Education, 20*(4), 39–47.

Erikson, Erik H. (1950). *Childhood and society.* New York: Norton.

Erikson, Erik H. (1968). *Identity: Youth and crisis.* New York: Norton.

Gill, Lunda L., & Magee, Carolyn. (1998, January 15). *Lawrence Kohlberg's levels and stages of moral development.* Retrieved on April 12, 2001, from Pepperdine University Web site: http://moon.pepperdine.edu/gsep/class/ethics/kohlberg/Stages_Moral-Development.html.

Gilligan, Carol. (1977). In a different voice: Women's conceptions of self and of morality. *Harvard Educational Review, 47*(4), 481–517.

Gilligan, Carol. (1982). *In a different voice: Psychological theory and women's development.* Cambridge, MA: Harvard University Press.

Gopnik, Allison, Meltzoff, Andrew N., & Kuhl, Patricia K. (2001). *The scientist in the crib: What early learning tells us about the mind.* New York: Perennial.

Greenspan, Stanley, & Greenspan, Nancy Thorndike. (1985). *First feelings: Milestones in the emotional development of your baby and child.* New York: Viking.

Harlow, Steve, & Cummings, Rhonda. (2000). Constructivist roots of moral education. *Educational Forum, 64*(1), 4–9.

Honig, Alice Sterling. (2002). *Secure relationships: Nurturing infant/toddler attachment in early care settings.* Washington, DC: National Association for the Education of Young Children.

Kohlberg, Lawrence (1969). Stage and sequence: The cognitive-developmental approach to socialization. In D. A. Goslin (Ed.), *Handbook of socialization: Theory in research.* Boston: Houghton Mifflin.

Kohlberg, Lawrence. (1978). Revisions in the theory and practice of moral development. In W. Damon (Ed.), *New directions for child development.* (no. 2, pp. 83–87). San Francisco: Jossey-Bass.

McClellan, Diane, & Katz, Lillian G. (1993). *Young children's social development: A checklist.* Urbana, IL: ERIC Clearinghouse on Elementary and Early Childhood Education.

Piaget, Jean. (1932/1965). *The moral judgment of the child.* New York: Free Press.

Sroufe, L. Alan. (1996). *Emotional development: The organization of emotional life in the early years.* Port Chester, NY: Cambridge University Press.

Thomas, A., & Chess, S. (1977). *Temperament and development.* New York: Brunner/Mazel.

Thomas, A., Chess, S., & Birch, H. G. (1970, August). The origins of personality. *Scientific American, 223*(2), 102–109.

Teachers in Early Childhood Education

 arly childhood teachers willingly undertake responsibility for the safekeeping and education of the young children in their care. Those responsibilities encompass a wide area of duties and privileges. Module Two, Teachers in Early Childhood Education, explores the personal and professional characteristics, knowledge, and skills of successful teachers, past and present, to examine your own qualities as you begin the exciting process of becoming an early childhood teacher.

By reading about the steps to becoming a teacher, you will find out more about what makes good teachers good. The opening chapter of this module invites you to reflect on your personal goals and reaffirm your decision to teach. The next chapter takes you back in time to gain understanding of the historical roots of early care and education by introducing some of the influential philosophers and educators who helped shape the field. The third chapter of the module offers a revealing glimpse into several contemporary approaches to early care and education that are currently in use in the United States and other countries. The final chapter of the module helps you gain awareness of and appreciation for the many roles played by teachers of young children. Welcome to teaching—a truly challenging and satisfying vocation.

I touch the future; I teach.

—Christa McAuliff, teacher and *Challenger* astronaut

After reading this chapter and completing the related activities, you should be able to

- Describe the process of becoming a teacher
- Identify your reasons and qualities for becoming a successful teacher
- Describe teachers' specialized knowledge base, core competencies, and skills
- Discuss professional standards
- Describe the benefits of field-based training and formal assessment
- Compare noncertified and certified teaching positions
- Consider educational and experiential requirements for various career opportunities
- Describe the link between teacher qualifications and program quality

View of the Early Childhood Teacher

Lucinda Washington smooths her skirt with the palms of her hands for the fifth time, chiding herself for being nervous. After all, speaking in front of groups has been part of her job for more years than she cares to count. The dean of the local college has asked Lucinda to talk to a group of early childhood education majors who are ready to begin their student teaching experiences.

Most of these young people live in the suburbs, but part of their required student teaching experience will be in the large urban school district where Lucinda teaches. Lucinda will tell these student teachers what they might encounter during their student teaching. Her more compelling goal today is to convince some of these enthusiastic future teachers to stay in the city school district. There is a real need for good teachers.

Applause startles Lucinda out of her reverie, and she realizes that the dean has already introduced her. Walking to the lectern, Lucinda tries to look confident and relaxed. She is a dedicated teacher herself, and she is happy to help start others on the same pathway. Looking at her audience, she begins: "Good morning boys and girls. It's good to see so many bright and shining faces this morning." As appreciative laughter ripples across the auditorium, Lucinda loses her nervousness and continues. "As most of you know, I have been teaching kindergarten for forty years—in the same school district. What you may not be aware of is that I am retiring this year, so there will be at least one teaching position open when you graduate! For more than twenty years, I have hosted dozens of student teachers just like you; some of them have been pleasures, and some of them trials. I'm sure all of you will be pleasures!"

102

CHAPTER 5

Lucinda gazes out at the attentive faces in the audience and considers what to say next. "The night before my first day of teaching, I was so scared and excited I hardly slept a wink. Now when the first day of school rolls around, I don't get scared but I still get excited. I told myself that if a school year ever started and I wasn't excited, that would be when I would leave the teaching field. Well, I still get excited, but forty years is enough. I wanted to make a space for you. Your dean has asked me to answer some of your questions about what you can expect in the city public schools. I would like to tell you that they are just like the schools most of you attended, but that wouldn't be true. We have shortages—of textbooks and supplies, of funds for extra projects, of chairs and desks sometimes, and, most of all, of good teachers. The one thing we never have a shortage of is children.

"If you entered teaching to teach children who want to learn, who need to learn, then the city public schools are the place for you. What can you expect? Expect hard work and moderate pay. Of course, you'll find that wherever you teach. Teaching young children is the most rewarding profession you will ever find. Where else could you work where people bring you dandelions and crayon drawings of you as a stick person? And that's just from your colleagues—think about what the children will do! As you carry out your student teaching, reflect on the difference you can make in the life of just one child. That's why we go into teaching; that's why we stay in teaching; that's why you should teach where you are needed most."

ach early childhood teacher makes the decision to teach in a different way and at a different time in life. For some, the idea of becoming a teacher emerges during childhood as they play school with neighborhood children; for others, the inspiration occurs when they are older and undergo meaningful experiences and encounter influential people. However you arrive at your decision to teach, the goal is at once noble and ordinary, for teaching is a distinguished profession that touches the lives of people.

This chapter examines the process of becoming a teacher of young children, from the decision to teach to the characteristics of successful teachers. The chapter also explores what effective teachers need to know and be able to do and how these qualities are assessed. There is a wide range of career opportunities from which you can choose within the field of early care and education, and responsibilities and qualifications for a variety of positions are explored. Finally, this chapter concludes with discussion about the link between the qualifications of teachers and the quality of child care and early education programs.

Becoming a Teacher of Young Children

The Decision to Teach

COMPETENCY GOAL VI
· Functional Area 13

While it is true that the formal process of becoming a teacher begins with making the decision to teach, many of you made informal commitments to children long before you announced your plans to become a teacher. What is it that impelled you to teach in the first place? Think about your own educational experiences and picture, in your mind, your favorite teacher. Did you picture one of your preschool or kindergarten teachers who sat beside you on the floor and read you stories about bears or dragons and other fascinating things? Or was your image of a teacher from your later schooling, who took time to really know you or who challenged your mind? What special qualities did your favorite teacher possess? Do you see some of those same qualities in yourself? This chapter invites you to reflect on your reasons for wanting to teach as you examine the personal and professional characteristics that will make you a successful teacher of young children.

Successful teachers display complex combinations of characteristics and professional abilities as they go about the daily process of teaching. Individuals who choose to become teachers of young children are challenged not only with meeting the intellectual needs of children who are entrusted to their care, but also with providing for their physical, emotional, and social well-being. Consider the public's stereotypical image of early childhood caregivers. Are you picturing elderly women who appear patient and nurturing? While it is true that most early childhood caregivers are female (Whitebook, Howes, & Phillips, 1989), being grandmotherly is not a job requirement! What about appearing patient and nurturing? Are certain personal traits absolutely necessary if you are going to be a successful teacher of young children?

Many researchers have asked the same question. For example, Spodek (1994b) reviewed criteria used by teacher education programs to evaluate teachers in training, or **preservice teachers**, before they were accepted into teacher education programs. Personal traits such as patience, warmth, enthusiasm for learning, and the desire to nurture are considered desirable teacher behaviors by many of the programs. Other traits identified as desirable for early childhood caregivers include having a positive outlook and being flexible (Katz, 1969). Taken collectively, these personal traits, or **dispositions**, demonstrate sensitivity to children as well as the desire to promote positive development (Harms, Clifford, & Cryer, 1998). Early childhood education's unique dual focus on care and education makes the nurturing aspects of teaching paramount in meeting the needs of young children.

In addition to reviewing the personal characteristics of preservice teachers, some studies have examined dispositions of practicing teachers. One group of researchers compared dispositions of teachers to teaching style, classroom climate, and effective teaching (Hamza, Khalid, & Farrow, 2000). These researchers found that having a positive outlook and being flexible were traits common to effective teachers. Another personal quality common to effective teachers was that they were "approachable," meaning that they were available to children, both physically and emotionally, as they taught. These findings are

Table 5.1   **Dispositions of Effective Teachers**

Category	Characteristics
Approachable	• Open, friendly, accessible
Confident	• Self-assured
Desire to nurture	• Responsive to emotional needs
Energetic	• Physical energy, lively, animated
Enthusiastic about teaching and learning	• Shows excitement, eagerness
Flexible	• Makes adjustments when situations warrant
Honest	• Shows integrity
Humor	• Reveals enjoyment, pleasure
Patient	• Tolerant, willing to let others do things in their own time
Positive outlook	• Upbeat, optimistic, proactive
Self-motivated	• Demonstrates initiative and interest
Warmth	• Welcomes interpersonal overtures

similar to those of other studies on successful teachers. Table 5.1 provides a summary of dispositions of successful teachers, as identified in the professional literature.

Take this opportunity to use knowledge of your own disposition to reflect on your potential for success within the field of early childhood. Hopefully, your reflection will affirm your decision to teach. This is not to imply that you must possess a particular

Successful teachers of young children embody dispositions, knowledge, and skills that enable them to build relationships with young children.

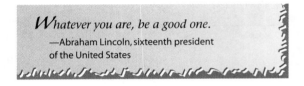

Whatever you are, be a good one.
—Abraham Lincoln, sixteenth president
of the United States

personality type to become a teacher of young children, but rather that you can use your self-knowledge to realistically plan what you will do to reach your full potential as a teacher.

Since the field of early care and education deals with young children from birth to age 8, caregivers may be involved in many settings where relationships with children are more or less strongly affected by the dispositions and personal traits of the caregivers. The quality of early care and education has been linked to "the nature of the relationship between caregiver and child" (Kagan, 1990, p. 5). Although relationships between learners and teachers are vital to quality education, teacher competence is also defined by level of knowledge.

Gaining Specialized Knowledge and Skills

Your post-high school studies provide both general knowledge and the specialized body of knowledge necessary to effectively carry out the responsibilities of providing developmentally appropriate care and education to young children. Although teacher education institutions do not fully agree on outcomes for preservice teachers who are completing their training (Stedman, 2000), guidelines regarding teacher preparation and evaluation are provided by professional organizations. These guidelines are commonly grouped into three broad categories: disposition, knowledge, and skills (NAEYC, 2001; Spodek, 1994b; Stedman, 2000; Willer, et al., 1991). Disposition, as mentioned previously in this chapter, describes one's collection of personal traits. **Knowledge** refers to what teachers know—general knowledge as well as the specialized body of knowledge associated with the field or profession. Knowledge answers the question "What does the teacher know?" **Skills** identify what teachers are able to do—those tasks and behaviors performed in carrying out job responsibilities. Knowledge and skills are more easily associated with specific observable behaviors, whereas disposition focuses more on personal attributes and is inferred from behaviors rather than observed directly.

Professional organizations, such as the National Association for the Education of Young Children (NAEYC), the National Council for Accreditation of Teacher Education (NCATE), and the Association for Childhood Education International (ACEI, 1997), have developed guidelines, or **standards**, for teacher preparation programs. These standards spell out components of the specialized knowledge base for early childhood teachers in training. In 2001, NAEYC and NCATE issued *NAEYC Standards for Early Childhood Professional Preparation* (NAEYC, 2001), which is a revision of NAEYC's 1996 standards (Hyson, 2000). These included five categories of standards:

- Promoting child development and learning
- Building family and community relationships
- Observing, documenting, and assessing to support young children and families
- Teaching and learning
- Becoming a professional.

For the purposes of discussion, this chapter will group professional recommendations and standards for specialized knowledge in teacher preparation programs into four overlapping categories: foundations of education; child development; teaching, learning, and assessment; and field-based observation and teaching practice (Sluss & Minner, 1999). The first category of this specialized knowledge base, foundations of education, includes study of the history and philosophies underlying the contemporary educational system of society. The foundations of education may also include the study of related academic areas such as psychology, sociology, and ethics. For foundations of early childhood education in the United States, many teacher preparation programs begin with a historical overview of the philosophies, theories, and theory applications of educators who have influenced contemporary early childhood education beliefs and practices. (Read Chapters 6 and 7 to learn about the historical and philosophical foundations of early childhood education.)

> *P*arents and the public have every right to expect that adults employed in early childhood programs have the knowledge, dispositions, and skills needed to provide high-quality services.
>
> —Barbara Willer, editor of NAEYC's *Position Statement: A Conceptual Framework for Early Childhood Professional Development* (1994, p. 9)

The second category of teacher preparation programs, knowledge of child development, is also provided as continuing education for early childhood practitioners from entry-level teachers to specialists in the profession. For prospective teachers like you, the study of child development includes more than just examination of the ages and stages of human development; it requires comprehensive understanding of the principles of human development. These principles are teachers' key to recognizing the predictable sequence of development in all children while also recognizing individual variations within the patterns of development. Such knowledge helps early childhood educators apply theories of child development as they carry out curriculum, or teaching plans, for groups of young children while still providing for the unique development of each child. Knowing the research on which child development theories are based is also important to future educators.

The third category of the knowledge base recommended for teacher preparation programs is knowledge of learning, teaching, and assessment theories and practices, a study that explores the varied roles of classroom teachers. Your studies will include teaching strategies, techniques for planning and carrying out instruction, creating and maintaining the learning environment, classroom management and behavior guidance, and assessment and evaluation. (Chapters 9 through 11 address these strategies and techniques.)

The fourth category of your growing knowledge base will include visits to the real world of teaching, where you will both observe actual early childhood classrooms and practice your teaching skills, with guidance, in those classrooms. Actual participation in early care and education settings will help you apply your newly acquired knowledge of children, learning, and teaching.

> *T*eaching is neither . . . knowledge nor . . . skill—it is both. It is knowledge and love of a subject combined with knowledge and love of children, leading to an intellectual pleasure in finding ways to bring children to discover knowledge.
>
> —Pattie Barth and Ruth Mitchell, *Smart Start: Elementary Education for the 21st Century* (1992, p. 125)

Assessing the Competencies of Preservice Teachers

CDA

COMPETENCY GOAL V
• Functional Area 12

COMPETENCY GOAL VI
• Functional Area 13

Field-based experiences in actual classrooms provide preservice early childhood teachers with opportunities to observe specialized skills in action, as experienced teachers facilitate learning, interact with children, and perform the many daily responsibilities inherent in teaching. As a result, you build your awareness of what it takes to be an effective teacher and gain first-hand practice in applying your knowledge and skills as you teach with the guidance of an experienced teacher. Through your practice teaching, your competency as an early childhood educator will be demonstrated. Competent teachers are those who use their knowledge of children and learning to provide quality education for learners. In other words, **competencies** encompass the abilities needed to apply specialized knowledge and skills within professional roles.

In many cases, before you formally enter the profession, your newly acquired teaching competencies will be assessed through use of preservice teacher evaluation instruments, usually standardized multiple-choice tests, that assess entry-level knowledge and skills of individuals completing teacher education programs. Other evaluation models may involve documenting the performance of practicing teachers in the classroom through observations, which are usually conducted by teacher education faculty or other experienced teachers. Examining teacher evaluation instruments can give you an overview of dispositions and competencies that teachers are expected to demonstrate on the job. Teacher evaluation instruments are usually based on standards set forth by professional organizations involved in the preparation and professional development of teachers.

Teaching Credentials and Certification

Formal authorization to teach is usually provided through a credentialing or **teacher certification** process whereby a state, through its department of education, issues you a license to teach once you have met their certification requirements. In the United States, entry-level requirements for teacher certification vary from state to state, depending on several factors. Generally, teacher certification is specific to the grade levels you wish to teach. In many states, certification in "early childhood education" means that you would teach children from birth to age 8, which would include kindergarten and the primary grades (grades 1 through 3). Other states identify early childhood education as birth to age 5, or through kindergarten. Special certifications may also be available in "early childhood special education," and those age ranges and grade levels will also vary among the states. At the initial certification level, most states require at least a four-year **bachelor degree program** in education if you plan to teach within the public school system in kindergarten or above. Some states that provide educational programs for children younger than 5 within their school systems require a bachelor's degree, while others accept a two-year **associate degree program** if you plan to teach children below kindergarten age. In many states, if you teach children younger than kindergarten age outside of the public school system, you may not require any formal teacher certification, although some programs specify that teachers have a specialized credential rather than teacher certification. The next section of this chapter explores the wide variety of career opportunities within the field, as well as national credentials for child-care teachers.

Career Opportunities within the Field of Early Care and Education

Dr. Seuss (1990), the well-known author of children's books, wrote a story called *Oh, the Places You'll Go!* The story follows an intrepid but unnamed character through a maze of interesting situations on the way to success. As you enter the exciting field of early care and education, you may feel a little like this storybook friend. Early childhood education is a broad field that is defined differently practically everywhere you go. But don't let this discourage you. What it means is that there are dozens of potential places you can go to be a teacher of young children, and although it may take some searching to find just the right match for you and your talents, it is out there.

COMPETENCY GOAL VI
• Functional Area 13

In fact, projections for the next decade suggest employment opportunities in the field of early care and education will continue to increase rapidly (U.S. Bureau of Labor Statistics, 2001), due primarily to the high percentage of mothers with children under age 6 in the work force (U.S. Bureau of Census, 2002). In October 1997, the White House Conference on Child Care indicated that the United States is facing a crisis in care and education of young children not only from the standpoint of shortages but also from the standpoint of quality. These concerns were supported by studies during the 1990s showing that some of the child care available in the United States was of less-than-satisfactory quality (Whitebook, Howes, & Phillips, 1998). Studies of quality and compensation of early childhood educators spearheaded by NAEYC and other early childhood advocates show that low wages, high staff turnover rates, and lack of consistent national and state standards are primary contributors to this situation (Whitebook, Howes, & Phillips, 1989, 1998).

In a proactive move, NAEYC has made recommendations for levels of staff training using a **career lattice** that specifies five different levels of education and experience for different staff positions in early care and education settings. The lattice begins with entry-level positions, or teaching assistants, and progresses to other levels, assistant teachers and teachers, as education and experience increase (Johnson & McCraken, 1994; NAEYC, 1994). (All levels of the lattice framework are illustrated in Table 5.2, p. 110.) For the assistant teacher and teacher, NAEYC recommends the **Child Development Associate (CDA)** credential as the minimum level of education and training. Some states also designate the CDA as the minimum qualification for child care teachers and/or directors. The CDA, a national credential awarded by the Council for Professional Recognition, identifies individuals who have completed a minimum of 120 clock-hours

Table 5.2   NAEYC's Career Lattice—Definitions of Early Childhood Professional Categories

Early Childhood Professional Level VI

- Successful completion of a Ph.D. or Ed.D. in a program conforming to NAEYC guidelines; or
- Successful demonstration of the knowledge, performance, and dispositions expected as outcomes of a doctoral degree program conforming to NAEYC guidelines.

Early Childhood Professional Level V

- Successful completion of a master's degree in a program that conforms to NAEYC guidelines; or
- Successful demonstration of the knowledge, performance, and dispositions expected as outcomes of a master's degree program conforming to NAEYC guidelines.

Early Childhood Professional Level IV

- Successful completion of a baccalaureate degree from a program conforming to NAEYC guidelines; or
- State certificate meeting NAEYC certification; or
- Successful completion of a baccalaureate degree in another field with more than 30 professional units in early childhood development/education including 300 hours of supervised teaching experience, including 150 hours each for two of the following three age groups: infants and toddlers, 3-to 5-year-olds, or the primary grades; or
- Successful demonstration of the knowledge, performance, and dispositions expected as outcomes of a baccalaureate degree program conforming to NAEYC guidelines.

Early Childhood Professional Level III

- Successful completion of an associate degree from a program conforming to NAEYC guidelines; or
- Successful completion of an associate degree in a related field, plus 30 units of professional studies in early childhood development/education including 300 hours of supervised teaching experience in an early childhood program; or
- Successful demonstration of the knowledge, performance, and dispositions expected as outcomes of an associate degree program conforming to NAEYC guidelines.

Early Childhood Professional Level II

- Successful completion of a one-year early childhood program.
- Successful completion of the CDA Professional Preparation Program; or completion of a systematic, comprehensive training program that prepares an individual to successfully acquire the CDA credential through direct assessment.

Early Childhood Professional Level I

- Individuals who are employed in an early childhood professional role working under supervision or with support (e.g., linkages with provider association or network or enrollment in supervised practicum) and participating in training designed to lead to the assessment of individual competencies or acquisition of a degree.

Source: From National Association for the Education of Young Children (1994), *NAEYC Position Statement: A Conceptual Framework for Early Childhood Professional Development, Young Children* (Washington, DC: Author), p. 69. Reprinted by permission.

of specialized education in child development and best practices in teaching, and 480 clock-hours of related field experience as a classroom teacher. In addition, CDA candidates go through a direct assessment process in which they are observed and assessed by specially trained early childhood professionals (Council for Professional Recognition, 1996). The Council for Professional Recognition has awarded over 100,000 Child Development Associate credentials since its inception. (Additional information about the CDA credential can be found in Appendix A.)

There are many career opportunities in early childhood education for people with CDA credentials and associate degrees; however, such educators, including preschool and child care teachers, currently earn lower salaries than individuals with bachelor's degrees (U.S. Department of Education, 2001). This is particularly true in those states that set only minimal standards of education and training for caregivers. Teaching staff members in early childhood programs that are not associated with public school districts are frequently classified as **noncertified personnel.** That is, they are not required to meet the same standards for education or experience required of **certified personnel,** teachers who have received certification to teach children over five years old in public school districts. (Chapter 8 provides additional information about minimum qualifications for teachers and other individuals who provide child care outside of public school systems.)

Home-Based Early Care and Education

Each week, in the United States, millions of young children attend some form of nonparental child care. Of the three main environments for nonparental child care, two are **home-based child care** and the third is center-based child care (Casper, 1996; Smith, 2000). The two home-based models of child care, or **family child care (FCC),** may refer to care given in either the child's home or the provider's home. You can find many employment opportunities within home-based settings to serve the care and education needs of young children directly.

Family Child Care Providers The **family child care provider** is the most common direct service provider of home-based care and education. Family child care providers generally care for one or more children in the provider's home, although some family child care providers travel to the child's home to provide service. In many cases, child care provided in a private home for children of a single family is not regulated by any state or federal agency. Most states do have some regulations for family child care (Halpern, 1987) if the provider cares for four or more unrelated children. Quality of home-based child care varies widely and largely depends on the educational qualifications of the provider. Although many family child care providers have education, specialized training, and/or experience in early care and education, the lack of national or state regulations regarding caregiver education often means that some family child care providers have little or no specialized training (Galinsky, Howes, Kontos, & Shinn, 1994).

National and regional professional organizations, such as the National Association for Family Child Care (NAFCC) and the National Association for the Education of Young Children (NAEYC), have spearheaded efforts to set voluntary training standards for early care and education providers. These agencies also provide a network of information and training opportunities to providers to improve the quality of care available from this largely unregulated industry. NAFCC and NAEYC also provide information about characteristics of quality child care to families seeking early care and education for their children.

Young children from economically disadvantaged situations participate in compensatory programs like Early Head Start and Head Start to increase their chances for success with formal schooling.

Early Head Start Programs Another example of home-based child care that provides employment opportunities in direct service to young children is the federal program **Early Head Start.** Early Head Start is associated with the federal **Head Start** program, which serves children and families who are economically disadvantaged. While Head Start focuses on center-based care for three- to five-year-old children, Early Head Start provides home-based services for families with children from the prenatal stage to age 3 and for pregnant women (Buell, Hallam, & Beck, 2001). Both programs have strong family involvement components, including **home visits** for center-based programs. Early Head Start providers are authorized to care for up to four infants and/or toddlers in a home-based setting. Guidelines identifying minimum provider qualifications and compensation are set by the U.S. Department of Education but are carried out by state agencies that have been awarded contracts by the federal government. Families must meet eligibility requirements before their children can receive services from Early Head Start providers, or **home visitors.** (Chapters 6 and 7 provide more detailed discussions of the history and curriculum of the Head Start and Early Head Start programs.)

Live-In Child Care Providers Sometimes family child care providers care for children within the children's home. If the caregiver lives in the family's home and receives room and board as part of the salary and benefits package, the provider is sometimes called a **nanny.** The term *nanny* is rarely used to refer to a family child care provider who cares for children within the children's home but does not reside with the family.

As with other types of home-based child care, professional organizations and agencies provide indirect services to children by acting as resources to both families seeking nannies and caregivers who work as nannies. Many of these agencies validate the credentials of potential nannies and recommend or provide specialized training if a viable candidate does not meet the minimum standards set by the agency. In many cases, the nanny is sponsored by a referral agency that serves as a point of contact for families seeking live-in child care providers.

Another type of live-in child care provider is the **au pair.** *Au pair* is a French term generally used to describe a person from another country who provides domestic services, including child care, in return for room and board. Traditionally, au pairs have little training beyond a brief cultural orientation, and they rely on letters of recommendation from school officials, community members, or former employers as the basis of their credentials. A contract, usually handled by an outside agency, indicating the length of time of the exchange is agreed on by the family and the au pair before the au pair comes to live with the family.

Center-Based Early Care and Education

The most widely used form of early care and education for preschool-age children in the United States, other than care by relatives, is **center-based child care** (Smith, 2000). It is here that you will find the most career opportunities. Center-based child care programs provide group care and education for young children in classroom settings. Millions of children under age 6 attend some form of center-based child care on a regular basis. Furthermore, industry analysts indicate that care for infants and toddlers is the fastest-growing aspect of center-based care and education. Center-based child care assumes many forms, including full- and part-day programs for infants and toddlers, preschool-age children, and school-age children.

Two common forms of center-based child care are **preschool programs** and **child care centers,** or **daycare centers.** The term *preschool* generally designates child care programs that offer less than full-day care and education services to children between ages 2 and 5. Preschools tend to focus more on socialization and education than on providing custodial care, or babysitting, services for working parents. Many preschool programs are associated with churches or other nonprofit agencies.

The term *child care center,* or **child development center,** generally refers to a full-day program that provides custodial child care services for working parents that include meals and rest periods as well as social and educational opportunities for young children. Child care centers may offer services for infants as young as four weeks and for preschool children ages 2 to 5, as well as before- and after-school care for six- to twelve-year-olds. The term *child care center* is preferred by many in the field over the term *daycare center,* because child care focuses on the child and daycare focuses on the time element rather than the care element.

Child care centers are owned, operated, and managed by a variety of individuals, agencies, and corporations. Sometimes child care centers are divided into two categories—for-profit and not-for-profit. Centers that are identified as for-profit are sometimes owned and operated by individuals who generate their personal income from fees charged for child care. These individuals may own a single facility or have multiple local sites, but they are not usually tied to any national corporations. In the United States, there are several regional or national child care "chains" that are owned by corporations that hire local directors to see to daily operation of one of their facilities. Many of these national child care centers have their own curriculum and staff training programs. Child care centers may also be classified as not-for-profit if they are operated by not-for-profit agencies associated with charitable or religious organizations.

Programs for Infants and Toddlers Early care and education programs that serve children under age 3 are considered **infant-toddler programs.** Developmentally oriented infant-toddler programs are responsive to individual children's psychomotor, cognitive, and affective needs, and these programs personalize care according to each infant's temperament and development. The primary goal of teachers in infant-toddler programs is to provide safe and healthy play and learning environments that allow children to form stable relationships with others. Consistency of caregiving is a priority, as is frequent communication with family members to ascertain that infants and toddlers receive the care they need. Recent findings on early brain development have special implications for teachers of children under age 3, when the brain is most responsive to appropriately stimulating interactions and experiences. In most states, group sizes for infant-toddler settings are smaller, and teacher-child ratios are lower than in classrooms for preschool-age children so that they receive more personalized attention through one-on-one interactions with caregivers. Although there are some child care centers that specialize in infant-toddler care, most center-based infant-toddler programs are within centers that also serve other ages of children.

Preschool and Prekindergarten Programs Center-based programs for children between ages 3 and 5 or 6 are called preschool programs, or **prekindergarten programs**. These programs vary widely according to setting, curriculum, and state. Some preschool and prekindergarten programs are half day (approximately four hours) while others are full day (eight to twelve hours). Curriculum in half-day programs usually focuses on activities and social interactions rather than on comprehensive care, which includes snacks, meals, and rest periods. Full-day programs generally incorporate meals and rest periods at suitable times as well as providing children with multiple opportunities to play, do activities, and interact with peers and adults.

A relatively recent trend in the United States is voluntary prekindergarten programs as part of public school systems. According to recent research, nearly a million children in the United States already participate in some type of state-sponsored prekindergarten program (Clifford, Early, & Hills, 1999). The National Center for Early Development and Learning, which has identified prekindergarten programs in forty-two states, partly attributes the rise in public-sponsored preschool to the No Child Left Behind Act (Children's Defense Fund, 2002), which was signed into law in January 2002 (Gallagher, Clayton, & Heinemeier, 2001).

School-Age Child Care Another important aspect of early care and education is **school-age child care (SACC)**, which provides care for five- to twelve-year-old children before and after the school day, on school holidays, and during school vacations. School-age child care provides safe and stimulating environments for children who are

Children in school-age child care display diverse needs, interests, and abilities.

too young to be left home alone while family members are unavailable. Many SACC programs also provide transportation to and from child care facilities and elementary schools. Curriculum for SACC programs varies from program to program but tends to focus on providing various options for activities, such as board games, arts-and-crafts projects, outdoor play, recreational reading, listening and responding to music, and building and construction projects. Some programs provide quiet spaces for children to complete schoolwork (homework), and helpers are available to assist children with their homework. These children are usually provided with snacks and meals appropriate to the amount of time they spend at the child care facility. During vacation periods, school-age child care programs often arrange stimulating field trips and other special events to engage children's interests.

Head Start Programs During the 1960s, as part of President Johnson's War on Poverty, a federally funded educational program for preschool-age children from economically disadvantaged backgrounds was established. The program was designed to deliver comprehensive care and education with the intention of providing these children with quality early childhood education to help them to catch up emotionally, socially, and academically with their peers prior to entrance into formal schooling. Briefly named Kiddie Korps, this national compensatory education program became known as Project Head Start. Since the 1960s, each presidential administration has re-funded and often expanded Head Start.

The pilot Head Start program began in 1965 as an eight-week summer program and served over 560,000 children between ages 3 and 5 and their families. Originally housed under the Office of Economic Opportunity (OEO), Head Start was reassigned in 1969 to the Department of Health, Education and Welfare (HEW), Office of Child Development. Currently, Head Start remains with HEW, under the Administration on Children, Youth and Families.

During the administration of President Nixon, Head Start programs were mandated to include young children with special needs; home-based program options were also authorized. By the time President Ford took office in 1974, Head Start programs had served over 5 million preschool-age children in less than ten years. During the Ford administration, performance standards for Head Start programs were established to ensure that high-quality curriculum and care were maintained at all Head Start sites. During President Carter's administration in the 1970s, Congress authorized Head Start bilingual programs that served over 6,000 children of migrant workers. The scope of Head Start continued to expand, and shortly after President Reagan took office in 1981, Head Start funding topped one billion dollars. By 1984, Head Start had served over 9 million preschool-age children in all 50 states and in many U.S. territories as well. Throughout the administration of President Bush (1989–1993), Head Start funds were increased by 600 million dollars to serve an additional 180,000 children and families, and during the 1990s under the administration of President Clinton, Head Start was reauthorized and expanded to provide full-day, full-year services.

Contemporary Head Start programs are designed to provide comprehensive care and education for children from low-income families through four primary avenues:

- Providing appropriate early education that promotes development through full-day, year-round center-based or home-based options
- Providing services to promote child health and development, including developmental and health screenings and by providing nutritious meals and snacks
- Involving families and forming partnerships with community agencies through ongoing communication, opportunities for family involvement, and community collaborations
- Providing social services through outreach and referral, including access to services and second-language assistance. (Head Start Bureau, 2001)

Curriculum in Head Start programs follows the *Head Start Performance Standards* (Head Start Bureau, 1996), which outline program operation, curriculum goals and strategies, and program assessment. Head Start classrooms provide diverse opportunities for promoting development in all developmental domains, including activities that support literacy and individual expression and communication through art, music, and movement (Taylor, 2000).

To maintain high-quality programming, the National Head Start Bureau provides training through a nationwide network as part of the professional development systems for its teachers and other staff members (Head Start Bureau, 2001). In addition, program quality is also monitored through the FACES (Family and Child Experiences Survey) instrument, which is designed to collect information on key indicators of performance, such as the learning environment and children's school readiness.

Kindergarten Programs In the United States, **kindergarten** is considered the beginning of formal schooling; all states provide public kindergarten programs, although kindergarten attendance is not compulsory in every state. (Chapter 6 provides information about the history of kindergarten beginning with its inception by German educator Friedrich Froebel.) Contemporary kindergarten programs in public school are one-year programs for five-year-old children and precede the first grade in elementary schools. Some kindergarten programs are half-day programs (about four hours), while many others are full-day programs. When kindergarten is part of the public school system, teacher certification requirements are generally the same as for elementary school teachers, although coursework may vary according to how the state defines early childhood education. Curriculum in public school kindergartens varies widely from developmentally appropriate practice to strong emphasis on academic preparation for first grade. In many states, kindergartens may also be operated by private or parochial agencies, in which case curriculum and teacher qualifications may be significantly different from those in public schools. Many kindergarten programs place strong emphasis on the development of literacy, mathematical awareness, and social skills.

Primary Schools The period of early childhood (birth through age 8) encompasses not only family child care, preschools, and child care centers but also kindergarten and the **primary grades** (first, second, and third grade). Most states require kindergarten and primary-grade teachers to have bachelor's degrees before they can seek teacher certification; however, each state sets its own teacher certification requirements for public and private school teachers. During the primary grades, emphasis is placed on reading, writing, mathematics, and problem-solving skills, although many other subject areas—such as science, social studies, physical education, art, music, and computers—may also be included. Children in grades 1 through 3 vary widely on their levels of development and abilities. During the last decade, some states began using a mixed-grade-level *primary block* classroom that might place kindergarten, first-grade, and second-grade students in one classroom. The exact composition of primary block classrooms is different in different states, and sometimes even within school districts within the same state. In addition to positions that require teacher certification, many states hire teacher assistants called **paraprofessionals** to work directly with kindergarten and primary-age children under the supervision of a certified teacher. Educational requirements for paraprofessionals vary widely from state to state, but many require a minimum of 60 semester-hours of college credit or an associate degree. Paraprofessionals usually receive some specialized training directly from school districts before working with children. This is particularly true if the paraprofessionals will be assigned as facilitators for young children with special needs.

Related Career Specializations

Services for Children with Special Needs Children under age 3 who have been identified with special needs are entitled to early intervention services, as outlined in the Individuals with Disabilities Education Act (see Chapter 1). In some cases, children require assistance as they are included with their peers, and many school districts hire paraprofessionals to act as facilitators for these children. In addition, certified teachers with bachelor's degrees, or higher, in early childhood special education and other specialists, such as speech therapists and occupational therapists, work directly with young children with special needs. Whenever possible, these services are provided in the child's natural environment, such as the home, child care center, or school. Many states have developed umbrella programs to coordinate resources for families so children can receive the full range of services they need. Because many of these programs receive federal funds, minimum standards for **service providers** are generally specified. Children who are identified with special needs during infancy continue to receive intervention services throughout kindergarten, elementary school, and high school, as long as those interventions are still needed. (Chapter 1 provides additional information about special education mandates and services for young children with special needs.)

Indirect Services for Young Children There are also many opportunities to provide care and education for young children and their families through **indirect services** such as program managers and child-care center directors, support staff, or **parent educators.** Parent educators provide some direct services to children, but their main responsibility is to help children's family members be their children's first teachers. State requirements for parent educators vary from a few college credits to a bachelor's degree, although most states require specialized training through the parents-as-teachers network that was listed in Professional Connections and Web Links in Chapter 3. Parents-as-teachers programs are voluntary for families; once a family decides to participate in these programs, a parent educator will visit the family's home periodically and discuss development, demonstrate activities and play behaviors to promote development, and conduct developmental assessments. Many parents-as-teachers programs begin during the third trimester of pregnancy and continue through the child's third, and sometimes fifth, birthday.

Summary

- Effective teachers of young children display a complex combination of personal traits and professional abilities.

Becoming a Teacher of Young Children

- Professional organizations recommend that early childhood teachers have specialized knowledge of foundations of education, child development, curriculum and assessment theories and practices, family and community relationships, professionalism, and supervised field experiences.

Assessing the Competencies
of Preservice Teachers

- Field-based experiences in actual classrooms provide early childhood teachers with opportunities to observe and perform many of the daily responsibilities of teachers.

- Many states require preservice teachers to take formal written examinations to assess their specialized knowledge and skills prior to awarding teacher certification.

Career Opportunities within the Field
of Early Care and Education

- NAEYC's career lattice identifies five levels of positions within early care and education programs.
- The Child Development Associate (CDA) is a national credential for teachers in early care and education settings that is awarded by the Council for Professional Recognition.
- Home-based early care and education opportunities include family child care, Early Head Start, and live-in child care positions, as well as parent educator positions.

- Center-based early care and education opportunities include child care centers and preschools, infant-toddler programs, prekindergarten and some kindergarten programs, and school-age child care.

- Opportunities within public schools include kindergarten, the primary grades, and several paraprofessional positions.

LEARNING ACTIVITIES

1 Activity: Bumper-Sticker Philosophy. How important is early childhood education? Think about what you hope to accomplish by being a teacher of young children. Try to condense your views into a "nutshell" philosophy and then design a colorful bumper sticker to send your message to the public. Share your bumper-sticker philosophy with classmates to generate a class discussion about the value of early care and education for children, their families, and society.

2 Role-Play: Who Is the Early Childhood Teacher? Pretend you are a reporter doing on-the-spot interviews with everyday people you might meet on a city street or at a shopping mall. Ask specific open-ended questions such as "What level of training or education should a child care teacher have?" as well as broader questions such as "What do you think about the salaries paid to daycare teachers?" With your classmates, role-play various individuals—such as teenage parents, grandparents, middle-aged businesspersons with no children, and so on—and respond to questions pertaining to what an early childhood educator should be like, should know, or should be able to do. Reflect on the role-play experience as you examine the diversity of opinions regarding the importance of early childhood education. Consider the impact of public opinion on the state of early care and education in the United States and other countries.

3 Activity: Wanted Poster. Building on the traditions of the Old West, design a large, colorful "Wanted" poster depicting the qualities and qualifications you believe are most desirable for the ideal early care and education teacher. Be sure to put a price on the individual's head to indicate the value of such a teacher. If possible, make a display out of the posters and use them as discussion starters for related class topics.

PORTFOLIO ARTIFACTS

1 Survey: Personal Inventory of Teacher Characteristics. Design a rating system, such as 10 for high and 1 for low, and compare your attitude and personal traits to the descriptors identified in Table 5.1 (p. 105). After completing your ratings, select one or more of the descriptors and write two teaching scenarios contrasting effective and ineffective teaching practices. For example, for the trait "approachability," an effective scenario might describe a teacher who sits on the carpet with a group of children and participates in give-and-take conversation with them as they discuss their project plans. An ineffective scenario would be where a teacher demonstrates lack of approachability by informing the class that no teacher assistance will be available during project planning because the project will be totally their responsibilities.

2 Interview: Novice and Experienced Educators. Prepare a set of at least five open-ended questions related to teaching practices, behavior guidance, home-school communications, and other aspects of classroom management. Using the prepared questions, interview a novice teacher who has less than two years' experience and an experienced teacher with three or more years of teaching practice with young children. Compare their responses, noting similarities and differences between the novice and experienced teachers. Take a moment to reflect on experiential factors that may have influenced their responses.

3 Sample: Analysis of Help Wanted Advertisements. Over the period of a month or more, collect several help wanted advertisements and announcements for teaching or caregiving positions from a variety of sources, such as newspapers, job fairs, school districts, or Web sites. Review the notices and compare job titles, job descriptions, education and experience requirements, and salaries. Develop a chart, or write a narrative, summarizing your findings. Afterward, take a few moments to reflect on the information you collected and reviewed. How did your expectations and your results differ? Do you notice any trends or patterns related to the care and education of young children?

Professional Connections and Web Links

Council for Professional Recognition
2460 16th Street, NW
Washington, DC 20009-3575
800-424-4310
http://www.cdacouncil.org

The Council for Professional Recognition, which was founded in 1985, is the agency that coordinates the Child Development Associate (CDA) credential program. Part of the council's mission is to improve the professional status of individuals who provide early care and education to children under age 5. The council also publishes a variety of print and video resources that can be used for self-directed learning or for staff training, including information and resources for Reggio Children/USA. The organization's Web site maintains a national directory of early childhood preparation programs.

National Association for Family Child Care (NAFCC)
P.O. Box 10373
Des Moines, IA 50306
515-282-9117
http://www.nafcc.org

The National Association for Family Child Care was established in 1994 and states as its mission "to promote quality child care by strengthening the profession of family child care." The organization also encourages family child care providers to become accredited and demonstrate that family child care offers higher-quality early care and education than required by most states. NAFCC's Web site provides information about its accreditation standards and process.

Suggestions for Further Reading

Elkind, David. (1987). *Miseducation: Preschoolers at risk.* New York: Knopf.

- Elkind provides a sensitive, but sobering, view of young children in contemporary society who are pushed beyond their true developmental levels by individuals who do not understand the concept of developmentally appropriate practice. Elkind addresses the misdeeds of families, schools, and society as they set unreasonable expectations for young children, thus diminishing the carefree childhood of earlier generations.

References

Association for Childhood Education International (ACEI). (1997). ACEI position paper: Preparation of early childhood teachers. *Childhood Education, 73*(3), 164–165.

Barth, Pattie, & Mitchell, Ruth. (1992). *Smart start: Elementary education for the 21st century.* Golden, CO: North American Press.

Casper, Lynne M. (1996). *Who's minding our preschoolers?* Fall 1993. Current Population Reports, HER P70-53. Washington, DC: U.S. Census Bureau.

Children's Defense Fund (CDF). (2002). *The state of children in America's union: A 2002 action guide to Leave No Child Behind.* Washington, DC: CDF.

Clifford, R. M., Early, D. M., & Hills, T. W. (1999). Almost a million children in school before kindergarten: Who is responsible for early childhood services? *Young Children, 54*(5), 48–51.

Council for Professional Recognition. (1996). *The child development associate: Assessment system and competency standards for preschool caregivers in center-based programs.* Washington, DC: Council for Professional Recognition.

Dr. Seuss. (1990). *Oh, the places you'll go!* New York: Random House.

Galinsky, E., Howes, C., Kontos, S., & Shinn, M. (1994). The study of children in family child care and relative care—Key findings and policy recommendations. *Young Children, 50*(1), 58–61.

Gallagher, J. J., Clayton, J. R., & Heinemeier, S. E. (2001). Education for four-year-olds: State initiatives. Chapel Hill: National Center for Early Development and Learning, University of North Carolina.

Halpern, R. (1987). Major social and demographic trends affecting young families: Implications for early childhood care and education. *Young Children, 42*(6), 34–40.

Head Start Bureau. (1996). *Head Start program performance standards.* 45 CFR, Part 1304. Washington, DC: U.S. Department of Health and Human Services, Administration on Children, Youth, and Families.

Hamza, M. Khalid, & Farrow, Vicky. (2000). Fostering creativity and problem solving in the classroom. *Kappa Delta Pi Record, 37*(1), 33–35.

Harms, Thelma, Clifford, Richard M., & Cryer, Debby. (1998). *Early childhood environment rating scale.* New York: Teachers College Press.

Head Start Bureau. (2001). *Head Start: A comprehensive child development program for children birth to age five.* Head Start Information & Publication Center. Retrieved September 24, 2001, from http://www.headstartinfo.org.

Hyson, Marilou. (2000). Growing teachers for a growing profession: NAEYC revises its guidelines for early childhood professional preparation. *Young Children, 55*(3), 60–61.

Johnson, Julienne, & McCracken, Janet B. (1994). *The early childhood career lattice: Perspectives on professional development.* Washington, DC: National Association for the Education of Young Children.

Kagan, Sharon L. (1990). *Excellence in early childhood education: Defining characteristics and next-decade strategies.* Washington, DC: Office of Educational Research and Improvement, U.S. Department of Education.

Katz, Lillian. (1969). Children and teachers in two types of Head Start classes. *Young Children, 24*(7), 342–439.

National Association for the Education of Young Children. (1994). NAEYC position statement: A conceptual framework for early childhood professional development. *Young Children, 49*(3), 68–77.

National Association for the Education of Young Children. (2001). *NAEYC standards for early childhood professional preparation: Initial licensure level.* Washington, DC: National Association for the Education of Young Children.

Sluss, Dorothy, & Minner, Sam. (1999). The changing roles of early childhood educators in preparing new teachers: Findings from three preparation programs. *Childhood Education, 75*(5), 280–284.

Smith, Kristin. (2000). Who's minding the kids? Child care arrangements: Fall 1995. *Current Population Reports, P70-70.* Washington, DC: U.S. Census Bureau.

Spodek, Bernard. (1994). The knowledge base for baccalaureate early childhood teacher education programs. In J. Johnson & J. B. McCracken (Eds.), *The early childhood career lattice: Perspectives on professional development.* Washington, DC: National Association for the Education of Young Children.

Stedman, Carl. (2000). *Identifying good teaching: What research tells us.* Indianapolis: Kappa Delta Pi.

Taylor, Helen H. (2000). Curriculum in Head Start. *National Head Start Bulletin, 67,* 1.

U.S. Bureau of Census. (2002). *America's children: Key national indicators of well-being, 2002. Part I: Populations and family characteristics.* Washington, DC: U.S. Census Bureau.

U.S. Department of Labor, Bureau of Labor Statistics. (2001). Report on the American workforce [on-line]. Available: http://www.bls.gov/opub/rtaw/rtawhome.htm [2002, February 12].

U.S. National Center for Education Statistics. (2001). *Digest of education statistics.* Washington, DC: U.S. Department of Education.

Whitebook, Marcy, Howes, Carollee, & Phillips, Deborah. (1989). *Who cares? Child care teachers and the quality of child care in America: National child care staffing study: Executive summary.* Oakland, CA: Child Care Employee Project.

Whitebook, Marcy, Howes, Carollee, & Phillips, Deborah. (1998). *Worthy work, unlivable wages: The national child care staffing study, 1988–1997.* Washington, DC: Center for the Child Care Workforce.

White House Conference on Child Care. (October 1997). *Remarks by President and Mrs. Clinton.* Washington, DC: Office of the Press Secretary.

Willer, Barbara. (Ed.). (1994). A conceptual framework for early childhood professional development. In J. Johnson & J. B. McCracken (Eds.), *The early childhood career lattice: Perspectives on professional development.* Washington, DC: National Association for the Education of Young Children.

Willer, Barbara, Hofferth, S., Kisker, E., Divine-Hawkins, P., Farquhar, E., & Glantz, F. (1991). *The demand and supply of child care in 1990 and a profile of child care settings.* Washington, DC: National Association for the Education of Young Children.

After reading this chapter and completing the related activities, you should be able to

- Describe how views on childhood have changed over the centuries

- Discuss social, economic, political, and religious factors that contribute to how societies view their children

- Describe the historical roots of child care and early education

- Associate individuals and their philosophies to theories and practices that shape contemporary early care and education

Historical Foundations of Child Care and Early Education

Somewhere in northern colonial America, circa 1713 . . .

Lisbeth Morris leaned forward and pushed the logs in the open-hearth fireplace closer together with an iron poker. The children would be arriving shortly, and she wanted the front room of her cabin to be warm for them. At 26, Lisbeth had been widowed for a year; her forty-year-old husband, Ethan, had died from a fever the previous winter. Now it was just Lisbeth and her two-year-old daughter, Abigail, who lived in the little cabin.

A few months after Ethan's passing, the town's elders had approached her to inquire if she would be willing to teach some of the town's younger children in her home. Lisbeth agreed, partly because the small fees and food goods she would receive from the families would help her take care of herself and Abigail until she remarried, and partly because she was so lonely without Ethan.

Their town of about thirty families did not have a schoolhouse, and most parents taught their own children to read and write, but not all parents could read, write, and cipher so some children had no one to teach them. Lisbeth, like most of the people in her town, believed that children should be taught to read so they could read the Scriptures for themselves. Lisbeth, who had learned to read and write from her governess when she was about eight, was lucky because she had two Bibles, hers and Ethan's, to use for schoolbooks. The only other book Lisbeth had was a copy of the New England Primer *given to her by the wife of one of the town's elders. The*

primer was especially good for the younger children, who enjoyed the rhyming couplets and pictures as they practiced their alphabet letters.

Looking back on the four months since she had turned her home into a dame school, Lisbeth realized that she looked forward to her time with the group of seven boys and girls who came to her home most every day but Sunday. The children were making progress learning to read and write simple words and were very good about reciting their Bible verses. Lisbeth felt a little pride, though she knew she shouldn't, at the children's accomplishments. If the town continued to add families as it had in the last three years, it would soon have fifty families, and then the town would have to build a schoolhouse and hire a teacher. Maybe she could be the schoolmistress; teaching gave her a purpose. With a little smile as she walked toward the door to let the children in, Lisbeth added to herself, "And, I'm good at it."

ver the centuries, classrooms designed for the care and education of young children have assumed different forms to suit the particular needs and beliefs of society. Contemporary early childhood programs retain some features of past programs, as illustrated in the vignette, while at the same time meeting the demands of today's world. The diverse array of early care and education practices in the United States reflects the multiple influences from which these practices evolved. By examining the historical roots and philosophical and theoretical underpinnings that have contributed to modern educational practices in our pluralistic society, teachers can better appreciate the complex nature of schooling. This chapter takes a chronological look at the people, events, theories, and practices most often associated with the foundation of early care and education.

Changing Views on Childhood

How a society views its children is reflected in the ways in which its children are educated. Over the centuries, society's image of childhood has undergone dramatic shifts in response to social, economic, political, and religious factors. Many events that contributed to these changing viewpoints on children and education arose from strife and conflict that also affected the family structure.

COMPETENCY GOAL VI
• Functional Area 13

Ancient Views on Childhood

Some philosophers of the ancient Western civilizations of Greece and Rome acknowledged childhood as an important part of the human life span. The renowned Greek philosopher Plato (c. 427–347 B.C.), and his notable student Aristotle (384–322 B.C.), described childhood as a time for learning because they believed that education shapes children's characters and prepares them for their roles in society (Osborn, 1991). Although not the prevailing view of their societies, Plato and Aristotle's thinking laid the foundation for state-sponsored educational programs for children that trained the mind, the spirit, and the body. Formal education in ancient Greece and Rome generally began around age 7. Prior to that, most children were given the freedom to indulge their playful natures among the women of the household (Castle, 1961). Once children reached age 7, responsibility for securing education and training shifted to the fathers or other males in the family.

> *Knowledge which is acquired under compulsion has no hold on the mind. Therefore do not use compulsion, but let early education be rather a sort of amusement; this will better enable you to find out the natural bent of the child.*
>
> —Plato, Greek philosopher, circa 300 B.C.

Of course, when Plato and Aristotle spoke of educating children for their roles in society, they were speaking primarily of male children who would as adults assume leadership roles in government or religion. To Plato, leadership by the most intelligent was a means of preserving one's culture; therefore, academies of higher learning were established where promising older boys and young men were taught to use logic and reasoning through intensive sessions of questioning and discussion. Plato believed that knowledge and virtue are closely linked and that education is the route to ultimate goodness. Like Plato, Aristotle believed that the quest for knowledge was noble, but he tempered this viewpoint by stating that goodness and virtue are most strongly mirrored by actions rather than rhetoric.

Like Greek society, ancient Roman civilization also focused on development of the intellect as a means to producing moral individuals. Development of the intellect was to be achieved through carefully selected courses of study, or **curriculum.** For the Romans, this consisted of reading, writing, grammar, arithmetic, music, and physical education—disciplines for both mind and body. Historical records indicate that some Roman cities provided elementary schools for both boys and girls between ages 7 and 12; however, higher education in secondary schools was reserved for male children between ages 12 and 20 (Castle, 1961).

The Roman system of public group education outside the home continued to spread across Europe until the fall of the Roman Empire in A.D. 476. As Germanic tribes overtook Roman strongholds, the Roman system of public education was replaced by strict Church-sponsored schools where boys were trained to become clergy, who were entrusted to preserve and copy religious manuscripts (Castle, 1961). For the centuries between the fall of the Roman Empire and medieval times, little historical evidence of the role of childhood in Western civilizations exists (Aries, 1962).

View of Children during the Middle Ages

During medieval times, European society was preoccupied with survival and warfare, on the continent and abroad. Learning and education were limited to the clergy. As people struggled with physical and financial hardships, attitudes toward childhood changed radically. The value of children was viewed in terms of their potential as laborers (Elkind, 1987). If, for some reason, children were not strong and could not labor as expected, they were deemed burdens.

One way families dealt with the burden of undesirable children was abandonment. Female infants were abandoned more often than males, not only because boys were viewed as stronger laborers, but also because girls, in most Western cultures, could not own or inherit property. Girls were more often viewed as financial liabilities rather than as assets to their families. As people began to believe that infants had souls, eliminating infants by abandonment or other deliberate acts was considered **infanticide**—the murder of infants (Colon, 2001). If abandoned children were found, they were taken to a home for children without parents. The practice of abandoning infants was so common that the term **foundling home** became synonymous with orphanage. However, foundling homes were not always a salvation for these children. Some historical accounts indicate that 50 to 90 percent of the children in these facilities died (Spielvogel, 2000). Mortality rates for infants and young children in general, even those in the care of their families, were high throughout the Middle Ages, which may partially account for the seeming lack of affection between parents and their offspring evident in historical records (Colon, 2001).

Roots of Child Care and Early Education

Children and Schooling during the Reformation

COMPETENCY GOAL VI
• Functional Area 13

Toward the latter part of the Middle Ages, in the fourteenth through sixteenth centuries, European culture underwent another philosophical shift in its perceptions of childhood. Societies once again began to place value on human existence. Gradually, this perceptual shift grew to encompass children, and many individuals recognized childhood as an important phase of life. From this enlightened perspective, philosophers and educators emerged who sought ways to nurture and educate society's youths.

One of the earliest voices of this changed perception was *Martin Luther* (1483–1546). A former Augustinian monk and professor of religion, Luther broke away from the Roman Catholic Church in Prussia (Germany) during what became known as the Protestant Reformation. He contended that all people should be allowed to read the Bible in the **vernacular**, their native language, rather than in Latin, so that they could

> *Now since the young must leap and jump, or have something to do, because they have a natural desire for it which should not be restrained (for it is not well to check them in everything) why should we not provide for them such schools, and lay before them such studies?*
>
> —Martin Luther, German religious reformer, circa 1520

interpret God's message personally (Osborn, 1991). Luther spoke out for a literate citizenry and maintained that this level of literacy could be achieved only through **universal education.** He advocated for free public primary schools for all children—boys and girls, rich and poor alike—believing that universal education was the only way to achieve the goal of a literate citizenry. Education, Luther maintained, should seek to develop not only the intellect, but also the spiritual and physical self.

Luther's ideas appealed to many individuals who were discontented with the doctrines and practices of the Roman Catholic Church. Among them was *John Calvin* (1509–1564), a Frenchman studying for the priesthood in Paris. Calvin drew unfavorable attention from the church and King Charles V by engaging in theological debates over the role of the Protestant reformers, and so fled France in 1536 without completing his training (Hodges, 2000). Calvin settled in Geneva, Switzerland, where he continued to publicly support church reform through his writings and teachings, only to be banished from Geneva in 1538.

Calvin resettled in Strasbourg, Germany, where he continued to write biblical commentaries until he was requested to return to Geneva. On his return, Calvin helped establish hospitals and schools. Calvin designed a municipal school system, with a curriculum that included reading and writing to enable children to read and understand the Bible and Protestant religious doctrine. Calvin, like Luther, believed that reading the Bible in one's native language led to understanding, and understanding led to salvation—the ultimate aim of education. To provide a forum for dissemination of Protestant doctrine, Calvin founded an academy of theology (later known as the University of Geneva) to educate others as religious leaders.

Schooling in Colonial America

Calvin's academy of theology helped spread the Protestant doctrine across Europe and ultimately to the eastern coast of North America to many of the New World colonies. The Pilgrims, one group of Calvin's followers, left England and sailed to America, where they could practice their religion with more freedom. The Pilgrims were called separatists in England because wanted to separate from the Church of England and interpret the Scriptures of the Bible in their own way. In 1620, the Pilgrims settled in the northern colonies in Plymouth, Massachusetts, where they established churches, laws, and schools according to their religious beliefs.

Another group of Calvin's followers, the Puritans, who wearied of religious persecution in England, immigrated to the American colonies ten years after the Pilgrims. The Puritans, so named because of their self-stated mission to purify and reform the Church of England, settled the Massachusetts Bay Colony in 1630. The Puritans were more rigid in their interpretation of the Bible and placed a strong emphasis on education because of its connection to salvation.

Both the Puritans and the Pilgrims believed in the Calvinist doctrine of predestination, which taught that humans were born into original sin. They believed that the only road to salvation was through knowledge of the Scriptures, which came from reading and interpreting the Bible. These beliefs strongly influenced life and schooling in colonial America, particularly in the northern colonies. If salvation came from reading the Bible, then it followed that children would need to be taught to read.

In 1642, the first education law of Massachusetts was enacted. The law specified that parents and others who had responsibility for children were also responsible for their education. A second Massachusetts law, passed in 1647, specified that towns with fifty families had to provide a teacher to teach children to read and write, and towns with a hundred or more families had to provide a teacher and a town school, or **common school**. The 1647 law was called the Ye Old Deluder Satan Act, because those who could read and interpret the Scriptures could find salvation and thus delude (escape) Satan. Common schools provided four or more years of education, beginning at age 7 (Hazen, 1997). In addition to reading, writing, and arithmetic, these schools instructed children in spelling and, of course, the Scriptures. More boys than girls attended common schools; girls were provided with rudimentary education in reading and writing though local dame schools.

Dame schools were taught in the home of a local widow (or dame) who was paid small sums of money or goods for her teaching. Like common schools, dame schools often met every day but Sunday, sometimes for as many as nine or ten hours a day. Curriculum in dame schools, which included children from ages 3 to 7, consisted of learning the alphabet, reading, simple arithmetic, and recitation from the Bible. Dame schools were the primary source of education for girls in the northern colonies (Beatty, 1995).

In keeping with the Puritan ethic, most schools were very strict and expected total obedience from children. Corporal punishment, through whippings and other physical means, was commonplace. Schoolmasters also used humiliation techniques like dunce caps and whispering sticks to control unruly students. Dunce caps were cone-shaped caps children were forced to wear if they failed to be prepared for lessons. Whispering sticks were small sticks of wood wrapped in cloth and placed, like a horse's bit, in the mouths of children if they spoke out of turn (Hakim, 2003). Sayings such as "Spare the rod and spoil the child" reflected the harsh physical and emotional punishment some children endured at the hands of their teachers, parents, and church leaders as the elders strove to keep children on the path of righteousness and salvation.

The Massachusetts education laws served as models for other colonies. By 1683, the middle colonies, such as Pennsylvania and New York, had also enacted laws for education. One such law stipulated that parents or others in charge of children must ascertain if children could read by the time they were twelve years old; those who failed to comply with the law were fined. Some of the schools in the middle colonies, which were colonized by the Dutch (people from the Netherlands), were more tolerant of children's behaviors, used less severe forms of discipline, and refrained from the use of humiliation (Hazen, 1997). These schools, often administered by Dutch Quakers, provided the same type of education for boys and girls.

The southern colonies were less concerned with education, particularly for girls, and tended to leave education of young children to house servants or slaves, nannies, or tutors. Wealthier families sometimes sent their male children to boarding schools in Europe. Generally, girls of wealthier families were expected to be able to read, write, and use arithmetic well enough to manage the household. Education for poor children and blacks was viewed as unimportant and was largely ignored during the 1600s.

Influence of the Renaissance on Early Education

During the latter part of the 1600s, views on children began to shift away from Puritan beliefs that children were innately evil and focused more on how children's early experiences influenced their natures. *John Amos Comenius* (1592–1670), a Moravian monk and educator (from an area that became known as the Czech Republic in 1933), believed that children's minds are pliable during the early years of life and that early learning shapes children into the adults they become. He offered advice to mothers about how young children learn, suggesting that they allow their children to play with other children, because learning occurs spontaneously during play. Comenius also recommended that mothers and teachers observe children at play, show sensitivity to children's personal developmental timetables, and vary teaching methods according to the age and inclinations of the children (Peltzman, 1998). When children demonstrate developmental readiness, he advised, they are ready to be trained to use their senses to actively learn about nature. Through his writings, Comenius described the "school of the mother's lap" as the first step in children's education. His ideas about teaching young children were generally well received throughout much of Europe.

Comenius also agreed with Luther's premise that children should be taught in their native language, especially up to age 6. Comenius viewed language as the key to learning; in fact, one of Comenius's abiding contributions to early care and education was writing and illustrating the first picture book for children. Published in 1657, the book,

Comenius wrote and illustrated *Orbis Pictus* (1657), the first picture book for children.

Orbis Pictus (*The World of Pictures*), presented illustrations of animals, plants, and objects accompanied by short captions (Peltzman, 1998). The educational ideas of Comenius signaled a further shift toward viewing childhood as a significant stage of life, a time when children need sensitive, nurturing adults to guide their development.

Seventeenth- and Eighteenth-Century Influences

John Locke (1632–1704) was an English physician and philosopher who moved from religious interpretations of behavior guidance toward more pragmatic and scientific views. Locke's stand for religious freedom resulted in his exile to the Netherlands. Locke believed that children are not born evil, as many religious persons contended; instead they are born **tabula rasa**—as "clean slates," neither evil nor pure but ready to be "written on" by parents, teachers, and society. Child rearing, educational practices, and other experiences determine children's dispositions.

CDA

COMPETENCY GOAL VI
· Functional Area 13

Some historians consider Locke the founder of modern educational philosophy because he used organized methods of observation to uncover how children learned, and his observations led him to suggest changes in child rearing and early education. For example, Locke suggested that infants should not be swaddled, or wrapped tightly in cloth, as was the custom of the day, but should instead be allowed to freely explore their surroundings using their senses, with only gentle guidance to keep them safe. Locke promoted educational methods that were suitable to the playful natures of children, and he recognized that there are individual differences among children. Because Locke believed that knowledge is received through the senses and then converted by reason, he suggested that parents and teachers respect and work within the natural order of each child's individual development (Braun & Edwards, 1972). According to Locke, nurture, not nature, is key to promoting positive development. Locke did not condone strict lessons and harsh punishment as ways of motivating children to learn; instead, he advised that children be motivated by **meaningful learning** experiences that hold personal significance.

Locke's views on the care and education of young children influenced many future generations of philosophers and educators. *Jean-Jacques Rousseau* (1712–1778), a noted philosopher of the eighteenth century, was strongly influenced by Locke. Rousseau agreed with Locke that early care and education should be flexible and individualized. However, Rousseau did not view children as neutral; rather, he viewed children as good and society, particularly government, as corrupt. Like Locke, Rousseau was exiled from his native France because he spoke out against prevailing practices of the government.

Rousseau's novel *Emile*, published in 1761, described how a boy, Emile, was reared on an island where his natural development remained untarnished by society, allowing his education to come about naturally from the

> *T*he great skill of a teacher is to get and keep the attention of his scholar: whilst he has that, he is sure to advance as fast as the learner's abilities will carry him; and without that, all his bustle and bother will be to little or no purpose.
>
> —John Locke, English philosopher, circa 1700
> (as cited in Braun & Edwards, 1972, p. 39)

senses and nature. Rousseau based his concept of **naturalism** on the idea that what is natural is also good. He believed that through their goodness, children view the world in distinctly different ways than adults. Rousseau was one of the first theorists to suggest that children's minds unfold through a series of phases, or stages, of development. For example, Rousseau explained that children learn first from concrete, active experiences and that learning abstractions and symbols should be delayed for later years (Peltzman, 1998). He contended that it is the responsibility of children's tutors to coordinate, or center, the education of their charges with these phases of development and, in general, to interfere as little as possible with the natural progression of development. Rousseau's concept of **child-centered teaching** builds curriculum in response to children's developmental needs and interests.

Rousseau's writings were widely disseminated and read, and his ideas influenced educational philosophy and practices for centuries, although Rousseau himself was only a teacher for a short time. Indeed, Rousseau, who wrote so eloquently of young children's need for protection from society, failed to provide such protection for his own five children, whom he abandoned to foundling homes. Nevertheless, Rousseau's impact on contemporary child-centered educational practices cannot be minimized.

> *T*he educator only takes care that no untoward influence shall disturb nature's march of development.
>
> —Johann Heinrich Pestalozzi, Swiss educator, circa 1800 (as cited by Kilpatrick, 1951)

One notable educator who was influenced by Rousseau's writings was his contemporary *Johann Heinrich Pestalozzi* (1746–1827), a Swiss humanitarian and educator who tried to use Rousseau's educational methods with his own son. However, when his son still could not read at age 11, Pestalozzi reexamined Rousseau's ideas (Peltzman, 1998). As a result, he developed an approach to early care and education that incorporated many of Rousseau's fundamental ideas within a new framework that was child-centered as well as practical. Like Rousseau, Pestalozzi believed that teachers should be kind and humane and should respect children's natural development as they gently guide children toward self-discovery. Pestalozzi believed that the aim of early childhood education is to help children develop their abilities to the fullest.

Pestalozzi maintained that the first year of life is of great importance for children's positive development. His book, *How Gertrude Teaches Her Children: An Attempt to Help Mothers Teach Their Own Children* (1801/1894), advised mothers of infants to educate according to nature and allow their children to actively explore using their senses and observation skills. Pestalozzi's advice to mothers reflects the same beliefs that characterized his school for poor and orphaned children.

Pestalozzi agreed with Rousseau's idea of child-centered teaching practices that are adapted to children's interests and abilities; further, he viewed children holistically, believing that their heads, hearts, and hands work together as they learn. From this position, Pestalozzi promoted the use of an **integrated curriculum** in which concepts are approached realistically, as wholes, rather than artificially, as discrete subject areas that do not overlap (Smith, 1999). For example, children who engage in a project to grow a vegetable garden will be learning science as they handle seeds and plants and observe how the weather affects plants. Additionally, when planting seeds, the children will use measuring skills to determine where to place the seeds or plants in relationship to each other. At times, the children may need to confer and make decisions about their garden plot, which means that they will use language and problem-solving as well as social skills. The gardening project integrates the subjects of science, math, and language in a realistic and meaningful manner and actively involves the children's heads, hearts, and hands.

Pestalozzi's humanitarian inclinations led him to promote the view that education belongs to all children, not only those from wealthy families. Education, he maintained, awakens intellectual and moral potential and can ultimately lead to social reform. Unlike Rousseau, Pestalozzi actually put into practice the educational methods that he proposed.

From 1774 to 1780, Pestalozzi provided training for poor children at his farm, Neuhof, in Birr, Switzerland, where he taught them spinning and weaving. After the school closed, Pestalozzi devoted himself to putting his educational ideas in writing until 1798, when he was asked to head an institution to train children who were left destitute by civil unrest. However, the school building in Stanz, Switzerland, was soon claimed by the French army, forcing the school to close after only one year of operation (Schwickerath, 1913/1997). Shortly afterward, in 1799, Pestalozzi was appointed guardian of several dozen war-orphaned children and established a school at the Castle of Burgdorf in Bern, Switzerland, in 1780 (Compton's Encyclopedia Online, n.d.). Pestalozzi maintained this school for five years until it was forced to close due to financial insolvency.

Pestalozzi was one of the first European educators to train others to teach groups of young children.

Pestalozzi's next opportunity to employ his educational practices came in Yverdon, Switzerland. The institute, a boarding school for children, most of whom were between the ages of 2 and 6, opened in the Castle of Yverdon in rural Switzerland in 1805; it functioned successfully for twenty years (Pestalozzi Documentation and Research Centre, n.d.). "Papa Pestalozzi," as some of the children called him, was a dedicated and caring teacher who believed in educating the whole child. In addition to playing and observing nature, groups of young children engaged in practical activities such as gardening, cooking, and weaving.

Pestalozzi's practical activities often began with an **object lesson.** Object lessons, which replaced traditional rote learning, begin with the children examining a familiar, concrete (real) object—such as a potato or a rock. After careful manipulation and examination of the object, the children describe what they observe and discuss what they already know about the item. Next, the teacher makes a brief oral presentation affirming the children's observations and adding new relevant information to extend the discussion as far as the children's development and interests indicate. Object lessons follow three simple guidelines:

- Begin with the *concrete* before progressing to the *abstract*.
- Move from the *simple* to the *complex*.
- Introduce the *known* before the *unknown*. (Gillett, 1966, p. 218)

In addition to teaching children at the institute in Yverdon, Pestalozzi offered formal specialized training in his teaching methods for adults who were interested in teaching young children. As Pestalozzi's **normal school,** or training school for teachers, grew in reputation, several interested educators of the day visited from Europe and the United States.

Early Care and Education in the Nineteenth and Twentieth Centuries

CDA

COMPETENCY GOAL VI
• Functional Area 13

The beliefs of philosophers such as Locke, Rousseau, Comenius, and Pestalozzi provided the ideological foundation for many of the child care and early education practices that predominated in the nineteenth and twentieth centuries. Their writings, and in some cases, teacher training programs had profound effect on the education of young children.

Birth of Kindergarten

The German educator *Friedrich Wilhelm Froebel* (1782–1852), the son of a Lutheran minister and an architect and forester by training, was intrigued by what he had heard about Pestalozzi's methods of education. Froebel attended Pestalozzi's teacher training institute from 1808 to 1810 (Peltzman, 1998). It was a reflective experience for Froebel because while he agreed with many of Pestalozzi's principles, he felt Pestalozzi focused too strongly on practical education as preparation for adulthood. In addition, Froebel felt that Pestalozzi needed to more clearly articulate his beliefs and teaching practices for early education.

What evolved from Froebel's ideas was a system for educating young children that seeks to provide learning environments where they can grow according to their own dispositions and inner development. Froebel named this system of education *kindergarten,* a German word that literally translates as "children's garden." Froebel predicted that children, when given opportunities for self-knowledge and self-expression through playful social interaction in nurturing homelike learning environments, will flourish and develop according to their own natures.

In 1837, Froebel opened his first kindergarten program for children from age 2 to 6 years. The kindergarten focused on four of Froebel's major ideals: creativity, self-expression, social participation, and motor (psychomotor) experiences (Froebel Web, 1998–1999a). Children achieved these ideals through playing games, singing songs, performing folk dances, listening to stories, drawing, playing with blocks, and studying nature. Froebel described active play as children's most direct route to learning (Gillett, 1966); in fact, Froebel believed that good teachers are those who use cues from children's play to guide them into activities that will help them grow intellectually and spiritually. Childhood, to Froebel, is a unique time in one's development—a time that should be esteemed.

> *Children are like tiny flowers; they are varied and need care, but each is beautiful alone and glorious when seen in the community of peers.*
>
> —Friedrich Froebel, German educator and "father" of kindergarten, circa 1820

Froebel's focus on the importance of play spurred him to develop sets of specially designed toys to help children organize and understand the world (Peltzman, 1998). These objects served as the forerunners of many of today's educational toys. Sets of blocks, balls, and cylinders, and related activities, were central to Froebel's kindergarten program. Froebel's belief that perceptual development drives cognitive development served as the impetus for the use of these toys and related activities, which he dubbed **gifts and occupations.** The toys, or gifts, were primarily geometric solids made of natural materials and were designed to symbolize the unity of nature (Froebel Web, 1998–1999a). The occupations were manipulative activities such as drawing, sewing, weaving paper, or molding clay and were intended to support perceptual motor development and foster aesthetic appreciation for shape, form, and balance (Brosterman, 1997). Froebel encouraged children to closely observe natural and manufactured objects and to use their senses to explore and actively manipulate those objects in order to gain understanding of the world.

> *Play is the purest, the most spiritual product of man at this stage, and is at once the prefiguration and imitation of the total human life—of the inner, secret, natural life in man and in all things.*
>
> —Friedrich Froebel, German educator, circa 1826

Froebel's efforts to make kindergarten available to more children were very successful, and less than ten years after the first kindergarten was established around 1837, Prussia (Germany) boasted more than forty kindergartens (Froebel Web, 1998–1999b). The rapid growth of Froebel's kindergarten programs created another need—trained kindergarten teachers.

In 1849, Froebel began offering courses to train individuals as kindergarten teachers (University of Surrey Roehampton, 2001). Although the Prussian leadership forced the closing of all kindergartens in 1851, by 1872, kindergarten school attendance in Germany had become required—that is, **compulsory education** was required for all children under age 6. Additionally, Froebel's teaching methodology was required coursework in teacher training programs throughout Germany. Froebel's influence continued to spread as his students, trained in Froebelian methodology, traveled to other parts of the Western world, including England and the United States. In addition to their knowledge of Froebel's philosophy and methods of early care and education, these newly trained teachers, many of whom were women, carried with them strong commitments to quality early childhood education.

Margarethe Meyer Schurz (1833–1876), who was a student at Froebel's training program in Germany, traveled to the United States with her husband, Carl. In 1856, she opened the first privately operated kindergarten in the United States in Watertown, Wisconsin. The kindergarten, held in Schurz's home and taught in German, was initially opened for her young daughter and four neighbor children. The kindergarten was closed for a time when the community objected to the use of the German language (Froebel Web, 1998–1999a).

Just as Froebel had encouraged interested educators to visit his kindergarten school, Schurz welcomed educators into her home to observe. In 1859, *Elizabeth Palmer Peabody* (1804–1894) visited the home of Margarethe Schurz to observe the implementation of Froebel's methods of kindergarten education. Peabody returned to Boston, Massachusetts, where she opened the first English-speaking kindergarten in the United States in 1860. She continued to operate the kindergarten until 1867, when she traveled to Germany, at the urging of Schurz, to study Froebel's teaching methods with his disciples. On her return to the United States, Peabody founded one of the first programs in the country for training kindergarten teachers. She was also instrumental in opening many of the kindergarten programs that were operating in the United States by 1885, including the first public school kindergarten.

Peabody convinced *William Torrey Harris* (1835–1908), the superintendent of St. Louis Public Schools, to open a free public kindergarten program in St. Louis, Missouri, under the direction of *Susan Elizabeth Blow* (1843–1916) (Graue, 2001). The Des Peres School, which opened in 1873, became a model of Froebel's methods of kindergarten education. In the mornings, Blow taught kindergarten; in the afternoons, she taught teachers about Froebel's philosophy and curriculum. Within ten years, every public school in St. Louis offered a kindergarten program for children from ages 3 to 6. Blow's classroom was described by visitors as colorful, active, and filled with play (Froebel Web, 1998–1999a).

Blow became a leading proponent for Froebel's kindergarten methods in the United States. In her efforts to maintain the purity of Froebel's methods, she organized the American Froebel Union in 1877 and served as the organization's first president. Additionally, her books, *Educational Issues in the Kindergarten* (1908) and *Kindergarten Ideal* (1897), described Froebel's vision of a homelike learning environment where children's creativity and self-expression are nurtured. Blow's books also describe the more practi-

The first public school kindergarten in the United States was located in St. Louis and operated and taught by Susan Blow, a stalwart follower of Froebel's methods of education.

cal aspects of the kindergarten program, such as teacher-facilitated exploration, or **guided exploration**, of the gifts-and-occupations method outlined by Froebel.

Nursery School Movement

Simultaneous with the rapid spread of kindergartens across Europe and the United States, another aspect of early care and education, the **nursery school**, was emerging. Begun in the 1800s, nursery schools provided for children's primary custodial care needs related to health, safety, and nutrition as well as for the educational needs of children under age 7. Historically, many nursery schools concentrated their humanitarian efforts on children whose families were economically disadvantaged due to societal and environmental factors such as droughts and famine (Spodek, 1985).

During the latter part of the 1800s and the early 1900s, the Industrial Revolution, brought about by the invention of automated machinery that allowed the mass production of goods, created major changes in what had been a primarily farming society (Osborn, 1991). Automated factories and mills needed workers to operate the machines of mass production, and the machines, in turn, required enormous quantities of coal for power, spawning a need for more workers in the coal mines. In Europe and the United States, families hoping to improve their economic lots moved from failing single-family farms to the cities to seek employment in factories, textile mills, and coal mines.

Instead of improving their lives, this change created a chain reaction that brought even greater hardships for children and families. To afford food and shelter for their families in the cities, both parents often worked in factories, mills, or mines for twelve hours or more per day, six days a week. Often, children as young as 7 toiled alongside their parents under the same grueling conditions. Additionally, overcrowded and unsanitary housing in heavily populated urban areas created threats to health, to which infants, young children, and the elderly were particularly vulnerable.

In England, sisters *Margaret McMillan* (1860–1931) and *Rachel McMillan* (1859–1917) accepted the challenge and devoted themselves to promoting healthy beginnings for infants and young children. Though born in the United States, they moved to Scotland with their mother, Jean, after their father and sister died from scarlet fever in 1865. Once settled in Scotland, the McMillan sisters attended school until their mother's death in 1877, at which time they took over the care of their grandmother. At age 18, Margaret went to England to receive training as a governess, while Rachel remained in Scotland until her grandmother's death in 1888, after which she joined her sister in London (SpartacusSchoolnet, n.d.).

Margaret, who had secured a position in a boarding school after her training, found a similar position for Rachel. In 1892, Margaret joined a medical inspection team for elementary schools in England and became concerned with the poor health of school-age children. She advocated for improved health and hygiene practices in the schools, as well as proper nourishment for the children through a system of school meals. Margaret McMillan's message to school officials was that healthy bodies precede healthy minds. By 1906, the government of England had passed the Provision for School Meals Act (SpartacusSchoolnet, n.d.).

Margaret and Rachel McMillan also turned their efforts to improving the health of younger children, and in 1914, the sisters founded the Deptford School, the first **open-air nursery school** in London. The sisters saw the open-air nursery school as a way to prevent the spread of disease and thus improve the health of young children. In addition to giving children opportunities to play in the fresh air, caregivers at the school bathed them, gave them clean clothes and sanitary places to nap, and fed them nourishing meals and snacks. The McMillan sisters also shared health and hygiene information with children's parents, hoping to improve living conditions for the whole family. The Deptford School, which remains open today, originally cared for about thirty children from eighteen months to seven years of age (SpartacusSchoolnet, n.d.).

Margaret McMillan referred to the nursery school as a "nurture school," where both the physical and intellectual well-being of children was fostered. Valuing imaginative play, the McMillans developed their own techniques for educating young children (Spodek, 1985). Their school provided opportunities for working-class children to play with clay, wooden blocks, and various natural materials to facilitate perceptual-motor development. Because the school emphasized spending time outdoors, the children also gardened, cared for animals, and participated in nature study. In addition to leading these activities, Rachel McMillan, who was responsible for the kindergarten class, introduced the older children to reading, writing, and arithmetic.

As attendance at the nursery school grew, Margaret McMillan saw the need for well-trained teachers for children under age 5. She began offering specialized training courses for teachers at the Deptford School. Two of her books, *Early Childhood* (1900) and *Through the Imagination* (1904), describe many of her beliefs and recommend practices for early care and education. Margaret and Rachel McMillan are credited with beginning what became known as the nursery school movement.

In 1921, seven years after the inception of the Deptford School, two American women, *Abigail Adams Eliot* (1892–1992) and *Edna Noble White* (1879–1954), visited with the McMillan sisters and observed operations at the open-air nursery school in London. Eliot and White became instrumental in the development of the early care and education system in the United States. Eliot, a social worker by training, studied Margaret McMillan's methods thoroughly before returning to the United States to complete her education at Harvard University.

In 1922, Eliot and *Elizabeth Winsor Pearson* opened the Ruggles Street Nursery School and Nursery Training Center (for teachers) in Roxbury, Massachusetts, which served the needs of children and families with low incomes. Curriculum at the school incorporated the methods of the McMillans, Froebel, and others that focused on child-centered learning. The Nursery Training Center became the Eliot-Pearson Department of Child Study at Tufts University in 1952.

On her return from London, Edna White established the Merrill-Palmer School of Motherhood and Home Training in Detroit, Michigan. The Merrill-Palmer Institute, as it was later named, provided parent education programs, beginning with prenatal development. The institute continues to serve as a center for child study and as a resource for teachers and others interested in early care and education.

Other nursery schools had opened in the United States prior to the Ruggles Street Nursery School and Nursery Training Center. As early as 1913, *Caroline Pratt* (1867–1954) established the City and Country School in New York City. In New York City, in 1919, *Lucy Sprague Mitchell* (1878–1967) and *Harriet Johnson* (1846–1900) helped establish a laboratory school associated with the Bureau of Educational Experiments that later became known as the Bank Street College of Education. Mitchell developed an early childhood curriculum that fostered development of the whole child—physical, social-emotional, and intellectual. (Bank Street's developmental-interaction approach to early care and education is discussed in Chapter 7.) Mitchell maintained that connecting the laboratory school to the college of education would help teacher education students bridge the gap between theory and practice. Johnson served as director of the newly established laboratory school and became actively involved with the teacher training aspects of the program.

Another pioneer in the field of early care and education in the United States was *Patty Smith Hill* (1868–1946). Hill, who was well trained in the Froebelian method of kindergarten, founded the Free Kindergarten Society in Louisville, Kentucky (Snyder, 1972). Later, she became a professor at Teachers College of Columbia University in New York. In 1921, Hill, like Mitchell, opened a laboratory school attached to the college of education. Hill began to question some of Froebel's practices, particularly the standard activities associated with the gifts-and-occupations method, and sought ways to restructure kindergarten and primary education.

Like Froebel, Hill valued play and recognized it as the vehicle through which children build understanding. However, Hill contended that children need more freedom in their explorations and opportunities for inquiry, which can be accomplished only

The Bank Street School, which was founded in New York City in the early 1900s, continues to provide quality programs for young children as well as teacher training.

through self-directed activities. Hill envisioned a child-centered curriculum filled with large periods of time for free play, creative art and music, block building, and outdoor play. Hill and her sister, Mildred, published a collection entitled *Song Stories for the Kindergarten* (1896), including the still-popular "Happy Birthday," so that other kindergarten teachers could incorporate music and movement into their programs (Quisenberry, Eddowes, & Robinson, 1991).

Hill's interest in restructuring kindergarten and her leadership within the International Kindergarten Union led to her wider participation in a movement to reform schools in the United States. This reform effort, which focused on moving away from traditional teacher-centered curriculum to a more modern learner-centered approach, was based on the premise that individuals living in democratic societies will benefit from educational practices that mirror the same democratic ideals.

Progressive Movement in the United States

John Dewey (1859–1952), an American philosopher and educator of the twentieth century, is often called the "father of the Progresssive movement" in the United States. Dewey, a teacher from Vermont, wrote an article for a prestigious education journal that attracted the attention of several influential educators, including William Torrey Harris, who had helped establish the St. Louis kindergarten program (Cremin, 1988). In Dewey's opinion the then-current system of education failed to consider the natural tendencies of children; however, it was not until several years later that Dewey fully articulated his views on contemporary teaching methodology, of **pedagogy.**

Dewey's thesis, *My Pedagogic Creed* (1897), published while he taught at the University of Chicago, delineated his beliefs about teaching and learning. Dewey viewed learning as an experiential process that emerges as individuals observe, inquire, discuss, interact, and construct understanding based on their active explorations (Cremin, 1988). Teachers are to advise, but not direct, the learning process; their role is to facilitate group cooperation and problem solving, thereby allowing children to make decisions about their own learning (Cuban, 1993). Dewey viewed education as part of life rather than as preparation for life; therefore, educators need to respond to individual children's personalities, interests, and abilities and provide them with continual feedback throughout the process of learning rather than delaying evaluation until a project or course of study is completed (Dewey, 1897). To Dewey, the process of education focuses on active problem solving and collaboration, not predetermined subject matter and competition (Dewey, 1938/1998).

> *I believe that the school must represent present life—life as real and vital to the child as that which he carries on in the home, in the neighborhood, and on the playground.*
>
> —John Dewey, American educator and leader in the Progressive movement, as cited in *The School Journal* (1897, p. 77)

In 1896, during his tenure at the University of Chicago, Dewey and his wife, Alice Chipman, established the Laboratory School of the University of Chicago, where the principles of progressive education could be applied and examined. The practice of establishing experimental schools to investigate learning and pedagogy was due, in part, to the influence of experimental psychologists who applied the scientific process to study child development.

Educational Trends in the United States

During the last hundred years, education in America has undergone many philosophical shifts in response to social, economic, and political events. Each decade has brought forth new directions for schooling, some more enduring than others, as briefly discussed in the following pages:

CDA

COMPETENCY GOAL VI
• Functional Area 13

• **The Child Study Movement**—Beginning in the early 1900s, understanding child development became a focus for many parents, teachers, psychologists, and schools. Child study, primarily through observation and interview, was conducted by various researchers, including physicians, psychologists, and educators such as G. (Granville) Stanley Hall (1844–1924) and Arnold Lucius Gesell (1880–1961). The detailed documentation of these studies formed the foundation of the "ages and stages" approach, which conceptualizes child development as generally predictable patterns and sequences.

- **Federal Government Involvement in Education**—Several events in the early and mid 1900s—such as World War I, the Great Depression, and World War II—contributed to the federal government's involvement in education. Efforts to relieve some of the financial hardships caused by economic decline led to the development of the Works Progress Administration (WPA), which provided over 6,000 jobs for teachers and others by supporting thousands of educational programs through the 1940s. Among the educational programs were over 2,000 government-sponsored nursery schools serving over 40,000 children (Colon, 2001; Hewes, 1976). A related government initiative, the Lanham Act of 1941, provided funds for 24-hour-a-day child care during World War II, for mothers who worked in industries that provided supplies and equipment to the U.S. war effort. These child care centers were closed at the end of the war.

- **The Space Race**—In 1957, when Russia successfully launched a satellite called *Sputnik* a year before the United States launched its satellite, *Explorer I,* the United States officially lost the race into space. As a result, education, particularly math, science, and foreign language instruction, came under scrutiny from the government and public alike. In response, the government sponsored research initiatives, under the National Defense Education Act of 1958, aimed at developing curriculum that would boost children's school performance, with the goal of ultimately restoring the United States to its place as a technological world leader.

- **The War on Poverty**—The 1960s marked the beginning of President Johnson's War on Poverty, which, under the Economic Opportunity Act of 1964, funded educational programs for children and families living in poverty. The Head Start preschool program (discussed in more detail in Chapter 5) received initial funding during this period. Unlike many other federally funded programs, Head Start has continued to receive federal funds since its inception.

- **Civil Rights Movement**—The 1950s and 1960s marked the beginning of the organized Civil Rights Movement, beginning with the 1954 *Brown* v. *Board of Education of Topeka* ruling that declared segregated education for blacks and whites was not "separate but equal" but rather discriminatory and unequal. The Civil Rights Act of 1964, which forbids discrimination on the basis of race, religion, or national origin, was an important step toward the desegregation of U.S. schools.

- **Educational Funds for Special Populations**—In 1965, the Elementary and Secondary Education Act (ESEA), which allocates funds to the states for educational programs directed at special populations, was enacted. Among the programs funded were
  - *Title I (now Chapter 1)*—educational programs for children from low-income families (enacted in 1965).
  - *Title VI*—educational programs for Native American children (enacted in 1966).
  - *Title VII*—educational programs for children who speak languages other than English as their native language (enacted in 1967).

- **Special Education**—During the 1970s, laws to guarantee the "free and appropriate public education" of children with disabilities were passed. The Education for All Handicapped Children Act of 1975, which was renamed the Individuals with Disabilities Education Act (IDEA) in 1990, mandated that the states develop and fund programs and instruction for children with disabilities. (Chapter 1 provides additional information about IDEA.) In addition, the Child Development Associate (CDA) program was funded, through the U.S. Administration for Children, Youth and Families, to credential child care workers who meet educational and experiential criteria set by the agency (Hymes, 1991). (Chapter 5 provides additional information on the CDA credential.)

- **Back-to-the-Basics Movement**—During the 1980s, education once again became the focal point for improving life in the United States. *A Nation at Risk* (National Commission on Excellence in Education, 1983), a report commissioned by President Ronald Reagan, presented evidence that the country's quality of education was in a state of decline and that higher standards were needed to ensure that the United States maintained its status as an educational leader among nations. In response, many states reformed their educational systems to include a stronger emphasis on basic skills needed for academic success. Around the country, schools designated longer periods of time each school day for reading, writing, and mathematics instruction and added instruction in the uses of technology. Additionally, many states incorporated formal testing strategies to monitor students' progress. The push for academics was not limited to elementary and high schools; some kindergarten and preschool programs shifted from play-based to preacademics curricula.

- **National Goals for Education**—During the 1990s, federal and state governments combined efforts to ensure that America's school children received a high standard of education. The result was Goals 2000: Educate America Act, which was signed by President Clinton in 1993; this law identifies eight national education goals, covering educational concerns from preschool through high school graduation. The first goal is, "All children in American will start school ready to learn."

- **Developmentally Appropriate Practice**—In 1987, the National Association for the Education of Young Children published its position statement on developmentally appropriate practice (DAP) for young children from birth to age 8. This statement, which was revised in 1997, proclaimed that early care and education programs needed to adopt teaching and learning practices that were age appropriate, individually appropriate, and culturally appropriate. (Chapter 1 provides additional information about DAP.)

- **Brain Research and Early Brain Development**—Extensive research about the development and working of the brain has contributed to awareness that the first five years of life are crucial to the healthy development of the brain. Many early care and education teachers consider information obtained from brain research as they make decisions about their programs. (Chapters 2 and 3 provide additional information about the development of the brain during early childhood.)

Understanding the historical roots of early care and education helps teachers build connections between past, present, and future practices. As views on childhood have changed over the centuries, the practices used to nurture and teach them have also changed. Within those changes, kernels of the past can be discerned and tied to today's ideas about the best ways to teach young children. Being aware of these underlying concepts enables us to use the lessons of the past to develop quality early care and education programs for today and the foreseeable future.

Summary

Changing Views on Childhood

- Some ancient Western civilizations, like Greece and Rome, viewed childhood as an important part of the human life span.
- During the Middle Ages, children were often viewed as economic and social burdens.

Roots of Child Care and Early Education

- Religious reformers Luther and Calvin believed that both boys and girls should be schooled so that they could read the Bible in their own language.
- Schooling in colonial America was heavily influenced by the religious doctrines of Calvin, as interpreted by the Puritans and the Pilgrims.

Seventeenth- and Eighteenth-Century Influences

- European philosophers such as Comenius, Locke, Rousseau, and Pestalozzi contributed to the idea that childhood is a time when children should be allowed to develop naturally.

Early Care and Education in the Nineteenth and Twentieth Centuries

- Influential leaders who visited or attended Froebel's kindergarten teacher training programs were instrumental in spreading his ideas about early education throughout Europe and the United States.
- Nursery schools in England, which focused on humanitarian efforts and used a play-based curriculum, served as models for many of the early care and education programs established in the United States during the 1900s.
- The Progressive movement in the United States reflected the views of John Dewey that education should focus on active learning, problem solving, and collaboration, not predetermined subject matter.

Educational Trends in the United States

- During the last hundred years, education in the United States has been influenced by various social, economic, and political events, which has prompted school reform.

LEARNING ACTIVITIES

1 Graphic Representation: Timeline. Construct a timeline showing the overlapping lives of key contributors to the field of early care and education. Use your timeline to determine which contributors were contemporaries. What else can you discover about the history of early care and education from your graphic representation? Share your insights with others in the class.

2 Discussion: Schooling throughout the Centuries. Through class discussion, generate a list of television shows and/or movies that include scenes of schooling in the United States from colonial times to the present day. Organize the list according to the era or decade the program represents. Compare how schools and teaching were depicted in the episodes you listed. For example, compare school scenes from "Little House on the Prairie" to "Walton's Mountain" or "The Brady Bunch." How realistic are the portrayals? Are teachers and schools shown from positive or negative perspectives? Discuss other aspects of schooling shown in these programs.

PORTFOLIO ARTIFACTS

1 Project: Who's Who in Early Childhood Education. Select one of the individuals discussed in the chapter about whom you would like more information. Research the individual's background and prepare a biographical sketch, including details from early years and adult life. Also summarize the individual's contributions to the field. Reflect on the people and experiences that sculpted the person's philosophy and practices in early care and education.

2 Interview: Recollections from the Past. Interview an experienced or retired early childhood teacher who has been involved with education at least twenty years. Ask about what schools were like when this teacher first began to teach. Use open-ended questions and provide examples. Continue the interview by asking about changes in schools, teaching, teacher preparation, or other factors related to education this person has experienced. After the interview, review the teacher's responses and reflect on what kind of educational changes you would expect over the next twenty years.

Professional Connections and Web Links

Froebel Web: An Online Resource
http://members.tripod.com/~FroebelWeb/

This site provides a timeline of Froebel's life and of the spread of kindergarten throughout Europe and the United States. It includes a selection of quotes, excerpts from correspondence, and descriptions of kindergarten programs related to Froebel. The site also provides a thorough description of each of Froebel's gifts and occupations.

The Life and Work of Jean-Jacques Rousseau
http://www.unige.ch/cite-uni/rousseau/
anglais/presaa.html

This unique Web site presents a visual biography of the life of French/Swiss philosopher Jean-Jacques Rousseau by presenting a series of postcards and other drawings to illustrate his life from birth to grave. The accompanying narrative is interesting and detailed, providing insight into Rousseau's complex nature.

Welcome to America: Life in the Colonies
http://www.education-world.com/
a_special/life_in_colonies2000.shtml

This site, sponsored by Education World, provides a regional view of life and schooling in the northern, middle, and southern colonies from the 1600s to the 1800s. In addition to elaborate information about life in the colonies, the site features lesson plans from colonial classrooms and colorful images of artifacts, such as the *Hornbook* and the *New England Primer*. Many of the topics provide activities to simulate growing up in colonial America. The site also provides links to other historical sites such as the Blackwell Museum.

Suggestions For Further Reading

Beatty, Barbara. (1995). *Preschool education in America: The culture of young children from the colonial era to the present*. New Haven, CT: Yale University Press.

- Beatty presents a comprehensive description of preschool schooling in the United States since the 1600s. The text includes many firsthand references from historical records, letters and journals, interviews, and other sources, which contribute to vibrant examples of early care and education from bygone eras. Beatty also includes several historical photos and sketches.

Brosterman, Norman (1997). *Inventing kindergarten*. New York: Abrams.

- Brosterman offers a well-researched, thoughtful presentation of Froebel's experiences with Pestalozzi and others that led to the advent of kindergarten. Through dozens of detailed illustrations and colorful photographs, Brosterman provides insight into each of Froebel's gifts and occupations and their connection to learning and artistic expression.

References

Aries, Philippe. (1962). *Centuries of childhood*. New York: Vintage.

Beatty, Barbara. (1995). *Preschool education in America: The culture of young children from the colonial era to the present*. New Haven, CT: Yale University Press.

Braun, Samuel J., & Edwards, Esther P. (1972). *History and theory of early childhood education*. Worthington, OH: Charles Jones.

Brosterman, Norman. (1997). *Inventing kindergarten*. New York: Harry N. Abrams.

Castle, Edgar Bradshaw. (1961). *Ancient education and today*. Baltimore, MD: Penguin Books.

Cremin, L. A. (1970). *American education: The colonial experience, 1607–1783*. New York: Harper & Row.

Cremin, L. A. (1988). *American education: The metropolitan experience, 1876–1980*. New York: Harper & Row.

Colon, A. R., with Colon, P. A. (2001). *A history of children: A socio-cultural survey across millennia*. Westport, CT: Greenwood Press.

Compton's Encyclopedia Online. (n.d.). *Pestalozzi, Johann Heinrich*. Retrieved on November 2, 1999, from http://www.optonline.com/comptons/ceo/03700_A.html.

Cuban, Larry. (1993). *How teachers taught: Constancy and change in American classrooms, 1899–1990*. New York: Teachers College Press.

Dewey, John. (1897). My pedagogic creed. *The School Journal, 54*(3), 77–80. Full-text article retrieved on December 7, 2002, from the informal education archives, http://www.users.globalnet.co.uk/~infed/e-texts/e-dew-pc.htm.

Dewey, John. (1938/1998). *John Dewey: Experience and education: The 60th anniversary edition*. West Lafayette, IN: Kappa Delta Pi.

Elkind, David. (1987). The child yesterday, today, and tomorrow. *Young Children, 42*(4), 6–11.

Froebel, Friedrich. (1885). *The education of man*. (W. N. Hailmann, trans.). New York: D. Appleton. (Original work published in 1826.)

Froebel Web, an Online Resource. (1998–1999a). *Friedrich Froebel time line*. Retrieved July 30, 2001, from http://members.tripod.com/~FroebelWeb/webline.html.

Froebel Web, an Online Resource. (1998–1999b). *Froebel Gifts*. Retrieved July 30, 2001, from http://members.tripod.com/~FroebelWeb/gifts/.

Gillett, Margaret. (1966). *A history of education: Thought and practice*. Toronto: McGraw-Hill.

Graue, Elizabeth. (2001). What's going on in the children's garden? Kindergarten today. *Young Children, 56*(3), 67–73.

Hakim, Joy. (2003). *From colonies to country, 1735–1791*. New York: Oxford University Press.

Hazen, Walter A. (1997). *Everyday life: Colonial times*. Parsippany, NJ: Good Year Books.

Hewes, Dorothy W. (1976). *NAEYC's first half century, 1926–1976*. Washington, DC: National Association for the Education of Young Children.

Hodges, Miles. (2000). *John Calvin*. New Geneva Center. Retrieved December 22, 2002, from http://www.newgenevacenter.org/biography/calvin2.htm.

Hymes, James L., Jr. (1991). *Early childhood education: Twenty years in review—A look at 1971–1990*. Washington, DC: National Association for the Education of Young Children.

Lucidcafe's Library (1996, June). *Jean-Jacques Rousseau: Swiss/French philosopher*. Retrieved October 13, 2000, from http://www.lucidcafe.com/library/96Jun/rousseau.html.

National Commission on Excellence in Education. (1983). *A nation at risk: The imperative for educational reform*. Washington, DC: U.S. Government Printing Office.

Osborn, D. Keith. (1991). *Early childhood education in historical perspective* (3rd ed.). Athens, GA: Daye Press.

Peltzman, Barbara Ruth. (1998). *Pioneers of early childhood education: A bio-bibliographical guide*. Westport, CT: Greenwood Publishing Group.

Pestalozzi, Johann Heinrich. (1894). *How Gertrude teaches her children*. (E. H. Lucy & F. C. Turner, Trans.) London: Swan Sonnenschein. (Original work published in 1801.)

Pestalozzi Documentation and Research Centre. (n.d.). *Pestalozzi's life*. Retrieved November 2, 1999, from http://www.einev.ch/pestalozzi/CRDP_english.html.

Quisenberry, James D., Eddowes, E. Anne, & Robinson, Sandra L. (1991). *Readings from childhood education* (vol. 2). Wheaton, MD: Association for Childhood Education International.

Schwickerath, Robert. (1913/1997). *Pestalozzi and Pestalozzianism*. Catholic encyclopedia electronic version by New Advent, Inc. Retrieved November 2, 1999, from http://www.knight.org/advent/cathen/11742b.htm.

Smith, Mark K. (1999). *Johann Heinrich Pestalozzi*. The informal education homepage. Retrieved November 2, 1999, from http://www.infed.org/thinkers/et-pest.htm.

Snyder, Agnes. (1972). *Dauntless women in childhood education, 1856–1931*. Wheaton, MD: Association for Childhood Education International.

SpartacusSchoolnet. (n.d.). *Rachel McMillan*. Retrieved July 30, 2001, from http://www.spartacus.school-net.co.uk/WmcmillanR.htm.

Spielvogel, Jackson J. (2000). *Western civilization since 1300* (4th ed.). Belmont, CA: Wadsworth/Thomson Learning.

Spodek, Bernard. (1985). Early childhood education's past as a prologue: Roots of contemporary concerns. *Young Children, 40*(5), 3–7.

University of Surrey Roehampton. (2001). *Froebel Archive for childhood studies: Friedrich Froebel*. Retrieved July 30, 2001, from http://www.roehampton.ac.uk.

After reading this chapter and completing the related activities, you should be able to

- List several contemporary approaches to early care and education
- Identify theoretical and philosophical bases for contemporary models
- Compare the roles of children, teachers, and learning environments in various approaches
- Describe the roles of families and communities
- Discuss the process of curriculum development

Contemporary Models of Early Care and Education

*M*s. *Rhoda Sherman, who has been teaching preschool for more than five years, walks quietly around her classroom, stopping beside each small group of children who are playing with a variety of toys and games and inviting them to the story rug. Several children put away their blocks, puzzles, and other toys and hurry to the story rug to secure the spots closest to the teacher, who is now sitting in a wooden rocking chair at the edge of a colorful circular rug. Ms. Sherman waits until most of the children are settled comfortably on the rug before holding up the large picture book that has been lying in her lap.*

"Children, our story today is called The Mitten. *Who can tell me what they think the story might be about?" Several children respond aloud that the story would be about mittens. "Yes, the story is about mittens," Ms. Sherman confirms, "and the mitten in this story is very special. Let's listen to the story and find out what is special about the mitten." Ms. Sherman props the big book against a large easel at her left side, repeats the title, and names the author (Jan Brett) before turning to the first page. She points to the colorful illustrations as she reads the book aloud in a lively manner. The children gaze at the illustrations with great interest, sometimes reaching out to touch the illustrations. As Ms. Sherman continues to read the book, she frequently points out interesting details in the illustrations, asking the children to describe what they see or to predict what they think will happen next.*

CHAPTER 7

As the story draws to a conclusion, Ms. Sherman asks the children, "What is so special about this mitten?" Most of the children eagerly respond that all kinds of animals live in the mitten. Samuel, who is almost five years old, informs everyone that the mitten would have to be really, really big to hold all of those animals. Several of the children giggle as they stretch out their arms to show how wide the mitten would need to stretch. Ms. Sherman smiles and regains the children's attention by saying, "Yes, Samuel is right. The mitten would need to be very large indeed—and today during center time you will have a chance to make it even bigger by adding more animals."

Several children murmur excitedly as Ms. Sherman continues her explanation. "I will leave this big book on the easel so you can look more closely at the pictures later on. I have put large sheets of paper, cut in the shape of mittens, in the art center, and anyone who chooses may add another animal to the story by drawing its picture on the mitten page with crayons or markers. Then, this afternoon while all of you are napping, I will put our very own Mitten Book *together so we can read it together before you go home today." As the children return to different areas of the classroom, some of them begin describing the types of animals they will draw during center time, while other children linger on the story rug to share their ideas with their teacher.*

Story time activities, like the one described in the vignette, happen every day in young children's classrooms around the world. Though the description of the activity is brief, you can discern some of the teacher's beliefs about how children learn by reflecting on her teaching practices and interactions with the children. Ms. Sherman invites the children to participate, she frequently involves them as the story is read, and she offers them the option to do a creative project related to the story, which will later be shared with the other children. Ms. Sherman gives the children opportunities to make decisions, but she also makes some decisions for the children, such as the selection of the book to read and the type of follow-up activity to do. Ms. Sherman's approach to this activity shows the influence of more than one philosophy or theory of learning.

Just as the history of early care and education (discussed in Chapter 6) presents a myriad of philosophies, theories, and practices, contemporary teaching practices also represent varied approaches to providing for the care and education of young children. The various approaches to early childhood education mirror different views of children, teachers, and learning environments. Even those approaches that spring from the same theoretical base interpret and apply assumptions about teaching and learning in different ways. Examining some of the more prominent approaches to contemporary early care and education helps teachers entering the field to consider and compare existing approaches to teaching young children.

Teachers in the field of child care and early education make decisions about their roles in classrooms based on their beliefs about how young children learn. Teachers who view children as active participants in the process of learning create play and learning environments that support direct involvement. Several contemporary approaches to early care and education embrace the concept of children as active participants in their own learning, while others view children in less active ways. This chapter presents a chronology of contemporary models, examines their origins and philosophical bases, and then explores practical applications of each of these approaches.

Montessori Method

CDA

COMPETENCY GOAL I
• Functional Area 3

COMPETENCY GOAL II
• Functional Areas 4–6

COMPETENCY GOAL VI
• Functional Area 13

As one of the oldest approaches to early care and education still in use today, the **Montessori method** is respected worldwide as a program of early childhood education. The Montessori method initially received limited support in the United States during the 1920s, due mainly to the momentum of the Progressive movement (discussed in Chapter 6). Initially employed primarily in private schools, this method became increasingly popular with Americans after World War II. The broader acceptance of the Montessori method can be attributed, in part, to the efforts of the American Montessori Society (AMS), founded in 1960 by Nancy Rambush, who amended some components of the model to make the method more appealing to Americans. Currently, in the United States alone, there are more than 3,000 private Montessori schools and several hundred public schools that embrace the Montessori method (Technical Support Consortium, n.d.).

Historical Foundations of the Montessori Method

Maria Montessori, founder of the Montessori method, opened her first school for young children in Rome in 1907. Named Casa dei Bambini (Children's House), the school provided for the care and education of approximately sixty children between the ages of 3 and 7. Montessori was not trained as an educator; she was, in fact, Italy's first female physician; however, her first medical assignments placed her in settings with children who were mentally challenged. As Montessori continued her hospital work and extended her education into the fields of philosophy and psychology, she developed a lifelong interest in how children learn.

In 1906, the Italian government appointed Montessori to open and operate a state-supported school for children living in poverty in the slum areas of Rome. Casa dei Bambini, established in 1907, gave Montessori opportunities to apply her ideas about teaching and learning to typically developing children. Montessori's approach to educating young children was influenced by the work of two French researchers, Jean Itard and Edouard Seguin, who used sensory stimulation in their work with children who

Maria Montessori, who developed the Montessori method, established Casa dei Bambini in Italy in 1907.

were mentally challenged (Montessori, 1967). Combining her knowledge of Itard and Seguin's work and her own extensive observation of children, Montessori documented an approach to early childhood education known as the Montessori method.

Montessori's View of Children as Learners

Montessori was interested in how children express their interests in learning through spontaneous activity, and she used her observations of their activity to develop a method of educating young children that supported their natural capacities for learning (Epstein, 1996). Montessori (1949) used the term the **absorbent mind** to describe the inquisitive nature of children's intellect. She observed that children learn best when provided with the freedom to indulge their curiosity rather than when limited by adult-imposed restraints. Montessori also noted several commonalties among young children and their approaches to learning. Montessori believed that children

- derive pleasure from repeating activities.
- concentrate for longer periods of time when actively engaged.
- show sensitivity to sensory stimulation.
- display spontaneous interest in learning.

Montessori Learning Environments

Montessori maintained that the most effective way to support children's natural inclination for exploration and learning was to carefully arrange and equip learning environments to complement children's development and nature. Montessori's notion of **prepared learning environments** remains a trademark of contemporary Montessori programs. Prepared learning environments are systematically organized for meaningful, independent learning experiences by including accessible **child-sized furnishings**, such as tables, chairs, and open shelves, and specially developed learning materials so children are free to pursue spontaneous activity with limited adult assistance or interference.

These manipulative learning materials are not only carefully sequenced according to complexity but also are self-correcting. The nature of these **didactic learning materials** supports self-paced learning experiences and *control of error,* because children receive immediate feedback as they interact with the objects, which thereby increases their inner motivation to become competent (Humphryes, 1998). For example, the "pink tower" is a set of ten pink wooden blocks, differing only in increments of size, that is to be stacked into a tower. The only way the ten-block tower will be stable is by beginning with the largest block as the base and proceeding to the next largest, and so on, until the smallest block is in place at the top of the tower. Montessori believed that children are self-motivated to learn and develop mastery over their environments and that they will persist with activities like the pink tower in order to achieve their personal learning goals. Once these goals are achieved, children will either repeat the activities to increase proficiency or seek out new learning challenges. Therefore, within the prepared environment, learning materials are displayed in an orderly fashion based on function and degree of simplicity or challenge (Humphryes, 1998).

> *Let us leave the life free to develop within the limits of good, and let us observe this inner life developing. This is the whole of our mission.*
> —Maria Montessori, *Dr. Montessori's Own Handbook* (1965, p. 134)

Montessori's series of didactic learning materials and experiences were designed to support three areas of development: motor education, sensory education, and language. Motor education, including body coordination, is supported through games and exercises. Sensory education focuses on objects, both natural and didactic, through which children move at their own paces from concrete, external manipulation and perception to abstract, internal understanding. Montessori believed that learning through the senses is integral to children's overall development. Language development occurs as children interact with teachers and other children in the multiage setting.

To Montessori, teachers are part of the prepared environment; their roles, beyond providing didactic learning materials, are to act as advisors or guides and serve as catalysts of learning rather than deliverers of information. In contemporary Montessori programs, teachers, who often stay with the same group of children for three years, routinely engage in **participant observation** as they observe children's self-directed activities, arrange learning environments, and provide instructional guidance as indicated by children's behaviors. Montessori believed that teachers who are knowledgeable in child development serve best as advisors and organizers of prepared learning environments, thereby freeing children to engage in spontaneous activity and scientific inquiry to satisfy their natural curiosity (Humphryes, 1998). Children not only have choices related to materials and activities, but they also have control over the amount of time they engage in activities. Montessori believed that children's self-discipline will emerge as they experience responsible freedom.

Through Casa dei Bambini, Montessori offered an early model of systematic teacher training. Teachers in training were expected to learn to effectively apply participant observation, demonstrate respect for and knowledge of children's natural sequence of development and motivation to learn, become skillful in development and maintenance of prepared environments, and understand and guide children's use of didactic learning materials.

Montessori classrooms are often organized into four areas of special function: practical life, sensorial, mathematics, and language (Humphryes, 1998). Practical life areas focus on care of self and environment, work habits and attention span, development of social behaviors, and control of movement. Sensorial areas foster development of the senses through interaction with varieties of sensorial materials. Mathematics areas focus on physical attributes of objects and concepts such as size, shape, and quantity and their associated symbols. Language areas provide preparation for writing through the development of the muscles of the hand and arm using materials such as movable alphabets, sandpaper letters, and tools for tracing (Montessori, 1966). Additionally, children explore concepts of culture, including the arts, and nature throughout the four areas, thereby fostering their aesthetic and scientific development (Lillard, 1996). The goals of Montessori education are to provide children with freedom for spontaneous activity as they develop inner discipline and set their own pace for learning, with security as they explore independence, and with success as they take on personal challenges.

Contemporary Montessori programs for infants and toddlers (up to age 3), preschool-age and kindergarten children (ages 4 to 7 years), primary (or lower-elementary), and intermediate (or upper-elementary) levels are represented in private and public school systems across the United States. Curriculum in contemporary Montessori programs is based on Montessori's views of human development, which she represented as a series of **sensitive periods** of intense change when children are more sensitive to stimulation followed by slower-paced periods of less sensitivity (Lillard, 1996). During sensitive periods, children focus intently on particular areas of interests, sometimes to the exclusion of other interests and activities (Humphryes, 1998). The program's **spiral curriculum**, carefully prepared by Montessori teachers who are specially trained in the Montessori method, follows the natural alternation of sensitive periods during which children are provided with opportunities for repeated, unhurried experiences in movement, language, biology, geography, history, mathematics, music, and art. Curriculum content overlaps traditional subject areas and is presented in an **interdisciplinary** manner that reflects the real world.

Throughout the 1900s, Montessori's pedagogy, or educational method, gained wide acceptance in Italy, England, the Netherlands, other European countries, and India as teachers, trained in her methods, opened Montessori schools around the world. Most training of teachers in the Montessori method was, and continues to be, through the Association Montessori Internationale (AMI), which has training centers situated in cities around the world. The AMI was founded in 1926 by Maria Montessori to safeguard the principles of her method and ensure that teacher training was true to those principles. In the United States, specialized training is also available through the American Montessori Society (AMS).

Bank Street Approach

CDA

COMPETENCY GOAL I
• Functional Area 3

COMPETENCY GOAL II
• Functional Areas 4–7

COMPETENCY GOAL III
• Functional Area 10

COMPETENCY GOAL IV
• Functional Area 11

COMPETENCY GOAL VI
• Functional Area 13

Teacher training and education is also integral to the **Bank Street approach**, or the **developmental-interaction approach**, developed in the United States in New York City during the early 1900s through the efforts of *Lucy Sprague Mitchell,* whose goal was to build a new kind of education that would improve society. Mitchell's approach was influenced by John Dewey's ideas of progressive education and learning through direct experience, Erik Erikson's theory of psychosocial development, and Jean Piaget's theory of cognitive development.

In 1916, Mitchell founded the Bureau of Educational Experiments, which was later renamed the Bank Street College of Education. In 1918, the Bureau of Educational Experiments housed the laboratory nursery school, directed by Harriet Johnson, where Mitchell researched and implemented the developmental-interaction approach. In 1926, the laboratory nursery school began serving as a clinical, or teacher training, site.

Bank Street's View of Children as Learners

The Bank Street approach defines curriculum broadly to encompass content, teaching methods, activities, materials, room arrangements, peer interactions, child-adult interactions, and home-school communication and involvement. The Bank Street approach views children holistically and makes the humanist goal of development of healthy self-concept paramount to children's psychomotor, cognitive, and affective development.

Mitchell's "Credo for Bank Street," which speaks of the potential of human beings to improve society, is mirrored in the developmental-interaction model, as teachers sensitively and flexibly support children's development of self-knowledge through direct experience and interactions with their play and learning environments. (See the Bank Street Web site at the end of this chapter.) Underlying the Bank Street approach is the assumption that motivation to make sense of our surroundings and to grow in meaningful understanding is inherent in all people (Mitchell & David, 1992). Therefore, children learn through experience as they actively explore and interact with their environments in order to connect meaningfully with the outside world.

The premise that the process of growth and maturation involves conflict also influences the Bank Street approach. Therefore, one of the objectives of the model is to meet children where they are developmentally and join with them in their explorations and interactions. This child-centered approach maintains that children are motivated to use their emerging abilities to create meaningful experiences and demonstrate competence.

Advocates of the Bank Street approach view children within a system of reciprocal influences beginning with themselves and branching outward from their families, to their schools, neighborhoods, communi-

> *With adults as well as children, interests and attitudes are not built up through words but through direct experiences.*
>
> —Lucy Sprague Mitchell, founder
> of the Bank Street College of Education
> and the developmental-interaction approach

ties, and society in general. (Chapter 13 offers discussion of these circles of influence, as theorized by Bronfenbrenner.)

Goals of the Bank Street Program

The Bank Street approach identifies four broad goals for its program. (See Table 7.1.) The first goal is to enhance children's competence by building their knowledge, skills, self-esteem, and emotional resiliency (DeVries & Kohlberg, 1990). Second, the Bank Street approach wants to help children develop their individuality by supporting their uniqueness and encouraging them to make decisions. The third goal of the Bank Street approach is to help children interact and communicate socially with others to develop a sense of belonging. The fourth goal of the model is to encourage all facets of children's creativity and help them develop awareness of the interconnected nature of their world so that they develop broad perspectives of life.

Teachers trained in the Bank Street approach learn techniques and teaching strategies to support these goals. For example, to support the goals of enhancing children's competence and fostering interaction and communication, classrooms are divided into sections reflecting an interest area, such as blocks, sensory play, literacy, music, and dramatic play. Classroom learning materials made by teachers and children are available along with commercial toys and materials. Children are invited to choose activities and to share learning experiences. Experiences in specific interest areas give children hands-on, concrete experiences and opportunities to interact with objects and with others. Typically, children initially select classroom activities that reflect their experiences outside the classroom; then, through the children's initiative, these experiences become part of their shared school experiences. The following vignette illustrates how a child's initial experience can evolve.

Four-year-old Lucas, who has just returned from a weekend visit with his grandfather, enters the classroom in a rush. Eager to gain his friends' attention, he calls out, "Guess what, guys? I can do a magic trick! My grandpa showed me how." As interested classmates and their teacher, Ms. Shirley Reynolds, gather around, Lucas performs a simple magic trick, amazing his friends by making a coin appear in the palm of his hand. Some of the other

Table 7.1 Goals of Bank Street's Developmental Interaction Approach

- To enhance children's competence
- To help children develop their individuality
- To help children interact, communicate, and develop a sense of belonging
- To encourage all facets of children's creativity
- To develop awareness of the interconnected nature of the world

Source: Adapted from A. Mitchell and J. David, Eds. (1992), *Explorations with Young Children: A Curriculum Guide from the Bank Street College of Education* (Mt. Ranier, MD: Gryphon House).

Young children build awareness of their world through hands-on exploration and interaction.

children excitedly describe their own experiences with magic and magicians. Still chattering animatedly, the small group of children gravitates toward the dramatic play interest area, where they begin to gather a variety of props like a man's hat, a couple of large scarves, and some cardboard tubes.

Ms. Reynolds smiles as she observes the children's activities and surmises that the dramatic play area is about to become a magic show. Sure enough, within a few moments, the dramatic play area has become a stage, with seating for the audience. The spontaneous magic show begins with Lucas, draped in a magic cloak fashioned from a doll's blanket, waving around his cardboard tube wand. "Ladies and gentlemen," he says dramatically, "the Great Lucas Magic Show is about to begin."

The activity described in this vignette may end as spontaneously as it began, or it may transform into an extended project as children demonstrate curiosity about optical illusions or other related concepts or themes. The Bank Street approach uses a **thematic curriculum** to integrate the exploration of general topics throughout classroom interest areas instead of artificially separating curriculum content into traditional subject areas. Thematic curriculum supports the fourth goal of the Bank Street approach—understanding the interconnected nature of the world. Teachers select themes for the curriculum based on the expressed interests of the children. This vignette offers one example of a possible thematic curriculum about magic and optical illusions.

Thematic curriculum can be preplanned by teachers or procured from commercial curriculum designers; however, in the Bank Street approach, themes are generated from the observed or expressed interests of learners and their current levels of knowledge about the facts and concepts involved. The result of this process is termed an **emergent curriculum.** This emergent curriculum is the basis for many child-centered approaches to early care and education.

Waldorf Approach

At approximately the same time that the Bank Street approach was being formalized in the United States by Lucy Sprague Mitchell and Harriet Johnson, another visionary educator, thousands of miles across the Atlantic Ocean, was developing another child-focused approach to early care and education. *Rudolf Steiner* (1861–1925), an Austrian by birth, first put his approach to education to use in 1919 in Stuttgart, Germany (then called Prussia). Some eighty years later, Steiner's **Waldorf approach** is the most widespread education system in use in nonsectarian private schools throughout the world.

In the early 1900s, after World War I, Germany, like most industrialized countries, was beset with the social consequences of the Industrial Revolution (also see Chapter 6). Schools for young children often suffered in a factory-based society that was more concerned with available laborers than with the education of children. In Stuttgart, Germany, Emil Molt, director of the Waldorf-Astoria cigarette factory, was concerned with both. He wanted to provide education for the children of his factory laborers, and it was at Molt's request that Rudolf Steiner first applied his educational philosophy in a school setting (Petrash, 2002).

CDA

COMPETENCY GOAL I
• Functional Area 3

COMPETENCY GOAL II
• Functional Areas 4–7

COMPETENCY GOAL III
• Functional Areas 8–10

COMPETENCY GOAL IV
• Functional Area 11

COMPETENCY GOAL VI
• Functional Area 13

Steiner's View of Childhood and Schooling

Steiner based his ideas about schooling on his theories about childhood. He viewed the development of children as a gradual process, which he divided into three seven-year phases (Almon, 1992). Each of the three phases of childhood has a primary force that dominates how children learn. Younger children, from birth to about age 7, channel their development through actions. During the active phase, children's primary means of learning about themselves and the world is through active play and imitation. The second phase, which includes children from ages 7 to 14, focuses on feelings as the main impetus for learning and purposeful activity. During this phase, children's imaginations are strongly connected to their development and learning. The third, and final, phase of childhood, from ages 14 to 21, centers on thinking and involves conceptual understanding brought about by asking questions and seeking answers about the nature of life as young people move closer to the potential they will realize as adults (Almon, 1992; Petrash, 2002).

Steiner, who was a strong advocate of the whole-child approach to education, proclaimed that education at all stages (preschool, grade school, and high school) must concern itself with balanced development of the hands, the heart, and the head. Steiner believed that education through balanced development was the only sure route to the willing, feeling, and thinking person. (By "willing," Steiner is referring to the willingness to engage in purposeful activity; he uses the image of hands to represent taking action.) Steiner's educational aim, to nurture the development of the whole child and thus maintain balance, is stated in the quote to the left.

> *The educator needs to remove the obstacles that stand in the way of the child's body and soul development in order to create an environment for the little one in which his or her spirit can in full freedom step forth into life.*
>
> —Rudolf Steiner, *Spiritual Ground of Education* (1990, p. 75)

Steiner believed that teachers using "enlightened educational practices" could aid parents as they helped their children develop into well-rounded individuals. All levels of Waldorf education are shaped by Steiner's "three golden rules":

- Receive each child with reverence.
- Educate the child with love.
- Let the child go forth in freedom. (Almon, 1994, pp. 28–29)

Goals of the Waldorf Approach

Preschool programs (sometimes called kindergarten) are multiage classrooms for children from ages 3 to 6 or 7. The programs follow the Waldorf approach and provide classrooms that are homelike in appearance, with subtle colors and lighting and furnishings and toys made of natural materials. Teachers encourage children to play, indoors and out, and use their imaginations. Academics have no place in the preschool classroom, although classrooms abound with language use, through informal conversations, songs, and storytelling. Caregivers invite children to listen to stories (often folktales), ask questions about the stories, retell the stories, tell their own stories, and dramatize the stories. Children develop story dramas with simple props such as a square of cloth or a stick found on the ground (Petrash, 2002). The program discourages elaborate and artificial props because they are thought to limit rather than support children's imaginative problem solving.

Teachers also encourage children to engage in craft making and other projects that require attention to detail as well as creativity. Children as young as three years old make rag dolls from yarn and use natural objects like pinecones and rocks to make imaginative seasonal displays or useful items. Throughout the school day, teachers observe children's play and demonstrate or give suggestions when children try new tasks. During much of the day, teachers engage in routine tasks, like preparing snacks or cleaning the room after projects. Steiner believed that very young children were particularly apt to learn through imitation, so teachers model daily tasks and invite children's assistance with tasks so that children learn that work is a part of each day's experience.

Some Waldorf preschool programs include kindergarten, while others identify kindergarten as a separate program; either way, the Waldorf fundamental beliefs about child development and education are maintained. Children in Waldorf kindergarten programs engage in many of the same activities that preschool-age children do; they play together informally and use their imaginations to create wonderfully complex play scenarios based on real experiences and stories. Children experience a wide variety of stories, including fairy tales, legends, myths, and biographies, which serves to broaden their cultural awareness (Almon, 1992). Kindergarten children also use their imaginary play to understand real and historical situations, which they dramatize with the assistance of classmates and teachers. Teachers participate in the children's play planning and offer information and demonstration as necessary.

Often, Waldorf kindergarten programs include children from three and one-half to six or seven years of age (Almon, 1992). The same teacher (or teachers) stays with the children throughout their kindergarten experience. As children reach the age to attend grade school (grades 1 through 8), younger children enter kindergarten in their places. The classroom has the same teacher, and about two-thirds of the same students at all times. In a Waldorf grade school, the children will most often have the same teacher for all eight years. The strategy of maintaining continuity of relationships between teachers and students over years is called **looping.** Looping has been a common practice in many European countries for several years but is less common in the United States, except in programs of European origin such as the Waldorf, Montessori, and Reggio Emilia approaches.

Reggio Emilia Approach

Another European approach to early care and education that, like the Montessori method, originated in Italy is the **Reggio Emilia approach.** Reggio Emilia is the name of a town in northern Italy that has come to represent an approach to early childhood education that embraces the contributions of young children to their own learning. The Reggio Emilia schools first gained international attention in 1991, after *Newsweek* magazine identified them as one of the ten best schools in the world (Hinckle, 1991). Over the next decade, several U.S. educators made pilgrimages to northern Italy to observe and learn about the Reggio Emilia approach to early care and education. What began as a cultural exchange resulted in a movement to reexamine early childhood education in America in light of the beliefs and practices of *Loris Malaguzzi* (1920–1994), founder of the Reggio Emilia approach to educating young children.

COMPETENCY GOAL I
• Functional Area 3

COMPETENCY GOAL II
• Functional Areas 4–7

COMPETENCY GOAL III
• Functional Areas 8–10

COMPETENCY GOAL IV
• Functional Area 11

COMPETENCY GOAL VI
• Functional Area 13

Origins of the Reggio Emilia Approach

Loris Malaguzzi, like many others returning home after World War II, was deeply affected by the devastation to his hometown of Reggio Emilia, Italy. Malaguzzi wanted to rebuild hope and community cohesiveness and believed that a community-based school for young children would be the vehicle to do so. Procuring funds from various sources, including the sale of abandoned military vehicles, Malaguzzi and the parents of young children opened the first city-managed Reggio Emilia school in the mid 1940s. The aim of the parent-managed program for young children was to encourage self-expression and active learning. More than fifty years later, thirty-three Reggio Emilia infant-toddler centers (up to age 3) and preschools (ages 3 through 6) flourish throughout Italy (Klein, 1999–2000).

The Reggio Emilia approach to early childhood education is constructivist, drawing its theoretical underpinnings from the ideas of Jean Piaget and Lev Vygotsky, psychologists who investigated interconnections between development of cognition and

Learning and teaching should not stand on opposite banks and just watch the river flow by; instead, they should embark together on a journey down the water.

—Loris Malaguzzi, Italian educator

language. (See Chapter 3.) The approach begins by recognizing the competence of all children and viewing the interdependence among children, families, and teachers as pathways to learning (Albrecht, 1996).

Compared with many other models of early childhood education, home-school communication and family involvement in Reggio Emilia neighborhood-based learning environments are more frequent and varied. Not only do family members visit, observe, and participate in their children's classrooms, but they also share decision making with teachers. Teachers attend meetings and training sessions side by side with family members. Because teachers typically stay with the same group of children for three years, family members and teachers have ample opportunities and time to build close, trusting relationships that directly benefit children (Albrecht, 1996). Another link between home and school is established by periodic *home visits* in which teachers visit children's homes. Family-school partnerships also extend into local communities, as children, family members, and teachers regularly make excursions into the community for social, cultural, and educational experiences.

Reggio Emilia Classrooms: The Environment as the Third Teacher

Reggio Emilia classrooms differ dramatically from traditional classrooms in the United States, which are designed for independent pencil-and-paper learning activities. Reggio classrooms are open, aesthetically inviting, and filled with a broad arrays of toys, materials, and resources for children to manipulate and explore as they decide how to creatively express their ideas, feelings, and interests in multiple ways. In addition to play and work spaces, Reggio schools have central open squares, or **piazzas**, where children congregate and interact with each other and with adults (Cadwell, 1997). A third feature of Reggio Emilia schools is the **atelier**, or art room, which houses a wealth of media for children to explore artistic techniques and communicate and represent ideas. The phrase "the hundred languages of children" (Edwards, Gandini, & Forman, 1993) represents the Reggio concept of "making thinking visible" via symbolic representation through media such as drawing, painting, sculpting, building, and dramatizing.

Teachers, who undergo nearly 200 hours of on-the-job and inservice training in Reggio Emilia environments, work together as **co-teachers** with shared goals and responsibilities (Albrecht, 1996; Edwards, Gandini, & Forman, 1993) rather than as lead teachers and assistant teachers. The co-teachers, together with the **atelierista**, or teacher trained in the visual arts, work as a team to scaffold children's learning experiences. These teachers view themselves as **co-constructors of knowledge** with children and embrace the total learning experience—both process and product. The **pedigogista**, or education coordinator, provides additional support and expertise by identifying professional development opportunities for teachers and family members.

Curriculum in Reggio Emilia schools is not predetermined; it develops from the ideas and interests of children, family members, and teachers. Emergent curriculum is extended through discussions and collaborations to form themes or units that last several days to several weeks. These long-term themes form the basis of the **project approach,** which facilitates children's imaginations, creativity, problem-solving skills, and communication skills as the progress of projects is documented by teachers and family members with sketches, photos, models, and captions (New, 1990). To further support the project approach, schedules in Reggio Emilia schools are flexible and determined by children's needs and interests.

High/Scope Approach

Another approach to early care and education that advocates for child-initiated activities is the **High/Scope approach,** which originated in the United States during the 1960s. Initially part of the educational research arm of the War on Poverty campaign sponsored by President Lyndon Johnson, the High/Scope approach has since evolved into the multifaceted High/Scope Educational Research Foundation. David P. Weikart, who founded the organization in 1970, explains that the foundation's name represents its "high purposes and far-reaching mission" to "improve the life chances of children and youth by promoting high-quality educational programs" (High/Scope Educational Research Foundation, n.d., pp. 1–2). Weikart and the foundation have developed active learning curricula for infants and toddlers, kindergarten, and the primary grades (grades 1 through 3) while continuing to support High/Scope's original focus—curriculum for preschool-age children. High/Scope's active learning curriculum is used throughout the United States and other countries in an estimated 300,000 formally endorsed High/Scope programs (Morrison, 1995). Additionally, High/Scope trainers have educated more than 33,000 teachers in the High/Scope approach (High/Scope Educational Research Foundation, 2000). The foundation continues to support research related to curriculum effectiveness and teacher training and actively advocates for high-quality preschool programs for young children.

CDA

COMPETENCY GOAL I
• Functional Area 3

COMPETENCY GOAL II
• Functional Areas 4–7

COMPETENCY GOAL IV
• Functional Area 11

COMPETENCY GOAL VI
• Functional Area 13

Development of the High/Scope Approach

The earliest and perhaps one of the most noteworthy studies involving the High/Scope Educational Research Foundation is the Perry Preschool Project. The research project, which took place in Ypsilanti, Michigan, and investigated the impact of preschool experiences on the subsequent school success of children living in poverty, was one of the first government-funded research studies of early childhood intervention programs (Weikart, 1989). The Perry Preschool Project, which operated between 1962 and 1967, randomly placed 123 preschool-age children who were identified as **at risk** for school failure into two groups. Approximately half of the children were assigned to the experimental group (*N* = 58) and attended a preschool program. The remaining children were designated as the control group (*N* = 65) and did not attend a preschool program. The curriculum used during the Perry Preschool Project was the forerunner of High/Scope's active learning curriculum. Initial findings indicated that those children in the experimental group, who had attended preschool, showed academic gains over children not attending preschool.

For the next twenty-three years, researchers from the High/Scope Educational Research Foundation continued to follow the lives of study participants, collecting data annually between the ages of 3 and 11 and again at ages 14, 15, 19, and 27 (Schweinhart, Barnes, & Weikart, 1993). Early findings showed that the educational performance of those children who attended preschool was higher from the end of the first year of preschool through age 7 than the educational performance of the children who had no preschool experience. Comparison of data related to participants' educational performance, social behaviors, and civic responsibility indicated that at age 27, participants who had attended the preschool program demonstrated higher levels of achievement in all areas than their counterparts who had not attended a preschool program.

Subsequent research by the High/Scope Educational Research Foundation, the Preschool Curriculum Comparison Study, examined the short-term and long-term effects of three different preschool curriculum models on academic achievement and social behavior during adolescence and adulthood. The three models were the High/Scope active learning curriculum (sometimes referred to as the cognitively oriented curriculum, or COC), the direct instruction (DISTAR) model developed by Bereiter and Englemann (1966), and the traditional thematic nursery school model (Epstein, Schweinhart, & McAdoo, 1996). The High/Scope active learning curriculum and the traditional nursery school curriculum models favor child-initiated activities, whereas the direct instruction curriculum model follows a highly structured format and does not permit child-initiated activities.

Short-term findings indicated that all three preschool curriculum models had similar positive effects on children's intellectual and academic performance (High/Scope Educational Research Foundation, 2002c). However, those gains gradually faded by the time the children were in third grade (Bredekamp, 1996).

Researchers from the High/Scope Educational Research Foundation continued to collect data from the Preschool Curriculum Comparison Project for several years. Long-term findings indicated that children from all three of the preschool curriculum models performed similarly in school and were equally likely to graduate from high school. However, further analysis of the data showed that as adolescents and adults, children who participated in either of the models that encouraged child-initiated activities (the High/Scope active learning or the traditional thematic nursery school curriculum) were

- more likely to aspire to higher levels of education.
- more likely to reach higher socioeconomic levels.
- more socially responsible.
- less likely to engage in delinquent behaviors.
- less likely to be arrested for felonies.

The study implies that high-quality preschool programs that support child-initiated activities positively affect individuals' future contributions to society (Schweinhart &

Weikart, 1997). (The upcoming section on direct instruction in this chapter provides additional information about the Preschool Curriculum Comparison Study.)

Theoretical Bases of the High/Scope Approach

The High/Scope curriculum is based on **constructivist theory**, which posits that learning occurs as individuals construct their own knowledge as they gain experience through interactions with objects and individuals in their environments. Based primarily on the theory of cognitive development espoused by Swiss biologist and psychologist Jean Piaget, the High/Scope approach maintains that children's cognitive development proceeds through a sequence of four discrete stages that are characterized by qualitatively different thinking processes. Piaget and many other constructivists view the sequence of development as fixed and consistent for all children but maintain that the rate of typical development varies along a continuum dependent on the individual child's maturation and experiences (Piaget, 1963).

Constructivists describe learning as the process of active engagement. The High/Scope curriculum incorporates this view throughout its curriculum model by providing **active learners** with a variety of options for learning through manipulating objects, interacting with others, and discovering for themselves properties of objects and relationships between objects and actions (Hohmann & Weikart, 2002). Children's knowledge emerges as they extend their physical experiences into mental representations and ultimately results in their development of conceptual understanding.

Concept understanding is also supported through children's play, particularly dramatic play. Based on the research of Sara Smilansky (1968), which investigated children's

As young children engage in active learning experiences and interact with others, they directly construct their own understanding of concepts.

play and its relationship to cognitive development, High/Scope developers incorporated learning through play into their curriculum model. As mentioned in Chapter 3, dramatic and sociodramatic play gives young children opportunities to actively demonstrate, explore, and extend their cognitive abilities.

Role of the Teacher

Much of the active learning in High/Scope classrooms is **child directed;** that is, children determine for themselves, within parameters, what they will do and how they will do it. For example, if a group of children playing in the sandbox decide they want to build a tunnel in the sand through which they can roll their toy cars, they discuss how to scoop out the tunnel and proceed with their digging. If they encounter challenges, such as the tunnel collapsing on their cars, they try to figure out how to change the tunnel to prevent its collapse. If their solutions are ineffective, they may seek help from their teacher, who will ask **open-ended questions** or make suggestions to guide the children rather than telling them how to fix the tunnel. Open-ended questions are phrased so that multiple responses are possible rather than a single correct response. For example, rather than asking "Did you try using a paper tube to brace the tunnel?" the teacher might ask "What are some of the ways you could put something between the sand and the cars to keep the tunnel from collapsing?" In response to the first question, children simply respond yes or no, but the second question is open ended and invites children to verbally explore possibilities before testing them.

Teachers implementing the High/Scope curriculum also act as **facilitators** of learning by organizing classroom environments in activity centers, or **interest areas,** filled with varieties of materials and equipment that invite active learning and problem solving through **hands-on learning** experiences with people and objects. Recommended interest areas encompass all developmental domains; they include the book area, block area, toy area, house area, woodworking area, and art area (Vogel, 2001). Within the activity areas, individuals or small groups of children direct their own learning experiences (Hohmann & Weikart, 2002), and teachers assume supportive roles to help children make decisions about their activities and follow them through to completion. No specialized materials are required; however, a variety of developmentally appropriate materials are integral to the High/Scope curriculum, which is based on active learning and physical manipulation of objects as the foundation for concept understanding.

As part of their daily routines, children make decisions about their activities using the three-part **plan-do-review** process. First, during planning time children consider what activities they plan to do and think about how they will proceed with their plans. Next, children follow through with their plans by carrying out selected activities during center-based work time (Vogel, 2001). After work time, children are presented with opportunities to reflect on, or recall, their learning experiences by describing what they did to other children and adults (Hohmann, Banet, & Weikart, 1979). Recall time usually involves a small group of children and an adult. Children are encouraged to describe both the successes and challenges they experienced during work time.

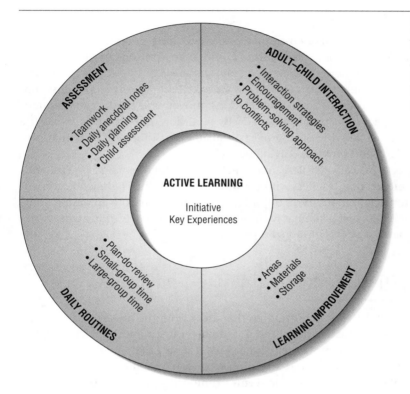

Figure 7.1 **High/Scope's ®
Wheel of Learning**

Source: From N. Vogel (2002), *Making the Most of Plan-Do-Review* (Ypsilanti, MI: High/Scope Press). Used with permission.

In addition to small-group opportunities such as planning time, center-based work time, and recall time, other components of the daily schedule include opportunities for large groups, such as **circle time** and outside time. Circle time provides opportunities for large groups of children to participate in singing, music making, and game playing. Some classrooms use circle time at the start of each day as a way for children to welcome each other and interact socially. Circle time also presents opportunities for sharing special events such as birthdays, new babies, and other exciting items that young children like to share with others. Outside time, another large-group experience, involves both children and adults in vigorous physical activities that involve the muscles of the upper and lower body (Hohmann, Banet, & Weikart, 1979).

Assessment is ongoing, as teachers observe children's behaviors and document demonstrated skills and competencies for each of the developmental domains throughout the plan-do-review process, circle time, and outside time (Schweinhart & Weikart, 1993). The High/Scope child observation record (COR) is coordinated with developmental areas, including social relations, creative expression, music and movement, language and literacy, and logic and mathematics. Behaviors in each of the developmental areas are rated on a five-point continuum designed to describe current levels of performance.

Open-Framework Model

The High/Scope program uses an **open-framework curriculum** model in which options for learning activities come from collections of appropriate learning experiences based on age-appropriate **key experiences** derived from ten areas of development encompassing all of the developmental domains. These areas include "creative representation, language and literacy, initiative and social relations, movement, music, classification, seriation, number, space, and time" (Vogel, 2001, p. 4). Key experiences serve as the frame for child-directed activities and projects available in all interest areas that promote decision-making and problem-solving behaviors.

The High/Scope Educational Research Foundation, which is based in Ypsilanti, Michigan, recommends that teachers who plan to implement the High/Scope curriculum participate in specialized inservice training workshops and follow-up training during implementation to become familiar with elements of the active learning curriculum and observation-based assessment model (Epstein, 1993).

Direct Instruction Model

CDA

COMPETENCY GOAL II
• Functional Areas 5–6

COMPETENCY GOAL V
• Functional Area 12

Another model for educating young children that arose from the research-based focus of the 1960s is the **direct instruction model.** The direct instruction model, a highly structured method of instruction that relies on formal teaching of curriculum, has some distinctive differences from the other approaches to early childhood education discussed in this chapter. First, unlike learner-centered models—like the High/Scope and Reggio Emilia approaches, which use input from the learners to develop curriculum—direct instruction is a **teacher-centered** model, using predetermined content that is sequenced by level of complexity without direct involvement of learners.

The direct instruction model also differs in how learners access the curriculum. In teacher-centered models, teachers formally deliver curriculum content to learners, usually through prepared (sometimes in the form of scripts) lectures or demonstrations, in small units of instruction that increase in difficulty or complexity as learners progress from one level to the next. In other words, learners in direct instruction models do not construct their own learning through experience; rather the teachers, who make all decisions regarding how instruction will take place and what the learners will do during the instruction, provide the content that children are expected to learn. Teachers specify how learners are to respond during the lesson, and learners receive immediate feedback concerning the accuracy of their responses. Teachers make decisions, based on learners' responses, as to whether they require further instruction at the same level of difficulty or if they are ready to move to the next level of content (Leontovich, 1999).

This process—direct instruction, learners' responses, and immediate feedback by teachers—serves as a system of control that shapes learners' behaviors. Control comes in the form of feedback through social praise or reward tokens (stickers or other prizes), which acts as **positive reinforcement.** The purpose of control through feedback is to maintain or increase desired behaviors, such as correct responses to teacher queries. The use of reinforcement to shape behaviors points to the third difference between this teacher-centered model and child-centered models. Direct instruction is based on **behaviorist** theory rather than constructivist theory; that is, direct instruction defines learning as a change in behavior (Skinner, 1953) rather than a developmental process by which individuals actively construct their own knowledge through interaction and experience (Piaget, 1963). Behaviorists believe that the environment plays the primary role in shaping all behaviors, including learning.

History of the Direct Instruction Model

The direct instruction model was developed during the 1960s by Siegfried Engelmann to teach his preschool-age sons. His sons responded so well to this method of instruction that Engelmann recorded one of the lessons and showed the film to Carl Bereiter at the University of Illinois. Bereiter, who was undertaking a project with preschool-age children at the time, was intrigued by the instructional method and hired Engelmann to teach in his preschool program (Grossen, n.d.). The focus of Bereiter's project was to find a way to improve the cognitive performance of preschool-age children who had been identified as disadvantaged due to socioeconomic status. Direct instruction, as the name implies, focuses on straightforward methods of instruction that target specific skills learners are expected to master.

One of the better known applications of direct instruction developed during the 1960s and 1970s was **DISTAR (Direct Instruction System for Teaching and Remediation).** DISTAR, a formal system for teaching reading developed by Bereiter and Engelmann (1966), was designed to accelerate learning through fast-paced, highly structured, teacher-directed lessons that provided immediate corrective feedback. The ultimate goal of DISTAR was student mastery of identified academic curriculum content—in this case, basic skills in reading (American Federation of Teachers, n.d.).

As the DISTAR model was tried out at actual school sites in field tests and was modified, it grew to encompass reading, spelling, language arts, and mathematics (Appalachia Educational Laboratory, n.d.). In order to ensure that their direct instruction model was being carried out accurately, Bereiter and Engelmann developed **scripted teaching plans** that specify word-for-word what teachers should say and do during the course of a lesson (Leontovich, 1999). Lessons are delivered to small groups of students who are grouped together according to their academic performance. Students with similar levels of performance form **homogeneous groups**, which enables teachers to have more control over curriculum content and pace of instruction, as opposed to **heterogeneous groups**, which include individuals with the differing levels of ability and performance you would typically find in a classroom. The scripts also indicate exactly how students are to respond to teachers throughout the lessons, so that teachers are able to systematically use feedback about students' performance to determine whether students have achieved mastery of targeted skills (Appalachian Educational Laboratory, n.d.). According to DISTAR developers, students are more likely to stay on task during these types of lessons, because the lessons are highly interactive, requiring frequent responses from students, either in unison or individually, as cued by teachers. More time on task equates with more time spent on teaching and learning, which results in accelerated learning (American Federation of Teachers, n.d.), the goal of direct instruction.

Research on Direct Instruction Methods

One of the first opportunities to demonstrate effectiveness of the direct instruction model occurred when it was one of the three models chosen for the Preschool Curriculum Comparison Study conducted by the High/Scope Educational Research Foundation (Schweinhart & Weikart, 1997), which began in 1967. The other models were High/Scope's active learning model (sometimes referred to as the cognitively oriented curriculum) and the traditional thematic nursery school model. The research project, which was discussed previously in this chapter, compared the short-term and long-term educational and social effects of preschool curriculum models on sixty-eight children who were living in poverty. Initial findings from the study indicated that children in all three of the curriculum models demonstrated improvements in academic and intellectual achievement through grade 3; however, those differences diminished after third grade (Bredekamp, 1996). Long-term effects of the preschool experience differed according to curriculum model. The **longitudinal study**, which collected data for several years after the preschool experience, reported that those children who participated in either of the curriculum models that endorsed child-initiated activities demonstrated higher levels of social responsibilities during adolescence and adulthood than those individuals who participated in the direct instruction model (DISTAR). However, Engelmann (1999) disputes High/Scope's report and cites inconsistent research techniques for data collection, analysis, and interpretation. Long-term effects notwithstanding, the direct instruction curriculum model did produce immediate gains in academic and intellectual scores for the children who participated in it.

DISTAR had another opportunity to test its direct instruction model during the massive billion-dollar Project Follow Through (planned variation) study commissioned by the U.S. Department of Education in 1967. The study, which involved over 20,000 children in kindergarten through grade 3, compared nine models (variations) of early childhood education by examining students' academic performance on a series of achievement tests and other measures (Leontovich, 1999). Results from the study, which was heavily criticized for its research design, were not widely disseminated. However, examination of the results shows that children who participated in DISTAR scored higher in reading, language arts, spelling, and math than children from any of the other models, which included High/Scope's active learning curriculum and the Bank Street approach (Nadler, 1998). According to Bereiter and Kurland (1981), Project Follow Through's planned variation experiment provided evidence supporting the academic effectiveness of the direct instruction model (I Can Read!, n.d.; J/P Associates, n.d.).

Many experts don't like the rigid structure of the Direct Instruction reform model, but a sizable body of research says it can raise achievement.

—Debra Viadero, "A Direct Challenge" (1999, 41)

Creative Curriculum Approach

Of the early care and education approaches discussed in this chapter, the **Creative Curriculum** approach is the most recent. According to Diane Trister Dodge, who developed the original model, the concept of a preschool curriculum framework based on classroom environment began to emerge in the 1970s when she collaborated with Helen H. Taylor at the Model Cities Centers in Washington, D.C. (Dodge, Colker, & Heroman, 2002). With the support of Taylor, Dodge and her colleagues were able to field test and fine-tune components of the curriculum before the first version was released.

The first and second versions of *The Creative Curriculum for Preschool* (1979 and 1988, respectively) focused on environmental aspects of curriculum, such as room arrangement and organization of key interest centers, as ways to improve early childhood curriculum. Using feedback from a variety of early care and education professionals and organizations, the third edition, released in 1992, maintained the environment-based focus of earlier versions and provided a curriculum framework that specified learning goals and objectives. The goals and objectives were coordinated with a comprehensive child development checklist, *The Creative Curriculum Developmental Continuum for Ages 3–5* (Teaching Strategies, Inc., 2001), for documenting children's development. The fourth edition, released in 2002, placed more emphasis on teachers' purposeful observation and documentation of children's behaviors and the role of such practices in planning curriculum (Dodge, Colker, & Heroman, 2002). The documentation system included in this edition enables teachers to more consistently align goals and teaching practices (Lunenburg, 2000).

CDA

COMPETENCY GOAL I
• Functional Areas 1–3

COMPETENCY GOAL II
• Functional Areas 4–7

COMPETENCY GOAL III
• Functional Areas 8–10

COMPETENCY GOAL IV
• Functional Area 11

Creative Curriculum Framework

The Creative Curriculum for Preschool specifies five curriculum components that revolve around the assumption that learning environments influence children's behaviors and therefore their development (Dodge, Colker, & Heroman, 2002; Goffin & Wilson, 2001). These components, which are firmly grounded in research and theory, overlap and interact to produce optimal learning environments for young children (Goffin, 2000). Each component contributes to the totality of *The Creative Curriculum for Preschool* by establishing play-based classroom environments that are responsive to the needs, interests, and abilities of individual children. Dodge et al. (2002, p. xiv) identify the following five components:

- How children develop and learn (developmental areas)
- Where children learn (learning environment)
- What children learn (body of knowledge)
- Role of the teacher
- Role of the family

Other curriculum approaches discussed in this chapter—such as the Montessori method and the Reggio Emilia and High/Scope approaches—take similar views of the role of the environment in establishing curriculum (Epstein, Schweinhart, & McAdoo,

1996). Like the High/Scope approach, *The Creative Curriculum for Preschool* clearly attaches each component of the curriculum framework to a theoretical base (Goffin, 2000), as illustrated in Figure 7.2.

The theoretical bases of the initial versions of *The Creative Curriculum for Preschool* included NAEYC's guidelines for developmentally appropriate practice (Bredekamp, 1987; Bredekamp & Copple, 1997) as well as the theories of Piaget, Erikson, and Maslow. (See Chapter 8 for information on Maslow's Hierarchy of Needs.) The theoretical base for the fourth edition of *The Creative Curriculum for Preschool* has been broadened to include the views of Vygotsky, Smilansky, and others. Additionally, Dodge, Colker, and Heroman (2002) have synthesized research findings related to early brain development and emotional resiliency throughout the curriculum framework.

Learning Environment

The Creative Curriculum for Preschool identifies three aspects of the learning environment: physical organization of the classroom, daily schedule, and relationships within the classroom community (Dodge, Colker, & Heroman, 2002). The physical aspects of the environment are perhaps the most noticeable features to an observer, because the classroom is arranged according to designated areas of interest and activity. Ideally, teachers divide the classroom into eleven specific interest areas, such as discovery and dramatic play, that are arranged and organized to foster child-directed play and social interaction. Teachers carefully plan placement as well as the organization of each interest area to provide children easy access to specialized materials and equipment and to each other.

Figure 7.2   **Framework of the Creative Curriculum for Preschool**

Source: D. T. Dodge, L. J. Colker, and C. Heroman (2002), *The Creative Curriculum ® for Preschool* 4th ed. (Washington, DC: Teaching Strategies), p. 16. Copyright 2002 by Teaching Strategies, Inc. Reprinted by permission. All rights reserved.

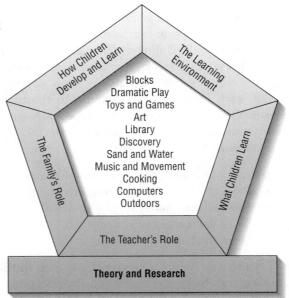

Young children gain valuable decision-making and social experience while engaging in self-directed play at interest centers.

Together, the interest areas meet the developmental needs of young children in four areas: physical, cognitive, language, and social/emotional. Individual interest areas may support one primary area of development more strongly than other areas. The eleven interest areas recommended for preschool classrooms are described in some detail in Table 7.2 (p. 170).

The second component of the Creative Curriculum learning environment, the **daily schedule,** or structure of the day, includes large blocks of unstructured **choice time** when children make decisions about where to play, how to play, and with whom to play. Caregivers encourage children to play in pairs or small groups in the interest areas, but solitary play is also possible. At other times during their day, children participate in other **daily events**, like large-group time, story time, meal time, rest time, and outdoor play. The daily structure also includes developmentally appropriate allowances for everyday routines, like arrival and departure, and for the process of transition between activities and locations (Dodge, Colker, & Heroman, 2002).

The daily structure augments the third aspect of the physical environment, relationships, by providing a variety of grouping arrangements throughout the day so that children have ample opportunities to build interpersonal connections with each other, teachers, and other adults in the classroom (Dodge, Colker, & Heroman, 2002). *The Creative Curriculum for Preschool* uses the center-based room arrangement and the daily structure to build a feeling of community within the classroom where children demonstrate respect for each other's feelings, choices, abilities, and needs. When situations arise in which children need guidance with their emotional/social behaviors, the Creative Curriculum method encourages a problem-solving approach. Multiple opportunities to interact positively with each other in the classroom build rapport among members of the learning community.

Table 7.2   Interest Areas for the Preschool Classroom

Areas of Development	
Interest Areas	**Suggested Materials**
Blocks	Wood/plastic blocks, human/animal figures, vehicles, and books related to building
Dramatic play	Male and female dress-up clothes, accessories, multicultural dolls, and child-sized furniture/toy appliances
Toys and games	Variety of puzzles/board games, toys that connect or stack, and small props
Art	Tools/materials for drawing and painting, variety of materials and objects for constructing three-dimensional art, and materials and tools to support sculpting activities
Library	Various types of children's books, including multicultural books and materials to support emergent literacy
Discovery	Classroom pets and habitats, scales, inquiry tools, nature collection, paper, and writing material
Sand and water	Sand, smocks, wide variety of containers, tools, and clean-up material
Music and movement	CD/tape/record player, children's music of various styles, instruments, and headphones
Cooking	Bowls, measuring equipment, cooking tools, and cookware
Computers	Computer(s), printer(s), software for children, paper, and diskettes
Outdoors	Sandbox, riding toys, garden and playground equipment

Source: Adapted from D. T. Dodge, L. J. Colker, & C. Heroman (2003), *The Creative Curriculum ® for Preschool*, 4th ed. (Washington, DC: Teaching Strategies), p. 16.

Creative Curriculum for Infants and Toddlers

The focus on relationship building that is so integral to *The Creative Curriculum for Preschool* (Dodge, Colker, & Heroman, 2002) is echoed in *The Creative Curriculum for Infants and Toddlers,* which was published in 1999. Throughout the curriculum framework for infants and toddlers, emphasis is placed on "building responsive relationships" (Dombro, Colker, & Dodge, 1999, p. iii) among all stakeholders—children, families, and teachers. As in the preschool curriculum framework, development of the physical classroom environment is key to the infant and toddler curriculum framework. The express purpose of the arrangement and organization of the room is to foster healthy relationships that allow young children's development to blossom.

The Creative Curriculum for Infants and Toddlers (Dombro, Colker, & Dodge, 1999) makes recommendations for the physical classroom environment related to safety, hygiene, and health and identifies environmental features that complement the special developmental needs of young infants, mobile infants, and toddlers. For example, young infants need opportunities for playtime on the floor, so providing soft washable mats is important. Mobile infants who scoot and crawl need lots of space for exploring as well as places to play with toys and cuddle with adults. Rather than specific interest centers like those in preschool classrooms, infants and toddlers need many opportunities to play with and explore a sampling of activities as the basis for their learning (Bergen, Reid, & Torelli, 2001).

Individuals who would like to use the Creative Curriculum approach can learn about the approach through self-study or with training assistance provided by Teaching Strategies, Inc. No formal coursework is required to use the approach, although training modules are available for individuals pursuing the CDA (child development associate) credential (Dodge, 1988).

Making Decisions about Curriculum Approaches

Examining contemporary approaches to early care and education enables you to gain broader awareness of the diverse interpretations and applications of theories related to child development, teaching, and learning (Katz, 1999). These models show how you may use theoretical principles as frameworks for building quality programs for the care and education of young children. (See Table 7.3.)

Table 7.3   Comparison of Early Care and Education Approaches

	Decade of origin	Child-centered curriculum	Special room arrangements	Interest areas or learning centers	Specialized learning materials	Multiage groups
Montessori method (Italy)	1900s	✓	✓		✓	✓
Bank Street approach (USA)	1920s	✓	✓	✓		
Waldorf approach (Germany)	1920s	✓	✓			✓
Reggio Emilia approach (Italy)	1940s	✓	✓			✓
High/Scope approach (USA)	1960s	✓	✓	✓		
Direct Instruction model (USA)	1960s				✓	
Creative Curriculum approach (USA)	1980s	✓	✓	✓		

Summary

- Contemporary approaches to early care and education vary according to their theoretical and philosophical bases.

Montessori Method

- The Montessori method uses a prepared environment equipped with specially designed didactic materials that enable children to work independently at their own paces.

Bank Street Approach

- The Bank Street approach views development holistically and provides learning environments where children demonstrate their competence and individuality through direct experiences and interactions.

Waldorf Approach

- The Waldorf approach emphasizes balanced education of the whole child—head, heart, and hands—through play and learning experiences.

Reggio Emilia Approach

- The Reggio Emilia approach supports emergent curriculum and open learning environments that encourage children to express themselves creatively.

High/Scope Approach

- The High/Scope approach provides an open framework curriculum based on children's development and center-based classroom environments that provide children with varied opportunities for hands-on learning.

Direct Instruction Model

- The direct instruction model is a highly structured curriculum based on the behaviorist perspective of learning.

Creative Curriculum Approach

- The Creative Curriculum approach creates child-centered learning environments by organizing the classroom into a variety of interest areas where children direct their own activities.

LEARNING ACTIVITIES

1 Discussion: Comparing Approaches to Early Care and Education. Divide the class into teams; each team selects and analyzes one of the curriculum models discussed in the chapter. Members from each team take turns describing key elements of their model in comparison to the other models. Key elements include, but are not limited to, view of the child, role of the teacher, structure of the environment, and development of curriculum.

2 Small Groups: Application. Form a small group with classmates and select one of the curriculum approaches discussed in the chapter. Briefly review the information about the model and then generate a list of materials and equipment that would be needed to set up an infant/toddler, preschool, or kindergarten classroom for the selected approach. With some curriculum models, it may be helpful to begin by sketching the classroom layout and then organizing the materials and equipment by area.

PORTFOLIO ARTIFACTS

1 Research: Curriculum Approaches. Conduct research to gain additional information about one of the early care and education approaches described in the text by visiting Web sites listed at the end of the chapter or searching the professional literature for journal articles or books. After

completing the research, write an annotated list of your newly identified resources, describing additional information about the model.

2 Graphic Representation: Personal Views on Early Care and Education. Select one of the early care and education approaches described in the chapter and list several of its key elements in the left column of a two-column chart. Use the right column of the chart to describe your views on these elements, highlighting similarities and differences.

3 Observation: Contemporary Practices in Early Care and Education. Visit an early care and education program in your community that employs a specific approach. If possible, gather program literature describing the model you are observing. After the observation, take time to reflect on the main elements of the model. Write a description of some of these elements, including your views on the use of developmentally appropriate practice (DAP) at the site you observed.

Professional Connections and Web Links

American Montessori Internationale (AMI/USA)
410 Alexander Street
Rochester, NJ 14607-1028
716-461-5920
http://www.montessori-ami.org

The Association Montessori Internationale (AMI) was founded by Maria Montessori in 1929 for the purpose of supporting the development of Montessori schools. The American branch of AMI serves as a reliable source of information about the Montessori method, provides access to approved Montessori publications and classroom materials, and disseminates information about training programs and scholarships for teachers and trainers. The Web site provides a history of AMI teacher training programs, details about Montessori pedagogy, and notices of upcoming training events in the United States. The site contains several historical photos of Montessori and her trainees.

American Montessori Society (AMS)
281 Park Avenue South, 6th floor
New York, NY 10010
212-358-1250
http://www.AmericanMontessoriSociety.org

The American Montessori Society (AMS), founded in 1960, serves as a national center for information about the Montessori method as it is applied in contemporary American culture. The society hosts annual meetings and regional seminars and workshops. AMS provides guidelines for AMS-affiliated teacher preparation programs that support team-teaching approaches and offers a procedure for accreditation. The Web site also maintains a list of children's programs and schools that are accredited. Additionally, the Web site provides background in-

formation and research findings about topics, such as multiage grouping, inclusion, music education, and learning and assessment. Various position statements on educational practices related to the Montessori method can be accessed from the site.

Association of Waldorf Schools of North America (AWSNA)
3911 Bannister Road
Fair Oaks, CA 95628
916-961-0927
http://www.awsna.org

The AWSNA is an organization of independent Waldorf schools (preschool through grade 12) and teacher preparation and certification programs. Its Web site provides general information about the Waldorf approach to education and its mission to preserve childhood and promote lifelong learning. The site provides links to other Waldorf-related associations and information about resources for families, teachers, and schools.

Bank Street School for Children
Bank Street College of Education
610 West 112th Street
New York, NY 10025-1898
212-875-4400
http://www.bankstreet.edu/html/sfc/children.html

The Bank Street School for Children is one of the children's programs associated with the Bank Street College of Education, which was founded in 1916. The school, which serves as a demonstration school and research site for the college's teacher preparation programs, provides educational programs for over 400 children between the ages of 3 and 13. The Web site provides information about child development and the school's approach to learning, which places emphasis on educating the whole child through developmentally appropriate, experience-based, interdisciplinary curriculum. The Web site also provides links to resources and other Web sites (through the college of education), such as the *New York Times* "learning network," which offers a collection of lesson plans.

High/Scope Educational Research Foundation
600 North River Street
Ypsilanti, MI 48198
313-485-2000
http://www.highscope.org

The Web site of the High/Scope Educational Research Foundation provides a collection of documents describing the High/Scope approach to education (infant/toddler through grade 5), including descriptions of many of the research projects conducted since the 1960s, such as the Perry Preschool Project. The part of the site devoted to early childhood education provides detailed descriptions of High/Scope's plan/do/review process, 58 key experiences for preschool-age children, and the child observation record (COR) assessment tool. The site also provides up-to-date information about training opportunities for educators, including institutes and conferences and annotated descriptions of publications, videos, and other staff training materials. The Web site provides on-line access to High/Scope position statements on issues in early childhood education.

Reggio Children International Center
via Guido da Castello, 12
42100 Reggio Emilia
Italy
522/455416
http://www.reggiochildren.com

This Web site is maintained by the Reggio Children International Center in Italy. It provides information about the Reggio Emilia approach to early childhood education as well as links to resources, exhibits, teacher training opportunities, and other Reggio children's programs around the world.

Reggio Children USA Office for Publications
c/o Council for Early Childhood Professional Recognition
2460 165th Street NW
Washington, DC 20009-3575
202-265-9090
http://www.cdacouncil.org/reggio/reggio-main.htm

Reggio Children USA serves as the distribution center for information, publications, and videos about the Reggio Emilia approach to early childhood education. The organization is connected to the Italian organization Reggio Children s.r.l., which sponsors study tours and other events designed to promote understanding of the approach. The organization was founded by Loris Malaguzzi in Italy in 1994 as the International Center for the Defense and Promotion of the Rights and Potential of All Children. The Reggio Children USA Web site links directly to the ERIC Clearinghouse on Elementary and Early Childhood Education (ERIC-EECE), which provides access to *ReChild,* the Reggio Children newsletter, several ERIC Digests, and various other publications and links. The site also maintains a list serve to promote electronic discussion about the approach and its use in the United States.

Rudolf Steiner College (Waldorf Education)
9200 Fair Oaks Boulevard
Fair Oaks, CA 95628
916-961-8727
http://www.steinercollege.org/waldorf.html

The official Web site for Rudolf Steiner College provides background information about Rudolf Steiner and the Waldorf approach to education as well as annotated lists of publications and other resources of interest to families, teachers, and Waldorf schools. In addition, the site provides detailed information about teacher preparation and certification programs and continuing education opportunities for practicing teachers. The site also maintains a searchable list of Waldorf schools in North America and information about employment opportunities from many of the 800 Waldorf schools worldwide.

Suggestions for Further Reading

Gandini, Lella, & Edwards, Carolyn Pope. (Eds.). (2001). *Bambini: The Italian approach to infant/toddler care.* New York: Teachers College Press.

• Gandini and Edwards provide an insightful look at early care and education practices for infants and toddlers in the United States and in Italy's locally based collaborative programs for children under age 3. Through a combination of narrative, interviews, and excerpts, the authors present a colorful, interesting, and reflective view of high-quality programming for infants and toddlers.

Petrash, Jack. (2002). *Understanding Waldorf education: Teaching from the inside out.* Beltsville, MD: Gryphon House.

- Petrash, an experienced Waldorf grade school teacher, masterfully weaves examples from his varied teaching experiences with basic information about Rudolf Steiner's Waldorf approach to education. Throughout the book, he explains and elaborates on Steiner's beliefs about child development and the role of education from preschool to high school in supporting the balanced development of the individual.

References

Albrecht, Kay. (1996). Reggio Emilia: Four key ideas. *Texas Child Care, 20*(2), 2–8.

Almon, Joan. (1992). Educating for creative thinking: The Waldorf approach. *ReVision, 15*(2), 71–78.

Almon, Joan. (1994, December). The needs of children in the 1990s: Nurturing the creative spirit. *Holistic Education Review,* 25–31.

American Federation of Teachers. (n.d.). *Seven promising programs for reading and English language arts: Direct Instruction (DI).* Retrieved on October 6, 2002, from American Federation of Teachers: http://www.aft.org/edissues/whatworks.

Appalachia Educational Laboratory. (n.d.). *Direct Instruction (K–6).* Comprehensive School Reform. Retrieved October 6, 2002, from http://www.ael.org.

Bereiter, Carl, & Engelmann, Siegfried. (1966). *Teaching disadvantaged children in preschool.* Englewood Cliffs, NJ: Prentice-Hall.

Bereiter, Carl, & Kurland, Midian. (1981). A constructive look at Follow Through results. *Interchange, 12.*

Bergen, Doris, Reid, Rebecca, & Torelli, Louis. (2001). *Educating and caring for very young children: The infant/toddler curriculum.* Williston, VT: Teachers College Press.

Bredekamp, Sue. (1996). 25 years of educating young children: The High/Scope approach to preschool education. *Young Children, 51*(4), 57–61.

Bredekamp, Sue. (Ed.). (1987). *Developmentally appropriate practice in early childhood programs serving children from birth to age 8.* Washington, DC: National Association for the Education of Young Children.

Bredekamp, Sue, & Copple, Carol. (Eds.). (1997). *Developmentally appropriate practice in early childhood programs (Rev. Ed.).* Washington, DC: National Association for the Education of Young Children.

Cadwell, Louise Boyd. (1997). *Bringing Reggio Emilia home: An innovative approach to early childhood education.* New York: Teachers College Press.

DeVries, Rheta, & Kohlberg, Lawrence. (1990). *Constructivist early education: Overview and comparison with other programs.* Washington, DC: National Association for the Education of Young Children.

Dodge, Diane Trister. (1988). *A guide for supervisors and trainers on implementing the Creative Curriculum for early childhood* (2nd ed.). Washington, DC: Teaching Strategies.

Dodge, Diane Trister, Colker, Laura J., & Heroman, Cate. (2002). *The Creative Curriculum for preschool.* Washington, DC: Teaching Strategies.

Dombro, Amy Laura, Colker, Laura J., & Dodge, Diane Trister. (1999). *The Creative Curriculum for infants and toddlers.* Washington, DC: Teaching Strategies.

Edwards, Caroline, Gandini, Lella, & Forman, George. (1993). *The hundred languages of children: The Reggio Emilia approach to early childhood education.* Norwood, NJ: Ablex.

Engelmann, Siegfried. (1999). Response to "The High/Scope Preschool Curriculum Comparison Study through age 23." *Effective School Practices, 17*(3), 18–23.

Epstein, A. S. (1993). *Training for quality: Improving early childhood programs through systematic inservice training.* Ypsilanti, MI: High/Scope Press.

Epstein, A. S., Schweinhart, Lawrence, & McAdoo, L. (1996). *Models of early childhood education.* Ypsilanti, MI: High/Scope Press.

Epstein, Paul. (1996). *Montessori's education vision.* Montessori Foundation.

Gandini, Lella, & Edwards, Carolyn Pope. (Eds.). (2001). *Bambini: The Italian approach to infant/toddler care.* New York: Teachers College Press.

Goffin, Stacie G. (2000). The role of curriculum models in early childhood education. ERIC Digest EDO-PS-00-8. ERIC Clearinghouse on Elementary and Early Childhood Education.

Goffin, Stacie G., & Wilson, C. (2001). *Curriculum models and early childhood education: Appraising the relationship* (2nd ed.). Upper Saddle River, NJ: Merrill/Prentice Hall.

Grossen, Bonnie. (Ed.). (n.d.). Overview: The story behind Project Follow Through. *ESP, 15*(1). Retrieved on October 6, 2002, from http://darkwing.uoregon.edu.

High/Scope Educational Research Foundation. (n.d.). *About the High/Scope Foundation.* Retrieved on October 15, 2000, from http://www.highscope.org/ABOMAIN.HTM.

High/Scope Educational Research Foundation. (2000). *High/Scope research: Examining and comparing effectiveness of educational programs.* Retrieved on October 15, 2000, from http://www.highscope.org/research/RESMAIN.HTM.

High/Scope Educational Research Foundation. (2002). *Research: Preschool Comparison Project: Different effects from different preschool models: High/Scope Preschool Curriculum comparison.* Retrieved on May 31, 2002, from http://www.highscope.org/Research/curriccomp.htm.

Hinckle, P. (1991). A school must rest on the idea that all children are different: Early childhood education in Reggio Emilia, Italy. *Newsweek, 118.*

Hohmann, Mary, & Weikart, David. P. (2002). *Educating young children: Active learning practices for preschool and child care programs* (2nd ed.). Ypsilanti, MI: High/Scope Press.

Hohmann, Mary, Banet, Bernard, & Weikart, David P. (1979). *Young children in action: A manual for preschool educators.* Ypsilanti, MI: High/Scope Press.

Humphryes, Janet. (1998). The developmental appropriateness of high-quality Montessori programs. *Young Children, 53*(4), 4–16.

I can read! (n.d.). Direct Instruction Research Summary: Research regarding Direct Instruction. Retrieved on October 6, 2002, from http://www.projectpro.com/ICR/Research/DI/Summary.htm.

J/P Associates. (n.d.). *Why DI?* Retrieved on October 6, 2002, from http://www.jponline.com/whydi.html.

Katz, Lilian G. (1999). Curriculum disputes in early childhood education. ERIC Digest EDO-PS-99-13. ERIC Clearinghouse on Elementary and Early Childhood Education.

Klein, Amy Sussna. (1999–2002). Different approaches to teaching: Comparing three preschool programs. *Earlychildhood LLC.* Retrieved on June 20, 2002, from http://www.earlychildhood.com/Articles/index.

Leontovich, Mary. (1999, August). *Title I report: Directly controversial: "Direct Instruction" makes enemies, converts.* Retrieved on October 6, 2002, from http://www.titlei.com/samples/direct.htm.

Lillard, Paula Polk. (1996). *Montessori today: A comprehensive approach to education from birth to adulthood.* New York: Schocken Books.

Lunenberg, Fred C. (2000). Early childhood education programs can make a difference in academic, economic and social areas. In Britannica.com, retrieved July 30, 2001, from http://search.britannica.com/magazine/article?content_id=158077&pager.offset=10.

Mitchell, Anne, & David, Judy. (Eds.). (1992). *Explorations with young children: A curriculum guide from the Bank Street College of Education.* Mt. Rainer, MD: Gryphon House.

Montessori, Maria. (1949). *The absorbent mind.* Madras: Kalashetra Publications.

Montessori, Maria. (1965). *Dr. Montessori's own handbook.* New York: Schocken Books.

Montessori, Maria. (1966). *The secret of childhood.* New York: Ballentine Books.

Montessori, Maria. (1967). *The discovery of the child.* New York: Ballentine Books.

Morrison, G. (1995). *Early childhood education today* (6th ed.). Englewood Cliffs, NJ: Merrill.

Nadler, Richard. (1998). Failing grade: Siegfried Engelmann developed an amazingly effective method of teaching. Why don't you know his name? Retrieved on October 6, 2002, from National Review: http://www.nationalreview.com/01jun98/nadler060198.html.

New, Rebecca S. (1990). Excellent early education: A city in Italy has it. *Young Children, 45*(6), 4–10.

New, Rebecca S. (1993). Reggio Emilia: Some lessons for U.S. educators. ERIC Digest EDO-PS-93-3. ERIC Clearinghouse on Elementary and Early Childhood Education.

Petrash, Jack. (2002). *Understanding Waldorf education: Teaching from the inside out.* Beltsville, MD: Gryphon House.

Piaget, Jean. (1963). *The origins of intelligence in children* (M. Cook, Trans.). New York: Norton. (Original work published in 1936.)

Schweinhart, Lawrence J., & Weikart, David P. (1993). Success by empowerment: The High/Scope Perry Preschool Study through age 27. *Young Children, 49*(1), 54–58.

Schweinhart, Lawrence J., & Weikart, David P. (1997). *Lasting differences: The High/Scope Preschool Curriculum Comparison Study through age 23.* Monographs of the High/Scope Educational Research Foundation, no. 12. Ypsilanti, MI: High/Scope Press.

Schweinhart, Lawrence J., Barnes, H. V., & Weikart, David. P. (1993). Significant benefits: The High/Scope Perry Preschool Study through age 27. Monographs of the High/Scope Educational Research Foundation, no. 10. Ypsilanti, MI: High/Scope Press.

Skinner, B. F. (1953). *Science and human behavior.* New York: Macmillan.

Smilansky, Sara. (1968). *The effects of play on disadvantaged children.* New York: Wiley.

Steiner, R. (1990). Spiritual ground of education. Blauvelt, NY: Spiritual Science Library.

Teaching Strategies, Inc. (2001). *The Creative Curriculum developmental continuum for ages 3–5: Individual child profile.* Washington, DC: Author.

Technical Support Consortium. (n.d.). *Best practices: A profile: Montessori.* Retrieved on October 6, 2002, from http://www.coe.wayne.edu/TSC/monte.html.

Viadero, Debra. (1999). A direct challenge. *Education Week, 18*(27), 41–43.

Vogel, Nancy. (2001). *Making the most of plan-do-review.* Ypsilanti, MI: High/Scope Press.

Weikart, David P. (1989). Hard choices in early childhood care and education: View to the future. *Young Children, 44*(3), 25–30.

After reading this chapter and completing the related activities, you should be able to

- Distinguish between teacher roles of caregiver and nurturer, learning facilitator, observer and assessor of development, professional, and advocate
- Discuss how teacher roles affect relationships with others and the development of young children
- Discuss NAEYC's Code of Ethical Conduct as it relates to teacher roles and educational settings
- Distinguish the stages of teacher development
- Describe how networking with other professionals supports professional development
- Identify related professional organizations
- Use self-evaluation techniques and reflection

Roles of Early Childhood Teachers

Suzanne Parsons sits next to her mentor teacher, Greg Robbins, and looks out the classroom window where several children and teachers are enjoying the warm spring weather. Pulling her attention back to her meeting with Greg, who is still looking at her professional portfolio, Suzanne takes a deep breath and waits for him to begin his review of her teaching performance over the last three months. During those months, Suzanne has developed a deep appreciation for Greg's contemplative manner and professionalism, but at the moment she just wishes he would say something. Closing the portfolio, Greg taps his fingers on the cover and asks, "Suzanne, tell me again why you became a teacher." Suzanne stares at him for a moment, somewhat confused by the question, since they had talked about her decision to teach many times in the first few weeks of her internship. Suzanne meets Greg's gaze and queries, "Greg, could I ask what that has to do with my performance assessment? I'll admit I didn't expect that question."

Greg laughs and then elaborates on his question: "What I'm asking is, do you still have the same reasons for wanting to teach? Remember you told me that you wanted to make a difference in a child's life. Do you still feel that way?" "Well sure, more than ever," replies Suzanne. Greg smiles. "Good, that is what I needed to know. I know you expect me to go through each part of your portfolio and tell you what I see in your teaching—but I believe you know yourself better than anyone else does, so I am going to ask you to describe yourself in each of these teacher roles. If there is something in your portfolio that demonstrates what you are saying in your self-evaluation, then we'll take a closer look at it. You can tell me how the

CHAPTER 8

artifact represents your abilities and ideas, and I will offer comments and suggestions for you to consider.

"We'll start with your role as a caregiver and nurturer; then we'll move on to the second role of facilitator of learning and so forth. We both know these teacher roles overlap, so don't be concerned if your comments address more than one role. I like to think of it as the 'whole-teacher' approach. Just like the whole-child approach, the separate roles are recognizable, but unless they are considered holistically, your view of the person is skewed. Being a good teacher means carrying out the multiple roles simultaneously and seamlessly. Are you ready to begin?" Suzanne, who is feeling much more relaxed now, answers enthusiastically, "Yes, I am. It's funny that I never thought of the whole-teacher thing. I considered each of the roles as a separate category. When I put my portfolio together, I had several artifacts that fit in more than one place and I got frustrated trying to decide where to place them. In the end, I made copies of a couple of things and put them in both sections as extras. What you said makes so much sense. Whenever I'm planning an activity, I make sure it's safe and interesting, I try to figure out how I will know how the child is doing, and I try to make sure the activity is sensitive to each child's needs and cultures. That's every role, isn't it?" Greg smiles and says, "Yes, you are on the right track. Tell me more."

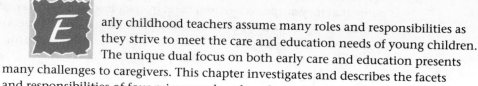 arly childhood teachers assume many roles and responsibilities as they strive to meet the care and education needs of young children. The unique dual focus on both early care and education presents many challenges to caregivers. This chapter investigates and describes the facets and responsibilities of four primary roles of teachers of young children—caregivers, facilitators, observers, and professionals and advocates. The chapter explores the unique features of each role and the relationship of each role to the well-being of young children.

Teachers as Caregivers and Nurturers of Young Children

Keeping young children safe is, of course, a primary function of early childhood teachers; young children depend on reliable adults in their worlds to safeguard them both physically and emotionally. Protecting children from harm and tending to their custodial needs is caregiving, but only in the strictest sense of the word. Teachers of young children provide caregiving within the framework of nurturing; that is, caregiving is not done in the functional sense alone. Instead, caregiving and nurturing are interwoven in the processes of valuing and respecting children for their uniqueness and of promoting their development so they can safely and confidently explore their abilities.

According to American psychologist Abraham Maslow (1908–1970), human beings are motivated by internal forces centered on a hierarchy of primary needs, meaning that needs at lower levels take precedence over needs at higher levels (Boeree, 1998). Individuals initially are most motivated to satisfy the lower levels of needs—the deficiency needs—before moving up the hierarchy to the next levels (Maslow, 1968). Figure 8.1 illustrates the levels of Maslow's **hierachy of needs**. The two lowest levels of the hierarchy are composed of basic survival needs for food, water, and shelter. Until those needs are met, individuals are less motivated by needs at higher levels (Maslow, 1970).

To fulfill their roles as caregivers and nurturers means that teachers' first priority is providing for children's physical needs. In other words, if children are hungry, they need to be fed; if they are thirsty, they need water. Although teachers cannot provide permanent shelter, they can provide temporary shelter in their classrooms and perhaps connect families with agencies to help them secure permanent shelter. When children's survival needs are met, they become more motivated by needs associated with physical and psychological safety; this is where the role of caregiver and nurturer becomes paramount.

Within early care and education settings, teachers design spaces where young children can safely play and learn without fear of physical hazards and with a sense of security that they are protected from harm by their teachers, who have their best interests at heart. Using knowledge of child development as a guide, teachers design classrooms that reflect the developmental needs of children who will be utilizing them. For example, teachers of two-year-old children prepare classrooms to provide space where children are free to move around so they can develop the large muscles of their bodies as they run and climb. At the same time, these teachers recognize that children of this age have little awareness of safe running and climbing versus unsafe running and climbing. Therefore, teachers provide soft resilient surfaces underneath climbing equipment to reduce the threat of serious injury and arrange equipment so children can be easily observed and closely supervised. These teachers create safe environments where the children can be active without undue risk. Providing for the physical safety of young children is a major emphasis of guidelines from professional organizations as well as regulatory agencies.

Another aspect of the need for safety has do to with psychological safety rather than physical safety (Maslow, 1968). Children's feelings of emotional security are supported in environments where they have opportunities to build stable, healthy relationships with others and where reasonable and consistent boundaries have been set for their explorations. Infants and toddlers are particularly sensitive to inconsistent staffing and practices because they are more reliant on caregivers than are older children. In early childhood programs where there is a high rate of staff turnover or

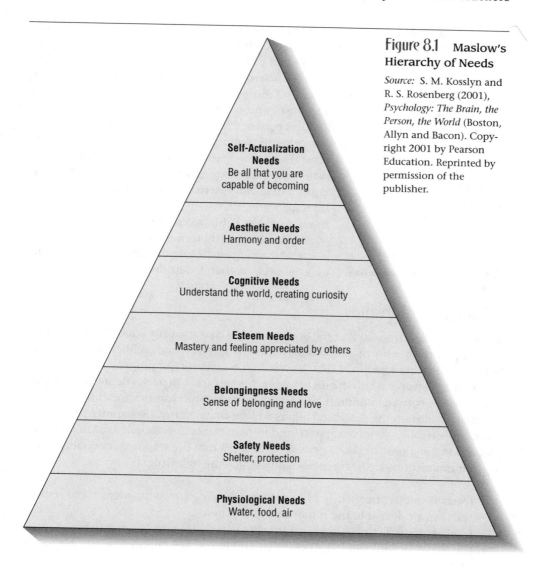

Figure 8.1 **Maslow's Hierarchy of Needs**

Source: S. M. Kosslyn and R. S. Rosenberg (2001), *Psychology: The Brain, the Person, the World* (Boston, Allyn and Bacon). Copyright 2001 by Pearson Education. Reprinted by permission of the publisher.

where caregivers respond to infants' needs inconsistently, very young children are more likely to feel anxious and less likely to confidently explore their environments (Honig, 2002).

In addition to the need for safety and security, children need to feel that they are accepted, which corresponds to the third level of Maslow's hierarchy of needs—the need for belonging. Children feel accepted in early care and education environments that are developmentally appropriate because such classrooms invite them to participate actively, without fear of reprisal for any minor infractions of adult-centered expectations or rules that are outside of their developmental range. For example, two-year-old children frequently use their bodies rather than words to express their emotions. Sometimes these expressions of emotion are full-fledged tantrums in which they lie on the floor and scream loudly; tantrums are to be expected with young children who, as yet, have limited spoken language abilities. Teachers who work with two-year-olds on a daily basis accept that they may occasionally become so distraught that they express their frustrations through tantrums. These teachers let the tantrums subside and then redirect the children to new activities when the incident has passed. Children are not punished or made to feel guilty; they are guided by the teacher to calm themselves before returning to their play. The need to belong, to feel accepted and loved, remains important throughout the life span. Acceptance implies that others welcome us for who we are rather than for whom they wish us to be. Sensitive caregivers show respect for children's individual natures and interests by following their cues and preparing responsive play and learning environments filled with open-ended experiences to accommodate diverse needs.

> *A musician must make music, an artist must paint, a poet must write, if he is to be ultimately at peace with himself. What a man can be, he must be.*
>
> —Abraham Maslow, *Motivation and Personality* (1954)

Building Relationships

Research supports the idea that the quality of child care and early education is partly determined by the quality of interactions between caregivers and children (Honig, 2002). In fact, the first standard in NAEYC's accreditation criteria (for program evaluation) relates to interpersonal relationships between children and teachers. The standard begins, "Interactions between children and adults provide opportunities for children to develop an understanding of self and others and are characterized by warmth, personal respect, individuality, positive support, and responsiveness" (National Academy of Early Childhood Programs, 1991). Observable indicators that the standard for quality child-to-adult interactions are being met would include the following:

- Teachers interact frequently with children, showing affection, interest, and respect.
- Teachers are available and responsive to children.
- Teachers speak with children in a friendly, positive, courteous manner.
- Teachers talk with individual children and encourage children of all ages to use language.
- Teachers use a variety of teaching strategies to enhance children's learning and development throughout the day.

Each of these indicators contributes to building solid, responsive relationships between children and teachers. These early social attachments form the patterns for relationship building that children will use in subsequent relationships (Honig, 2002). Several respected program evaluation models, such as Creative Curriculum's "Self-Assessment Goals and Objectives for Caregivers/Teachers," include elements that identify stable relationships between children and teachers as indicators of high-quality early care and education (Dombro, Colker, & Dodge, 1999).

Regulation and Licensing of Early Care and Education Programs

Safeguarding children's physical and psychological well-being is also a major function of regulatory agencies charged with inspecting and licensing child care centers. In the United States, there is no national system in place to regulate and license child care centers (Kagan, 1990); however, each state designates agencies to develop, implement, and enforce regulations for home-based and center-based child care and early education programs. These **licensing regulations**, which vary widely from state to state, set minimum requirements for safety, health, and nutrition. (See Chapter 11 for additional information about safety, health, and nutrition in early childhood programs.)

In addition, each state specifies allowable maximums for group size and staff-child ratio, because these factors directly affect level of supervision, which, in turn, affects children's safety. *Group size* refers to the maximum number of children permitted in individual classrooms, and the *staff-child ratio* refers to the number of children assigned per staff member. Maximum allowances for group sizes and staff-child ratios vary not only from state to state, but also by ages of the children. Many states set group size caps for children younger than three years but do not limit group sizes for children age 3 and over. Because smaller group sizes and lower staff-child ratios have been identified as key indicators of quality, not only for safety issues but also for child-teacher interactions, the National Association for the Education of Young Children (1991) has made recommendations for "maximum staff-child ratios with group size." Their recommendations are as follows:

- Infants (birth to 12 months)—group size 8, ratio 1:4
- Toddlers (12 to 24 months)—group size 12, ratio 1:4; or group size 10, ratio 1:5
- Two-year-olds (24 to 30 months)—group size 12, ratio 1:6
- Two-year-olds (30 to 36 months)—group size 14, ratio 1:7
- Three-, four-, or five-year-olds—group size 20, ratio 1:10
- Kindergartners—group size 24, ratio 1:12
- Six- to eight-year-olds or nine- to twelve-year-olds—group size 30, ratio 1:15

There is concern that in many states, some programs for young children are exempt from licensing and thus are not required to follow state regulations. Exempted programs may include those associated with religious organizations, such as churches, and those entities that provide programs for young children only on a part-day basis, such as preschool programs that meet four or fewer hours per day. In these cases, few safeguards are in place to ascertain that these programs are providing safe and high-quality programs for young children. Although there are many high-quality exempt programs across the United States, there are few safety nets to stop those programs that choose to provide less-than-satisfactory environments for young children. NAEYC's (1987a) position statement on licensing and regulation summarizes its concerns and recommends that all child care programs be licensed to ensure high-quality child care for all children.

Another aspect of licensing regulations is setting minimum educational and experiential requirements for teachers in home-based and center-based child care programs; however, more than thirty states require no training related to child development or early childhood education (Children's Defense Fund, 2002). Of the states that do set minimum qualifications for child care staff, those qualifications range from a few hours of on-the-job training to formal credentials or degrees. Higher levels of specialized education and training of teachers have been linked to early childhood program quality in several studies (Whitebook, Howes, & Phillips, 1998). Because there is so little agreement among the states, the National Association for the Education of Young Children (NAEYC) has made recommendations for levels of education and experience for teachers in early childhood programs. (See Chapter 5 for additional information about NAEYC's recommendations for teacher education and experience.) Qualified teachers contribute to high-quality child care and early education, not only in the realm of children's physical and psychological safety and well-being, but also with relationship to their learning experiences.

Teachers as Facilitators of Learning

CDA

COMPETENCY GOAL II
• Functional Areas 4–7

When children's needs for survival, safety, and belonging have been met, they are ready to learn. Teachers as facilitators of learning keep in mind children's basic needs as they shape classroom spaces and organize developmentally appropriate play and learning opportunities for young children. According to Maslow (1968), the fourth level of need in the hierarchy is the need for self-esteem, which is best supported when children view themselves as competent and recognize their contributions to others as valuable. Additionally, children will seek confirmation of their abilities through approval and recognition by others. Play and learning environments that support self-directed play send children the message that they are trusted to make good decisions about their own activities and learning.

As children gain confidence in their abilities to learn, they are more likely to accept cognitive challenges and to extend their explorations, which relates to Maslow's fifth level of the hierarchy of needs—the need for intellectual achievement that comes from understanding. Part of the reason children are motivated to learn about new concepts and try out new skills is because they feel the need to be successful learners and to have others acknowledge their accomplishments. About the same time that children begin to display self-conscious emotions, such as shame and guilt, they are also able to demonstrate self-approval or pride. Open-ended learning experiences that encourage creativity and problem solving support children's need to demonstrate their abilities. For example, a four-year-old boy who has tried unsuccessfully several times to construct a paper airplane that will fly likely will be eager to demonstrate to classmates and teachers his successful paper airplane and explain how he created it. Because the child used his own abilities to problem solve, rather than relying on a teacher telling him how to solve the poroblem, his sense of competence and intellectual achievement was enhanced. Early learning experiences that encourage children to actively explore and extend themselves intellectually provide for children's optimum growth and development.

Child-Centered Teaching Practices

In order to plan and implement developmentally appropriate activities and experiences for young children, teachers need to consider not only what concepts or skills children are going to learn about, but also how the learning is going to take place—the teaching and learning strategies teachers use (Bredekamp & Copple, 1997). A third vital factor to consider as a facilitator of learning is how to determine children's current level of performance, which involves the observation, documentation, and interpretation of behaviors and using information gleaned from these measures to inform practice. Early childhood education practices that are child centered begin with the child rather than with the teacher or a predetermined curriculum; therefore, knowledge of the child is essential. (Chapter 9 provides additional information about curriculum strategies that are child centered.) Teachers gain a view of the whole child as they observe and interact with children in a variety of situations.

Early childhood education is concerned with promoting the positive development of the whole child; that is, it aims to support all of the developmental domains. Early childhood educators acknowledge that the psychomotor, cognitive, and affective domains overlap and interact with one another and that young children learn best when they are fully engaged in their own learning (Bredekamp & Copple, 1997). In order to promote development across developmental domains, early care and education settings need to provide activities and experiences that encourage children to participate actively and construct their own understandings.

Reflective Teaching and Decision Making

Within the role of teacher as facilitator lies the role of teacher as decision maker. Teachers who are effective facilitators of children's learning make dozens of decisions daily; some are spontaneous, and others are considered more deeply. These decisions encompass every aspect of the early care and education environment, and most are informed by our knowledge of child development and best practice. For example, the act of selecting a picture book to share with a group of preschool-age children seems like a minor matter. However, in this situation the teacher must decide whether the content of the story is developmentally appropriate, how the story will be read, when it will be read, and how long it will take to read it, among other considerations. The teacher ultimately makes a decision to read the book or not, based on knowledge of child development as well as knowledge of the children in the classroom—their ages, individual needs, and diverse linguistic and cultural backgrounds. Of course, listing all of the factors to consider in this decision makes the process seem cumbersome and time consuming. However, experienced teachers move through the process so quickly that decisions like these seem almost spontaneous. Some situations call for a more deliberate decision-making process; for example, deciding to refer a child for assessment for special needs requires more consideration than deciding which children's book to read.

Reflecting on decisions during the decision-making process or after they are made is a form of assessment that allows teachers to be intentional in their choices and actions. Reflective decision making is the underlying premise of NAEYC's program for voluntary accreditation of early childhood programs.

Accreditation of Early Care and Education Programs A national system for program evaluation that encourages the use of reflective teaching and decision making is the voluntary accreditation process. NAEYC mounted a national effort to encourage early childhood programs to voluntarily assume leadership in providing high-quality early care and education programs. Through its National Academy of Early Childhood Programs, NAEYC has developed criteria and procedures for voluntary accreditation for many types of early care and education programs (NAEYC, 1991). Programs that want to receive accreditation begin the process by completing a self-study document that asks programs to rate themselves on indicators in eight broad areas related to quality early care and education programs. (This document can be viewed on NAEYC's Web site listed at the end of this chapter.) After completing the self-study and indicating that the standards have been met, the program submits the study to the academy, which reviews the document before organizing a team comprised of local early childhood professionals to validate the information presented in the self-study document.

Teachers as Observers and Assessors of Children's Development

CDA

COMPETENCY GOAL II
• Functional Areas 4–7

COMPETENCY GOAL III
• Functional Areas 8–9

COMPETENCY GOAL IV
• Functional Area 11

COMPETENCY GOAL V
• Functional Area 12

COMPETENCY GOAL VI
• Functional Area 13

Although each of the roles of teachers discussed in this chapter are of equal importance, the role of observer and assessor of children's development is perhaps the most encompassing. Careful observation of children provides valuable information about their development in psychomotor, cognitive, and affective domains, which enables early childhood teachers to differentiate instruction and more effectively meet the needs of the whole child. Data collected from observations can be scrutinized and used to identify potential areas of special need for children and to communicate with family members about their children's developmental progress. However, the uses of observation are not limited to children's development; they can also be used to provide objective information about teacher performance and professional development. A third area where observational data are useful is in assessing the effectiveness of learning environments. Observation can be used to assess learning environments not only in terms of safety and health, but also with regard to such diverse factors as cultural sensitivity, accessibility for individuals with special needs, popularity of learning centers, opportunities for creative expression, and many more possibilities. Conducting thorough, objective observations helps to maintain the overall quality of early care and education programs.

Observation and Documentation of Children's Behavior and Development

Observing young children as they play and interact with others within their home, play, and learning environments offers many benefits to teachers, children, and their families. **Observation** of children's behaviors provides caregivers with documented, in-depth evidence of children's growth and development (Beaty, 2002). Observation focuses on what children can do, rather than what they are as yet unable to do. In addition to aiding the efforts of caregivers to assess children's developmental progress, observation helps caregivers make informed decisions about the children's current and future learning experiences. Children benefit because caregivers are able to individualize learning experiences, based, in part, on their observations of behavior. Additionally, observation enables caregivers to pinpoint stages of development and document developmental concerns so that early intervention strategies can be delivered in a timely manner. Families of young children also benefit from observations, as caregivers share valuable information about children's development. In turn, family members enrich caregivers' understanding of their children by sharing personal observations and reflections about children's accomplishments, challenges, and role within the family.

> *The most important single factor influencing learning is what the learner already knows. Ascertain this and teach him accordingly.*
>
> David Ausubel, *Educational Psychology: A Cognitive View* (1968)

Being an Effective Observer **Naturalistic observation**—that is, observation of children's day-to-day behaviors in their natural settings—offers the most authentic form of observation. **Authentic assessment** avoids contrived or artificial situations and experiences and attempts to observe and record children's typical behaviors as they happen. Naturalistic observation avoids the use of situations in which children's behaviors may be influenced by environmental factors. The observer attempts to be unobtrusive and to document children's behaviors without interfering in the situation (Cohen & Stern, 1978).

For example, teachers who want information about children's emotional development—perhaps how they express their feelings—could orchestrate activities that place children in situations where they would be asked to respond emotionally. For instance, the teacher could read aloud a storybook about two children who wanted the same toy and ask the children listening to the story what they would do if they wanted the same toy as someone else. The children's responses would provide the teacher with some information about the children's abilities to solve problems and express emotions. However, the children's responses in this contrived situation might be influenced by the proximity of the teacher or by the fact that the situation is pretend and not real.

Compare this scenario to one in which the teacher observes children on the playground as they interact with peers. Two preschool-age children have been sitting in the sandbox together, digging with shovels. Simultaneously, both children reach for a plastic dump truck. Now the teacher will be able to observe how these children naturally react in a real situation where both want the same toy. The teacher documents not only the behaviors observed but also the conversations of the two children as they attempt to solve the problem. It is clear that this real-life situation, rather than the contrived one using the storybook example, will give the teacher more accurate information about the natural behaviors of these children's emotional and problem-solving abilities.

The contrived situation using the storybook example provides important clues about the children's behavior in relation to potentially emotional situations, but it does not provide a complete picture of the children's emotional development unless their responses are considered in combination with other observations from a variety of situations. Teachers have to consider various factors that might influence children's behavior, such as the setting, the other individuals involved, the time of day, or even children's health at the time of the observation. To be able to accurately interpret information gleaned from observations, teachers must consider both internal and external factors that might influence behavior (Cohen & Stern, 1978). By reviewing a collection of observations taken over a period of time, teachers are better able to identify patterns of behavior and make well-informed decisions about children.

Teachers can record their observations of children's behavior in many ways; generally, the purpose of the observation determines the mode of **documentation.** Most documentation is written, although audio and visual documentation is sometimes used. Teachers can also collect samples of children's drawings, writings, and other work to provide a record of behavior and performance.

Regardless of the format in which the behavior is documented, there are three essential pieces of information that need to be included. First, all observations should be *dated.* Recording the actual time the behavior occurred is also helpful. Documenting the date on all evidence of behavior enables the teacher to sequence the observations

Teachers gain valuable information about children's development and interests as they observe their play activities.

and construct a developmental timeline or pattern of behavior. Second, all observations should *identify the individual(s) being observed.* In addition to the individual's name, it is helpful to record the child's age (to the nearest month) as well as a brief objective description of the individual(s) included in the observation. (Care must be taken to safeguard the confidentiality of individuals; this issue is discussed in more detail later in this chapter.) The third piece of information essential to documentation of behaviors is the *name of the person who conducted the observation and recorded the information.* The person who conducted the observation may be able to elaborate on the written documentation if additional details are needed before the behaviors can be interpreted. Taken together, these three pieces of information provide a frame of reference for the observation and a way to organize and validate the information.

Written documentation needs to provide an **objective** description of actual behaviors observed by the teacher or other adult. Objective observations record accurate, detailed descriptions of behaviors while avoiding **subjective** comments (Beaty, 2002). Subjective comments include opinions, interpretations, and conclusions and will make documentation of observed behaviors less accurate and therefore less useful.

The desire to offer opinions along with descriptions of observed behavior is quite natural, but such subjective material detracts from the usefulness of the observation. Suppose the teacher records the following statement: "Amy is usually friendly and playful, but today she is really crabby." You learned nothing about Amy's actual behavior from this observation. The teacher did not record what he saw and heard; rather, he formed an opinion of Amy's behavior based on his previous knowledge of the child. While it is appropriate to record the change in Amy's behavior, this record will not be useful to other caregivers or to Amy's family, because the actual behaviors or situations in which the behaviors occurred were not documented.

Another type of subjective documentation occurs when the teacher interprets the behaviors observed. For example, if the teacher's documentation of an observed event states that "the child appeared angry," the teacher has interpreted but not actually offered an objective description of the child's behavior. If the teacher documents that "the child stomped her right foot repeatedly while clenching her hands into fists," the reader of the observation gets a more detailed description of the actual behaviors without the observer's interpretation of the behavior. When teachers are familiar with the children they are observing, their interpretations of behavior may be useful; however, these comments should be separated from the actual record of behavior. Many observation or documentation forms provide a separate space or column for "comments" by the observer. These comments may elaborate on the situation surrounding the targeted behavior or even offer explanations, but these comments should be separated from the objective record of the behaviors.

What if the teacher added to the statement about the child stomping her foot and making fists the following reason: "She wanted to be first to ride the new tricycle and another child was first instead." The teacher has not described any additional behaviors but instead has attempted to draw conclusions about what events provoked the child's behavior. The teacher's conclusions may be accurate but they are still subjective and, as such, should be separated from the objective documentation of actual observed behaviors.

Another oversight that may occur when documenting behaviors is lack of details. Suppose the caregiver documented the following behavior: "Susie and Johnny played ball." This statement is accurate; it describes an actual behavior rather than interpreting or drawing conclusions. But the statement still lacks something. Picture in your mind exactly what Susie and Johnny are doing with the ball. Are they sitting and rolling the ball back and forth? Are they standing and tossing the ball back and forth? Is each perhaps engaged in a different behavior? Maybe Susie is holding a bat ready to swing and Johnny is pitching the ball to her. The statement "Susie and Johnny played ball" is too generic; it lacks details. Because it provides no details about the behavior, the reader of the observation fills in the blanks and mentally visualizes a behavior that hasn't been described. Consider the difference when the following details are added: "Susie and Johnny stood about three feet apart on the concrete patio. Susie used both hands to bounce the basketball to Johnny. Johnny caught the basketball with both hands and then bounced it back to Susie, using only his right hand. Johnny laughed as he bounced the basketball back to Susie and said, 'This is a fun game. Let's do it some more.' " These added details provide more information on the behaviors and reduce the chances of inaccuracy. These details enable the reader of the documented behaviors to get information about Susie and Johnny's physical motor development, social development, and cognitive/language development.

Documenting Behavior and Development   There are various formats that can be used to document observations of behavior and development. The most general form for recording observation data is the **running record.** Running records are continuous documentation of behaviors for a block of time. The observer begins by recording the general information, such as the date and beginning time of the observation, and then uses a three-column method to record observed behaviors. (See Figure 8.2a.) The time a behavior occurs is listed in the far left column, labeled "Time," and new times are entered when there are significant shifts in behavior, such as a change of location or a behavior that differs significantly from what has been happening. It is not necessary to record the time every minute. For example, at 9:02 you observe that the child is sitting alone on the carpet, rolling toy vehicles into an empty box, and this behavior continues for five minutes, when the child suddenly stands up and dumps all of the vehicles into the trash can. This behavior differs significantly from what you had been observing, so you record 9:07 on the running record as you objectively document the actual behavior in the middle column, labeled "Observation Notes." The far right column, labeled "Comments," is for notes to yourself about connections to previous behaviors or remarks that will help you recall what you were thinking when you recorded the observed behavior. For example, in this situation where the child is alone on the carpet, the observer might record a comment such as "It is really unusual that he is playing by himself; he typically plays with at least two other boys." This comment may help in later review of the running record of this incident. Running records can be used to record behaviors of individuals, groups, or events (Billman & Sherman, 2003).

Figure 8.2 Observation and Documentation Records

(a) **Running Record**

Person conducting the observation _____

Date of observation _____

Time of observation _____

Time	Observation Notes	Comments

(b) **Anecdotal Record**

Child's Name _____

Date of observation _____

Time of observation _____

Setting/circumstances _____

Person conducting observation _____

Observation Notes _____

_____

Comments _____

_____

Another commonly used method for recording behavior is the **anecdotal record.** Anecdotal records are written documentation of single significant events, such as reaching developmental milestones or marked changes in behavior. Behaviors recorded on anecdotal records are usually unplanned and occur spontaneously. (See Figure 8.2b.) Anecdotal records generally describe the behavior of one child rather than a group of children. In some situations, more than one child may be involved, but the focus is on a single child and a single behavior. Anecdotal records are particularly useful with infants and toddlers who display several milestone behaviors within a few months of development. Anecdotal records taken over a period of months may reveal a pattern of development when considered as a timeline of development.

Both running records and anecdotal records are narrative forms of documentation—that is, they are written descriptions of observed behaviors. Other forms of documentation—such as checklists, rating scales, and rubrics—are not narratives; rather they are specially organized lists that allow teachers to rapidly record observed behaviors. Checklists record only the absence or presence of behaviors. For example, a checklist for locomotor behaviors might state "Child walks without assistance." If the child does walk without assistance, the teacher records a check mark next to the behavior; if the child has not been observed walking without assistance, no check mark is recorded. Although checklists do not provide an in-depth look at behavior, they are useful for comparing changes in developmental behaviors over time (Leonard, 1997). (Chapter 11 provides an example of a checklist used to do daily safety inspections of playgrounds.) Rating scales and rubrics are checklists that have added qualifiers to provide additional information about observed behaviors. For example, a checklist statement might read "Child speaks in complete sentences." If the child only uses complete sentences sometimes, what should the teacher record? Rating scales and rubrics provide categories such as "most of the time" and "seldom," which allow teachers to record the degree of behavior and thus make the information more useful for assessing children's development.

Systematic Observation and Assessment Whatever the method of recording, observation and assessment need to be ongoing and cyclical in order to be effective. Information about children's behaviors needs to be collected routinely and reviewed systematically to provide the most complete portrait of their development over time.

Teachers as Professionals and Advocates

COMPETENCY GOAL VI
· Functional Area 13

Another factor that contributes to the difficulty of defining the field of early childhood education is the traditional separation between child care and "formal" early childhood education, which some equate with education that begins in kindergarten. The breadth of early care and education settings available for children from birth through age 8 results in vast differences in qualifications and compensation for early childhood educators. These differences are one factor that causes child care to be considered as separate from early childhood education. NAEYC attempts to bridge the gap between the categories of "child care" and "early education" by suggesting that early childhood professionals are both caregivers and educators and that "early care and education" is a more accurate descriptor of what we do as teachers of young children.

Ethical Considerations in Early Care and Education

NAEYC's code of ethical conduct (1998b, p. 1), which was adopted in 1989 and amended in 1977, represents the collective efforts of many early care and education experts to define the rules of behavior for the profession of early child care and education.

The code identifies core values derived from agreed-on standards of ethical behaviors, as follows:

- Appreciating childhood as a unique and valuable stage of the human life cycle
- Basing our work with children on knowledge of child development
- Appreciating and supporting close ties between the child and family
- Recognizing that children are best understood and supported within the context of family, culture, community, and society
- Respecting the dignity, worth, and uniqueness of each individual (child, family member, and colleague)
- Helping children and adults achieve their full potential in the context of relationships that are based on trust, respect, and positive regard

Accepting and abiding by the code of ethical conduct for our profession will ascertain that the best interests of children and families are at the core of our decisions and actions.

Professional Development and Advocacy

As teachers become more confident in their roles as caregivers and nurturers, observers and assessors, and facilitators of learning, they are likely to extend their interests and influence outside the walls of their classrooms. Successful, experienced teachers often take the lead in the professional development of novice teachers and in community-based efforts to promote the well-being of children and families.

Developmental Stages of the Early Childhood Teacher Katz (1977) suggests that teachers progress through four stages of development—survival, consolidation, renewal, and maturity. Development from one stage to the next is dependent on both real-world experience and additional specialized training. Katz identifies types of professional development that are most critical for teachers at each stage of development. For example, during the survival stage, novice teachers may feel overwhelmed and unprepared to deal with the realities of teaching. Their professional development is best supported by frequent one-on-one contact with successful experienced teachers who act as mentors by providing on-site consultation and scaffolding and modeling of effective teaching and classroom management strategies. At the second stage, consolidation, novice teachers begin to narrow their focus by acknowledging specific instructional concerns and using problem-solving strategies to manage them. These teachers benefit from availability of various resources, such as peers, other educators, and professional publications, to seek solutions to specific problems. By the time they reach the third stage, renewal, teachers are more confident about their abilities and are ready to expand their repertoire of teaching practices. These

> *One of the beauties of teaching is that there is no limit to one's growth as a teacher, just as there is no knowing beforehand how much your students can learn.*
>
> Herbert Kohl, *Growing Minds: On Becoming a Teacher* (1990)

teachers actively seek out new ideas and perspectives by joining professional organizations, attending conferences, and taking advantage of inservice opportunities available through their schools. During the renewal stage, teachers are also likely to extend their formal education by enrolling in college programs and seeking more advanced degrees. During the final stage of development, maturity, teachers are ready to serve as leaders in their fields by increasing their involvement in professional organizations, conducting workshops or seminars for other educators, and serving as mentors for new professionals entering the field.

Seeking Opportunities for Professional Development and Advocacy

The aim of professional development is to maintain and extend the knowledge base, skills, and competencies of individuals employed in the field. Opportunities for professional development are available in many venues. For example, child care centers and schools often provide orientations for novice teachers and specialized inservice seminars and workshops for all teachers on a regular basis. Larger entities, such as school districts or corporations that own and operate child care facilities, may have well-developed professional development agendas that provide multiple possibilities for professional growth, which teachers can select from on the basis of their personal needs and interests. Smaller organizations, such as privately owned child care centers, may rely on local and national professional organizations or higher education institutions to sponsor professional development seminars, workshops, and conferences.

Professional growth and development may also be obtained by furthering one's formal education through college and university coursework or degrees or through self-directed study by using the hundreds of resources available from professional and commercial sources. Often, involvement with professional organizations, such as the National Association for the Education of Young Children (NAEYC) or the Association for Childhood Education International (ACEI), provide for professional development through leadership opportunities within the organization. These contacts frequently extend into the community and allow professionals to connect, or network, with each other. The organizations provide advocacy opportunities as well. Advocacy represents a willingness to take positive action to promote a worthwhile cause; in the field of early care and education, the overarching cause is to promote the development and well-being of young children and their families. (Chapter 12 provides additional information about advocacy activities as an extension of family involvement.) Most professional educational organizations have well-established advocacy committees that work diligently to maintain and improve the quality of early care and education and the status of professionals.

> *Because society has not yet fully recognized and acknowledged the value of high-quality early childhood programs, we must communicate the importance of our work not only in testimony to policymakers but also in day-to-day conversations with parents, supervisors, colleagues, and everyone else we encounter.*
>
> —Lawrence J. Schweinhart and David P. Weikart,
> *Success by Empowerment: The High/Scope Perry Preschool Study through Age 27* (1993, p. 54)

Summary

- Teachers of young children assume many vital roles, such as caregiver and nurturer, facilitator of learning, observer and assessor of development, and professional and advocate.

Teachers as Caregivers and Nurturers of Young Children

- Relationships among teachers and young children directly impact the quality of early care and education.

Teachers as Facilitators of Learning

- Teachers promote development of the whole child by facilitating self-directed play and learning experiences.

Teachers as Observers and Assessors of Children's Development

- Developmentally appropriate observation and assessment of young children are continuous, systematic, and varied.

Teachers as Professionals and Advocates

- NAEYC's code of ethical conduct defines ethical assumptions and responsibilities for professionals in the field of early childhood education.
- Early childhood teachers progress through stages of development as they gain experience, training, and education.
- Networking with others in the field provides many professional development opportunities.
- Accreditation plays a significant role in maintaining quality child care.
- Professional organizations promote professional development and advocacy.
- Reflection and self-evaluation techniques promote personal and professional development.

LEARNING ACTIVITIES

1 Discussion: Nurturing Infants and Toddlers in Group Care. Discuss specific caregiving behaviors and practices you should be able to observe in early care and education settings where teachers nurture infants and toddlers in their care. Contrast these with nonnurturing behaviors and practices that should not be used in early childhood settings for infants and toddlers because they would be detrimental to children's development.

2 Viewpoints: Scenarios in Ethical Conduct. As a class, generate a list of potential ethical dilemmas (or decisions) you might face as an early care and education teacher. After a reasonable number of dilemmas have been identified, take a class vote to decide which ones you would like to discuss. Divide up into four teams; each team will represent a different perspective, such as classroom teacher, program administrator, child's family member, child, social worker, licensing representative, or law enforcement official. Restate the dilemma so everyone understands the situation. Then, staying in the character your team has chosen, explain the team's perspective of the situation. Follow up with discussion or debate.

PORTFOLIO ARTIFACTS

1 Project: Collection of Observation Recording Forms. Visit one or more early care and education programs and ask for blank copies of some of the observation and documentation forms the program uses to record and assess the behavior and development of young children. Review each of the forms and write one or two sentences about how you might be able to use this observation tool in your classroom.

2 Reflection: Autobiography. Contemplate your earliest memories of wanting to teach. What individuals or events influenced you? Write a brief autobiography highlighting the "sparks" of inspiration that influenced your decision to become a teacher. Complete your autobiography with a description of what goals you would like to accomplish during your first five years of teaching.

Professional Connections and Web Links

National Academy of Early Childhood Programs
National Association for the Education of Young Children
Accreditation
1509 16th Street NW
Washington, DC 20036-1426
800-424-2460
http://www.naeyc.org/accreditation

The NAEYC Web site provides information about its national accreditation system for early childhood centers and schools. Through the National Academy of Early Childhood Programs, NAEYC operates the voluntary accreditation process, which involves three steps: self-study, validation visit, and accreditation decision. The Web site provides answers to frequently asked questions about the process and access to self-study materials and other resource materials for programs applying for accreditation. In addition, the Web site provides updates on the accreditation process, information about validator training, and a searchable list of NAEYC accredited programs.

National Child Care Information Center (NCCIC)
243 Church Street, NW, 2nd Floor
Vienna, VA 22180
800-616-2242
http://nccic.org

The National Child Care Information Center (NCCIC) is a project of the Child Care Bureau, which is part of the U.S. Administration for Children and Families, and serves as a dissemination vehicle for information related to children and child care in the United States. The site maintains a national database of information and resources, as well as some full-text publications on over twenty topics relevant to the field of early care and education. Topics include brain development, early childhood work force, faith-based child-care resources, Hispanic resources, tribal child care, research, and statistics and data.

National Network for Child Care (NNCC)
Iowa State University Extension
Ames, IA 50011
515-294-4111
http://www.nncc.org

The National Network for Child Care (NNCC), whose Web site is hosted by the Iowa State University Extension, is part of the Cooperative Extension System and serves as a resource for current research, reports, statistics, and resources. The site also provides access to news releases related to topics in early care and education, such as child abuse and neglect, child care staffing issues, and quality child care. In addition, the site provides access to statistics about young children and child care that are compiled by reliable sources throughout the country and includes licensing regulations from each of the states. NNCC also disseminates information related to welfare reform and child advocacy efforts.

Suggestions for Further Reading

Beaty, Janice J. (2002). *Observing development of the young child* (5th ed.). Upper Saddle River, NJ: Merrill/Prentice Hall.

- Beaty provides a clearly written overview of the purposes and practices underlying observation of young children's behaviors. She provides varied examples of how to document behavior, such as anecdotal records, running records, and rating scales. Beaty also includes a selection of checklists organized into developmental categories, such as emotional development and spoken language, that can aid both novice and experienced teachers alike in developing a systematic assessment plan.

Billman, Jean, & Sherman, Janice. (2003). *Observation and participation in early childhood settings: A practicum guide* (2nd ed.). Boston: Allyn and Bacon.

- Billman and Sherman's book is designed to support teacher education students who are participating in a field-based practicum. The book begins with a brief overview of the purposes of observation and its role in the overall assessment system. Subsequent chapters focus on specific applications of observation in various child-care and early education settings and include sample formats for documenting children's behavior and development. The book suggests many activities that students can undertake to learn more about observation and participation in the field of early childhood education.

Honig, Alice Sterling. (2002). *Secure relationships: Nurturing infant/toddler attachment in early care settings.*

Washington, DC: National Association for the Education of Young Children.

- Honig provides information explaining attachment and the importance of relationship building during the first three years of life. The book examines attachment from the perspective of children, family members, and child caregivers. The book also provides practical suggestions about building and maintaining secure relationships with infants and their families.

References

Beaty, Janice J. (2002). *Observing development of the young child* (5th ed.). Upper Saddle River, NJ: Merrill/Prentice-Hall.

Billman, Jean, & Sherman, Janice. (2003). *Observation and participation in early childhood settings: A practicum guide* (2nd ed.). Boston: Allyn & Bacon.

Boeree, C. George. (1998). *Personality theories: Abraham Maslow.* Retrieved on September 2, 2002, from http://www.ship.edu/~cgboeree/maslow.html.

Bredekamp, Sue, & Copple, Carol. (Eds.). (1997). *Developmentally appropriate practice in early childhood programs.* Washington, DC: National Association for the Education of Young Children.

Cohen, Dorothy H. E., & Stern, Virginia. (1978). *Observing and recording the behaviors of young children.* New York: Teachers College Press.

Dombro, Amy Laura, Colker, Laura J., & Dodge, Diane Trister. (1999). *The Creative Curriculum for infants & toddlers* (Rev. ed.). Washington, DC: Teaching Strategies.

Helm, Judy Harris, Beneke, Sallee, & Steinheimer, Kathy. (1998). *Windows on learning: Documenting young children's work.* New York: Teachers College Press.

Honig, Alice Sterling. (2002). *Secure relationships: Nurturing infant/toddler attachment in early care settings.* Washington, DC: National Association for the Education of Young Children.

Kagan, Sharon L. (1990). *Excellence in early childhood education: Defining characteristics and next-decade strategies.* Washington, DC: U.S. Department of Education, Office of Educational Research and Improvement.

Katz, Lillian. (1977). *Talks with teachers.* Washington, DC: National Association for the Education of Young Children.

Kosslyn, Stephen M., & Rosenberg, Robin S. (2001). *Psychology: The brain, the person, and the world* (2nd ed.). Boston: Allyn & Bacon.

Leonard, Ann Marie. (1997). *I spy something! A practical guide to classroom observations of young children.* Little Rock, AR: Southern Early Childhood Association.

Maslow, Abraham H. (1968). *Toward a psychology of being.* New York: Van Nostrand.

Maslow, Abraham. (1970). *Motivation and personality.* New York: Harper & Row. (Original work published in 1954.)

National Academy of Early Childhood Programs. (1991). *Accreditation criteria and procedures of the National Academy of Early Childhood programs.* Washington, DC: National Association for the Education of Young Children.

National Association for the Education of Young Children. (1987). *Position Statement: Licensing and public regulation of early childhood programs.* Washington, DC: Author.

Phillips, Carol Brunson. (Ed.). (1991). *Essentials for child development associates working with young children.* Washington, DC: Council for Professional Recognition.

Schweinhart, Lawrence J., & Weikart, David P. (1993). Success by empowerment: The High/Scope Perry Preschool Study though age 27. *Young Children, 49*(1), 54–58.

Shores, Elizabeth F., & Grace, Cathy. (1998). *The portfolio book: A step-by-step guide for teachers.* Beltsville, MD: Gryphon House.

Whitebook, Marcy, Howes, Carollee, & Phillips, Deborah. (1998). *Worthy work, unlivable wages: The national child care staffing study, 1988–1997.* Washington, DC: Center for the Child Care Workforce.

The Emerging Learning Environment

ust walking into an early childhood classroom evokes a sense of nostalgia for many adults. Tiny chairs and tables waiting to be occupied, the scent of crayons lying haphazardly beside brightly colored drawings, a collection of inviting toys within easy reach—all recall a simpler existence. Behind the seeming simplicity of these play and learning settings lies one of the greatest challenges early childhood educators face. How can one learning environment meet the many needs of a group of highly active and unique children?

Early care and education teachers balance multiple considerations in order to create optimal play and learning environments for young children. Armed with a knowledge of child development and a deep understanding of how children learn, caregivers prepare developmentally appropriate classrooms that evolve with the children as they grow and develop. Module Three, "The Emerging Learning Environment," equips you with information and resources to design and develop early care and education curriculum and settings that promote positive development of the whole child. As the title of the module implies, early childhood classrooms are not static environments that, once formed, remain developmentally appropriate forever. Quality settings for young children must be fluid and flexible to meet the ever-changing needs of their participants.

The opening chapter of this module connects your knowledge of developing children to the construction of early care and education curriculum that invites children to play and learn by supporting their emerging literacy and curiosity and by fostering independence and self-guidance. The second chapter explores other aspects of effective early care and education environments, such as selecting and arranging furnishings, as well as play and learning materials, and scheduling daily activities. The last chapter of the module provides useful information about safety, health, and nutrition for young children and offers suggestions for maintaining early care and education settings that are sensitive to the needs of individual children and their families.

The three chapters of this module provide the pieces of the puzzle you will need to construct developmentally appropriate early care and education opportunities for young children. Unlike the typical puzzle, however, these pieces can fit into many viable solutions to create early learning environments as unique and responsive as the children who participate in them.

It is the supreme art of the teacher to awaken joy in creative expression and knowledge.

—Albert Einstein, German-born American scientist and mathematician

- Define the components of a curriculum and how curriculum models reflect teacher beliefs about children's learning

- Suggest developmentally appropriate curriculum practices that support self-directed play and learning

- Describe the concept and give examples of practices that support emergent literacy

- Describe the premise behind emergent curriculum

- Explain how thematic curriculum supports young children's learning

- Describe the concept of learning by discovery and its connection with problem solving

- Give examples of developmentally appropriate behavior guidance techniques

- Discuss the importance of facilitating children's independence

Developing Curriculum for Young Children

When student teacher Pilar Alverez was assigned to the multiage preschool classroom at her college's child development center, she expected to see little children sitting in little chairs at little tables coloring with fat crayons and practicing their alphabet letters. Instead, as she enters Samantha Chandler's classroom, it seems as if no two children are doing the same thing. Some children are coloring, but not with fat crayons at little tables; they're sprawled on the carpet, drawing something that looks like a gigantic fish on a piece of mural paper at least six feet long. A few children stand around a large, clear, shallow tub filled with something that looks remarkably like blue gelatin. In another corner of the room, two boys and a girl wear fishing hats and vests as they sit in a large cardboard box "boat," rowing across a lake, which is actually a blue sheet spread on the floor.

Feeling a little uneasy, Pilar looks around the classroom in hopes of spotting her host teacher, whom she met at the get-acquainted reception last week. Ms. Chandler, an experienced teacher of twenty years, is with a group of about eight children who are wearing green-and-brown skirts made of crepe paper and doing the hula. As soon as they make eye contact, Ms. Chandler smiles and says, "Welcome, Ms. Alverez! The children have been looking forward to meeting you. Put your things on the desk and come over and join us. We need another hula dancer."

CHAPTER 9

arly childhood classrooms are busy, multifaceted places where children and teachers actively partici-pate in the wonderfully noisy and messy process of learning. In this vignette, the student teacher's expectations are typi-cal of the way most people think about early care and education settings. Ms. Alverez is not completely wrong; there are actually times when children do sit at little tables and color with fat crayons. Sometimes they even practice their al-phabet letters, but such activities comprise only a small portion of the happenings in programs designed for children from birth to age 5. This chapter explores the process of developing a curriculum for young children that complements their emerging language and thinking abilities. The chapter also examines positive techniques for guiding children's behavior while supporting their independence.

Defining and Developing Curriculum

For many individuals, childhood represents a carefree period of life filled with days of play, exploration, and discovery. Some view children's play as activity without intent or purpose; however, both Piaget (1962) and Vygotsky (1934/1984) believed that the play experiences and social interactions of childhood are essential to the development of thought and language. All new experiences and interactions build on existing knowl-edge, as children actively construct and reconstruct their personal understandings. Early childhood teachers who, like Piaget and Vygotsky, view children as active agents in their own learning take care to create curriculum that supports children's efforts to learn about themselves, others, and their world.

COMPETENCY GOAL I
• Functional Area 3

COMPETENCY GOAL II
• Functional Areas 4–7

Defining Curriculum

At the simplest level, *curriculum* is defined as a course of study; however, in thinking about curriculum in the broader context, we find that it encompasses much more—curriculum is everything that is taught or learned. For most early childhood educators, the true definition of curriculum, which lies between these two extremes, includes what is taught, how it is taught, and how it is evaluated. "What is taught" refers to the **con-tent** of instruction, while "how it is taught" refers to the instructional **methods** teach-ers use to deliver the content to learners. "How it is evaluated" relates to **assessment** strategies that educators use before instruction, throughout the instructional process, and at the end of an instructional segment.

For public school classroom teachers, including kindergarten teachers in most states, curriculum content is often partially determined by the local school district, and some portions of curriculum content may be required, or **mandated,** by state departments of education. In early childhood programs that are not part of state public school systems, curriculum content may be based on the specific curriculum models (such as those discussed in Chapter 7) endorsed by program sponsors. For example, teachers employed in a certified Montessori program would be expected to teach curriculum content as it is specified by the Montessori method.

Sometimes instructional methods as well as content are determined by curriculum models, as would be the case with a certified Montessori program. In other situations, teachers have more leeway on the teaching methods they use than they do on the curriculum content. In many instances, what is considered **best practice** determines the methods. Best practices are instructional methods that have been endorsed by a professional organization or agency that is recognized as an authority on the subject. In early childhood education, the National Association for the Education of Young Children (NAEYC) is the most widely recognized authority on best practices for children from birth to age 8. In 1997, NAEYC published a revised statement of best practice called developmentally appropriate practice (DAP), which was discussed in detail in Chapter 1 (Bredekamp & Copple, 1997). DAP is not considered a curriculum model like those described in Chapter 7; rather, NAEYC intends that educators use DAP as a tool for determining which instructional methods are most appropriate in their particular settings.

Some curriculum models prescribe guidelines for both content and methods. For example, High/Scope's active learning model provides content parameters through its key experiences that are aligned with areas of development, and it outlines instructional methods, such as the plan-do-review process and the use of choice time and well-defined interest areas. The High/Scope model's curriculum framework also recommends the use of observation and documentation as the assessment arm of its curriculum.

In recent years, interest in assessment of learners' abilities has increased notably. Across the United States, many school districts mandate specific measures of assessment to document children's academic progress. In some states, results of these assessments are used to evaluate the performance of teachers, the assumption being that effective teachers produce academically successful students. The increased popularity of teacher-centered direct instruction models (beginning in kindergarten) that regularly measure students' progress through formal testing can be linked to the testing movement.

Many early childhood specialists disagree with the use of formal tests with children ages 0 to 5 years, noting that testing methods are not compatible with developmentally appropriate practices. NAEYC recommends that educators use informal observational techniques to document children's developmental progress and to make informed decisions about curriculum (Bredekamp & Copple, 1997). (Chapter 8 includes more detailed information about observational techniques and their uses.)

Characteristics of Developmentally Appropriate Curriculum

According to NAEYC, curriculum for young children is developmentally appropriate when it complements their natural learning tendencies and cultural sensibilities and meets their developmental and individual needs (Bredekamp & Copple, 1997; NAEYC, 1995). Included among the natural tendencies of young children are the inclination to satisfy their curiosity by asking questions and to seek solutions to questions through play. Therefore, for young children, play serves as the primary vehicle through which they explore and discover new objects, events, concepts, and relationships. From the perspective of children, learning is not the purpose of play; play serves its own purpose. Many of the complexities of play were discussed in Chapters 1 and 3; this chapter revisits the topic of play in relationship to developmentally appropriate curriculum for young children.

What makes play the most developmentally appropriate practice for teaching young children? First, play is self-directed activity; children engage in play because they want to, not because they are asked to do so by their family members or teachers. Because play is freely chosen, children's attention is more likely to be focused and self-sustaining during play. When children play, they are totally involved—they are mentally, emotionally, socially, and (usually) physically active, and they pursue learning that is meaningful to them. Therefore, play is called holistic—it supports development of the whole child. Additionally, play occurs throughout the course of children's daily activities, so it is naturally integrated and comprehensive (Bredekamp & Copple, 1997).

With play, particularly pretend play, children are able to challenge themselves as they take on new roles and view things from other perspectives. Their play episodes give them opportunities to be successful and to feel competent. Pretend play releases their imaginations and enables them to make connections between what is and what could be. Of the models discussed in Chapter 7, the Waldorf and the Bank Street approaches place the most focus on imaginative play, maintaining that pretend play gives children opportunities to challenge themselves while at the same time developing deeper understanding of their world. Another benefit of play as the primary method through which children learn is that play supports the use of communication strategies, particularly oral language, as children interact and develop play scenarios (Owocki, 2001).

Promoting Emergent Literacy

By the time they are three years old, most children have mastered many of the intricacies of oral language. What is more, mastery of their native tongue has occurred without formal schooling or direct instruction. The native tongue is not necessarily English; over nine million children in the United States live in homes where languages other than English are spoken (NAEYC, 1995). (See Appendix B, NAEYC's *Position Statement: Responding to Linguistic and Cultural Diversity*.) Additionally, there is an increasing likelihood that young children will fluently speak two (**bilingual**) or more languages (**multilingual**)

CDA

COMPETENCY GOAL I
• Functional Area 3

COMPETENCY GOAL II
• Functional Areas 5–6

COMPETENCY GOAL III
• Functional Area 8

> *For the optimal development and learning of all children, educators must* accept *the legitimacy of children's home language,* respect *(hold in high regard) and* value *(esteem, appreciate) the home culture, and* promote *and* encourage *the active involvement and support of all families, including extended and nontraditional family units.*
>
> —National Association for the Education of Young Children, *Position Statement: Responding to Linguistic and Cultural Diversity* (1995, p. 2)

before entering formal schooling. Teachers of young children need to be especially conscientious about helping "children feel good about themselves as speakers of each language" (Council for Professional Recognition, 1996). As discussed in Chapter 3, young children learn to speak from individuals around them who use spoken language in the course of daily activities. As with other facets of human development, development of language is a gradual process that is dependent on children's natural abilities and their experiences (Owocki, 2001). The developmental process whereby children become increasingly aware of the interconnectedness of listening, speaking, reading, and writing is called **emergent literacy.**

Many of an infant's first steps into language result from imitation and exploration, through playing with the sounds of languages to which they are exposed (such as babbling), or from trial-and-error experiences (such as using one-word sentences to communicate needs or wants). Toddlers' abilities to understand spoken language exceed their abilities to use spoken language. That is, their listening vocabulary, or **receptive vocabulary**, is larger and more developed than their speaking vocabulary, or **expressive vocabulary.** For example, toddlers may be able to understand (receptive vocabulary) the request, "Please go and get the big red ball from the toy box"; however, their spoken response (expressive vocabulary) might be "Go ball." (Chapter 3 provides additional information on the development of oral language.)

The learning patterns that apply to oral language also apply to written language (Goodman, 1986). During the preschool years, young children explore written language in much the same way that infants and toddlers explore oral language. The pretend play of preschool-age children often explores the uses of written language. For example, young children pretending to visit a restaurant might use books or magazines to represent written menus and scribble on small pads of paper when taking orders from diners. In this way, they are emulating the behaviors of literate adults they have observed, and although these children cannot actually write or read, they are exploring some of the facets of written language. The pretend play of these children indicates their broadening consciousness of written symbols, **print awareness**, as well as their recognition of the connections between speech and writing (Schickedanz, 1986).

Other activities in which young children engage also indicate emergent literacy (Owocki, 2001). For instance, when young children listen to someone read to them from a book, they often point to written symbols rather than the pictures, thereby demonstrating their understanding that symbols, not pictures, represent language. They also pretend to read familiar books aloud, speaking the memorized text and sporadically turning the pages, thus fitting their speech to the appropriate illustrations. Children's level of emerging literacy varies according to their abilities, maturation, and social and cultural experiences.

Pretend play provides many opportunities for young children to extend their emerging literacy skills.

As their awareness of the connections between reading and writing and listening and speaking processes grows, so does their interest in the symbols of written language (McGee & Richgels, 2000). They begin to notice details associated with letters and numerals and to point out similarities and subtle differences between symbols. Gradually, their abilities to use *visual discrimination,* or to differentiate symbols by comparing details, enable them to label some of the symbols with names. Initially they might point to a symbol and say, "I have one of those in my name." Then, as they gain more experience with written symbols they might point to a word and say, "That's an *m;* I have one of those in my name, too."

Teachers who appreciate the significance of emergent literacy strive to fill their classrooms with materials and activities that support young children's exploration and experimentation with oral and written language. These **literacy-rich environments** for learning provide many opportunities for young children to observe and use reading and writing in natural ways. For example, in addition to a wide selection of quality children's literature, the classroom may offer magazines, newspapers, stationery and envelopes, posters, menus, catalogs, recipe cards, shopping lists, order forms, and dozens of other supplies and props to encourage reading and writing behaviors. Care should be taken that the literacy materials selected provide a fair representation of gender and culture (Derman-Sparks, 1989). For example, include menus from a variety of restaurants to acknowledge cultural diversity, and select catalogs and magazines that present gender-fair images—such as males and females playing sports, reading books, cooking dinner, and caring for children. Table 9.1 (p. 207) provides a more comprehensive list of materials and activities to support emergent literacy.

Figure 9.1   Samples of Prewriting

Source: From J. A. Schickedanz, P. D. Forsyth, and G. A. Forsyth (1988), *Understanding Children and Adolescents,* 3rd ed. (Boston: Allyn and Bacon). Copyright 1988 by Pearson Education. Reprinted by permission of the publisher.

Table 9.1   Creating Literacy-Rich Environments

A variety of tools to write with

crayons
pencils
colored pencils
pens (erasable)

markers (washable)
chalk
dry-erase markers
rubber stamps and stamp pads

A variety of materials to write on

charts
labels
blank books
lists
signs
unlined paper (various sizes)
construction paper (various colors)

mural paper
personal slates
chalkboards
white boards
magnetic board
magnetic letters
flannel boards, felt letters

A variety of things to read

picture books
storybooks
informational books
concept books (alphabet, numbers)
poems
song books, newspapers, magazines

pamphlets, brochures
posters
cookbooks
menus
instructional books

A variety of real-life literacy props

stationery, envelopes
notepads
receipt books
stenopads
clip boards
coupons, advertisements
telephone books
encyclopedias
wipe-off charts, graphs

checkbooks (mock)
recipe cards
index cards
file folders
business cards
stamps, stickers
greeting cards
playing cards

Materials and activities to support emergent literacy should extend to all areas of the classroom, just as listening, speaking, reading, and writing extend to all facets of our lives. Library corners are an integral component of literacy development in early care and education settings; by devoting a part of the classroom to a literacy center, teachers demonstrate that they value language in all of its forms.

Literacy centers need to be cozy, accessible, inviting places where children can feel comfortable while reading and sharing books, listening to stories, writing stories, or choosing other options available to them. Literacy centers usually include several permanent features, such as a selection of developmentally and culturally diverse and gender-fair children's books and soft furnishings for reclining. These centers also often include special interest items related to themes or special events (Evans, 1998). For example, if some of the children in the classroom are about to become big brothers or sisters, a selection of books about new siblings would be appropriate, along with other literacy items associated with a new baby, such as birth announcements, thank-you cards, and growth charts. Adding such types of special interest materials and activities to the language learning center enriches children's play experiences and encourages self-expression and creativity.

Curriculum Strategies

CDA

COMPETENCY GOAL II
• Functional Areas 4–7

In addition to fostering emergent literacy, child care and early education programs seek to support children's creative and cognitive development, as well. Child care and early education classrooms may use any of several child-centered curriculum strategies to accomplish these goals.

When curriculum planning takes into account the interests, needs, and abilities of the learner, such as in the example of the new sibling described above, learning often becomes more meaningful to children. A popular child-centered curriculum strategy among early childhood educators is to develop content from topics suggested by the learners themselves, thereby creating curriculum that is both interesting and challenging to the children. This strategy is most often used with preschool-age and kindergarten children, although some models and individuals use this approach with infants and toddlers.

Emergent Curriculum

The child-centered process of spontaneously developing curriculum, as well as methods, from the interests of the learners is called *emergent curriculum*. Teachers observe children as they engage in self-directed activities in the classroom and listen closely to their conversations in order to gather information about their interests, questions, and current levels of knowledge about the topics under consideration. In some situations, teachers hold impromptu meetings with small groups of children to ask them about what they are learning and what they would like to investigate next.

Teachers integrate the children's ideas into a flexible curriculum framework without taking control of the content away from the learners. They solicit information from the learners and make decisions about which supplies and resources will be most useful to learners as they pursue their interests. Teachers also de-

> *Optimal learning is driven by curiosity, which leads to exploration, discovery, practice, and mastery. In turn mastery leads to pleasure, satisfaction, and confidence to once again explore. The more the child experiences this cycle of wonder, the more she can create a lifelong excitement and love of learning.*
>
> —Bruce D. Perry, M. D., Ph.D.

termine how they will scaffold the children's play and learning experiences so that children will continue to develop and acquire skills in the psychomotor, cognitive, and affective domains. Documentation of the learning process is particularly important with emergent curriculum, since there are few predetermined outcomes.

Several of the models discussed in Chapter 7 depend primarily on emergent curriculum. For example, the Reggio Emilia approach encourages children to represent their ideas in multiple ways through child-directed projects. Teachers document each step of the learning process from the time the children conceive their ideas, through their initial attempts at representation, to the conclusion of the projects as children are ready to move to new ones. Making careful observations, teachers record the children's actions and ideas in the form of written annotations, sketches, photographs, and flowcharts. The recorded history of the projects becomes a means through which teachers, family members, and the children themselves can visually review their learning. When curriculum takes into account the interests and needs of learners, it becomes more meaningful to children.

Thematic Curriculum

Early childhood teachers who are working in programs where the focus is on developmentally appropriate practices but where no specific curriculum model is endorsed sometimes apply the emergent curriculum strategy to some segments of the curriculum planning process. For example, a teacher may have established particular learning outcomes for the children but will use the children's own ideas about topics or themes as means to achieve those outcomes. This type of curriculum development is called *thematic curriculum*. The theme or topic becomes the unifying force of the curriculum content and overlays most of the activities, projects, and subject disciplines in which children engage (Jones & Nimmo, 1994). Teachers gather materials, arrange classroom spaces, and orchestrate activities that emerge from the theme so children can engage in learning experiences that provide them with opportunities to learn new skills, practice established skills, and gain rich firsthand information as they explore and build on their existing knowledge of the theme. Themes typically revolve around children's interests and curiosities that arise as they play and interact with others at home and school. As in traditional nursery school programs, themes are often related to changes in the seasons or to other commonly occurring events in the lives of children, such as getting a new pet, riding in a car, or visiting grandparents. Thematic curriculum provides many opportunities for sensitive exploration of diverse lifestyles, ethnicity, and culture (Derman-Sparks, 1989). For example, a thematic curriculum about grandparents could be extended to include other significant adults who play grandparentlike roles in children's lives. The theme can also serve to build children's awareness of how grandparents are viewed in various families, countries, and cultures.

A planning technique frequently associated with thematic curriculum involves the use of a graphic organizer called a web, which allows teachers to visually construct the connections between various aspects of the theme (Jones & Nimmo, 1994). The **thematic curriculum web** begins with the name of the theme written as the hub in the center of the page, usually surrounded by a circle. Then, as the brainstorming process proceeds, teachers write related ideas or activities in other circles around the hub. Figure 9.2 presents an example of a curriculum web about the theme "windy weather." In this case, the related circles are organized according to interest areas in the classroom. Thematic curriculum webs can also be organized by formal disciplines (such as math, science, and social studies) or developmental areas (such as language, fine motor, and social skills).

Figure 9.2   **Thematic Curriculum Web**

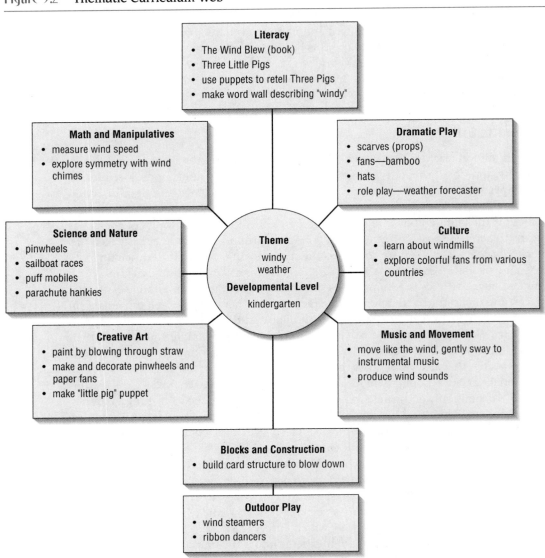

Learning through Discovery

Self-expression and creativity are encouraged by a curriculum strategy known as **discovery learning.** Cognitive psychologist Jerome Bruner developed the discovery learning instructional strategy in the late 1960s. The premise behind discovery learning is that children learn best as they are seeking meaning and making discoveries (Bruner, 1961). According to Bruner, learning by discovery remains the primary mode of learning throughout life.

Like Piaget, Bruner believed that children progress through stages of cognitive development. The first stage, the **enactive stage**, lasts from birth to about 18 months of age; during this stage infants grow cognitively as they explore actions and objects through their senses. The second stage, the **iconic stage**, begins at about 18 months of age and lasts until approximately age 6. During the iconic stage, children develop cognitively as they experiment with concrete objects and discover new information. During the third stage, from age 6 or 7 onward, called the **symbolic stage**, individuals draw meaning from abstract concepts through the use of logic and problem solving (Bruner, 1961).

> *F*or whether one speaks to mathematicians or physicists or historians, one encounters repeatedly an expression of faith in the powerful effects that come from permitting the student to put things together for himself, to be his own discoverer.
>
> —Jerome Bruner, *The Act of Discovery* (1961, p. 22)

Bruner believed the instructional strategy of discovery learning can be applied at every stage of cognitive development, because the main tenet of discovery learning is that learners who actively participate in the collection and organization of information build their own structures of knowledge (Bruner, 1986). The modes through which learners collect information vary with development, but at each stage learners actively pursue and organize knowledge for their own uses. Teachers open exciting new avenues for learning when they encourage young children to be discoverers, and their inquisitive attitude focuses on exploring, finding out about things, and adding to what they already know. Children feel like capable and powerful learners rather than incapable and restricted recipients of knowledge. Discovery learning often begins with a question. Rather than directly answering the question, teachers in child-directed learning environments act as facilitators by sharing their knowledge and experience through suggestions and open-ended questions and by providing children with access to the tools they need to complete their investigations.

According to Bruner (1961, 1986), classroom environment strongly influences the attitude of discovery. In classrooms that promote discovery learning, children have access to materials, supplies, and equipment that will aid their explorations. For example, if kindergartners want to discover some of the properties of water, they will need access to water, clear containers to hold water, clear flexible tubes, funnels, sponges, various objects that float or sink, and many other materials. If most of these materials are readily available, then children can concentrate on finding out about water rather than waiting for someone to tell them about it. Bruner describes learners who are self-motivated to learn about something through discovery, like the kindergarten children in the example, as **self-propelled thinkers.**

Each time one prematurely teaches a child something he could have discovered for himself, that child is kept from inventing it and consequently from understanding it completely.

—Jean Piaget, psychologist

Children who are self-propelled create their own learning as they actively engage in the process of figuring things out. One systematic way of figuring things out is through the process of **problem solving.** Problem-solving abilities emerge almost as soon as infants are born; from their very first attempts to seek nourishment or comfort, they are learning how to find solutions to their needs. Discovery learning encourages a problem-solving attitude in which children use trial-and-error strategies to explore concepts and view making errors as part of the process rather than as failure. Many individuals have outlined steps in the problem-solving method. Barbara Coloroso (1994) identifies six steps in the problem-solving process:

- Identify and define the problem.
- List viable options for solving the problem.
- Evaluate the options (by exploring each option's pluses and minuses).
- Choose one option.
- Make a plan and do it.
- Evaluate the problem and the solution. (adapted from Coloroso, 1994, p. 109)

Problem solving is an important component in discovery learning, as illustrated in the previous *finding out about water* example, but it can also be used in a variety of other situations including those related to social skills and behaviors.

Guiding Behavior and Facilitating Independence

CDA

COMPETENCY GOAL III
· Functional Areas
8–10

One of the challenges of childhood is learning to get along with others. Though this task may sound straightforward, in reality it is both complex and gradual. Young children are not born knowing how to behave in socially acceptable ways; the concepts of social behavior are learned, just as other concepts are learned—through experience and maturation.

Developing Social Competence

During the first months of life, the behaviors of infants are strongly influenced by their physical and emotional needs; they react in response to their needs for nourishment, rest, and nurturing and are dependent on their caregivers to meet these needs. Because infants have limited language and mobility, their experiences are restricted to those orchestrated by the adults who tend to them. However, just a few weeks after birth, infants learn to distinguish one familiar caregiver from another and adjust their responses accordingly. This marks the beginning of voluntary emotional behavior. For instance, infants sometimes show preferences for one caregiver over another, and these preferences may be task specific. For example, some crying infants are comforted more easily by their fathers than by other caregivers. Gradually, infants learn to adjust their behaviors to specific individuals and situations in order to have their needs met in the most expedient ways. As adults, who respond to infants' cues, notice these differentiated behaviors, they may convey to infants that one pattern of behavior is preferable to another. As described in Chapter 3, children's socioconventional knowledge is constructed and reconstructed as a result of these interactions. The ability to effectively adapt our social, emotional, and cognitive behaviors in response to others is *social competence.*

Sometimes it is difficult to determine when the behaviors of young children are deliberate and when they are the result of inexperience. For example, during the first year of life, the socially acceptable way for children to gain the attention of their caregivers is to cry. However, when they begin to talk, children are expected to use words, rather than crying, to tell their caregivers what they need or want. How do young children learn to distinguish between such socially acceptable and socially unacceptable behaviors?

Most often children rely on their primary caregivers to scaffold their learning of socially acceptable behavior, or **prosocial behavior,** just as they rely on their caregivers to help them learn other things. Guiding the behavior of young children in developmentally appropriate ways is a great challenge of parenting and teaching. Strategies and practices that caregivers can use to help children learn prosocial behaviors are called **behavior guidance.** Caregivers who use developmentally appropriate behavior guidance techniques take into consideration the child's age and developmental level, as well as cultural contexts, when making decisions about how to respond to a child's socially acceptable and unacceptable behaviors (NAEYC & NAECS/SDE, 2002).

Understanding Misbehavior and Responding with Positive Guidance Strategies

The term **misbehavior** is sometimes used to describe behaviors that are not considered socially acceptable. Although adults may be able to distinguish acceptable behavior from misbehavior quite easily, children are often left in a quandary as to which of their most recent behaviors is, indeed, misbehavior. Sometimes, the most logical first step when dealing with children's unacceptable behaviors is simply to find out if children are aware that their behaviors are unacceptable and if they know what acceptable behaviors to use in place of the unacceptable behaviors. For example, if a three-year-old boy, on his first day of preschool, leaves the classroom without the teacher's permission, he may be doing so because at home he is allowed to go from one room to another without asking the permission of his parents. Without any former experience of going to school, he does not know that the teacher expects him to stay in one room unless he is granted permission to leave. The child has not really misbehaved; he simply behaved in the way he has always done, which does not happen to be appropriate for this setting. Therefore, some gentle explanation and assistance from the teacher will help him learn what to do when he wants to leave the classroom in the future. It may seem like common sense that adults first find out whether children know the standards of acceptable behavior before holding them accountable, but we sometimes make assumptions about what children know and do not know on the basis of our own experience.

After the caregiver has determined that the behavior in question is indeed misbehavior, then understanding of the reasons behind the misbehavior is the next important step in developmentally appropriate behavior guidance. Using the **goals of misbehavior** framework developed by Dreikurs and Stolz (1964), this chapter discusses how knowing the origins of misbehavior informs practice and allows teachers to respond with strategies for guiding behavior that are appropriate for each child and situation (Council for Professional Recognition, 1996). According to Dreikurs and Stolz, children typically act out to achieve one of the following goals of misbehavior: attention, power, revenge, or relief of inadequacy.

The first goal of or reason behind misbehavior usually focuses on gaining the attention of others in order to communicate or interact. Responsive caregivers can anticipate many of children's needs for attention and prevent some outbursts by routinely providing sufficient positive attention. In situations where children's need for attention is not circumvented by preventive measures, caregivers can help children identify more acceptable ways than misbehavior to gain the attention they want. Young children seeking attention do not always know the difference between positive and negative attention, so reprimanding children for attention-getting behaviors still meets their goal to gain attention. Therefore, even if caregivers reprimand them, the children will continue to use the attention-getting behaviors with which they experienced success. Once teachers become familiar with the patterns of children's behaviors, they will often be able to anticipate when a child is about to engage in attention-getting behaviors and provide positive attention to the child before the unacceptable behaviors begin. If the attention-getting behaviors are inconsequential, sometimes the most appropriate response is nonattention—*to ignore* the behavior and provide no reinforcement whatsoever. If the behavior consistently fails to gain attention, the child will usually abandon the behavior. Ultimately, the better solution is to help children learn other, more socially acceptable methods for gaining attention and to encourage their independence so that they become more self-reliant.

A second reason children misbehave is to achieve power (Dreikurs & Stolz, 1964). Such misbehavior usually involves conflict with others. Often, young children believe their needs are more critical than the needs of others; their natural egocentrism limits their abilities to view situations from perspectives other than their own. Typically, young children's struggles for power involve choices that impact others, such as deciding who goes first or who gets to play with a particular toy. Caregivers can frequently identify power struggles by the child's use of first-person pronouns such as *me, my,* or *mine.* Struggles for power between children occur when each child's egocentric point of view clashes. These clashes can escalate, because young children have not developed mature impulse control. With children under age 3, the most effective response to a power struggle is often to divert the children's attention to another task or object by offering them fixed choices—the opportunity to choose among acceptable alternatives (Rice, 1995). Using such **redirection** of behavior limits interruption to the play and dilutes the struggle for power.

As children enter the preschool years, however, caregivers can use these struggles for power as opportunities to help children learn to apply problem-solving, or **conflict res-**

olution, strategies (Hemmeter, Maxwell, Ault, & Schuster, 2001). Conflict resolution techniques scaffold children's attempts to be problem solvers and negotiators and foster attitudes of nonviolence; success at resolving conflict boosts their social competence and allows for self-regulation (Kaiser & Rasminsky, 2003). The conflict resolution process is similar to the techniques used in problem solving. The first step is to define the situation so that all parties concur on what issues need to be resolved. Then each party calmly states their proposed solutions while avoiding any negative or aggressive statements. If the parties agree to a solution, the conflict is resolved, and the children can return to their activities. With preschool-age children, conflict resolution may need to be guided by the teacher, because children's natural egocentrism restricts their abilities to consider multiple perspectives. Teachers can help children articulate their views and solutions, but whenever possible, children should arrive at their own solutions so that they gain real experience in dealing with social conflict in nonviolent ways (Rice, 1995).

Although it may sometimes seem more time efficient, and thus tempting, to solve the conflict for the children, such a resolution is only temporary, because the children have not learned any new prosocial behaviors from the encounter and will require intervention from authority figures each time a new issue arises. Power struggles may also occur between children and adults. Adults, whose level of cognitive development allows them to view multiple perspectives, can model negotiating skills so that these situations between children are resolved cooperatively, rather than leaving one child as the winner and one as the loser.

A third goal of misbehavior identified by Dreikurs and Stolz (1964) is revenge. When individuals feel they have been treated unfairly or when they experience emotional pain, they sometimes attempt to strike out at others in retribution. Young children cannot always identify the sources of their negative feelings and may seek revenge against nearby individuals, whether or not they were actually involved. This factor makes the caregiver's task more difficult, because the reason behind the misbehavior is more obscure. The goal of revenge may manifest itself in aggressive, disruptive, or destructive behaviors. When these behaviors are directed toward people rather than objects, safety issues become paramount.

Additionally, because young children have difficulty differentiating between emotions such as guilt and anger, they may not be able to explain their feelings accurately to caregivers. In these situations, caregivers must safeguard the other individuals involved and help the children who are misbehaving to find other ways to restore their emotional balance. One way to do this is by helping children talk about what they are feeling and by acknowledging that it is normal to have negative feelings from time to time. Caregivers can help young children distinguish between their negative feelings and their resulting negative behaviors in order to focus on changing the negative behaviors to more prosocial ones without making children feel that expressing emotions is not acceptable. Providing opportunities for *discussion* to talk about emotions through role-play, puppets, and other activities is one way to give children the tools they need to express themselves more clearly (Dettore, 2002).

Taking time to discuss the situations and emotions of the characters in children's books is another effective strategy for dealing with children's emotions and negative behaviors. This technique, called **bibliotherapy**, provides an excellent avenue for understanding feelings and learning about prosocial behavior. Many children's storybooks have plots that involve young children's attempts to deal with emotions in socially accepted ways. By sharing these books with young children, individually or in small groups, caring adults can encourage children to talk about or role-play how people can deal with situations involving emotions. Children also can be invited to describe their own experiences with the same feelings; this allows them to practice verbally expressing their emotions. Through role-play, children can become more aware of the facial expressions and body language associated with various emotions so they can better recognize emotions in others. A sampling of classic children's picture books about emotions follows:

- Anger, embarrassment, affection: *Alexander and the Terrible, Horrible, No Good, Very Bad Day* by Judith Viorst (Aladdin Paperbacks, 1987)
- Fear of the dark: *Bedtime for Frances* by Russell Hoban (Harper & Row, 1960)
- Positive self-esteem: *I Like Me* by Nancy Carlson (Houghton Mifflin, 1988)
- Sibling rivalry, jealousy: *If It Weren't for Benjamin I'd Always Get to Lick the Icing Spoon* by Barbara Shook Hazen (Human Sciences Press, 1979)
- Telling lies, dealing with disapproval, friendship: *Molly's Lies* by Kay Chorao (Seabury Press, 1979)
- Dealing with anger: *My Mom Hates Me in January* by Judy Delton (A. Whitman, 1977)
- Sadness, grief: *Nana Upstairs and Nana Downstairs* by Tomie de Paola (Putnam, 1973)
- Sibling rivalry, feeling left out: *Peter's Chair* by Ezra Jack Keats (Scholastic, 1967)
- Friendship, anger, dealing with conflict: *The Quarreling Book* by Charlotte Zolotow (Harper & Row, 1963)
- Feeling different, self-esteem: *Tacky the Penguin* by Helen Lester (Trumpet Club, 1988)
- Affection, love: *What Mary Jo Shared* by Janice M. Udry (A. Whitman, 1966)
- Feelings of insecurity: *Will It Be Okay?* by Crescent Dragonwagon (Harper & Row, 1977)
- Gender bias, confusion: *William's Doll* by William DuBois (Harper & Row, 1972)

Another goal of misbehavior, also related to negative emotions, is to avoid feelings of inadequacy (Dreikurs & Stolz, 1964). As children become less egocentric and more aware of others, they begin to compare themselves to others and to perceive themselves as they think others do. When children hold negative views of themselves or have low self-concepts, these feelings of inadequacy sometimes lead to misbehavior. (Chapter 4 provides additional information about affective development.)

Throughout early childhood, children face innumerable challenges related to their psychomotor, cognitive, and affective development. Although children's development follows the same predictable sequence, rates of development vary among children due to a variety of factors. As a result, children acquire knowledge and skills at different ages and to different degrees. Inevitably, children begin to notice differences between their abilities and performances and those of their peers. Feelings of inadequacy arise if they view their performance as inferior to those of others. Sometimes other children or adults, intentionally or unintentionally, point out these differences. However children become aware of their perceived inadequacies, they sometimes behave unacceptably to draw attention away from their "inferior" performances. Children who feel inadequate typically respond by refusing to engage in particular activities or impeding the attempts of others to do so. For example, preschool-age children who feel that they are not able to jump rope as well as the older children on the playground may grab the jump rope and hide it from the other children. Hiding the jump rope serves two purposes. It prevents the older children from demonstrating their "superior" skills, and it will prevent "failure" for the younger children. When faced with misbehaviors focused on relieving feelings of inadequacy, caregivers need to be particularly conscientious about showing appreciation of all children's abilities and efforts. Appreciation can be demonstrated through **praise**. Praise is a way of positively acknowledging someone or something. Praise, which is generally a verbal comment such as "Your paper-bag puppet is so creative, especially the way you used the yarn for his hair," should always be sincere and delivered directly to the individual (privately if possible) or group in a normal tone of voice. Praise is more effective when it is specific rather than general. For example, telling a child "good job" lets the child know you appreciate what he has done but does not really identify what he did that was good. However, a statement such as "Marcus, you sure are doing a good job of setting the lunch table" is detailed enough to let Marcus know exactly what behavior you are acknowledging. Classroom activities that focus on the process rather than the product, such as creating torn-paper collages or building block structures in a unique way, support the efforts and creativity of young children rather than focusing on performance or compliance to standards set by adults. Therefore, praise is best when it focuses on process or effort rather than products or results. Additionally, praise should avoid making comparisons between children (Kaiser & Rasminsky, 2003). Though verbal praise is the most common form, praise can also be demonstrated in nonverbal ways such as smiling, making eye contact, showing "thumbs up," or giving a hug. Praise, when used effectively, is a powerful tool to support children's positive behaviors and self-image.

Logical Consequences

Even though caregivers regularly use prevention and intervention techniques such as redirection, conflict resolution, discussion, bibliotherapy, and praise, children will still engage in some socially unacceptable behaviors. When this occurs, caregivers rely on other developmentally appropriate behavior guidance strategies, such as the use of naturally occurring or related consequences (Coloroso, 1994). Dreikurs and Stolz (1964) refer to this strategy as **logical consequences**. For example, if some children repeatedly throw their modeling dough on the floor and stomp on it, even though they are aware that modeling dough is used for molding and sculpting and not for throwing and stomping, at least two logical consequences can be employed. First, the children could forfeit their opportunities to use the modeling dough for the rest of that free-play period. Alternatively, the children could be required to clean the modeling dough off the floor before receiving more modeling dough. In both cases, the consequences are related to the children's unacceptable actions. The premise of this behavior guidance strategy is that the children will associate their actions with the logical consequences. Therefore, if they want to have access to modeling dough for molding and sculpting and if they would like to avoid scraping modeling dough off of the floor, then they will stop throwing the modeling dough and stomping on it. Coloroso (1994) suggests that logical consequences are most effective when they come from natural social consequences (for example, if you spill water, you wipe up the spill) rather than from an authority figure, unless the social consequences are impractical or potentially harmful to someone. The success of behavior guidance techniques such as these depends on many factors in addition to the developmental level and cultural context of the children and the goals of the misbehavior (Freeman, 1998). Caregivers should use behavior guidance techniques consistently and fairly so children will have reasonable expectations for behavior and more opportunities for self-regulation and independence.

Observational Learning and Behavior

Another way that children learn social behaviors is by observing the behavior of others. Family members, teachers, and other children all serve as models of behavior for young children who, in turn, imitate the observed behaviors. Behaviorist Albert Bandura (1986) refers to this as **observational learning.** Observational learning is impacted not only by the behaviors modeled but also by the observed consequences to the modeled behavior. Sometimes observational learning occurs because caregivers plan it, as when they say "Please" and "Thank you" throughout the course of the day, thereby deliberately **modeling** desirable behaviors so children will use *imitation* to try out their use of these polite terms. However, observational learning can also be the result of unintentional modeling, as when older children or popular media characters use profanity and younger children repeat the language in similar situations. Teachers of young children have to be diligent about the behaviors they model so that they do not inadvertently teach children undesirable behaviors.

Summary

Defining and Developing Curriculum

- Broadly defined, curriculum encompasses all aspects of the learning situation, including content, teaching methods, and assessment strategies.

Promoting Emergent Literacy

- Emergent literacy describes the gradual, and overlapping, processes of learning how to listen, speak, read, and write.

Curriculum Strategies

- Emergent curriculum is developed from the ideas and interests of the learners.
- Thematic curriculum uses a theme as the unifying instrument when developing curriculum in various subject or interest areas.
- Discovery learning encourages children to construct and reconstruct their own understandings.

- Problem-solving approaches enable young children to successfully participate in self-directed discovery activities.

Guiding Behavior and Facilitating Independence

- Social competence is demonstrated by children's abilities to make friends and get along with others.

- Children's misbehavior is often directed toward the goals of attention, power, revenge, or relieving feelings of inadequacy.
- Positive behavior guidance techniques facilitate children's self-regulation and independence.

LEARNING ACTIVITIES

1 Graphic Representation: Curriculum Web. Alone, or with a small group, select a topic that would be of interest to preschool- or kindergarten-age children, such as "dinosaurs" or "transportation." After deciding on the developmental level to focus on, draw a thematic curriculum web (like the one in Figure 9.2, p. 210) that includes activities in various learning centers or subject areas about the theme. If time permits, draw the web on the board and share your ideas with other classmates. Invite classmates to add to or make suggestions for modifying your web to involve them in the planning process.

PORTFOLIO ARTIFACTS

1 Project: Bibliotheraphy. Preview one or more of the children's books from the list provided in this chapter (on p. 216) and then read the book aloud to a small group of children of the appropriate developmental level. Use open-ended questions to encourage the children to talk about the episodes in the book in which the characters are experiencing negative emotions. Afterward, reflect on the benefits of using bibliotherapy in early childhood settings. Extend the project by adding the titles of other children's books to the list.

2 Interview: Promoting Problem-Solving Behaviors. Interview an experienced early childhood educator about effective techniques to encourage children to use problem-solving behaviors. Use open-ended questions to solicit specific examples from the teacher's personal experiences with these techniques. After recording the teacher's responses, reflect on which of these techniques you might choose to incorporate into your personal repertoire of teaching practices.

Professional Connections and Web Links

International Reading Association (IRA)
International Headquarters Office
800 Barksdale Road
P.O. Box 8139
Newark, DE 19714-8139
302-731-1600

The International Reading Association, which has members in ninety-nine countries, is a professional organiza-tion dedicated to promoting literacy by improving the quality of reading instruction through training and research. Membership in the IRA is open to classroom teachers, reading specialists, researchers, librarians, parents, and others interested in promoting literacy and lifelong reading. The organization also publishes brochures, books, position statements, and the journal *The Reading Teacher*.

National Black Child Development Institute (NBCDI)
1101 15th Street NW, Suite 900
Washington, DC 20005
202-833-2200
800-556-2234
http://www.nbcdi.org

The National Black Child Development Institute, a non-profit organization founded in 1970, identifies its mission as improving and protecting quality of life for African American children and their families. The organization sponsors diversity training for professionals, parent empowerment training, and leadership training for community members advocating for black children and their families. The organization also advocates "wholistic violence prevention strategies" through its trainings and publications. NBCDI publishes a biannual newsletter called *The Black Child Advocate* and an annual "Calendar of Children."

Suggestions for Further Reading

Kaiser, Barbara, & Rasminsky, Judy Sklar. (2003). *Challenging behavior in young children: Understanding, preventing, and responding effectively.* Boston: Allyn and Bacon.

- Kaiser and Rasminsky present a comprehensive overview of theories about children's challenging behaviors and describe management strategies recommended by various experts. Additionally, their book gives clear, straightforward information about factors that contribute to children's behaviors and offers reasonable suggestions for preventing and responding to them effectively. The authors also include information about the role of family and culture in children's behavior.

Neuman, Susan B., Copple, Carol, & Bredekamp, Sue. (2000). *Learning to read and write: Developmentally appropriate practices for young children.* Washington, DC: National Association for the Education of Young Children.

- This book begins by stating the position of the International Reading Association (IRA) and the National Association for the Education of Young Children (NAEYC) on developmentally appropriate literacy practices. Subsequent chapters recommend teaching practices, ideas, and activities to support "readers and writers in the making." Through pictures and samples of children's drawing and writing, the authors provide many examples of emergent literacy.

References

Bandura, Albert. (1986). *Social foundations of thought and action: A social cognitive theory.* New York: Prentice Hall.

Bredekamp, Sue, & Copple, Carol. (Eds.). (1997). *Developmentally appropriate practice in early childhood programs* (Rev. ed.). Washington, DC: National Association for the Education of Young Children.

Bruner, Jerome. (1961). The act of discovery. *Harvard Educational Review, 31*(1), 21–32.

Bruner, Jerome. (1986). *Actual minds: Possible worlds.* Cambridge, MA: Harvard University Press.

Coloroso, Barbara. (1994). *Kids are worth it! Giving your child the gift of inner discipline.* New York: Avon Books.

Council for Professional Recognition. (1996). *Child development associate: Assessment system and competency standards for preschool caregivers in center-based programs.* Washington, DC: Council for Professional Recognition.

Derman-Sparks, Louise, & ABC Task Force. (1989). *The anti-bias curriculum: Tools for empowering young children.* Washington, DC: National Association for the Education of Young Children.

Dettore, Ernie. (2002). Children's emotional growth: Adults' role as emotional archaeologists. *Childhood Education, 78*(5), 278–281.

Dreikurs, Rudolph, & Stolz, V. (1964). *Children the challenge.* New York: Hawthorne Books.

Evans, Karlin S. (1998). Combating gender disparity in education: Guidelines for early childhood educators. *Early Childhood Education Journal, 26*(2), 83–87.

Freeman, Nancy K. (1998). Look to the East to gain a new perspective, understand cultural differences, and appreciate cultural diversity. *Early Childhood Education Journal, 26*(2), 79–82.

Goodman, Kenneth. (1986). *What's whole in whole language?* Portsmouth, NH: Heinemann.

Hemmeter, Mary Louise, Maxwell, Kelly L., Ault, Melinda Jones, & Schuster, John W. (2001). *Assessment of practices in early childhood classrooms (APECC)*. New York: Teachers College Press.

Jones, Elizabeth, & Nimmo, John. (1994). *Emergent curriculum*. Washington, DC: National Association for the Education of Young Children.

Kaiser, Barabara, & Rasminsky, Judy Sklar. (2003). *Challenging behavior in young children: Understanding, preventing, and responding effectively*. Boston: Allyn and Bacon.

McGee, Lea M., & Richgels, Donald J. (2000). *Literacy's beginnings: Supporting young readers and writers*. Boston: Allyn and Bacon.

National Association for the Education of Young Children (NAEYC). (1995). *Position statement: Responding to linguistic and cultural diversity*. Washington, DC: NAEYC.

National Association for the Education of Young Children (NAEYC) & National Association of Early Childhood Specialists in State Departments of Education (NAECS/SDE). (2002). *Joint position statement: Early learning standards—Creating the conditions for success*. Washington, DC: NAEYC.

Owocki, Gretchen. (2001). *Make way for literacy!* Portsmouth, NH: Heinemann, and Washington, DC: National Association for the Education of Young Children.

Piaget, Jean. (1962). *Play, dreams, and imitation in childhood*. New York: Norton.

Rice, Judith Anne. (1995). *The kindness curriculum: Introducing young children to loving values*. St. Paul, MN: Redleaf Press.

Schickedanz, Judith A. (1986). *More than the ABCs: The early stages of reading and writing*. Washington, DC: National Association for the Education of Young Children.

Vygotsky, Lev. (1984). *Thought and language*. (Alex Kozulin, Trans.). Cambridge, MA: MIT Press. (Original work published in 1934.)

After reading this chapter and completing the related activities, you should be able to

- Describe the interpersonal, physical, and temporal dimensions of classroom climate
- Describe the components of the interpersonal dimension that promote relationships
- Identify the factors in selecting and organizing materials and equipment for early childhood classrooms
- Identify the considerations in preparing and arranging play and learning environments
- Suggest guidelines for establishing developmentally appropriate schedules, routines, and transitions
- Describe how classroom climate impacts the development of the whole child

Preparing the Climate of Early Care and Education Classrooms

It was my first day as a kindergarten teacher. I had spent hours preparing my classroom for the twenty-three four- and five-year-olds who would be arriving within minutes. The closest description I have for my feelings at the time would be "stage fright." Twenty years later, as I reflect back on that exciting day, the term "stage fright" actually does fit the situation pretty well. I had been "setting the stage," anticipating a year filled with playing and learning, laughing and growing. My students and I would spend hundreds of hours together in that classroom in the upcoming months, and much of what would happen in that classroom would depend on the physical environment. Had I thought of everything—arrangement of tables, chairs, and other furniture; supplies and access to them; personal and group spaces; as well as a seemingly endless list of other considerations? At 7:45 A.M., as the opening bell was still ringing, the children and their family members filled the doorway, looking just as expectant as I felt. The colorful and inviting learning centers drew the children's eyes, but family members sought out the personal spaces I had carefully labeled with each child's name. Around the room I saw shy smiles and heard bold giggles and also a few quiet sobs, but most of all I saw anticipation—it was going to be fine.

arly learning environments reflect the knowledge and beliefs of the teachers who orchestrate them. Although architects and school planners design the physical dimensions and fixed features of classrooms, the teachers and children who occupy them are responsible for the climate of the learning spaces. Within the walls of classrooms, many play and learning scenarios unfold as children and teachers grow and develop with each new experience. As the year progresses and the needs and interests of the learners evolve, teachers responsively adapt the learning environments to meet the ever-changing needs of the children who will play and learn within them.

Effective teachers shape every detail of play and learning environments according to their views about children and learning. Teachers who view children as active participants in their own learning set up their classrooms to encourage active exploration and personal construction of knowledge. Many related factors—such as relationships between children and teachers; selection, placement, and arrangement of toys, supplies, and furniture; and sequence of activities and other events—influence the character of early childhood settings. Collectively, these factors produce an overall impression of play and learning spaces, or the **classroom climate**, a term often used to describe the composite character of learning environments. Our views about how children grow and learn are the main guideposts we use to make decisions about the classrooms we prepare for young children.

Interpersonal Dimensions of Classroom Climate

Your beliefs about your role as a teacher shape the climate of the classroom. These beliefs are, in turn, grounded in your beliefs about childhood and children as learners and are strong indicators of the types of interactions that will occur in the learning environment. Interactions may include child-to-child, child-to-adult, and adult-to-adult situations and experiences. The **interpersonal dimension** of classroom climate focuses on relationship building among children and adults. Choices you make about teaching practices and curriculum strongly affect the interpersonal dimension of the classroom. Curriculum that is highly child directed, such as emergent curriculum, offers children many opportunities for child-to-child interactions as they engage in self-directed learning experiences in flexible small- and large-group situations. Children and teachers also experience quality interactions as teachers facilitate learning in supportive rather than directive roles.

CDA

COMPETENCY GOAL I
• Functional Area 3

COMPETENCY GOAL II
• Functional Area 6

COMPETENCY GOAL III
• Functional Areas 8–10

COMPETENCY GOAL IV
• Functional Area 11

For example, a teacher who has been observing a group of preschool-age children collaboratively build a huge structure out of pipe cleaners sees them suddenly stop constructing and show frustration because one side of the structure has collapsed for the second time. Of course, the teacher could take a directive course of action and simply tell the children how to keep the structure from collapsing. However, if the teacher firmly believes that children learn best through self-directed play, the teacher assumes a supportive role, leading the children to some possible solutions by asking open-ended questions and scaffolding the problem-solving process. By taking a supportive role in this child-to-teacher interaction, the teacher clears the way for the children to continue making decisions while actively directing their own play. When teachers interact without assuming control of situations, the interaction between children and teachers is two way—both groups contribute and both groups benefit by the interchange. **Reciprocal teaching** strategies like these positively affect children's classroom participation (Slavin, 2003).

> *I have believed . . . in the right of children to grow and learn in ways that are true for children.*
> —Caroline Pratt, *I Learn from Children* (1948)

The developmental levels of the children is another factor to consider when children and teachers interact. Infants, toddlers, and two-year-olds have limited spoken language abilities and rely more heavily on child-to-teacher interactions than child-to-child interactions. Although children younger than three years of age may play near each other, they are more likely to seek the secure base of familiar adults whenever they need reassurance or assistance.

It is especially important for teachers of very young children to be alert to both the verbal and nonverbal cues of the children as they interact with them. Sometimes, adults fail to consider when their interactions with very young children might be supportive and when they might be interruptions rather than reciprocal interactions. This situation sometimes arises when the **custodial needs** for physical caregiving, such as changing diapers and feeding, take precedence over the total needs of the children. For instance, infants and toddlers need diaper changes routinely throughout the day, and teachers often record these caregiving procedures on checklists or daily logs. Sometimes caregivers develop the habit of changing diapers in the same order so that no child misses a diaper change. While this system may be efficient, it does not consider the total needs of the children if caregivers allow the routine to interrupt children while they are engaged in self-directed play or worthwhile interactions. When selecting which children to diaper, teachers need to take into account how the children are engaged as well as whether they need diapering at that time. Since infants and toddlers generally have short spans of focused attention, waiting a minute or two to change diapers could make the difference between interaction and interruption.

Caregiving routines provide excellent windows of opportunity for child-to-teacher interactions. Even though teacher-child ratios are smaller in infant/toddler programs than in preschool and kindergarten programs, opportunities for one-to-one interaction are still limited. However, diapering and feeding, which, of necessity, are frequently one-to-one procedures, give teachers precious moments to build and maintain strong interpersonal relationships with each child. These few moments spent holding, touching, and rocking individual infants and toddlers form strong foundations of trust and affection. This "up-close-and-personal contact" also helps teachers become more familiar with children's verbal and nonverbal communication styles and capacities. According to physician and researcher Bruce Perry, the process of being aware of and responsive to others, which he calls *attunement,* lies at the heart of successful teaching (Perry, 1996–2002).

Early care and learning environments also provide various opportunities for adult-to-adult interactions between teachers as they collaborate while planning, implementing, and assessing instruction. In addition, teachers discuss their observations of children's behavior and development in order to make informed decisions about teaching and learning. Adult-to-adult interactions also take place between teachers and members of children's families. Some of these interactions are unplanned, such as the brief conversations that take place when parents accompany their children into the classroom during arrival or departure, while other interactions are planned, such as family-teacher conferences to discuss children's progress. (Chapter 12 provides a comprehensive look at the importance of effective communication between home and school.)

Although toys, supplies, and furniture are physical objects, they also reflect the interpersonal dimensions of play and learning spaces because they influence how individuals interact. For example, puppets and a puppet stage invite interaction and conversation, while an easel designed for one child to use at a time is more likely to encourage solitary activity, involving only incidental conversation with passersby. Both types of experiences are valuable to children's development, and both are shaped by physical elements within the classroom.

Physical Dimensions of Classroom Climate

The interpersonal dimension affects, and is affected by, the second dimension of classroom climate, the **physical dimension.** The physical dimension involves creating learning environments that safely support the needs of developing children through selection of appropriate toys, supplies, and furnishings and the arrangement of those items in indoor and outdoor play and learning spaces. Rather than viewing play and learning environments merely as rooms filled with child-sized furniture and bright, colorful toys, educators see early care and education environments as dynamic, responsive settings that support the children and teachers who use them.

CDA

COMPETENCY GOAL I
• Functional Area 3

COMPETENCY GOAL II
• Functional Areas 4–7

COMPETENCY GOAL V
• Functional Area 12

Selecting Materials and Equipment for Young Children

Appropriate selection of toys, supplies, and furnishings for early care and education environments requires understanding of how children develop and learn (Bronson, 1995). As one of the more obvious aspects of the physical dimensions of classrooms, the materials and

Children learn by interacting with their environment and actively transforming their relationships with the world of adults, things, events, and, in original ways, their peers.

—Loris Malaguzzi, Italian educator

equipment you provide for children send a clear message to observers about your views on early childhood education. **Materials** refers to toys and supplies that need to be replaced or replenished frequently, such as construction paper and other consumable items that can be used up. **Equipment** refers to long-lasting items such as tables, chairs, shelving, and changing tables that only need to be replaced occasionally; equipment is durable. Teachers select materials and equipment according to how these items will be used to implement quality care and education.

Developmentally Appropriate Materials and Equipment When preparing early childhood settings for quality play and learning experiences, teachers use age appropriateness as the baseline for selecting toys, supplies, furnishings, and equipment, while also keeping in mind the unique needs of individual children (Gould & Sullivan, 1999). Early care and education teachers recognize the importance of preparing learning environments that are individually appropriate as well as age appropriate (Bredekamp & Copple, 1997).

Toys and equipment that are age appropriate have less potential for causing injury to children (Bronson, 1995). The safety of toys and equipment is particularly relevant for children under the age of three years, who are more likely to place small items in their mouths and less likely to have the cognitive abilities to be aware of potential hazards. Each year, thousands of children are injured in toy-related accidents to their eyes, hands, and other body parts due to sharp points, jagged edges, projectiles, small broken pieces, and other risk factors. (Chapter 11 provides safety guidelines for selecting and using materials and equipment in early childhood classrooms.)

Additionally, sufficient varieties and quantities of play and learning materials related to each of the developmental domains are essential to support development of the whole child. Materials that can be used in many ways are most suitable to early childhood classrooms, because they make allowances for the range of development represented by the children who attend (Chandler, 1994). For example, simple puzzles are appropriate for preschool classrooms because they encourage problem solving, but they are less versatile than snap-together blocks, which can be used and reused by young children time after time. The blocks are considered open-ended play materials because there are several possible successful outcomes, whereas the puzzles are designed to have only one successful outcome. Play and learning materials that are open ended are more likely to support more than one developmental domain. One way to determine if the classroom has materials to support each of the developmental domains is to sort the materials according to areas of the classroom that primarily support the psychomotor, cognitive, or affective domain. Many early care and education programs designate areas of their classrooms for particular purposes and place related toys, supplies, and equipment within those areas (Dodge, 2002). A subsequent section of this chapter provides additional information about organizing early childhood classrooms according to developmental domain.

As with materials, selection of durable classroom equipment and furnishings begins by considering the ages and developmental levels of the children who will be using the play and learning spaces and determining their custodial as well as educational needs. Classrooms designed for infants and toddlers require specialized equipment—such as high chairs, cribs, swings, stationary walkers, changing tables, and potty chairs—to accommodate the special feeding, sleeping, diapering, and toileting of children under three years of age. Classrooms designed for preschool-age children have fewer custodial requirements but require child-sized tables, chairs, shelving, and cubbies that provide open access to supplies and toys to facilitate children's independence (Dodge, 2002; Phillips, 1991). Classrooms for children in kindergarten should have appropriately sized tables, chairs, shelving, and some type of storage space for personal items. Heavy pieces of equipment or furniture need to be sturdy and stable to avoid possible injuries to children, who may lean or climb on these items. These large items are quite expensive, so it is important to buy equipment that is both durable and easily cleaned and sanitized.

Before making decisions about equipment and furnishings, always consider the intended audience and function of the equipment. Who will be using the equipment? How will the equipment be used? Will children and adults be using the equipment? Let your knowledge of child development and teaching and learning theory guide you to make informed decisions about the furnishings and equipment in your classroom.

Antibias Curriculum   Another consideration when selecting materials and equipment is how they reflect diversity. Recognizing the uniqueness of children encompasses valuing the diversity of families, cultures, and communities (Banks, 2002). Culturally appropriate play and learning environments for young children avoid use of materials and practices that show bias related to culture, ethnicity, gender, language, or religion. Louise Derman-Sparks and ABC Task Force (1989) use the term **antibias curriculum** to represent this ideal. The impact of antibias curriculum is not limited to the physical dimensions of learning environments but also encompasses the interpersonal dimensions through teaching and learning practices. Consider the situation presented in the following vignette.

Four-year-old Luis Rodriguez is the youngest of three children. His parents, who were born in Mexico, immigrated to the United States six years ago so that Luis's father could find better employment. Luis attends a Head Start program near the family home. Luis speaks fluent Spanish and English and often helps his mother, Juanita, communicate with his teacher. Mrs. Rodriguez speaks English well, but Luis's teacher, Ms. Chemeka Winston, sometimes has trouble understanding her heavily accented English. "Señora Juanita," as the children call her, participates in Luis's classroom as a volunteer and is warmly received by the other children, especially when she shares folk stories she learned from her parents and grandparents. As soon as Ms. Winston observed the children's interest in the Mexican folk tales, she requested several books from the school and public libraries to share with her students. For some tales, Ms. Winston found both English and Spanish versions. Building on the children's interest, she asks Luis and Señora Juanita to help her label some of the objects in the classroom in Spanish so that she and the other children can learn more of the language. Luis is excited to share what he knows and patiently repeats the names of objects for his classmates. Mrs. Rodriguez is comfortable in the classroom and knows that Luis is flourishing. Ms. Winston feels fortunate to have Luis and Señora Juanita as part of her Head Start program.

Learning environments that reflect antibias curriculum strategies, such as the one illustrated in the vignette, enrich the lives of all of the children and adults who participate by celebrating diversity. Early childhood teachers need to develop awareness of their own biases as they develop culturally sensitive learning environments (Derman-Sparks & ABC Task Force, 1989).

The term *antibias* is not meant to imply that teachers of young children are prejudiced or harbor ill will toward any population segment; it simply means that all individuals have tendencies to view things from their own experiential bases. For example, individuals who have grown up in families where women work as police officers are more likely to use gender-neutral terms such as *police officers* and *firefighters* rather than the gender-biased terms *policemen* and *firemen,* which imply that all police officers and firefighters are male. However, if everyone within a child's family or circle of friends uses only *policemen* and *firemen* (terms that have been used traditionally for decades), the child may not be sensitive to this gender bias. Although these individuals generally intend no disrespect to female police officers or firefighters, the use of gender-specific terms is not something they routinely notice. As teachers become conscious of the antibias perspective, they become more sensitive to the nuances of language and avoid terms and statements that imply bias for gender, race, lifestyle, and other culturally sensitive factors.

Classrooms reflect cultural sensitivity and respect for diversity when they offer a variety of play and learning materials that are antibias in nature (Derman-Sparks & ABC Task Force, 1989). For example, such classrooms include male and female dolls representing many cultures, children's books showing different kinds of families and individuals in nontraditional roles, and dramatic play props for both boys and girls. (Additional information about antibias curriculum is available in Chapter 9.)

Arranging Play and Learning Environments

Developmentally appropriate learning environments are prepared to foster positive development of the whole child through self-directed activity and play, which is facilitated not only by the materials and equipment selected, but also by the way these items are set up and distributed throughout the classroom. **Room arrangement** is the term used to describe the organization of materials and equipment within the learning environment. As discussed in Chapter 1, play is an integral part of childhood, and through play children spontaneously discover, explore, and construct new understandings. Therefore, developmentally appropriate room arrangements invite children to investigate and actively engage in learning experiences as they interact with others (Dodge, 2002; Isbell & Exelby, 2001).

General Classroom Features When designing early care and education environments, caregivers consider a variety of essential factors related to the interpersonal, physical, and temporal dimensions of classroom climate. The developmental level of the children serves as the initial guide when caregivers arrange play and learning spaces. However, the basic structure of the classroom places certain restrictions on room arrangements. Permanently placed structural features (such as walls, windows, doors, electrical outlets, carpeting, and tile) are **immovable features** of classrooms, whereas **movable features** (like equipment and furnishings) allow for more flexibility in room arrangement. The selection of movable features is partly determined in relationship to the permanent structures.

After considering the general layout of immovable features and selecting developmentally appropriate materials, equipment, and furnishings, caregivers turn their attention to arrangement of those items within early childhood settings. Another factor to contemplate when arranging classrooms is **mobility**. Mobility allows children to move freely between areas of the classroom and have unimpeded access to entrances and exits. Mobility factors relate to typically developing children as well as children with special needs. Inclusive early care and education environments need to ensure that children with special needs can access the equipment and spaces to the fullest extent possible, as do their typically developing peers (Chandler, 1994).

Other factors to consider when setting up early childhood classrooms are function, group size, and noise level. For example, play spaces designated for building with large wooden blocks need to be relatively roomy to accommodate the gross motor

Inclusive early care and education environments consider the mobility needs of all children when making decisions about room arrangement.

movements of one or more children as they reach, lift, and bend while building. Building block areas also require large, flat, open zones in which to build block structures. In addition, block building is naturally a noisy process, so carpeted floors that cushion sounds are better for block building than tile floors. The factor of noise level also suggests that placing block areas next to areas for quiet activities like reading books might not be suitable. Sometimes decisions about placement of equipment depend on pragmatic considerations such as lighting or access to hand-washing facilities. For example, areas designated for creative expression through art, such as easel painting and collage making, not only need to be near sinks for hand washing, but also work best when located on floor surfaces that can be easily cleaned and sanitized.

Generally, some definition of classroom spaces according to function or use is preferable to large open areas without boundaries, because young children usually feel more secure with some flexible structure (Dodge, 2002). Boundaries can be indicated by placement of low open shelves, other furnishings, or floor coverings such as rugs. Of course, early childhood classrooms are busy places that serve many functions, so tables used for modeling dough activities early in the morning may also serve as lunch or snack-time tables later in the day. Consequently, storage spaces for materials and convenient clean-up options are also important.

Early childhood classrooms are truly multipurpose rooms, and the movable features of the classroom allow children and teachers flexibility in the use of space (Isbell & Exelby, 2001). Some activities designed for larger groups of children, or in some cases all of the children in the class, require large, open spaces. Movable pieces of equipment make quick rearrangements of space possible so children can participate in large-group music and movement activities, circle times, or other activities that need extra space.

Center-Based Room Arrangements   Most programs for infants, toddlers, and preschool-age children and some kindergarten classrooms use center-based approaches and develop areas designated for particular types of activities. **Learning centers** or **activity centers** group together relevant materials and equipment to facilitate self-directed activity and play. A well-planned assortment of learning centers can easily support all of the developmental domains as children move from one center location to another during their day. Although learning centers may be geared primarily to support one particular developmental domain, they will likely support the other domains as well. The following learning centers, which are typically found in early childhood classrooms, are grouped according to the developmental domain that takes priority. A brief description of some of the materials and equipment commonly found in these centers is provided, but these lists are by no means comprehensive. (Please note that not all materials listed are suitable for all age groups or developmental levels.)

Play and Learning Spaces to Promote Psychomotor Development   The psychomotor domain, which is discussed in Chapter 2, includes physical development of gross, fine, and perceptual motor skills and sensory functions such as seeing, hearing, feeling, tasting, and touching. The following learning centers and related materials and equipment offer children multiple opportunities to use the large muscles of their arms, legs, and torsos as well as the small muscles of their hands, feet, and face. Additionally, children will use their senses in conjunction with motor skills and gain experience in visual-motor coordination. Still other activities will support use of the senses and motor skills to explore and manipulate objects and substances.

- *Sensory areas* usually include shallow, transparent tubs or specially designed sensory tables than can be filled with a variety of substances with various textures, such as water, sand, or other nontoxic substances. Depending on the substance, various implements useful for scooping, filling, pouring, emptying, and measuring can be used to extend sensory experience.

- *Blocks and construction zones* are designated areas for building with large wooden unit blocks and often include props, such as toy vehicles, traffic signs, and small human and animal figures made of wood or plastic. Sometimes these areas are designated with a specially designed rug showing landscapes or patterns of roadways. Block areas may also include various other types of building materials, such as snap-together blocks, plastic or wooden "logs" that are notched to fit together, and dozens of other similar items to provide practice with building and assembling structures.

- *Manipulatives and table toys areas* include a wide variety of toys and objects that can be manipulated or handled. Typical manipulatives are beads and laces, puzzles, shape sorters, small items for sorting and counting, and collections of items such as plastic milk jug caps, old keys, rocks, and seashells.

- *Creative music and movement areas* provide materials and equipment for listening to music, responding to music, and creating music. These areas frequently have tape recorders or CD players, along with an assortment of instrumental and vocal music appropriate for young children. In addition, various rhythm instruments—such as wood blocks, bells, maracas, tambourines, and small drums—are available to children. Props—such as streamers, bracelets or anklets with bells, and scarves—are commonly available to encourage children to move in response to music.

- *Indoor gross motor areas* usually consist of large open spaces where groups of children can gather together with enough room for active movement with hula hoops, jump ropes, traffic cones (for making obstacle courses), balls, or group games. In some classrooms, particularly those for children under age 3, indoor gross motor areas have small climbing structures placed on cushioned mats.

- *Outdoor play areas* provide age-appropriate playground equipment such as swings, slides, and climbing structures, and sandboxes and riding toys such as tricycles. Grassy areas for running and playing and paved areas for riding vehicles, bouncing balls, and jumping rope are sometimes available as well.

Play and Learning Spaces to Promote Cognitive Development The cognitive domain, which is covered in Chapter 3, includes thinking skills, problem solving, logico-mathematical reasoning, concept development, memory, and language and literacy development. Learning centers that support the cognitive domain provide children with opportunities to question, explore, experiment, figure things out, and build understanding. In addition, as children interact with other children and adults, they use their language skills to describe, explain, and inquire.

- *Literacy areas,* or *library corners,* usually provide comfortable furniture or pillows so children can enjoy books and other literacy materials alone or with other children and adults. Literacy areas also include a balanced selection of children's picture books, storybooks, poetry, and informational concept books and other reading materials, including child-made books, to meet the needs and interests of children at various levels of development. Literacy areas frequently support written language as well by providing various implements and media for drawing and writing and offer some exposure to alphabet and number symbols. Some literacy areas provide listening stations with headphones so children can listen to books on tape or song stories. (Chapter 9 provides additional information on literacy-rich environments.)

- *Puppetry corners* are often incorporated into literacy or dramatic play areas and provide various types of simple hand puppets to encourage children to use language as they create or dramatize stories and plays or as they simply play with the puppets. Some puppetry corners include a puppet theater or furniture that can be used as a puppet stage.

- *Math and manipulatives areas* include many of the items mentioned for the manipulatives and table toys areas, including various objects for counting, sorting, classifying, and constructing patterns. In addition, math and manipulatives areas may provide tactile numerals, number posters, sorting trays, graphing mats, and simple board games that involve counting or other math skills.

- *Inquiry areas,* or *curiosity corners,* are designed to encourage children to observe and study nature and science and to explore communities and cultures. Materials to support observation and the study of nature and science frequently include magnifying glasses, balance scales, prisms, microscopes, and other tools to support scientific inquiry. Collections of natural objects (such as rocks, seashells, pinecones, feathers, leaves) are added, as indicated by children's interests. In addition, models of animals and objects of interest may be available. Exploration of communities and cultures often involves globes, maps, and informational books with photographs or illustrations about people and how and where they live (Banks, 2002). Artifacts from various cultures—such as clothing, cooking utensils, toys, tools, and other items—may also be included. In some classrooms, science and "social studies" areas may be separate rather than combined.

- *Computer areas* having computers and related computer programs are frequently in place in early childhood classrooms. Depending on the type available, computer programs may support development in many areas. Typically, computer programs used in early childhood programs focus on language and math skills such as identifying alphabet letters and sounds and counting. Computer programs are also available to support problem solving and creativity. Computer programs that engage children mentally and physically are preferable to those that merely expect children to observe and occasionally respond. If computers are available in the early childhood classroom, they should be equally available to all interested children.

Play and Learning Spaces to Promote Affective Development The affective domain, which is discussed in Chapter 4, includes emotional, social and moral development; therefore, learning centers to support the affective domain encourage social interaction, expression of feelings, and opportunities for children to learn about themselves and others. Additionally, as children learn about themselves and others, they develop social competence and gain greater awareness of similarities and differences among people.

- *Circle time areas* are not learning centers in the usual sense, but rather areas of the classroom set aside for interactive group activities. The size of the group may vary according to the purpose of the activity, space available, or preferences of children and teachers. Circle times are organized in different ways, according to the curriculum philosophy and approach used in the classroom, but they are generally meant to give children opportunities to socialize and build a sense of community through shared activities such as singing, doing finger plays, listening to stories, or sharing experiences. Children and teachers often sit close together on the floor or on chairs, which are clustered around the teacher or other adult. The length of circle time is related to children's development levels; circle time usually occurs once or twice per day. Circle time areas are frequently used for other purposes throughout the day.

- *Dramatic play areas* are designed to give children opportunities to pretend and engage in role-play, usually with props and costumes. Many dramatic play areas are set up like miniature home living areas and include kitchens and living rooms. Child-sized replicas of tables, chairs, stoves, refrigerators, closets, baby beds, and other household furnishings are arranged invitingly and supplied with a wide variety of props, such as dishes, baby blankets, multicultural dolls, food models, and other household items.

Room arrangements that support self-directed play are often organized into interest areas or learning centers.

Dress-up clothes—including hats, shoes, purses, and other garments to depict both male and female roles—are available. A full-length unbreakable mirror is also helpful to support children's role-playing and self-awareness. Dramatic play areas support children's social development as they plan and carry out play episodes. As discussed in Chapter 3, dramatic play also supports cognitive development, as children use their imaginations and problem-solving skills to maintain their pretend play.

- *Creative expression/art areas* provide children with an assortment of supplies, art media, and tools for drawing, painting, constructing, sculpting, and print making. The focus of creative expression/art areas is on the process of expression rather than on the finished art project. Children use art materials to represent their ideas and emotions rather than to replicate predetermined products. Examples of process art experiences include drawing murals, painting with watercolors, creating collages, manipulating modeling dough, and making designs with objects. The possibilities for creative expression through art are endless.

Developmentally appropriate practice recognizes that the developmental domains are interrelated; therefore, it is natural that learning centers provide for overlapping experiences while being predominantly related to one domain. The learning centers described in this chapter will look different, have different materials and equipment, and be used differently in various classrooms. That is as it should be, for each early childhood environment is a reflection of the children and teachers it encompasses.

Temporal Dimensions of Classroom Climate

CDA

COMPETENCY GOAL I
· Functional Area 3

COMPETENCY GOAL III
· Functional Area 10

A third dimension of classroom climate relates to time-related aspects of early care and education, such as the planned sequence of the day, the amount of time allotted to various types of activities and procedures, and the process of changing from one event to another. These time-related factors comprise the **temporal dimension** of classroom climate and are central to the effective functioning of child-centered play and learning spaces.

Planning Schedules, Routines, and Transitions

Just as the interpersonal and physical dimensions of the classroom need to be developmentally appropriate, so does the temporal dimension. For example, the planned sequence of events and activities for the day, known as the *daily schedule,* needs to account for many factors, such as children's ages and the size of the group. In addition, the daily schedule must consider the needs of individual children as related to attention span, level of activity, rest requirements, and other personal and cultural distinctions. In accord with the daily schedule, the recurring procedures, or *routines,* established for carrying out everyday events (such as arrival, mealtime, hand washing, and rest periods) should reflect understanding of child development and be based on reasonable expectations for children's behavior. A third element of the temporal dimension is linked to both the daily schedule and routines; this element is called a transition. **Transitions** are the "in-betweens," those times when children and teachers are expected to shift from one activity or location to another. When transitions are not developmentally appropriate, they sometimes create stressful situations for children and teachers and may create disharmony among children. Well-planned daily schedules, routines, and transitions reinforce the efficient operation of child-centered early care and education environments.

Typical Daily Schedules In addition to being developmentally appropriate, well-planned daily schedules need to be balanced for type of interactions, level of activity, and degree of child-directed and teacher-directed options. For example, throughout the day, preschool-age children would benefit from opportunities to participate in small-group and large-group situations; it is desirable to provide options for playing alone. The daily schedule should alternate the types of grouping arrangements and the periods of time set aside for these group activities instead of using only one grouping arrangement or scheduling all small-group interactions at one time of day and all large-group interactions at another. Activity or energy level is another factor to consider; again, it works best to alternate the sequence of activities. For example, if indoor group motor time is immediately followed by outdoor playtime, children may become tired because both activities use high levels of movement and energy. Therefore, it would be better if activities that require moderate levels of activity, such as small-group **center time**, when children engage in activities in learning centers, would precede outdoor play. Another aspect of the daily schedule that works best when arranged in alternating sequence is the degree of child-directed and teacher-directed activities. For instance, if the schedule provides large blocks of time for self-directed play in both the morning and afternoon, then short periods of teacher-directed events like story time or circle time could be scheduled in between the periods of self-directed play, or *choice time*.

Another consideration when planning the structure of the day relates to the amount of time allocated to various types of activities and events. The first guideline is the developmental level of the children; infants and toddlers stay interested and involved for shorter periods of time than preschool or kindergarten-age children, so the schedule would designate smaller blocks of time for younger children. Of course, the degree of involvement also needs to be considered; generally, children can sustain active self-directed play for longer periods of time than they can for activities that are passive or directed by adults. When there is a mismatch between the amount of allocated time and the children's level of development or degree of activity, then challenging behaviors may occur more often. For example, kindergarten children playing a group game that involves turn taking and waiting may be able to handle the idleness for short periods of time, but if the activity goes on too long, those children who become restless may seek other outlets for their energies. Yet these same kindergartners may be able to play outdoors or engage in dramatic play for long periods of time without any restlessness.

Routines and Transitions The efficient daily structure in early care and learning environments is dependent primarily on developmentally appropriate practice, which recognizes that children feel secure within predictable, yet flexible, daily schedules that allow children to move from one event to the next without undue disruption. Many of the recurring daily events, or routines, can be efficiently planned so that whenever possible, children are active participants in these procedures. Many routines are functional; that is, they serve a real purpose for the efficient operation of the program. For example, many public schools require that teachers do a daily count of the number of children who want chocolate milk or regular milk with their lunches. One approach would be to call out each child's name and ask the question, but this would mean that several children would be waiting while only one is responding. Another way to collect this information and at the same time encourage children to be independent is to use a self-report system where children record their preference on a simple two-column picture graph as they arrive. Then the teacher can look at the graph, record the milk count, and see who is absent all at one time. Some functional daily routines relate to self-care procedures such hand washing, toileting or diapering, meals, and rest time. By preparing effective procedures for these routines, teachers can avoid potential problems throughout the day. For instance, children need to wash their hands several times a day—before eating, after toileting, and after messy activities, to name a few situations. Rather than having all of the children wash their hands at once, which necessitates lining up and long wait times, teachers can arrange that individuals or small groups of children do hand washing while the rest are still engaged in activities. If two teachers are available in the classroom at the same time, routines are much more manageable, because teachers can share responsibilities for supervising both routine and ongoing activities.

Once the daily schedule has been constructed and procedures for routine activities have been planned, teachers need to formulate some strategies for guiding children from one activity or event to the next. These transition strategies are not only important to the smooth flow of the daily schedule, but also to the overall temporal dimension of the learning environment. Transitions represent periods of change; for many children, such change creates tension or uncertainty, as one activity ends and another begins. Effective transition strategies help children adjust to change, provide closure, and limit interruptions to play and learning.

Four basic transition strategies are alerting, cueing, providing transition alternatives, and reducing idle time. Alerting and cueing are similar, because they both give children advance notice that a change is imminent. Alerting is usually done verbally with statements such as "Very soon it will be time for snack, so we need to begin putting away toys and cleaning off tables." Alerting is more effective when it is attached to events (such as snack time) rather than to time ("in five minutes"), because young children rarely comprehend the concept of time. Cueing, which is often part of a routine, is a prearranged signal rather than a direct statement of what children "need to do." For example, children and teachers can decide in advance that when it is time to clean up toys at the end of center time, the teacher will begin singing the "clean-up" song. Then, as they clean up their toys and projects, children will join in the singing, which continues until most of the toys are returned to their storage bins. Cueing is more participatory than alerting, but both strategies are needed, because not all transitions can be preplanned. The transition strategies of providing transition alternatives and reducing idle time are actually complementary. That is, by providing transition alternatives (things to do while waiting), you automatically reduce the amount of time children are unoccupied. For example, when preschool-age children are preparing for rest time, some will be toileting while others will be sitting or lying on their cots listening to quiet music or looking through picture books. As children return from the restrooms, they select a book and go to their cots, too. When all of the children have completed their nap-time preparations, the teacher may dim the lights, ask the children to lie down, and read a relaxing story to the group. As the children become drowsy, they place their books beside their cots and close their eyes. By the end of the story, some children will be asleep, while others will continue to rest. The transition alternative between the toileting and rest-time routines provides children with a replacement behavior (looking at books) so that they do not have to fill in idle periods of time with other behaviors that might be less conducive to the restful situation the teacher is attempting to create. Well-planned transitions are the key to the smooth implementation of the daily schedule.

The three main components of the temporal dimension—daily schedule, routines, and transitions—work best when they are planned and implemented within the framework of the total play and learning environment. Although these elements of the day may not actually be curriculum, they definitely affect curriculum as well as overall classroom climate.

Teachers who believe that classroom climate directly impacts children's development continually analyze the many aspects of the interpersonal, physical, and temporal dimensions of their early childhood classrooms to provide optimal experiences for young children. Quality early care and learning environments are responsive, complex, multi-faceted places where childhood is valued and young children are viewed holistically.

Summary

Interpersonal Dimensions of Classroom Climate

- The dimensions of classrooms overlap to produce overall classroom climate.
- The interpersonal dimensions of classrooms relate to child-to-child, child-to-adult, and adult-to-adult interactions and relationships.

Physical Dimensions of Classroom Climate

- The physical dimensions of classrooms relate to materials, equipment, and room arrangement.
- Materials and equipment should reflect developmentally appropriate practice.
- Antibias curriculum uses materials, equipment, and practices that show cultural sensitivity and celebrate diversity.

- Room arrangement influences children's play and self-directed learning.
- Learning centers facilitate child-centered curriculum and promote development within each of the developmental domains.

Temporal Dimensions of Classroom Climate

- The temporal dimensions of classrooms relate to schedules, routines, and transitions.
- Classroom climate impacts children's development by influencing how they interact, use materials and equipment, and direct their activities and play.

LEARNING ACTIVITIES

1 Role-Play: Child-to-Adult Interactions. In a small group, identify a typical interaction between a small group of children and their teacher during center time in which the teacher's approach facilitates play, such as by asking open-ended questions or offering suggestions. Devise two scenarios to depict this interaction. In one scenario, model developmentally appropriate child-to-adult interactions; in the other scenario, demonstrate the same interaction using less developmentally appropriate practice. Role-play both scenarios for classmates without identifying which scenario is more developmentally appropriate. Invite classmates to analyze both scenarios and identify those teacher behaviors that were more effective for extending children's play.

2 Small Group: Brainstorming. After organizing into small groups, select one of the learning centers discussed in the chapter. Review the information and then brainstorm a list of possible additional materials and equipment that could be used to provide adaptations for young children with special needs. Categories of specials needs may include

- developmental delays.
- sensory impairments (vision, hearing).
- motor impairments (conditions that affect the use of the muscles such as cerebral palsy and muscular dystrophy).
- cognitive functioning and attention (mental retardation, autism, attention deficit disorder).

PORTFOLIO ARTIFACTS

1 Model: Room Arrangement. Use the underside of a shoebox lid to define the immovable features (walls) of an early childhood classroom. Draw other immovable features (such as windows, doors, and sinks) directly onto the cardboard lid. Cut pieces of construction paper to serve as models of classroom equipment (movable features) and arrange them in the model classroom in ways that are developmentally appropriate for the age range of your choice. Label the learning centers that you have incorporated into your classroom. Take a photo of your model classroom to include in your portfolio, and reflect on the process of room arrangement and how room arrangement is

influenced by teacher attitudes toward learning and teaching.

2 Project: Daily Schedule. Using the classroom model you designed in portfolio artifact 1, construct a developmentally appropriate daily schedule that includes activities, events, routines, and transitions. Prepare a brief description for each segment of the schedule, explaining how you determined the sequence so that it provided balance for level of activity and degree of participation. You may also want to explain how you determined how much time to allocate to each activity or event.

Professional Connections and Web Links

Child Care Information Exchange
P.O. Box 3249
Redmond, WA 98073-3249
800-221-2864
http://www.ChildCareExchange.com

The Child Care Information Exchange publishes a journal, *Child Care Information Exchange,* and other publica-

tions for directors and teachers in various child care settings. In addition, their Web site provides a searchable index for, and access to, over 800 articles collected from their journal for over twenty-five years. The articles relate to early childhood program managers as well as classroom teachers.

Suggestions for Further Reading

Gould, Patti, & Sullivan, Joyce. (1999). *The inclusive early childhood classroom: Easy ways to adapt learning centers for all children.* Beltsville, MD: Gryphon House.

- Gould and Sullivan present a well-organized and informational book about including children with special needs into early childhood classrooms that use center-based approaches. The book begins with an overview of various categories of disabilities and then proceeds through the classroom, center by center. For each learning center, the authors provide a checklist or narrative description of potential adaptations that in most cases are simple and effective.

Isbell, Rebecca, & Exelby, Betty. (2001). *Early learning environments that work.* Beltsville, MD: Gryphon House.

- Isbell and Exelby clearly depict the critical role of the environment in promoting the positive development of young children. Using personal experiences and research, the authors discuss multiple aspects of play and learning spaces. The photographs, illustrations, and narratives serve as invitations to design early childhood environments that are responsive to the needs of children.

References

Banks, James A. (2002). *An introduction to multicultural education.* Boston: Allyn and Bacon.

Bredekamp, Sue, & Copple, Carol. (Eds.). (1997). *Developmentally appropriate practice in early childhood programs* (Rev. ed.). Washington, DC: National Association for the Education of Young Children.

Bronson, M. B. (1995). *The right stuff for children birth to 8: Selecting play materials to support development.* Washington, DC: National Association for the Education of Young Children.

Chandler, Phyllis A. (1994). *A place for me: Including children with special needs in early care and education settings.* Washington, DC: National Association for the Education of Young Children.

Derman-Sparks, Louise, & the ABC Task Force. (1989). *The anti-bias curriculum: Tools for empowering young children.* Washington, DC: National Association for the Education of Young Children.

Dodge, Diane Trister. (2002). *The new room arrangement as a teaching strategy.* Washington, DC: Teaching Strategies.

Gould, Patti, & Sullivan, Joyce. (1999). *The inclusive early childhood classroom: Easy ways to adapt learning centers for all children.* Beltsville, MD: Gryphon House.

Isbell, Rebecca, & Exelby, Betty. (2001). *Early learning environments that work.* Beltsville, MD: Gryphon House.

Perry, Bruce D. (2002–1996). Attunement: Reading the rhythms of the child. Retrieved September 3, 2002, from http://teacher.scholastic.com.

Phillips, Carol Brunson. (Ed.). (1991). *Essentials for child development associates working with young children.* Washington, DC: Council for Professional Recognition.

Slavin, Robert E. (2003). Educational psychology: Theory and practice (7th ed.). Boston: Allyn and Bacon.

After reading this chapter and completing the related activities, you should be able to

- Identify factors affecting the safety and well-being of children
- Give examples of preventive and protective strategies and teacher behaviors that promote children's safety
- Explain the role of supervision in safe play and learning environments
- Identify policies and practices that promote the health and healthy lifestyles of young children
- Explain the relationship of immunizations to children's health
- Describe effective hand-washing practices and universal precautions for infection control
- Identify policies, guidelines, practices, and standards for healthy nutrition
- Identify ways to help young children develop nutritional awareness, including the USDA's Food Guide Pyramid
- Describe teaching practices and family-school partnerships to promote health and nutrition

Safety, Health, and Nutrition for Young Children

After introducing herself, Ms. Susie Gardner, director of Sunnyvale Early Childhood Center, welcomes the anxious looking young couple into her crowded but colorful office. Once Greg and Carla Sherman are seated, Susie offers a brief explanation for the detour into her office. "Before taking your scheduled tour of the center, I thought we might spend a few moments talking about your expectations for child care and answering any questions that we didn't cover when we spoke on the phone yesterday."

Speaking hesitantly, Carla begins, "Well, we did have a few additional questions. Tommy, our son, just turned three, and this will be the first time that he will be in the care of anyone besides a family member, and we were wondering about your security procedures." "That's right," says Greg. "How do you make sure no one else picks him up but us? How do you keep track of the comings and goings around here? Will our son be safe here?"

"Those are important questions; I'm glad you asked," replies Susie. "Safety is always our first concern here at Sunnyvale, and not just physical safety but emotional safety, too—for the children and family members. Our program has many safety procedures in place, and our teachers and other staff members are thoroughly trained during their orientation in those procedures. You, as Tommy's parents, decide who will be permitted to pick him up or visit him while he is at school. You will provide the names of approved individuals and other pertinent information on the enrollment form and on the family identification card. Additionally, we ask you to provide current photographs of those individuals for verification purposes, and we will ask the individuals for picture identification cards if the staff person on duty does not recognize them. Except for

one hour in the morning and one hour in the afternoon when a staff member is stationed at the door to greet arrivals, the doors are locked from the outside, and visitors have to press a call button and be buzzed in to enter. Both of you, of course, may visit Tommy at any time without calling in advance. Our door is always open to you, and we hope that you have many opportunities to visit in the classroom or join us for snack or lunch sometime."

Noticing that Tommy's parents are looking much more relaxed, Susie continues, "Hopefully, I have been able to ease some of your concerns about Tommy's safety. Let's begin the tour, and I will answer other questions as they arise. I would like to point out some of our other safety features and share information with you about our health practices and our tasty, nutritional meals and snacks. At Sunnyvale Early Childhood Center, we truly believe that a quality program considers the whole child, so everything, from the morning greeting to the play and learning experiences to the meals and naps, is carefully orchestrated to provide the best experience possible for each of our children and their families."

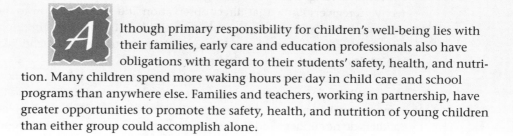 lthough primary responsibility for children's well-being lies with their families, early care and education professionals also have obligations with regard to their students' safety, health, and nutrition. Many children spend more waking hours per day in child care and school programs than anywhere else. Families and teachers, working in partnership, have greater opportunities to promote the safety, health, and nutrition of young children than either group could accomplish alone.

Preparing Safe Play and Learning Environments

Teachers serve as guardians for the young children in their care; therefore, concern for children's safety is a primary responsibility that encompasses all facets of early care and education programs. Safety takes priority over all other aspects of early care and education. Informed caregivers are alert to potentially harmful situations at all times and use both preventive and protective strategies to safeguard children, indoors and outdoors, from physical and emotional threats to their well-being. Further, they recognize that safety factors are directly related to children's developmental levels and that no matter what the child's age, continuous, diligent supervision is paramount. The challenge of keeping children safe requires ongoing awareness and commitment to the goal of providing play and learning environments where children safely interact with others as they explore their surroundings (Lowman & Ruhmann, 1998).

CDA

COMPETENCY GOAL I
• Functional Areas 1–3

COMPETENCY GOAL III
• Functional Area 8

COMPETENCY GOAL IV
• Functional Area 11

COMPETENCY GOAL V
• Functional Area 12

Preventive Strategies to Safeguard Children

Preventive safety strategies seek to anticipate and avoid the potential for harm. Selecting safe equipment and materials for early care and education settings is a primary preventive strategy (Council for Professional Recognition, 1996). Avoiding use of particular materials or equipment because it is potentially hazardous for certain ages or individuals is a preventive safety strategy. Caregivers' knowledge of child development helps them identify toys and other materials that are age appropriate, and their knowledge of specific children in their classrooms helps them choose items that are individually appropriate as well. For example, teachers of infants and toddlers are unlikely to select tiny building blocks for their classrooms, because children of this age are prone to placing small objects in their mouths, and small objects present potential risks as **choking hazards** (Lowman & Ruhmann, 1998). The objects may accidentally be swallowed and become lodged in their throats and block air passages. Teachers in the primary grades, however, are more likely to select blocks or construction toys with smaller pieces because school-aged children have more highly developed fine motor skills and are far less likely to put the blocks in their mouths.

Thoughtful arrangement of play and learning spaces is a second preventive safety strategy (Council for Professional Recognition, 1996). First and foremost, early care and education settings need to be arranged to facilitate adequate **supervision** by adults. Effective caregivers know that direct observation and alert attention to individuals, objects, and events is vital to the safety of children throughout childhood. Therefore, caregivers arrange rooms so children are always within viewing and hearing range of the adults supervising the environment.

The degree of supervision required depends on children's ages (Lowman & Ruhmann, 1998). Infants and toddlers need constant and diligent supervision, whether they are awake or asleep, because they are unable to protect themselves. Infants and toddlers do not understand their environments enough to make independent decisions about what is or is not safe. Their limited abilities to communicate also place them at high risk. However, most infants and toddlers have somewhat limited and predictable mobility, so **childproofing** the areas they use is a reasonable preventive strategy (CPSC, 2002). Childproofing areas means that caregivers keep the needs, abilities, and limitations of infants and toddlers in mind and prepare the environment so that it is as free from potential safety hazards as possible. For example, caregivers prepare safe environments for infants and toddlers by installing physical barriers (such as gates on stairwells and covers on electrical outlets) and by removing obstacles (such as adult-sized tables and chairs) to protect children (CPSC, 2002). These changes still support children's needs to actively explore their surroundings. So, while infants and toddlers still require supervision in areas that have been childproofed, they have less risk of encountering potential hazards and more freedom for safe exploration (Isbell & Exelby, 2001).

A common misconception is that infants and toddlers require more supervision than preschool-age children; however, the statistics of accidents by age disprove this idea. In the United States, accidents are the main cause of injury that requires treatment in emergency rooms to preschool-age children, who are curious and frequently follow their impulses to investigate interesting sights and sounds (CPSC, 2002). Since preschool-age children are very mobile and can open doors and latches and climb over gates or other obstacles, they are likely to face more hazards than infants and toddlers. Though the mobility and dexterity of preschool-age children are more developed, they still do not have fully developed cognitive abilities that allow them to consistently make sound decisions about safety. Part of this lack of awareness of hazards is due to their limited experiences with danger, and part is due to their egocentric view of situations, which restricts their abilities to determine the relative safety of many situations. Because teachers know that curiosity is a major catalyst to learning, they attempt to anticipate and support children's tendencies to investigate while also supervising them, because teachers know that curiosity is a major contributor to injuries and accidents.

Achieving balance between keeping young children safe from harm and encouraging their independence is sometimes a challenge but well worth the effort. Creating carefully planned and organized play and learning environments that are safe but that still invite curious children to be somewhat independent as they play and explore requires knowledge of child development across the psychomotor, cognitive, and affective domains (Harms, Clifford, & Cryer, 1998).

Protective Strategies to Safeguard Children

Awareness of the needs, interests, and characteristics of children not only helps teachers shape safe play and learning environments, but also enables them to maintain safe conditions while classrooms are in use. Taking preventive safety measures is the initial step in safeguarding children, but caregivers need to use additional strategies to monitor, inspect, and maintain safe conditions (Lowman & Ruhmann, 1998). Supervision is not only an ongoing preventive strategy, it is also the primary **protective safety strategy** used by teachers of young children.

In addition to knowledge of developing children, teachers need to know safety guidelines or mandates set by local, state, or national agencies (Cardwell, Citron, & Dreier, 1999). Groups of individuals with relevant expertise usually develop *standards* linked to particular issues, such as safety, health, or nutrition; these are then approved by professional organizations. Standards indicate the quality, and, in some cases, the *minimum* acceptable level of quality, judged appropriate by experts in the field.

At the local level, fire districts often set fire safety standards for their municipalities. Buildings used for children, such as schools and daycare centers, sometimes have standards or regulations specific to their populations. For example, the local fire district may require that children in child care centers leave their shoes on while napping in the event of a fire emergency. Although school districts and administrators of early childhood programs generally provide information for staff members about these standards, the ultimate responsibility for applying child safety standards falls to those individuals who spend the most time with the children—teachers.

State-level agencies, such as departments of education or departments of health, also propose standards that affect the care and education of young children (Jastrow, Briley, & Roberts-Gray, 1998). As discussed in Chapter 8, child care centers often have to adhere to regulations or standards linked to safety, health, and nutrition before they can be licensed to provide early care and education services. Safety standards for licensure typically focus on issues related to children, caregivers, and physical facilities, including

- Fire safety devices (smoke detectors, fire extinguishers) and evacuation plans
- Access to emergency services (telephones, two-way radios, etc.)
- Building design
- Building security
- Environmental hazards (for example, no lead-based paint or asbestos)
- Natural disaster preparedness (earthquakes, floods, severe storms)
- Staff background screens (for abuse/neglect charges or criminal records)
- Staff training in first aid and CPR (cardiopulmonary resuscitation)

The federal government enacts some standards, but in child care centers and schools, standards are more often determined by state departments of health, education, or family services and by national professional organizations. For example, the National Association for the Education of Young Children (NAEYC) includes compliance with safety standards as part of its voluntary accreditation process, and the National Program for Playground Safety (NPPS) sets guidelines for outdoor play spaces (Thompson, 2000).

Children list outdoor playtime as one of their favorite things to do at child care centers and schools, but more injuries happen on playgrounds each year than anywhere else. Many of these injuries are attributed to poor staff training and inadequate supervision of children (Cardwell, Citron, & Drier, 1999). Unsafe playground equipment, inadequate surface cushioning under climbing equipment, and poor maintenance of equipment account for another large percentage of playground injuries (Kiwanis International Program Development Department, n.d.). The National Program for Playground Safety (NPPS) offers detailed guidelines for safely using playground equipment and surfaces, and for supervising outdoor play (Thompson, 2000). NPPS also recommends use of playground safety checklists to maintain hazard-free playground environments. (See Figure 11.1 for an example of a brief safety checklist for playground equipment that could be completed each day before children use the playground.) Additionally, the U.S. Architectural and Transportation Barriers Compliance Board (2001) provides guidelines and specifications for compliance with the tenets of the Americans with Disabilities Act (ADA).

The most effective protective strategy for both preventing and handling accidents and emergencies is to train and inform staff members on specialized safety procedures, such as first aid and CPR, and have them practice these behaviors and skills. For example, having access to safety devices such as fire extinguishers is an important protective measure, but unless individuals in the building know when and how to use fire extinguishers, serious consequences can still occur (Cardwell, Citron, & Dreier, 1999). Without specialized safety training and practice, individuals will not be prepared to take the appropriate action. **Preparedness** is a term that describes a state of readiness—in this case to handle accidents and emergency situations (Terrass, 2002).

The highest priority for a caregiver is to stay calm during emergency situations; this can be one of the most difficult goals to achieve. By their nature, emergency situa-

Figure 11.1   **Playground Equipment Daily Safety Checklist**

1. ☐ Each piece of equipment is securely anchored.
2. ☐ No loose or broken pieces of equipment are apparent.
3. ☐ No protruding or uncapped parts of equipment are visible.
4. ☐ No rotting or splintered wood on equipment.
5. ☐ No flaking paint or varnish on equipment.
6. ☐ No sharp metal edges or points protruding.
7. ☐ No cracks or broken components are visible on equipment.
8. ☐ Surfaces of equipment are dry and not slippery.
9. ☐ Sufficient cushioning material (10"–12" depth) in place under equipment.
10. ☐ No trash, glass, or other foreign objects on or around equipment.

Comments about items: _____

_____

Recommended actions: _____

_____

Actions taken: _____

_____

Person conducting inspection: _____

Date: _____   Time: _____

tions are unplanned, and the element of surprise can impede action. Part of preparedness training for caregiving staff should include emergency drills and inspections, during which staff members model what they would say or do in the event of a real emergency (Cardwell, Citron, & Dreier, 1999). For example, most schools routinely practice fire evacuation procedures several times a year by sounding the fire alarm and announcing the practice drill. Teachers, children, and all other individuals leave the building in an orderly manner according to predetermined and posted exit routes. Once away from the building, teachers take their students to designated safe areas and take attendance while they wait for the "all clear" announcement before returning to their classrooms. Building administrators, or in some cases fire fighters, observe and time the evacuation procedures to ensure that the building staff carries out the drill as planned. These drills help school personnel identify the strengths and weaknesses of the planned emergency procedures while there is still time to change the procedures without endangering children and staff.

Documenting the date and performance of routine safety practices, such as fire drills or inspections of playground equipment, demonstrates the ongoing safety consciousness of the program. Other types of written records are also important to the facility's preparedness. For example, forms completed by family members at the time of enrollment are used to identify emergency contacts for children and to alert school staff to special medical circumstances (Chang, 2002). These forms can circumvent potentially harmful situations, such as releasing children to unauthorized adults or allowing paramedics to give children medications to which they are allergic (Council for Professional Recognition, 1996; Terrass, 2002).

Another type of written record related to safety is the **incident report.** (See Figure 11.2.) Incident reports are used to keep track of the specific circumstances of safety-related incidents, such as accidents and emergencies (Chang, 2002). These forms are not only important for documenting mishaps but also for use during the planning process, because they can serve as evidence that it is necessary to develop preventive measures related to unsafe situations (Cardwell, Citron, & Dreier, 1999).

Figure 11.2   Incident/Accident Report

Child(ren)'s name(s): _____

Setting: _____

Date of incident: _____   Time of incident: _____

Description of incident: _____

_____

_____

_____

Actions taken: _____

Notifications made (if necessary): _____

_____

Incident observed by: _____

_____

Incident reported by: _____

Date of report: _____

Recommended follow-up: _____

_____

Practicing Healthy Procedures

Many factors influence the overall health of America's children, including access to immunization and health care, socioeconomic levels of families, awareness of healthy hygiene practices, balance of daily nutritional intake, and level of physical activity. Most of these factors are outside the direct control of children who depend on their primary caregivers to oversee their health needs.

CDA

COMPETENCY GOAL I
• Functional Area 2

COMPETENCY GOAL IV
• Functional Area 11

COMPETENCY GOAL V
• Functional Area 12

The first five years of life represent a crucial period for developing healthy minds and bodies; yet, according to the Children's Defense Fund (CDF, 2002, p. 13), one in eight children in the United States has no health insurance, which severely restricts their access to health care. Without health insurance, many children and families lack basic preventive health care, which not only increases their likelihood of illness but puts other individuals at risk as well.

Healthy Practices in Early Care and Education Settings

Before enrollment, many child care programs request **health histories** from families, to obtain an overview of children's general state of health from birth. Family members are asked to describe any ongoing health issues (such as chronic asthma, seizures, or frequent nosebleeds) so school staff are well informed about the children's individual needs. Some health histories, particularly those for infants and toddlers, also ask about daily routines, such as children's sleeping habits (whether they sleep with a pacifier or favorite blanket) and their eating habits (their food and drink preferences). This collection of information provides school personnel with information necessary to meet the health needs of individual children.

> *We are obliged to make sure every child gets a healthy start on life. With all our wealth and capacity, we just can't stand by idly.*
> —Colin Powell, U.S. Secretary of State (2000)

Many early care and education programs conduct periodic **health appraisals** of enrolled children. In some cases, particularly in daycare centers, nurses or other staff members carry out **daily health checks** as children arrive. Daily health checks are quick visual surveys that focus on the appearance of children's skin, eyes, nose, mouth, and palms to determine if they are exhibiting any symptoms of illness. Other facilities rely on the observation skills of teachers to identify children who are ill. In addition to informal health checks, programs perform or sponsor routine **health screenings** for vision, hearing, and certain physical conditions. Health screenings are usually administered by certified health personnel and serve as "first alert systems" to quickly identify children who may need more extensive medical examination to confirm they have health conditions that need treatment.

Communicable Diseases among Children

Young children are somewhat more susceptible to infectious or **communicable diseases,** like chickenpox and measles, which can be spread from one individual to another, than are older children and adults. Because children are apt to touch objects and put their fingers in their mouths, they are more likely to come in contact with germs. In order to reduce the likelihood of spreading serious illnesses, most early care and education programs require children to have up-to-date **immunizations** before they begin attending school (American Academy of Pediatrics, 2002). Immunizations, which are generally administered by medical personnel through injections, enable individuals to build resistance to specific diseases. Some states also require annual physical examinations by authorized medical personnel. In addition to immunization records, school administrators may request information about children's current state of health and any chronic or serious medical conditions, such as seizure disorders or diabetes.

Schools in the United States generally require health records from child care personnel to ensure that they are free of infectious diseases and do not pose health threats to children (American Academy of Pediatrics, 2001). In addition to annual physical examinations by certified medical personnel, many states require diagnostic **tuberculosis skin tests** for children and adults who work in schools, hospitals, or restaurants. Tuberculosis (also called TB) is a highly infectious disease that affects the lungs. Tuberculosis was very prevalent in the United States for the first half of the twentieth century until routine skin tests made early detection and treatment possible. Although staff members may not have to complete health histories, they are often asked to supply information about their current levels of health, including any chronic or serious medical conditions that would interfere with the performance of their job responsibilities or that might pose a risk to others.

In addition to identifying types of medical information required, school health policies outline preventive practices to ensure healthy learning environments. Whenever groups of individuals share common space for periods of time, the risk of spreading infectious disease increases. One highly effective way to control the spread of infectious diseases is through hand washing. Most infectious diseases, such as colds and flu, are spread by individuals' contact with contaminated objects or host individuals. In many cases, hands are the contaminated objects. The two major routes for disease transmission are **airborne transmission** and **fecal-oral transmission.** Airborne transmission is spread through tiny droplets of fluid from the mouth (saliva) or nose (mucus) that are usually expelled during coughing or sneezing; airborne transmission may also contribute to foodborne disease outbreaks (FDA/USDA, 2002). Infants and toddlers are also likely to spread or contact germs through saliva when they suck on bottles, pacifiers, or other objects. Fecal-oral transmission results when germs in fecal matter are spread, during diapering or toileting procedures, to the mouth.

Consistent use of effective **hand-washing techniques** by staff members and children reduces the likelihood that infectious diseases will be spread. Young children are notorious for their poor hand-washing techniques, so teachers need to not only model effective techniques but also to encourage and supervise children as they wash their hands. Poor personal hygiene is a major contributor to the spread of infectious diseases (FDA/USDA, 2002). Table 11.1 outlines effective hand-washing techniques.

Another hygiene technique recommended by the Centers for Disease Control and Prevention (CDC, 2002) to protect individuals from infection is the use of **universal precautions** when handling any types of body fluids, such as urine, blood, vomit, or feces (which may contain blood). Universal precautions for infection control begin with the assumption that all body fluids are potentially infectious (OSHA, 1998). Acting in

Table 11.1 Effective Hand-Washing Techniques

- Wash hands using warm, running water.
- Apply liquid soap.
- Lather soap and rub front and back of hands and wrists (for at least 20 seconds).
- Continue rubbing lather between fingers and under nails.
- Rinse thoroughly under running water.
- Dry hands with a clean disposable towel (or use air dryer).
- Use disposable towel to turn off faucets.
- Dispense towel in a covered trash receptacle.

Source: U.S. Food and Drug Administration/U.S. Department of Agriculture. (2002). *Healthy People 2010.* Washington, DC: U.S. Department of Health and Human Services.

accordance with this assumption provides an extra margin of safety for individuals who may come into contact with body fluids on a regular basis. In early care and education settings, diapering and assisting children with toileting are everyday occurrences that require the use of universal precautions (Lowman & Ruhmann, 1998; Texas Child Care, 2000). Another frequent occurrence when working around active young children is injury that causes bleeding; children often stumble, fall, or run into objects and receive scrapes and cuts as a result. The first step in administering first aid to injured children is to follow the procedure for universal precautions to control infection. The Occupational Safety and Health Administration (OSHA) requires that individuals who work closely with body fluids be trained in the use of universal precautions to protect the health of themselves and others (OSHA, 1998). (See Table 11.2.)

Although protective and preventive practices—such as immunizations, daily health checks, hand washing, and universal precautions—reduce the spread of contagious

Table 11.2 Universal Precautions for Infection Control When Handling Blood and Other Body Fluids

- Wash hands with soap, using effective hand-washing techniques.
- Always wear well-fitting, disposable latex gloves.
- Disposable latex gloves should be discarded after a single use.
- Remove glove by grasping the cuff and pulling it off inside out.
- Discard used gloves in covered trash receptacles.
- Wash hands with soap, using effective hand-washing techniques.
- Dispose of contaminated materials properly:
  - Seal soiled clothing in plastic bags to be laundered at home.
  - Discard disposable diapers by sealing them securely in plastic bags.
- Clean all surfaces with disinfectant bleach solution.

Source: U.S. Department of Labor, Occupational Safety and Health Administration. (1998). *Universal Precautions—Blood-Borne Pathogens.* Washington, DC: Author.

diseases, some infectious illness will still occur. School health policies provide guide-lines for handling illnesses. These policies often specify whether children may continue to attend school or should be excluded from school until the illness no longer poses a threat to others. Exclusion policies for illness are generally based on guidelines from lo-cal departments of health or from the Centers for Disease Control and Prevention (CDC), which maintain a database of infectious (communicable) diseases that describes symptoms, treatments, and approximate number of days that each illness remains con-tagious. Illness policies for children and staff with communicable diseases should be similar; both children and staff should be excluded from school settings while they are still contagious (CDC, 2002; Chang, 2002).

For many common childhood communicable diseases, such as measles and chicken pox, immunizations are highly effective in preventing individuals from be-coming infected. For children in the United States, the American Academy of Pediatrics (AAP, 2002) recommends an immunization schedule that begins during infancy and includes booster shots throughout childhood to maintain immunity. Table 11.3 lists several childhood illnesses and recommended immunization schedules.

Table 11.3   Recommended Immunization Schedule for Children in the United States (2003)

	Birth	2 months	4 months	6 months	12–15 months	4–6 years
HBV[a]	✓	✓		✓		
DTaP[b]		✓	✓	✓	✓	✓
HIB[c]		✓	✓	✓	✓	
IPV[d]		✓	✓	✓		✓
MMR[e]					✓	✓
PCV[f]		✓	✓	✓	✓	

[a] Hepatitis B virus—infects the liver; vaccine usually given as a series of three injections.

[b] Diptheria, tetanus (lockjaw), and pertussis (whooping cough); vaccine given in a series of five injections.

[c] Haemophilus influenzae—type B bacteria, the leading cause of meningitis in children; vaccine given in series of four injections.

[d] Inactivated poliovirus—a gastrointestinal viral infection that can result in permanent paralysis; vaccine given in series of three injections.

[e] Measles, mumps, and rubella (German measles); vaccine given in two injections.

[f] Pneumococcal infections, like pneumonia and bacterial meningitis; vaccine given as series of four injections.

Source: Constructed from the 2003 immunization schedule of the American Academy of Pediatrics (AAP) and the Centers for Disease Control and Prevention (CDC).

Promoting Nutrition and Healthy Eating

Throughout our lives, our health is strongly affected by the types and quantities of foods we eat. During early childhood, a period of rapid growth and development, infants and children are particularly sensitive to nutrition. **Nutrition** is the study of foods and how the body processes them. Foods that contribute to the healthy operation of the body are said to be nutritious because they are rich in food substances called **nutrients,** such as carbohydrates, fats, proteins, minerals, vitamins, or water. Nutrients contribute to the health of the body by building and maintaining body tissues, regulating body functions, and providing energy.

When infants and children receive adequate nutrition, their bodies and brains are able to grow and develop at normal rates. However, if they receive inadequate nutrition, their growth will be slowed, their motor and cognitive development may be delayed, and they may lack energy and appear listless (Brown & Marcotte, 2002). **Malnutrition (**or **undernutrition)** stems from not having sufficient quantities of food or from not having the right kinds of food needed to obtain all of the nutrients necessary for normal growth and development. For many young children, schools provide nearly half of their daily nutritional needs; even so, over ten million children in the United States experience hunger on a regular basis. The effects of **hunger,** "a painful condition associated with the lack of food," are particularly detrimental to young children's growth and development and may continue to affect their adolescent and adult health status as well (Brown & Marcotte, 2002, p. 15).

Another aspect of malnutrition is **obesity,** which is defined as being 20 or more percent above your normal body weight. Obesity is often associated with consuming too much food. However, children who are obese may still be malnourished because, although they are eating too much food, they are not eating the types of food their bodies need for the nutrients to maintain healthy body function. Children who are malnourished often lack energy, which reduces their interest in physical activity and thus contributes to weight gain. (Nutrition guidelines are discussed later in this chapter in the section on dietary guidelines.)

Keeping families informed about their children's eating patterns helps them make decisions about supplementing their children's diets at home, if necessary. Posting weekly school menus or including the menus in take-home newsletters or calendars can help inform parents of what children are eating. In addition, teachers can advise family members with brief notes or telephone calls if they have concerns about children's food intake or eating behaviors (Brown & Marcotte, 2002).

CDA

COMPETENCY GOAL I
• Functional Area 2

COMPETENCY GOAL IV
• Functional Area 11

In addition to supporting a stimulating educational environment, early childhood educators can maximize a child's learning potential by advocating for nutrition education, acting as role models for healthy eating habits, and recognizing when a child may be at risk for undernutrition.

—J. Larry Brown and Lori P. Marcotte, Center on Hunger, Poverty and Nutrition at Tufts University (2002, p. 20)

Special Considerations Related to Food and Eating Practices

Families have responsibilities to inform schools if their children have special needs with relation to foods. **Food allergy** and **food intolerance** represent two areas of special needs associated with food. Food allergies are triggered when body systems produce histamines in reaction to particular foods. In some cases, food allergies trigger breathing problems and can be serious and even deadly; other times, less severe allergic reactions, such as sneezing or skin rashes, can occur (Welsh, 2000). All food allergies need to be taken seriously, because each reaction has the potential to become serious. Examples of foods that have been documented to cause allergic reactions are milk and milk products, eggs, peanuts, and shellfish (ACAAI, 2001). (More information about food allergies can be found at the ACAAI Web site listed at the end of this chapter.) Food intolerance occurs when body systems have difficulty digesting particular foods or components of food. Food intolerance is rarely fatal but can cause mild to strong discomfort. For instance, intolerance to lactose (a component of cow's milk) is relatively common and can cause stomach cramps or diarrhea. A third area of special needs relates to chronic medical conditions that are directly linked to particular types of foods. For example, children and adults with diabetes have to be very careful about the amount of sugar and starch they consume. Early care and education programs need to work with families to develop cooperative plans to ensure that children are not offered foods that have the potential to make them ill. Special needs related to foods should be considered as carefully and confidentially as other types of special needs to ensure children's health and to avoid making them feel uncomfortable among their peers.

Two other factors that influence food choices are religious beliefs and family preferences, such as with kosher and vegetarian diets. Early childhood programs need to demonstrate respect for individual families' food preferences and comply with their requests as much as possible. If such food requests place an undue burden on school programs, it may be necessary to confer with families to find the best way to accommodate their requests. Open communication promotes sensitivity to family choices and shows appreciation for diversity.

Food can also promote cultural awareness by inviting families to share their customs and recipes. Caregivers can encourage young children to try new foods by introducing them gradually to other food options in the same food groups. Young children seem to take comfort from familiar foods and may initially be hesitant to try new ones. However, if they are exposed to new foods more than once, without pressure, they will likely try the new food.

Dietary Guidelines

Nutritional guidelines for school programs come from the U.S. Department of Agriculture (USDA), which specifies dietary guidelines according to nutrient groups. The USDA uses a graphic model, called the **Food Guide Pyramid**, to explain these food groups. In 1999, the USDA presented a version of this model particularly for children between ages 2 and 6. (See Figure 11.3.) Using a simplified format, the Food Guide Pyramid for Young

Figure 11.3   USDA Food Guide Pyramid for Young Children

Source: U.S. Department of Agriculture, Center for Nutrition Policy and Promotion, January 2000.

Children gives examples of foods in each of the food groups and includes information about serving sizes for children.

In the United States, millions of school meals are served to young children every weekday; thus, it is essential that teachers of young children have a firm understanding of the nutritional needs of young children and of the nutritional values of commonly served foods. In child care centers, where children may spend more than eight hours per day, teachers also need to model healthy eating habits. Family-style meals in day-care centers provide opportunities both to support social development and promote nutrition education. In many states, licensing regulations require teachers to sit and eat with the children in order to observe children's eating patterns and to model healthy eating habits.

Informing and Teaching about Safety, Health, and Nutrition

COMPETENCY GOAL I
• Functional Areas 1–3

COMPETENCY GOAL IV
• Functional Area 11

COMPETENCY GOAL V
• Functional Area 12

COMPETENCY GOAL VI
• Functional Area 13

One of the responsibilities of being an early childhood educator is to help families become aware of ways that they can contribute to their children's overall development. Within the areas of safety, health, and nutrition, teachers have many opportunities to share information with families and to learn from families as well.

Communicating with Families about Safety, Health, and Nutrition

Most early childhood programs provide family members with written information about guidelines and practices related to safety, health, and nutrition. In child care and school programs, these materials are usually provided prior to enrollment, and family members are asked to read the information before making decisions about enrollment. When written policies and guidelines are collected and organized into coherent packets of related information, the booklets are call **handbooks.** Giving family members handbooks, rather than individual information sheets, is generally more effective for sharing vital information. Handbooks are less likely to be overlooked in the abundance of notices that schools send home with children. Helpful reading aids—such as tables of contents, indices, and consecutively numbered pages—make handbooks valuable tools for the family as well as for staff members. To ensure that information is accurate and amended as needed, each page of the handbook should state the date the page was most recently updated. Handbooks also provide early care and education programs with excellent opportunities to promote the safety, health, and nutrition of children by sharing information with family members about community resources available to them. (Chapter 13 provides additional information about community resources.) While most early care and education programs continue to distribute printed handbooks, some programs have supplemented or replaced written handbooks with computerized on-line versions available on program Web sites that family and staff members can access through the Internet. On-line versions of handbooks are more easily updated and provide an excellent means of connecting families to information about community resources through convenient Web links; however, not all families have Internet access, and some individuals prefer written materials.

Teaching Children about Safety, Health, and Nutrition

Children gradually learn about safety, health, and nutrition as they encounter situations, at home and school, concerning various aspects of these concepts. Teachers have frequent opportunities to verbalize or model safety, health, and nutrition practices through the course of daily routines and procedures, such as holding onto the handrail when climbing stairs, washing hands with soap before eating, and making wise food choices (Jastrow, Briley, & Roberts-Gray, 1998). These **teachable moments** provide excellent informal teaching opportunities for helping children learn and practice appropriate safety, health, and nutrition behaviors.

Children can also learn concepts about safety, health, and nutrition through formal learning experiences that teachers can arrange to coincide with curriculum themes or topics or to occur as adjuncts to learning center activities. For example, dramatic play areas can be enriched with prop boxes filled with materials related to safety, health, or nutrition themes, such as going to the dentist or shopping for nutritious groceries. The props encourage children to role-play different scenarios and gain additional understanding of the concepts. Children's books, both fiction and nonfiction, also provide information and ideas about safety, health, and nutrition concepts.

Summary

- Human factors—such as lack of supervision and poorly trained staff members—can negatively affect the safety, health, and nutrition of children. Diligent supervision and well-trained staff members can promote children's safety, health, and nutrition.

Preparing Safe Play and Learning Environments

- Physical factors—such as materials, equipment, room arrangement, and building conditions—affect the safety of children.
- Preventive safety strategies—such as childproofing and avoiding developmentally inappropriate materials and equipment—help to safeguard young children.
- Protective safety strategies—such as continuous supervision and routine maintenance of equipment, both indoors and outdoors—help to safeguard young children.
- Emergency preparedness encompasses planning, training, and practicing of techniques and routines.

- Effective supervision by caregivers is central to maintaining safe, healthy play and learning environments for young children.

Practicing Healthy Procedures

- Preventive medical care reduces the potential for illness.
- Many schools require up-to-date immunizations before children are allowed to attend their programs.
- Health records are required by schools and usually include information about each child's immunizations, current level of health, and health history.
- Early care and education programs use preventive practices, such as daily health checks and health appraisals, to track children's health and to protect others from potential health risks.
- Illness exclusion policies for infectious diseases are based on guidelines from departments of health and the Centers for Disease Control and Prevention (CDC).

- Effective hand-washing techniques reduce the spread of infectious disease.
- Universal precautions for infection control are based on the assumption that all body fluids are potentially infectious.
- Universal precautions for infection control protect both children and staff.
- Children imitate healthy practices modeled by program staff.

Promoting Nutrition and Healthy Eating

- Early care and education programs follow nutrition guidelines from departments of health and the U.S. Department of Agriculture (USDA).
- The USDA's Food Guide Pyramid for Young Children identifies nutrient groups and recommended number of daily servings to maintain balanced diets.

- School mealtimes provide opportunities for children to learn about nutrition and healthy-eating practices.
- Families and schools can work as partners to promote children's health and nutrition.
- Health is affected by nutrition and activity level.

Informing and Teaching about Safety, Health, and Nutrition

- Communicating with family members about policies, procedures, standards, and resources related to safety, health, and nutrition is an important aspect of quality early care and education.
- Teacher behaviors such as modeling and verbalizing promote children's awareness of concepts related to safety, health, and nutrition.
- Both informal and formal learning experiences and teaching practices help children learn about safety, health, and nutrition.

LEARNING ACTIVITIES

1 Role-Play: Handling Emergencies. In small groups, brainstorm a list of emergencies that might occur in early care and education settings. Select one or more of the emergencies and role-play classroom teachers handling them. Use one scenario to model calm, efficient handling of the emergency that follows a preparedness plan; use the second scenario to demonstrate ineffective handling of the emergency situation. Invite classmates to analyze both scenarios and suggest improvements.

2 Brainstorming: Nutrition Activities. In a small group, brainstorm a list of activities that could be used with young children to teach about healthy nutrition by using the USDA's Food Guide Pyramid for Young Children that is illustrated in Figure 11.3 (p. 253). Also discuss how mealtimes could be used to build young children's nutritional awareness on a daily basis.

PORTFOLIO ARTIFACTS

1 Observation: Safety Perspectives. Make arrangements to visit an early childhood classroom. Examine the classroom environment for safe and potentially unsafe characteristics. Include materials, equipment, room arrangement, and line-of-sight for supervision. After you have recorded your findings, move to another location in the room and squat down until you are at the approximate eye level of the children who use the

classroom. Remaining at children's eye level, repeat your safety inspection of all aspects of the classroom space. What differences in safety did you note? Reflect on how viewing the room from the perspective of the children affects your awareness of potential threats to safety.

2 Sample: Children's Health Records. Visit one or more early care and education programs and collect blank samples of health record forms, such as immunization schedules and health histories that programs require families to complete before children are allowed to attend school. Review the forms and reflect on how the types of information requested can be used by schools and classroom teachers to safeguard children's health. Also consider issues of confidentiality related to the health information requested by schools for both children and staff.

3 Project: Children's Book Duets about Nutrition. Visit your local library or bookstore and locate children's books about nutrition and healthy eating. After browsing through several books, identify a special topic in nutrition for which you have found

a fiction and a nonfiction book. Read both books and prepare a "book duet" that includes complete bibliographic information and at least one project or activity appropriate for children under age 6. For example, the book *Bread, Bread, Bread* by Ann Morris (Mulberry Books, 1993) is part of the nonfiction Around the World Series, and *Everybody Bakes Bread* by Norah Dooley (Carolrhoda Books, 1996) is a fiction storybook about how everyone in the neighborhood prepares and eats different kinds of bread. A related learning activity could be a "tasting party," where children sample small bites of a variety of breads, including pita bread and tortillas and some of the other breads described in these books.

Professional Connections and Web Links

American College of Allergy, Asthma & Immunology (ACAAI)
85 West Algonquin Road, Suite 550
Arlington Heights, IL 60005
847-427-1200
http://www.acaai.org

The ACAAI Web site provides information about quality health care for individuals with allergies and asthma. The site maintains an on-line "allergy watch alert" and information directed toward allergy and asthma sufferers, physicians, schools, and the general public. The ACAAI site also provides a link to an on-line medical library, Medem, which provides information about symptoms and treatment of "asthma and other allergic diseases," including indoor and outdoor allergies, pet allergies, and food allergies. The Medem medical library can be accessed directly at http://www.medem.com.

Centers for Disease Control and Prevention (CDC)
1600 Clifton Road Northeast
Atlanta, GA 30329
404-639-3311
http://www.cdc.gov

This federal Web site is maintained by the Centers for Disease Control and Prevention (CDC), which is part of the U.S. Department of Health and Human Services. The CDC monitors health threats, conducts research and collects data related to disease prevention, and promotes awareness of health issues. Its mission is "to improve the health of the people of the United States." One of the

most helpful features of the CDC site, for teachers of young children, is its Health Topics A–Z, which provides up-to-date information about a variety of health topics, including communicable diseases and chronic health conditions, such as allergies and asthma, that are related to environmental conditions. The CDC site also provides links to several of its partner agencies, such as the National Center on Birth Defects and Developmental Disabilities (NCBDDD) and the National Center for Injury Prevention and Control (NCIPC).

Childcare Health Program
1625 Alcatraz Avenue, Suite 369
Berkeley, CA 94705
510-923-9513

The Childcare Health Program Web site is designed to serve as a resource link between California child care programs and community agencies, so they may better serve families. The organization maintains ongoing activities, such as specialized training for child care providers regarding diversity curriculum and disaster preparedness. Childcare Health Program has also developed a template, complete with national standards and California licensing regulations, to be used to personalize parent and staff handbooks for child care programs. This site will be useful to individuals outside the state of California as well, because of its extensive links to national programs concerned with the development, safety, health, and nutrition of young children.

Children's Defense Fund (CDF)
25 E Street, N.W.
Washington, DC 20001
202-628-8787
http://www.childrensdefense.org

The CDF is a private, nonprofit organization that states its mission as serving as an "effective voice for all the children of America." It publishes annual reports, based on statistics gathered from dozens of sources, on the state of children's well-being in America and suggests ways that individuals and groups can make differences in the lives of children. Many of the statistics relate to access to quality child care. This Web site also provides information about their Movement to Leave No Child Behind, a grassroots effort to ensure that all of America's children have a fair and healthy start in life.

Healthy Child Care America Campaign (HCCA)
Healthy Child Care America Campaign
American Academy of Pediatrics
Department of Community Pediatrics
141 Northwest Point Boulevard
Elk Grove, IL 60007
888-227-5409
www.aap.org/advocacy/hcca

The Healthy Child Care America Campaign (HCCA), which is a cooperative effort of the American Academy of Pediatrics, the U.S. Department of Health and Human Services Child Care Bureau, and the Maternal and Child Health Bureau, has identified ten steps for its Blueprint for Action. The action plan is designed to promote the healthy development of children by providing information for linking health care professionals, child care providers, and families with community resources.

KidsHealth
The Nemours Foundation
1600 Rockland Road
Wilmington, DE 19803
302-651-4046
http://kidshealth.org

This versatile Web site, sponsored by the Nemours Foundation, offers a wealth of accurate health-related information (in English and Spanish) for children, adolescents, and parents. Although the site is not geared specifically to educators, many of the topics are useful to individuals working in the early care and education field. Topics in-clude hand washing, control of infectious diseases, allergies, immunization schedules, first aid and safety, and positive parenting. Many of the articles, which are available in printer-friendly versions, are excellent sources of information to share with families.

National Program for Playground Safety
University of Northern Iowa
Cedar Falls, IA 50614
800-554-PLAY (7529)
http://www.uni.edu/playground

This Web site offers a selection of brochures, safety bulletins, and videos about playground safety as well as suggestions for playground design and maintenance. NPPS also posts an on-line newsletter that can be accessed at www.uni.edu/playground/newsletter.html.

U.S. Consumer Product Safety Commission (CPSC)
CPSC, Office of Information and Public Affairs
Washington, DC 20207
1-800-638-2772
www.cpsc.gov

The U.S. Consumer Product Safety Commission (CPSC) conducts research, collects statistics, and disseminates information about public safety. It offers a complete list of publications about safety issues related to infants, children, and adolescents, many of which are available in English and Spanish. Topics include child care [centers] safety checklist, childproofing, car seat safety, infant bedding, and bicycle safety. Many brochures are available in individual and bulk quantities at no cost. CPSC also maintains a database of information about product recalls, including toys, safety gates, cribs, home playground equipment, and car seats.

U.S. Department of Agriculture (USDA)
Center for Nutrition Policy and Promotion
3101 Park Center Drive, Room 1034
Alexandria, VA 22302-1594
703-305-7600
http://www.usda.gov/cnpp

This government Web site offers information about required daily amounts of nutrients and minerals as well as information about the USDA Food Pyramid and the Food Guide Pyramid for Young Children. The USDA also provides information about federal food programs for public schools and nonprofit daycare centers.

Suggestions for Further Reading

Chang, Albert. (2002). *Caring for our children* (2nd ed.) Elk Grove Village, IL: American Academy of Pediatrics, American Public Safety Administration, and U.S. Health Resources and Services Administration.

- This book, which provides 658 safety, health, and nutrition guidelines and standards for child care programs, is a joint publication of the American Academy of Pediatrics, the American Public Health Association, and the U.S. Health Resources and Services Administration. This well-organized volume covers a wide range of essential topics in staff health assessment, healthy food preparation and storage, and risk factors for child abuse and neglect. The book also includes NAEYC's position statement on licensing and public regulation of child care.

Kendrick A. S., Kaufman, R., & Messenger, K. P. (Eds.). (1996). *Healthy young children: A manual for programs.* Washington, DC: National Association for the Education of Young Children.

- This well-organized manual designed for early childhood programs provides information on promoting and protecting young children's health and safety. The book also includes information related to healthy practices that can be employed by staff and family members to reduce the spread of infectious diseases.

Ray, A., Harms, T., & Cryer, Debby. (1996). *Nutrition activities for preschoolers.* Menlo Park, CA: Innovative Learning Publications.

- This illustrated book describes nutrition-related activities to do with preschool-age children in a variety of interest areas or learning centers, such as blocks, art, music, and pretend play. Many of the projects include opportunities for children to assist with snack and meal preparation. The introduction provides general information on nutrition and healthy eating for children.

References

American College of Allergy, Asthma & Immunology (ACAAI). (2001). *Children's Allergies.* Medem Medical Library. [on-line] Retrieved on February 2, 2003, from http://www.medem.com/MedLB.

Brown, J. Larry, & Marcotte, Lori P. (2002). Nutrition & cognitive development in young children. *Earlychildhood News, 14*(6), 15–18, 20–21.

Cardwell, Anne, Citron, & Dreier, Steve. (1999). How secure is your center? *Child Care Information Exchange, 130,* 66–69.

Centers for Disease Control and Prevention (CDC). (2002, November). *Health topics A–Z.* Retrieved February 2, 2003, from http://www.cdc.gov/.

Chang, Albert. (2002). *Caring for our children* (2nd ed.). Elk Grove Village, IL: American Academy of Pediatrics, American Public Safety Administration, & Health Resources and Services Administration.

Children's Defense Fund (CDF). (2002). *The state of children in America's union: A 2002 action guide to Leave No Child Behind.* Washington, DC: Author.

Council for Professional Recognition. (1996). *The child development associate: Assessment system and competency standards for preschool caregivers in center-based programs.* Washington, DC: Council for Professional Recognition.

Harms, Thelma, Clifford, Richard M., & Cryer, Debby. (1998). *Early childhood environment rating scale* (Rev. ed.). New York: Teachers College Press.

Isbell, Rebecca, & Exelby, Betty. (2001). *Early learning environments that work.* Beltsville, MD: Gryphon House.

Jastrow, Susie, Briley, Margaret, & Roberts-Gray, Cindy. (1998). Food safety: Is your kitchen clean? *Texas Child Care, 21*(4), 8–13.

Kiwanis International, Program Development Department. (n.d.). *A service project for young children: Priority one playgrounds.* Indianapolis, IN: Kiwanis International.

Lowman, Linda H., & Ruhmann, Linda H. (1998). Simply sensational spaces: A multi-"S" approach to toddler environments. *Young Children, 53*(3), 11–16.

Terrass, Mary. (2002). Planning for disaster: Keeping children safe and healthy. *Earlychildhood News, 14*(1), 22–23.

Texas Child Care. (2000). Summer sanitation: Review basic practices for preventing disease. *Texas Child Care, 24*(1), 2–7.

Thomas, Nancy G., & Berk, Laura E. (1981). Effects of school environments on the development of young children's creativity. *Child Development, 52,* 1133–1162.

Thompson, Donna. (2000). *Planning a play area for children.* Cedar Falls, IA: National Program for Playground Safety (NPPS).

U.S. Architectural and Transportation Barriers Compliance Board. (2001). *Guide to ADA accessibility guidelines for play areas.* Washington, DC: U.S. Access Board.

U.S. Consumer Product Safety Commission (CPSC). (2002). CPSC and CNA join together to offer free home childproofing brochure. Retrieved May 11, 2003, from http://www.cpsc.gov/CPSCPUB/PREREL/PRHTML99/99066.html.

U.S. Department of Labor, Occupational Safety and Health Administration (OSHA). (1998). *Universal precautions—Blood-borne pathogens.* Washington, DC: Author.

U.S. Food and Drug Administration (FDA) & U.S. Department of Agriculture (USDA). (2002). *Healthy people 2010.* Washington, DC: U.S. Department of Health and Human Services.

Welsh, Michael J. (2000). *Your child's allergies and asthma: Breathing easy and bringing up healthy, active children.* New York: Villard.

Connecting with Families and Communities

Children are intimately connected to their families, and through their families, to their communities. As a teacher of young children, you will have countless opportunities to extend your influence beyond the boundaries of the schoolyard in ways that positively affect the quality of children's lives. The two chapters of Module Four, "Connecting with Families and Communities," offer you information and insight into the intricate relationships among children, families, schools, and communities.

The first chapter of this module describes a variety of ways teachers and schools can support family relationships by involving families in their children's educational experiences right from the start. Once a firm foundation is in place, family members are more likely to continue playing active roles in their children's schooling. In turn, children, teachers, and schools benefit from the broader cultural context that occurs when the community is brought into classrooms. The closing chapter of this module explores the diverse array of community resources available to children and families and the role of teachers and schools in bringing them together.

Education is for improving the lives of others and leaving your community and world better than you found it.

—Marian Wright Edelman, Founder of Children's Defense Fund

Connecting with Families

After reading this chapter and completing the related activities, you should be able to

- Discuss the state of children and families in the United States
- Describe the role of families and ways to involve them in early care and education
- Describe informal and formal methods of home-school communication as well as the benefits and challenges
- List considerations in planning family-teacher conferences
- Give examples of two-way and one-way communication strategies
- Discuss the roles of volunteers in early childhood education
- Describe ways families serve as resources for schools
- Identify the goals of parent education
- Suggest ways that early care and education environments can be oriented to and responsive to children and their families

Tugging on her father's hand, five-year-old Sue Lynn practically drags her father down the long hallway toward the kindergarten. She is so excited about her first day of "big school" that she was dressed and ready before her father came to wake her up. Mr. Lee Chinn glances at his watch and hopes that Sue Lynn's teacher, Ms. Nicole MacKenzie, is ready for his energetic and excitable daughter. He and Ms. MacKenzie had already spoken twice on the telephone about Sue Lynn before school started, and the teacher had seemed very caring and willing to do what she could to help Sue Lynn succeed in kindergarten. Although Sue Lynn looks, and usually acts, like a typical happy-go-lucky five-year-old child, at times she will burst into tears for no apparent cause or become very withdrawn and silent. He and Sue Lynn are still adjusting to life without Kara, his wife and Sue Lynn's mother, who died suddenly six months ago.

Ms. MacKenzie assures him that Sue Lynn's behavior is part of the normal grieving process and that she and the other school personnel will be sensitive to his and Sue Lynn's loss. The teacher had even mailed him a packet with information about how young children deal with death and a list of children's books to share with his daughter. The information had been very helpful, and he and Sue Lynn had started attending a support group for families whose loved ones had died. Ms. MacKenzie had also suggested that he might volunteer in the classroom occasionally to see how his daughter is adjusting and to let Sue Lynn know that he is, and always will be, involved in her schooling. Now, Sue Lynn is waiting impatiently for him outside the classroom doorway, clutching the family photograph they had been asked to bring on the first

CHAPTER 12

day of school. The first thing Mr. Chinn notices on entering the classroom is the large, colorful bulletin board entitled "Important People" and the group of excited children and parents who are clustered around it. He expects to see pictures of presidents or community helpers and so isn't prepared for the collage of family snapshots tacked to the board with captions like "People Who Are Important to Bobby." There is a space labeled for every child's family photos, and the teacher has left a space for Sue Lynn's family's photos too. Mr. Chinn breathes a sigh of relief. Any teacher who recognizes how important family members are to young children is certainly the right type of teacher for his pride and joy.

Young children are connected to their families in many ways. Early childhood teachers recognize the unique bonds between children and their families and strive to create learning environments that provide accessible pathways for communication and involvement. Knowledge of children's home lives and cultures helps teachers develop holistic views of the young children in their care. The traditional portrayal of families as fathers, mothers, and siblings fails to capture the rich diversity of family structures in the United States and other countries. Teachers who look forward to opportunities to interact with a wide array of families are rewarded with unique glimpses into real family life.

Young Children and Their Families

The landscape of the American family has shifted from generations of families living in close proximity to small pockets of relatives living at distances from each other. The changes stem from a variety of influences, including economics and technology (Kohler, 1998). Whatever the causes, many families, which once were relatively self-sufficient because of their multigenerational support bases, now depend on support services from their communities to meet their needs (Children's Defense Fund, 2001). In many communities, schools have stepped in to fill the child care roles once filled by relatives and are also sometimes called on to serve as referral agents to social services. The mobility of society also creates situations where families new to the community are unfamiliar with the services available to them, and so in many cases schools have undertaken many of the roles once carried out by social service

CDA

COMPETENCY GOAL IV
• Functional Area 11

COMPETENCY GOAL VI
• Functional Area 13

agencies, such as food assistance programs and counseling services (Gonzalez-Mena, 2001).

When schools assume new responsibilities, teachers' roles are also affected. Most preservice training programs for teachers include coursework related to how schools and teachers will communicate with, involve, and serve families in their communities, although the amount of time devoted to these crucial skills is often minimal. The first step to sensitive and effective home-school relationships is understanding and respecting families in all aspects of their diverse cultures (Gonzalez-Mena, 2001).

> *Instead, our image of the child is rich in potential, strong, powerful, competent, and most of all, connected to adults and other children.*
> —Loris Malaguzzi, Italian educator

Many families today are small units consisting of parent figures and children; these **nuclear families** often lack the support of relatives or **extended families**. In the 1950s, a nuclear family was usually mother, father, and their offspring. Today, members of a nuclear family may or may not have the same biological ties. Increases in numbers of divorces, remarriages, and single parents have broadened the concept of **family** to include diverse individuals blended into groups who are emotionally, and usually economically, dependent on one another.

With the rise of single-parent families and increased costs of living, many children live in homes where each parent figure is employed outside the home. Families in this situation need alternative ways to provide for the care of children. The Children's Defense Fund (CDF, 2002) reports that as of December 2001, nearly 500,000 children in the United States were on waiting lists for child care assistance. Reports from the U.S. Census (Smith, 2000) indicate that 14.4 million children under age 5 routinely attend some type of child care program. Further, another seven million are left home alone on a regular basis (CDF, 2002). These figures highlight the critical need for more high-quality child care in the United States.

Increased awareness of the state of children in the United States helps early childhood teachers become more sensitive to the everyday challenges that children and their families face. The Children's Defense Fund (CDF), a nonprofit agency devoted to educating the nation about the needs of children, collects and analyzes statistics related to the well-being of children and their families. Each year, CDF publishes a report about economic, political, and social conditions affecting America's children. Table 12.1 highlights some of those statistics.

What do these statistics mean to teachers of young children? Being aware of what children face each day in the United States builds a sense of compassion for our country's youngest citizens and their families. Many of the children who attend early care and education programs come from families that are struggling to maintain the basics, such as shelter, food, and medical care, even as they take on the daily challenges of parenting. Teachers can serve as positive links between schools and families as they carry out their shared responsibilities for the care and education of young children.

Table 12.1   Each Day in America

- 5 children or teens commit suicide.
- 9 children or teens are killed by firearms.
- 34 children or teens die from accidents.
- 77 babies die.
- 401 babies are born to mothers who received late or no prenatal care.
- 1,310 babies are born without health insurance.
- 1,329 babies are born to teen mothers.
- 7,883 children are reported abused or neglected.

Source: Adapted with permission from Children's Defense Fund (2002), *The State of Children in America's Union: A 2002 Action Guide to Leave No Child Behind.* (Washington, DC: CDF), p. 14. Reprinted by permission of the publisher.

Communicating with Families

COMPETENCY GOAL IV
· Functional Area 11

When families entrust schools with their children, they expect that school personnel will keep them informed about all facets of their children's care and education. Though fulfilling these expectations may seem straightforward and routine, doing so actually entails a multitude of details and related responsibilities. Even in this age of technology, communication remains a challenge, particularly for school personnel who interact daily with so many families. However, the benefits derived from keeping families informed and involved in their children's care and education cannot be underestimated.

Research on school effectiveness has repeatedly shown that children whose families are involved in their education are more successful in school and are more likely to graduate from high school (Bempechat, 1990; Steinberg, 1996). Because patterns of home-school communication and family involvement are set during the first years of schooling when children are still totally dependent on their families to safeguard them (McFarland, 2000), early care and education providers are uniquely positioned to start families along paths that lead to ongoing communication and positive involvement with schools throughout their children's education.

Informal and Formal Communication

Family involvement begins with open channels of communication between families and schools. Some of the most beneficial interactions between families and teachers occur spontaneously through unplanned

> *There must be a profound recognition that parents are the first teachers and that education begins before formal schooling and is deeply rooted in the values, traditions, and norms of family and culture.*
>
> —Sara Lawrence Lightfoot, author and professor of education

meetings, casual notes, and phone calls rather than through planned forms of communication such as newsletters, handbooks, conferences, meetings, and events. Teachers in preschools and child care centers often have more opportunities for these types of **informal communication** with families than teachers in public or private kindergarten and primary programs, who often rely on **formal communication** means. By the time children attend kindergarten, many schools provide bus transportation to and from school, which reduces the number of times family members routinely enter school buildings. However, families generally use private transportation when taking their children to preschools and child care centers, and they accompany their children directly into the classrooms, thus giving early care and education providers frequent opportunities for informal communication.

Greetings at arrival and departure times present daily opportunities for informal communication with families (McFarland, 2000). These short, unplanned conversations and nonverbal communications, such as waves and smiles, may seem insignificant to individuals outside the field of early childhood education, but to the children, families, and teachers involved, these moments of contact form the bases for strong home-school relationships.

*M*s*. Edith Matthews, the infant/toddler teacher at Pleasant Day Child Development Center, smiles when she hears Benjamin's voice in the hallway. She steps quickly toward the doorway to help Benjamin's father unload and store away the diaper bag and car seat before holding out her arms in invitation to the infant. Eight-month-old Benjamin readily falls from his father's arms into Ms. Matthews's arms as he continues to babble away in a language all his own. Benjamin's father, Mr. Rubin Goldstein, comments to Ms. Matthews that Benjamin jabbers from the moment his eyes open in the morning and continues until bedtime, except when he is eating—and sometimes even when he is eating! Ms. Matthews laughs and tells Benjamin that he must have lots of important things to say. The infant smiles, drools, and begins to babble once again. As Ms. Matthews sets Benjamin on the carpet near a pile of colorful toys, she casually mentions to his father that infants of this age are beginning to associate certain sounds with particular objects and actions and adds that before long Benjamin's jabbering will be language that others can understand. Rubin gives Benjamin a good-bye kiss and thanks Ms. Matthews for helping him see the connection between his son's nonstop jabbering and his language development. Ms. Matthews tells Mr. Goldstein to have a good day at work and mentions that she has a booklet on language development that she will place in Benjamin's diaper bag, if Mr. Goldstein and his wife would care to read it. As he leaves the classroom, Rubin replies, "That sounds great. Maybe I'll have Benjamin read it to me!"*

Though the exchange described in the vignette took less than five minutes, Ms. Matthews was able to take advantage of Benjamin's arrival as a time to communicate informally with his father. From her first smile, Ms. Matthews let Benjamin and his father know she was happy to see them, and she was able to receive and share information about Benjamin's development to help his father better appreciate the noisy process of learning language. By offering Mr. Goldstein some printed material on language development, she acknowledged the family's role in Benjamin's development and empowered the father to find out more about his son's emerging language. This example represents only one of the many discussion topics that arise at such unplanned, informal meetings when family members accompany their children to and from early care and education programs.

Other opportunities for informal communication, such as casual notes and phone calls, occur through the course of daily events in early care and education settings. Sometimes these notes and telephone calls are used as reminders of upcoming events or courtesy calls to let family members know when their children need some type of supplies. Though the main purpose of the notes or phone calls is purely functional, when teachers take a few extra minutes to share new information or insights about the children's development, the usefulness of the calls and notes is extended to act as a form of informal communication.

Family-Teacher Conferences

Another way to communicate with families about their children's development and school progress is the formal means of **family-teacher conferences.** Family-teacher conferences (also known as **parent-teacher conferences**) are planned, scheduled, private meetings organized for the express purpose of having face-to-face exchanges with children's parents or primary guardians to update them on their children's current level of performance and to receive input from the families about relevant topics (Newman, 1997/1998). Though participation by families is generally optional, many preschools and child care centers offer annual or semiannual family-teacher conferences to discuss growth and development issues through reviewing developmental checklists or artifact portfolios. Once formal schooling begins in kindergarten, family-teacher conferences tend to become more structured and to center on periodic, formal, written evaluations such as progress reports or grade report cards. Family-teacher conferences provide a venue for families and teachers to exchange information, ask questions, and make informed decisions about children's current and future care and education.

> *O*ur children need to be treated as human beings—exquisite, complex and elegant in their diversity.
>
> —Lloyd Dennis, radio talk show host

The effectiveness of family-teacher conferences depends on several factors, including logistical considerations, family matters, and teacher expertise. Logistical details include scheduling (days and times staff are available), length of appointments, and location of meetings at places that offer privacy and no interruptions. Factors related to family matters involve work schedules, transportation, other children in the family, and health-related issues (Kohler, 1998). Language challenges, such as limited proficiency with English, may also affect the communication process during family-teacher conferences. Teacher expertise in handling family-teacher conferences also influences the success of such meetings; teachers gain this expertise through preservice and inservice training, as well as through their prior experience with conferences

(Epstein & Sanders, 1998). Teachers' individual styles of communication, abilities to organize information, and time spent in preparation also influence outcomes of family-teacher conferences (Coleman & Wallinga, 2000).

Two-Way and One-Way Communication

Face-to-face discussion, whether formal and planned or informal and impromptu, provides the best avenue for exchange of information between families and caregivers. Interactions that result in the exchange of information are described as **two-way communication.** Educators generally prefer to use two-way communication strategies to **one-way communication** strategies, because mutual exchange of information encourages reciprocal relationships and creates feelings of partnership between home and school (Filp, 1998). Face-to-face discussions, telephone calls, and parent-teacher conferences are examples of two-way communication strategies. Notes, newsletters, and informational fliers are forms of one-way communication. One-way communication strategies are effective tools for keeping families informed about their children's care and education, but they can limit feedback. Of course, teachers can modify many one-way communication strategies to provide options for responses from recipients. For example, classroom newsletters (one-way communica-

Table 12.2   **Samples of Informal and Formal Communication Techniques**

Informal Communication Techniques	Formal Communication Techniques
Two-way communication	*Two-way communication*
Arrival and departure greetings	Family-teacher conferences
Family socials	Family education meetings
Phone calls by situation	Phone calls by appointment
E-mail notes	Surveys, questionnaires
	Suggestion boxes
	Advisory boards
One-way communication	*One-way communication*
Casual notes	Developmental profiles
	Grade report cards
	School performances
	Web pages
	Newsletters and fliers
	Daily updates
	Bulletin boards
	Take-home activities
	Lending libraries

tion) that are primarily designed to inform families about upcoming events and developments can incorporate surveys, questionnaires, response cards, or suggestion forms that invite responses, thus transforming the newsletters into two-way communication (Thornburg, 2002).

Benefits and Challenges of Effective Communication

Effective ongoing communication between home and school provides many benefits for children, families, and schools. Children are the most obvious beneficiaries, because teachers and families unite in their efforts to provide optimal care and education for them. Families benefit from ongoing communication because they remain up-to-date about their children's development and school progress and have more opportunities to seek the guidance of trained school personnel to assist them with concerns related to their children's care and education (Beckman & Hanson, 2002). Schools and teachers benefit from ongoing communication, particularly two-way communication, because as they learn more about their students' home lives, they are better able to view families as partners in the process of education (Epstein & Sanders, 1998; Filp, 1998).

Although the benefits of effective communication make the effort worthwhile, maintaining open communication between schools and families is not without challenges. Factors such as scheduling conflicts and investment of time can be barriers to effective communication. The potential for miscommunication between individuals with different perspectives always exists and increases when diverse cultures and value systems are involved (Gonzalez-Mena, 2001). Because family-teacher conferences are often convened to discuss concerns about children's development or school progress, elements of emotional stress enter the picture, as both family members and teachers attempt to represent children's best interests. These challenges to effective communication between families and schools are more easily met if relationships of trust and respect already exist between the parties (Kohler, 1998).

Involving Families

Teachers find many opportunities to build trusting relationships with families as they provide quality care and education for young children. **Family-oriented practices** recognize family members as partners and participants in the process of caring for and educating their children.

Opportunities for School Involvement

Family involvement assumes many forms, with varying degrees of participation that give family members a full range of ways to support the early care and education efforts of teachers and schools (Thornburg, 2002). Responsive schools provide involvement options that allow family members to tailor their participation to their personal

CDA

COMPETENCY GOAL IV
• Functional Area 11

COMPETENCY GOAL VI
• Functional Area 13

availability, concerns, and talents. Families can contribute to children's success in schools through home-based, school-based, or community-based family involvement (Epstein, 1995).

Home-based opportunities for family involvement enable family members to help their children at home with school projects and studies to support the efforts of schools. Seemingly simple practices—such as making sure children have the school supplies they need or taking time from other responsibilities to read aloud with young children each evening—are basic forms of home-based family involvement. Sometimes teachers suggest specific ways families can help their children succeed in school (Coleman & Wallinga, 2000); other times, children themselves seek guidance and opportunities to practice emerging skills with caring adults at home. Teachers guide family members in coordinating their home-based involvement with school experiences to provide children with a united support system.

Traditional school-based forms of family involvement usually focus on bringing family members into the schools in some capacity. Sometimes school-based family involvement is simply participating in school events such as carnivals and field trips; other times, family members attend children's performances in music programs, school plays, or other projects that are presented at school sites (Georgiou, 1998).

Family members who have time and enjoy hands-on opportunities for involvement may serve as school volunteers. They assist teachers, librarians, food service workers, or office personnel with the day-to-day operations of schools (Georgiou, 1998). Volunteering might be occasional, such as serving as room parents for holidays and special events, or ongoing throughout the school year.

School volunteers who serve regularly in classrooms or libraries and who interact directly with children generally participate in some type of structured orientation before beginning their volunteer services. These orientations guide volunteers in appro-

Programs such as this seniors' volunteer program in San Francisco provide opportunities for children to build intergenerational relationships with community members.

priate ways to interact with children in school settings. Many early care and education teachers find classroom volunteers to be great assets to them and the children. Young children thrive when they have attention from caring adults who listen to them and scaffold their learning. School volunteers also benefit from their experiences by gaining insights into the internal workings of early childhood education and observing first-hand the challenges and pleasures of teaching young children.

Parent Education Programs

Sometimes family members want to know more about how young children learn and about the ways they can support their children's development. These family members are ready to take advantage of school-based **parent education** opportunities. The major goal of most parent education programs is to empower family members to continue to be their children's first teacher by giving them knowledge and skills to further support their children's development, education, and school success (Coleman & Wallinga, 2000). A secondary goal of these education programs is to help family members parent effectively (Kelley-Laine, 1998). Some schools have fully developed parent education programs that offer a selection of meetings and workshops throughout the year; other schools sponsor periodic workshops as needs or opportunities arise. Whether parent education programs are extensive or moderate, they send strong messages to family members that they are partnering with teachers and schools to provide the best educational experiences possible for all children.

Opportunities for Advocacy

Sometimes family members want to reach more children and families as well as more schools than the ones in which their children are enrolled. In these cases, family involvement becomes community based, as family members contribute to broader decision making about children's care and education. At the community level, these family members might assume positions in advisory councils, task forces, or advocacy groups.

Advisory councils examine information relevant to school policies or plans and suggest how schools should act or respond. Advisory councils influence decision making but are not directly responsible for the ultimate decisions although school program administrators usually value their input (Kelley-Laine, 1998).

Task forces are usually formed for a single purpose; members of task forces can be volunteers or appointees and frequently include school personnel and community representatives as well as family members, thus representing multiple perspectives on issues. Schools can organize task forces to investigate a topic of concern or interest. For example, a task force might be formed to research playground safety before a school makes decisions about redesigning a playground and purchasing equipment. Once the task force collects and reviews pertinent information, members prepare written or oral reports to advise school officials of their findings. Sometimes task forces make recommendations for school personnel to consider. Once the decision has been made and the project is completed, the task force is disbanded, since its purpose has been met.

Advisory councils and task forces provide extensive school-sanctioned opportunities for family members to be actively involved in the larger educational process.

Advocacy groups offer opportunities for family involvement outside the immediate system of care and education. (Chapter 8 discusses advocacy as an avenue for professional development for teachers and other school personnel.) Sometimes advocacy groups include both family members and school personnel who have united for a common cause, such as increasing funding for a full-day kindergarten program. Depending on the cause, advocacy groups may also be associated with special interest groups or professional organizations. Often, family involvement through advocacy grows out of powerful personal experiences. For example, the advocacy organization Mothers Against Drunk Driving (MADD) was formed as a mother's response to the death of her child, who was killed by a drunk driver. This nonprofit organization exemplifies how

Figure 12.1   **Advocacy Groups Related to Children's Issues**

- Annie E. Casey Foundation (AECF)
  www.aecf.org
- Association for Childhood Education International (ACEI)
  www.acei.org
- Center for Effective Parenting (CEP)
  www.parenting-ed.org
- Child Welfare League of America (CWLA)
  www.cwla.org
- Children's Advocacy Institute (CAI)
  www.caichildlaw.org
- Children's Defense Fund (CDF)
  www.childrensdefense.org
- Connect for Kids
  www.connectforkids.org
- I Am Your Child
  www.iamyourchild.org
- Mothers Against Drunk Driving (MADD)
  www.madd.org
- National Association for the Education of Young Children (NAEYC)
  www.naeyc.org
- National Association of Child Care Resource and Referral Agencies (NACCRRA)
  www.naccrra.org
- National Black Child Development Institute (NBCDI)
  www.nbcdi.org
- National Center for Missing and Exploited Children (NCMEC)
  www.ncmec.org

- National Center for Children in Poverty (NCCP)
  cpmcnet.columbia.edu/dept/nccp
- National Children's Alliance (NCA) (formerly National Network of Children's Advocacy Centers)
  www.nca-online.org
- National Clearinghouse on Child Abuse and Neglect Information
  www.calib.com/nccanch/
- National Information Center for Children and Youth with Disabilities (NICHCY)
  www.nichcy
- National Latino Children's Institute (NLCI)
  www.nlci.org
- National Network for Child Care (NNCC)
  www.nncc.org
- National School-Age Care Alliance (NSACA)
  www.nsaca.org
- Prevent Child Abuse America
  www.preventchildabuse.org
- Stand for Children
  www.stand.org
- Voices for America's Children (formerly National Association of Child Advocates)
  www.voicesforamericaschildren.org
- USA Child Care (USACC)
  www.usachildcare.org
- Zero to Three
  www.zerotothree.org

the efforts of a few determined advocates can rally others to the cause. Of course, not all advocacy groups arise from catastrophic events, but they are all motivated, mission-driven groups of individuals supporting common causes. Figure 12.1 lists some advocacy groups related to child development, parenting, and early care and education.

Advocacy offers wide-reaching outlets for connecting children, families, schools, and communities. Together with other types of family involvement, advocacy allows family members to select their own avenues for participation in their children's education (Coleman & Wallinga, 2000).

Creating Family-Oriented Early Childhood Environments

Programs for young children that use family-oriented practices in forming partnerships with families also need to be responsive to the diverse traditions, values, and cultures that are part of families. One of the first steps in establishing responsive school environments is to foster attitudes of cooperation, rather than separation. Cooperation builds partnerships with family members, strengthens family bonds, and increases children's awareness that parents and teachers work together to provide the best possible play and learning environments for them.

CDA

COMPETENCY GOAL IV
• Functional Area 11

Establishing and maintaining a cooperative attitude requires respect among all involved parties and acknowledgment that both home and school contribute to the well-being and education of young children. On occasion, of course, the goals of the school and the goals of the family may seem at cross-purposes; how-

Culture is a treasure which follows its owner everywhere.
—Chinese proverb

ever, diligent and thoughtful discussion and negotiation can overcome these challenges. Often, classroom teachers have closer and more regular contact with family members than other school personnel; therefore, teachers may be more aware of the views of family members. Thus, teachers may have to act as advocates for parents when schools develop policies or procedures that potentially conflict with the values, beliefs, or best interests of families. For example, on examining the school calendar a teacher may notice that the first meeting of the Parent Teacher Organization is scheduled for the evening that also marks the beginning of an important religious observation for several of the families in the school. Family members would have to choose between attending their religious observances or their children's school function, which could cause dissension in the family and unfavorable feelings toward the school. When the teacher brings this to the school's attention, it changes the date of the meeting and reviews the school calendar for the rest of the year to make sure other school functions have not been inadvertently scheduled the same way. Willingness to change and make adjustments to accommodate the diverse needs and preferences of children and families demonstrates a proactive approach that invites individuals to participate in planning and organizing school functions.

Opportunities to use family-oriented practices are not limited to programwide decisions. At the classroom level, teachers also contribute to the overall attitude of cooperation and mutual respect in the ways they interact and communicate with children and their families. Establishing consistent methods of two-way communication, like weekly or monthly classroom newsletters with ample opportunities to contribute input, ensures that family members feel like partners in their children's education. Informing parents and family members about various ways they can become involved inside and outside the classroom adds to the sense of working together that is so vital to successful early care and education.

As discussed in Chapters 9 and 10, teachers also need to be aware of and sensitive to the diversity of community so that teachers' personal biases do not negatively influence the choice of books, toys, dolls, posters, and other learning materials used in the classroom. Teachers' decisions about curriculum content, methods, materials, and assessment should reflect a celebration of diversity rather than a narrow view. For example, when teachers read fairy tales to children, they can include versions of the same tale from other cultures rather than presenting only one version of the tale, usually an American or European version. The story of Cinderella, for example, is well known in its French version; however, there are literally dozens of Cinderella stories from around the world. By including multiple versions of the popular fairy tale, teachers demonstrate their appreciation for literature from many cultures.

> *The secret of education is respecting the pupil.*
> —Ralph Waldo Emerson, American poet

Well-planned and well-implemented efforts to involve families at all levels of their children's early care and education set a pattern for successful home-school partnerships that will benefit children, families, and schools for many years to come. Teachers who exemplify respect for all cultures and celebrate diversity through open communication and frequent invitations for families to participate can strengthen the bonds with family members and between children, families, and teachers.

Summary

Young Children and Their Families

- During the last century in the United States, family structures have shifted from extended families to nuclear families.
- Schools serve as community referral agencies to children and their families.

Communicating with Families

- Effective home-school communication provides benefits and presents challenges to children, families, and schools.

- Two-way communication strategies support the mutual exchange of information.
- Family members serve as school volunteers in many valuable capacities.
- Family involvement can be home based, school based, or community based.

Involving Families

- Family-oriented practices in schools build partnerships with families.
- Schools that use family-oriented practices demonstrate respect for diversity.

Creating Family-Oriented
Early Childhood Environments

- Attitudes of cooperation acknowledge that both home and school contribute to the well-being and education of young children.

- Opportunities to use family-oriented practices occur at program and classroom levels.

- Decisions that teachers make about curriculum content, methods, materials, and assessment should reflect a celebration of diversity.

LEARNING ACTIVITIES

1 Interview: Expectations about Parenting. Draw names to identify partners for this "expectations about parenting" interview. First, each individual will jot down five expectations about parenting. For example—Parents should put their children's needs ahead of their own. After a few minutes, partners can share their parenting expectations with each other and rank the expectations in order of importance. Finally, each pair of students will identify their top three parenting expectations and share the list with all classmates. Engage in class discussion about some of the expectations and try to narrow the list to the three most important expectations of parenting for the class as a whole. Reflect on how teachers' expectations about parents and parenting can influence their relationships with families.

2 Small Groups: Discussion. Form a group with three or four classmates and select a curriculum theme that would interest young children. Using a brainstorming approach, generate a list of ways the theme could be extended to include the participation of family members inside or outside the classroom. If time permits, discuss ways that the theme or topic could also be used to celebrate cultural and linguistic diversity. For example, the theme of "shoes" could explore types of shoes worn in different countries, cultures, and climates as well as social practices related to shoes. Children and family members could be invited to bring in various types of shoes and describe how the shoes represent diversity.

PORTFOLIO ARTIFACTS

1 Sample: Classroom Newsletters. Call or visit at least three early care and education settings and collect samples of their classroom newsletters. Compare the newsletters and describe your overall impression of each, based on your knowledge of effective home-school communication. Analyze the newsletters and determine whether they are intended as one-way or two-way communication strategies. Then, modify one of the newsletters so that it will better facilitate two-way communication.

2 Observation: Advocacy for Children. Check the local community calendar and locate information about local advocacy groups for children's issues. Collect informational literature, if available, from the group, visit their Web site for informa-

tion about their advocacy efforts, and/or attend a local meeting. After this experience, take a few moments to reflect on the role of advocacy groups in the field of early care and education. Consider whether you could envision yourself involved with advocacy groups and answer why or why not.

3 Project: Application. Using the Internet or other means, collect several calendars or other sources of information about diverse cultural celebrations and observances, such as Kwanza and Cinco de Mayo, and make a perpetual calendar for use when planning activities or projects for your classroom. (A perpetual calendar lists recurring dates by month.)

Professional Connections and Web Links

Urban Programs Resource Network
University of Illinois Extension:
Helping Children Succeed in School
University of Illinois at Urbana-Champaign
905 S. Goodwin (547 Bevier Hall)
Urbana, IL 61801
217-244-0191
http:/www.urbanext.uiuc.edu/

The Urban Programs Resource Network was developed by educators at the University of Illinois Extension as part of an outreach program to parents to help them become aware of the positive relationship between parent involvement and school success for children. Topics of articles include parent-teacher communication, parental involvement in school, school stress, and learning styles. Although the articles and resources are geared toward family members, teachers will also benefit from the clear,

reasonable explanations about home-school communication and involvement.

Mothers Against Drunk Driving (MADD)
511 E. John Carpenter Freeway, Suite 700
Irving, TX 75062
800-GETMADD (438-6233)
http://www.madd.org

Mothers Against Drunk Driving (MADD), a nonprofit organization that was founded in 1980 by Candy Lightner and a small group of mothers, has grown into one of the largest grassroots crime victims' organizations in the world, with chapters in many cities throughout the United States and other countries. The organization's main mission is to save lives by building public awareness of the dangerous consequences of drunk driving and underage drinking.

Suggestions for Further Reading

Gonzalez-Mena, Janet. (2001). *Multicultural issues in child care* (3rd ed.). Mountain View, CA: Mayfield Publishing.

- This book provides a tool that early childhood educators can use in developing awareness of and sensitivity to diversity and cross-cultural communication.

Each chapter presents issues in child care and discusses them in light of cultural perspectives that may have been overlooked in traditional discussion of the topics. The book also provides suggestions for further reading and research.

References

Beckman, Paula J., & Hanson, Marci, J. (2002). Community participation of children with disabilities. In Samuel L. Odom (Ed.), *Widening the circle: Including children with disabilities in preschool programs* (pp. 109–119). New York: Teachers College Press.

Bempechat, J. (1990). *The role of parent involvement in children's academic achievement: Review of the literature*. Paper prepared for the Office of Planning Research and Evaluation Service. U.S. Department of Education and the ERIC Clearinghouse on Urban Education. Boston, MA: Harvard University.

Children's Defense Fund (CDF). (2001). *The state of America's children: Yearbook 2001*. Washington, DC: Author.

Children's Defense Fund (CDF). (2002). *The state of children in America's union: A 2002 action guide to Leave No Child Behind*. Washington, DC: Author.

Coleman, Mick, & Wallinga, Charlotte. (2000). Connecting families and classrooms using family involvement webs. *Childhood Education, 76*(4), 209–214.

Epstein, Joyce L. (1995). School-family-community partnerships: Caring for the children we share. *Phi Delta Kappan, 76*, 701–712.

Epstein, Joyce L., & Sanders, Mavis, G. (1998). What we learn from international studies of school-family-community partnerships. *Childhood education, 74*(6), 392–394.

Filp, Johanna. (1998). From mutual blame towards trust: Changing school-family relationships in Chile. *Childhood Education, 74*(6), 346–350.

Georgiou, Stelios N. (1998). Opening school doors: Teacher-parent-student relations in Cyprus. *Childhood Education, 74*(6), 362–366.

Gonzalez-Mena, Janet. (2001). *Multicultural issues in child care* (3rd ed.). Mountain View, CA: Mayfield.

Kelley-Laine, Kathleen. (1998). Parents as partners in schooling: The current state of affairs. *Childhood Education, 74*(6), 342–345.

Kohler, Hartmut. (1998). Parents as partners in schooling in Germany: The urgency of fundamental design. *Childhood Education, 74*(6), 372–374.

McFarland, Laura. (2000). Involving fathers in the preschool classroom. *Texas Child Care Quarterly, 24*(2), 2–7.

Newman, Rita. (1997/1998). Parent conferences: A conversation between you and your child's teacher. *Childhood Education, 74*(2), 100–101.

Smith, Kristin. (2000). Who's minding the kids? Child care arrangements: Fall 1995. Current Population Reports, P70-70. Washington, DC: U.S. Census Bureau.

Steinberg, L. (1996). *Beyond the classroom.* New York: Simon & Schuster.

Thornburg, Kathy R. (2002). Building families: Building community. *Child Care Information Exchange, 148,* 65–68.

Community Connections

After reading this chapter and completing the related activities, you should be able to

- Describe the interrelationships among children, families, schools, and communities
- Identify ways in which early care and education programs serve as referral services for children and families
- Cite examples of agencies and organizations that serve as resources
- Identify ways in which early care and education programs and communities act as reciprocal resources
- Cite examples of community-based resources and programs that can enrich early care and education experiences
- Explain how family-school-community partnerships reinforce children's overall well-being

Ten years ago: Two-day-old Nathaniel lay still in his layette in the neonatal intensive care nursery; his twenty-year-old mother, Lisa, hovered nearby, still recovering from the emergency surgery that saved her son's life and brought him into the world nearly two months early. At less than four pounds, Nathaniel's tiny brain and body waged a mighty battle against death; it appeared as if death would win, as a team of medical personnel revealed the extent of Nathaniel's brain injuries.

Today: Ten-year-old Nathaniel might not be the best player on his recreational soccer team, but he is certainly one of the most enthusiastic. Holding his right forearm protectively close to his chest, he races toward the soccer ball, ready to stop the ball's progress at all costs. In spite of the cerebral palsy that affects the right side of his body, Nathaniel manages a speed that seems to defy his awkward gait, as he and his teammates converge on the ball. "Pow," he yells as he comes to a complete stop before giving the ball a solid kick. "High five, Mom!" he shouts to his mother as she watches proudly from the stands.

 he vignette describes a situation all too common across the world— tiny infants born too soon, struggling against odds that would give adults pause. Families in crisis turn to their immediate and extended families for support, but what if no family members are available or if the crises extend outside the experiences, abilities, and means of family members? In these cases, families turn to resources within their communities. For Lisa, the young mother described in the vignette, traversing the maze of community resources that can potentially support her and her son is a daunting experience. Early care and education programs are uniquely situated to serve as liaisons and referral services for families such as Lisa's and to incorporate resources from the community into school outreach programs (Kelley-Laine, 1998).

Infants begin their lives within the protective nests of their families; soon they are exposed to extended family, and before long they are integrated into schools, churches, synagogues, or mosques, and other community structures. By their third birthdays, many children have playmates not only from their own families, schools, and neighborhoods, but also from their association with other children through organized activities outside their homes, such as dance lessons, soccer games, and other activities. In such ways, children gradually are integrated into the fabric of their communities. Early care and education programs are particularly well positioned to give children opportunities to gain awareness of other individuals, families, and cultures. Families of young children also benefit from school-based community involvement and can use these resources to enrich their own lives and the lives of their children.

> *E*ducation is the most powerful weapon which you can use to change the world.
> —Nelson Mandela, former president of South Africa

Children, Families, and Communities

During the crucial early years, young children are cradled within the protecting arms of parents and other close family members. This immediate circle of family helps to shape children's ideas about themselves and others. As children learn to walk and talk, they develop the primary means to interact with others, and soon their realm widens to encompass individuals outside family boundaries. Though children's first forays into communities are made with their families, these outside encounters nonetheless give children diverse examples of people, places, and events that differ from their familiar home experiences.

CDA

COMPETENCY GOAL III
• Functional Area 9

COMPETENCY GOAL IV
• Functional Area 11

Urie Bronfenbrenner (b. 1917), an American psychologist who was born in Russia, proposed a systems model of human development showing ever-expanding spheres of influence over children's development (see Figure 13.1, p. 280). At the center of this **ecological model,** children's most immediate environment, the **microsystem,** consists of the closest family members, their relationships with the children, and physical objects

Figure 13.1   Bronfenbrenner's Ecological Model

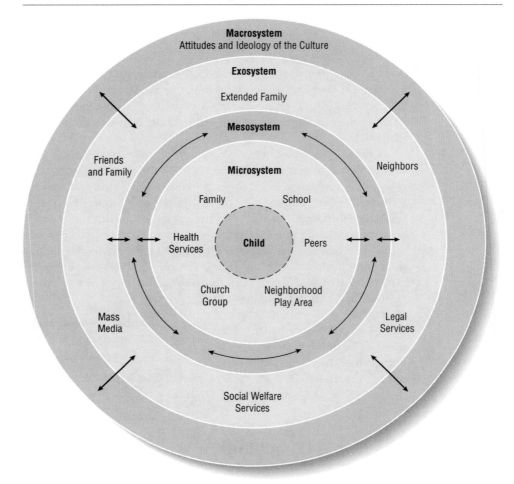

Source: From J. A. Schickedanz, P. D. Forsyth, and G. A. Forsyth (1988), *Understanding Children and Adolescents,* 3rd ed. (Boston: Allyn and Bacon). Copyright 1988 by Pearson Education. Reprinted by permission of the publisher.

to which children are exposed in their home environments. Moving outward from the microsystem, the next circle of influence is the **mesosystem,** which represents the two-way relationships between children and their families and those individuals directly connected to the children on a regular basis, such as their schools and other familiar settings. The mesosystem includes reciprocal influences from children and families toward other individuals they encounter and from these other individuals toward families. For example, a father's employer may insist that he work overtime every Friday for a month; this would mean that the father, a single parent, could not pick up his infant from the child care center because it would be closed by the time he could get there. Therefore, the father must find someone else to pick up his child or tell his employer that he cannot work later because of his child care arrangements. Either way, both parties in the mesosystem are affected. Beyond the mesosystem is the **exosystem**, which represents individuals and physical settings that do not directly interact with the children but are linked to them by their mesosystems. For example, very young children rarely accompany their mothers or fathers to work, but work environments influence the parents, who, in turn, influence the children. The outermost circle of the ecological model, the **macrosystem**, represents the larger influence of society, including cultural attitudes and values. Children are influenced by the macrosystem because it surrounds and influences all of the interior circles (Bronfenbrenner, 1979, 1986).

Bronfenbrenner's ecological model suggests that children are strongly influenced by, and have an influence on, their families, friends, teachers, and other individuals with whom they interact. This model also suggests that communities, and society in general, exert influence on children, both directly and indirectly. Understanding this model can help teachers of young children see that children's development is influenced by their environments—not only those environments closest to them, but those removed from them by distance as well. For example, although a grandmother may not directly go to her grandchild's preschool classroom, she may still influence her daughter's ideas and behaviors about preschool during their weekly conversations. In turn, the daughter may incorporate her mother's views into her own expectations about preschool, and the way she feels about the preschool program her child attends may change as a result. When teachers and early care and education programs appreciate the linkages between children, families, schools, and society, they are better prepared to scaffold children's emerging participation into the communities of the world (Bronfenbrenner, 1985).

Communities as Resources for Families

As described in Chapter 12, families today often use **community resources** and services as the bases of support when their extended families are not available or are unable to assist them. Community resources are public and private agencies at local, state, regional, national, and, sometimes, global levels that help to fill the void created by changes in family structure and to provide specialized services to children and families. Community-based support services are designed to prevent, protect, and improve situations that cause hardship to families. These services may be in any of three areas—economic, social, and educational. Several specific programs, such as resource and referral agencies and parents-as-teachers programs, are discussed in later sections of this chapter; however, this chapter provides a sampling of community resources and services available in most states for each of the three service areas.

Community Resources That Address Economic Needs

Economic services help provide families with basic needs—such as food, shelter, employment, transportation, health insurance and access to medical care, child care, and

CDA

COMPETENCY GOAL IV
• Functional Area 11

COMPETENCY GOAL V
• Functional Area 12

other services for which lack of financial resources is the primary barrier. Examples of community resources within the category of economic services include

- *Dress for Success*—administered by the international not-for-profit organization of the same name. This program provides women with interview tips, and with one outfit of business attire for job interviews and another when hired.
- *Food Stamp Program (FSP)*—administered by the U.S. Department of Agriculture (USDA). This program provides food coupons for low-income families to exchange for nutritious foods in neighborhood retail food stores.
- *Housing and Urban Development Program (HUD)*—administered by the U.S. Department of Housing and Urban Development (USHUD). This program helps eligible low-income families obtain financing for housing and/or home improvement.
- *Temporary Assistance to Needy Families (TANF)*—part of the welfare reform initiative, administered by different agencies in various states. TANF, formerly known as ADC (Aid to Dependent Children), provides temporary housing assistance, subsidized child care, and education and/or training for heads of households to enable individuals to move off welfare.
- *Welfare-to-Work*—administered by the U.S. Office of Personnel Management. This program helps welfare recipients gain necessary education and training to qualify for employment that will enable them to move off welfare.
- *Women, Infants, and Children (WIC)*—administered by the USDA. This program provides coupons for food supplements (to be redeemed at local retail food stores), health care referrals, and nutrition education to low-income women who are pregnant, who are breastfeeding, or who have recently given birth, as well as to infants and children who are identified as at nutritional risk.

Community Services That Address Social Needs

Social services that are designed to safeguard children and families include health clinics for prenatal care and preventive medical care, such as immunizations, family violence intervention programs, legal aid, mental health services, parenting classes, substance abuse programs, and specialized services for individuals with special needs. Examples of community services within the social category include

- *Family violence prevention and protection programs*—provide information, referrals, safe havens to victims of family violence, and hotlines for reporting of suspected abuse
- *Crisis nurseries*—provide immediate, but temporary, care for infants and children who are in risky situations
- *Early childhood special education programs*—provide information, referral, screening, and intervention services to children with special needs and their families
- *Health clinics*—provide free or low-cost health screenings, immunizations, and referrals to children and families with regard to health issues
- *Teen parenting programs*—inform, educate, and support teenagers and their children

Community Services That Address Educational Needs

The focus of educational services is twofold. First, educational services provide adults with basic education, including ESL (English as a second language) and ELL (English language learners) classes, plus specialized training to enter or reenter the work force or to maintain employment. The second focus of educational services is to support the care and education needs of children who are economically disadvantaged or have special needs. Examples of community resources within the education category include

- *Early Head Start*—administered by the National Head Start Bureau under the U.S. Administration for Children and Families. This program provides home-based (family) child care and/or center-based comprehensive care and early education to children under three years of age and to pregnant women who are living in low-income-eligible households.

- *Even Start Family Literacy Initiative*—administered by the U.S. Department of Education. This program supports the states in developing and implementing their own research-based literacy initiatives for families that are economically or educationally disadvantaged.

- *Head Start*—administered by the National Head Start Bureau under the U.S. Administration for Children and Families. This compensatory program provides center-based comprehensive care and early education for children (ages 3 to 5 years) living in low-income-eligible households.

- *Parents-as-teachers (PAT) programs*—administered by state departments of education and/or local school districts in various states. This program provides home-based educational services delivered by specially trained parent educators to children (prebirth to age 5) and their families. No income eligibility is required.

- *English language assistance programs*—available through most local school districts and community colleges. These programs provide English language instruction for adults through ESL (English as a second language) or ELL (English language learners, formerly known as LEP—limited English proficiency) classes.

- *General education diploma (GED)*—available through most local school districts and community colleges. These programs provide classes for adult learners to prepare them for the general education (high school equivalency) exam.

Community resources and services overlap in an intricate network, with nebulous boundaries between federal, state, and local authority, responsibilities, and funding sources. To traverse the confusing maze of programs, community resource agencies and organizations develop collaborative **service delivery systems** that cut through some of the bureaucratic red tape so that individuals who qualify can receive services in a more timely manner. Often, state governmental agencies act as liaisons, coordinating state programs and guidelines with federal programs and their mandates so that state departments of health, family services, or education can effectively administer federal services. For example, the Medicaid health insurance and access program has federal eligibility requirements for citizenship, residency, and income. Each state designs its Medicaid program to meet the federal guidelines, as well as any additional guidelines the state may have enacted. Individuals applying for Medicaid assistance deal directly with local branches of the appropriate state agency, and the state agency acts on behalf of the federal one. Although service delivery systems streamline the application process by helping individuals access and receive community resources more efficiently, potential clients may still encounter problems. Difficulties can arise from factors such as lack of transportation, child care, or stable home address or telephone number for contact information; inability to read and write English well enough to complete necessary paperwork; and myriad other possibilities. Many national, state, and local agencies approach some of these concerns proactively. For example, some state offices provide assistance with transportation or child care. In addition, many federal and state forms are currently available in Spanish as well as English. Although these efforts do not remove all drawbacks to service access and delivery, these cooperative efforts do model respect for diverse family situations.

One way that families in need deal with the tangle of community resources and services is to look to schools for guidance and referrals (Kelley-Laine, 1998). To meet these needs, some schools have adopted **partnership practices** that connect families and community services, with schools serving as the common link (Epstein & Sanders, 1998). Through collaboration, partnership practices focus on ways to make the best use of resources for the benefit of all stakeholders.

> *Why should society feel responsible only for the education of children, and not for the education of all adults of every age?*
> —Eric Fromm, social scientist

Teachers are pivotal to the success of partnership practices because they have the most direct contact with children and their families (Coleman & Churchill, 1997). However, for teachers to serve in resource and referral capacities, they need specialized training on how to access economic, social, and educational services from both public and private organizations (Coleman & Wallinga, 1999/2000) as well as knowledge about the service delivery systems of these agencies. Family Support America, formerly the Family Resource Coalition of America (1996), suggests that delivery of services should shift from federal, regional, and state control toward local autonomy, so that public and private agencies can work together to become more responsive to children, families, and schools within their communities.

Families in need can also access help through **resource and referral agencies.** This national network bolsters community efforts to connect families with children to appropriate community resources and services. Resource and referral agencies (sometimes called R & R agencies) are strong advocates of family-focused practices and have spearheaded the movement for all individuals and organizations to take responsibility for improving the lives of children and families. As part of their mission, R & R agencies mount public awareness campaigns to educate the general public about the importance of quality child care. Combined efforts of families, schools, and communities serve not only to improve children's success in school but also to help families and schools build strong ties to communities (Epstein & Sanders, 1998).

Communities as Resources in Early Care and Education

Families and schools exist within communities and have shared responsibility for children's welfare and socialization (Kelley-Laine, 1998). Communities are also ripe with potential for enriching children's learning through their community services, businesses, cultural venues, environmental efforts, and recreational facilities. Early care and education programs tap into these community resources through a variety of outlets (Epstein, 1995).

COMPETENCY GOAL III
• Functional Area 9

COMPETENCY GOAL IV
• Functional Area 11

One of the more common means of accessing educational and enrichment services in the community is through **field trips**, where groups of children, chaperoned by teachers and sometimes by family members, visit selected sites or attend special events sponsored by community organizations. These forays into communities also provide opportunities for family involvement as family members provide valuable assistance to children and teachers alike (McFarland, 2000). Sometimes family members serving as volunteers on outings can assume teaching roles as they share their expertise in community resources such as museums or conservation sites. Family volunteers from diverse cultures may also help children and teachers view community resources in the context of their cultures, offering insights to which children might not otherwise be exposed (Coleman & Wallinga, 2000; Gollnick & Chinn, 2002). Typical field trip experiences might include

- *Cultural experiences*—art museums and art exhibitions; history museums and heritage celebrations; musical and dance performances, plays, and other dramatic performances
- *Environmental experiences*—local parks and recreation facilities; national parks and conservation areas; botanical gardens, zoos, aquariums, farms, and biological preservation areas
- *Community awareness experiences*—fire and police stations and hospitals; local businesses such as grocery stores, plant nurseries, restaurants, and manufacturing facilities

Sometimes, rather than venturing into the community for educational or enrichment opportunities, educators opt for bringing community resources to the schools. Three typical avenues for providing these services are lending programs, speakers' bureaus, and special performances or presentations. When these services are provided by community resource agencies, they are often called **outreach programs.** Sometimes agencies provide outreach programs without charge, as part of their community service—for example, local police officers who visit classrooms to talk about pedestrian safety. However, some outreach programs charge minimal fees to cover expenses; still others charge individual or group fees per usage.

Outreach programs may also disseminate information through **lending libraries,** programs that allow teachers to borrow specially developed curriculum materials and resource kits to enrich children's learning and cultural experiences. For example, historical societies often put together prop boxes, or traveling trunks, filled with artifacts about historical figures or events, which teachers can borrow, use in their classrooms, and return. Museums, science centers, zoos, and botanical gardens also develop and lend out various forms of prop boxes. Lending programs may also provide teacher resource books, articles, or multimedia resources such as slides, videos, films, and computer software.

A second type of outreach program, speakers' bureaus, provides individuals who share their expertise with others through speeches, discussions, or demonstrations. **Guest speakers** are available for a variety of interesting topics related to the mission or goals of the community resource agency. For example, a guest speaker from the state conservation agency might talk to children about their role in protecting the environment and make suggestions for outdoor activities that could help them become more aware and appreciative of their natural surroundings.

Some community resource agencies provide more elaborate types of outreach programs, such as cultural performances with demonstrations of music and dance representing a particular heritage. Additionally, some groups sponsor **community-based volunteer programs,** such as adoptive grandparent programs and family literacy projects in which the agency arranges for volunteers to go to homes or schools to interact with children. In many cases, the agencies prescreen the volunteers and provide at least rudimentary training before assigning them to families or schools. Guest speakers, special performances, and classroom volunteers with no ties to a particular community resource agency are engaged by schools.

Joint efforts of families and schools through **service projects,** such as town cleanup days, give children firsthand experiences at supporting their communities even as communities support them and their families. Service projects often involve environmental themes or community-based recreational facilities, such as neighborhood parks and playgrounds (Beckman & Hanson, 2002), that benefit all stakeholders.

Service projects sometimes generate enough support from families that they become long-term advocacy projects involving family members in discussion forums and action groups to support causes that offer far-reaching benefits to children, families, schools, and communities (Coleman & Wallinga, 2000; Kohler, 1998). Chapters 8 and 12 provide information about advocacy opportunities for educators and family members, respectively.

As teachers, our access to young children provides us with many opportunities to build bridges of awareness and cooperation between families and communities that will enrich the lives of all stakeholders. Schools play a central role, not only in providing quality care and education for young children, but also in extending their view of the world and its many wonders.

Summary

Children, Families, and Communities

- Children, families, schools, and communities develop interrelationships that are mutually beneficial.

Communities as Resources for Families

- Early care and education programs serve as community referral services for children and families.
- Communities provide services for children and families to meet economic, social, and educational needs.

Communities as Resources in Early Care and Education

- Early care and education programs use communities as resources for learning through a variety of channels.
- Family-school-community partnerships are united efforts to support children's overall welfare.

LEARNING ACTIVITIES

1 Graphic Representation: Ecological Theory. Using Figure 13.1 (p. 280) as a model, draw a set of concentric circles to represent each of the levels of influence affecting children. Beginning with the innermost circle and moving outward, chart your personal development through this ecological model. At each circle, list specific individuals, organizations, and community events that influenced your development. Contribute to class discussion by sharing examples from your graphic representation.

2 Demonstration: Guest Speakers. With permission from your course instructor, volunteer to locate and invite a guest speaker from a community resource agency to make a ten- to fifteen-minute presentation in your class to share information about services and resources available through this agency.

PORTFOLIO ARTIFACTS

1 Interview and Observation: Community-Based Social Services Agency. Visit the site of a public or private community-based social services agency that provides families with assistance on economic, social, or educational concerns. Be prepared to ask questions about types of services available, eligibility requirements, and waiting periods. Collect informational literature from the organization and determine its mission, target population, and methods of referral. Describe how awareness of this agency's services might prove valuable to you in your role as an early childhood educator.

2 Project: Field Trip and Outreach Opportunities. Contact a local organization or agency—such as a museum, zoo, or nearby national park—and gather information about availability and guidelines for class field trips and/or outreach programs sponsored by the agency. Also, investigate special memberships, discounts, or resources available to classroom teachers. If time permits, visit the site to gain firsthand knowledge of this community resource. After you have reviewed the information, reflect on how the field trip or outreach program could benefit young children and be linked to curriculum goals.

Professional Connections and Web Links

National Association of Child Care Resource
and Referral Agencies (NACRRA)
1319 F Street, N.W., Suite 810
Washington, DC 20004
202-393-5501
http://www.naccrra.org/

The National Association of Child Care Resource and Referral Agencies connects community-based efforts and resources to promote quality child care with a referral service for families who use the information provided to select a program that meets their needs. NACRRA also mounts national campaigns to inform and educate the general public about the positive impact of quality child care on children's overall development. Several brochures, booklets, and research reports about the larger role of child care in the community are available.

Child Care Action Campaign (CCAC)
330 7th Avenue, 17th floor
New York, NY 10001
212-239-0138
http://www.childcareaction.org

The Child Care Action Campaign is a national advocacy organization that works through multiple channels to support the development of policies and programs to increase the availability of affordable, quality child care.

Suggestions for Further Reading

Robinson, Adele, & Stark, Deborah. (2002). *Advocates in action: Making a difference for young children*. Washington, DC: National Association for the Education of Young Children.

• This book offers practical guidance for individuals who want to advocate for young children. It overviews federal, state, and local policies on advocacy and gives descriptions of advocacy efforts taking place in the United States.

References

Beckman, Paula J., & Hanson, Marci J. (2002). Community participation of children with disabilities. In Samuel L. Odom (Ed.), *Widening the circle: Including children with disabilities in preschool programs* (pp. 109–119). New York: Teachers College Press.

Bronfenbrenner, Urie. (1979). *The ecology of human development*. Cambridge, MA: Harvard University Press.

Bronfenbrenner, Urie. (1986). Ecology of the family as a context for human development: Research perspectives. *Developmental Psychology, 22,* 723–742.

Bronfenbrenner, Urie. (1985). The three worlds of childhood. *Principal, 64*(5), 7–11.

Children's Defense Fund (CDF). (2002). *The state of children in America's union: A 2002 action guide to Leave No Child Behind*. Washington, DC: Author.

Coleman, Mick, & Churchill, Susan. (1997). Challenges to family involvement. *Childhood Education, 73*(3), 144–148.

Coleman, Mick, & Wallinga, Charlotte. (1999/2000). Teacher training in family involvement: An interpersonal approach. *Childhood Education, 76*(2), 76–81.

Coleman, Mick, & Wallinga, Charlotte. (2000). Connecting families and classrooms using family involvement webs. *Childhood Education, 76*(4), 209–214.

Epstein, Joyce L. (1995). School-family-community partnerships: Caring for the children we share. *Phi Delta Kappan, 76,* 701–712.

Epstein, Joyce L., & Sanders, Mavis G. (1998). What we learn from international studies of school-family-community partnerships. *Childhood Education, 74*(6), 392–394.

Family Resource Coalition of America. (1996). *Guidelines for family support practice*. Chicago, IL: Author.

Gollnick, Donna M., & Chinn, Philip C. (2002). *Multicultural education in a pluralistic society* (6th ed.). Upper Saddle River, NJ: Merrill/Prentice Hall.

Gonzalez-Mena, Janet. (2001). *Multicultural issues in child care* (3rd ed.). Mountain View, CA: Mayfield.

Kelley-Laine, Kathleen. (1998). Parents as partners in schooling: The current state of affairs. *Childhood Education, 74*(6), 342–345.

Kohler, Hartmut. (1998). Parents as partners in schooling in Germany: The urgency of fundamental design. *Childhood Education, 74*(6), 372–374.

McFarland, Laura. (2000). Involving fathers in the preschool classroom. *Texas Child Care, 24*(2), 2–7.

Competency Goals and Functiona[l...]
Child Development Associate (CD[A...]

CDA Competency Goals	Functional Areas
I. To establish and maintain a safe, healthy learning environment.	1. **Safe:** Candidate prov[...] 2. **Healthy:** Candidate [...] environment that con[...] 3. **Learning Environmen[...]** and routines as resource[...] able enviornment that e[...]
II. To advance physical and intellectual competence.	4. **Physical:** candidate prov[...] tunities to promote the ph[...] 5. **Cognitive:** Candidate pro[...] and opportunities that encourage curiosity, exploration, and problem solving appropriate to the developmental levels and learning styles of children. 6. **Communication:** Candidate actively communicates with children and provides opportunities and support for children to understand, acquire, and use verbal and nonverbal means of communicating thoughts and feelings. 7. **Creative:** Candidate provides opportunities that stimulate children to play with sound, rhythm, language, materials, space and ideas in individual ways to express their creative abilities.
III. To support social and emotional development and to provide positive guidance.	8. **Self:** Candidate provides physical and emotional security for each child and helps each child to know, accept and take pride in himself or herself and to develop a sense of independence. 9. **Social:** Candidate helps each child feel accepted in the group, helps children learn to communicate and get along with others, and encourages feelings of empathy and mutual respect among children and adults. 10. **Guidance:** Candidate provides a supportive environment in which children can begin to learn and practice appropriate and acceptable behaviors as individuals and as a group.
IV. To establish positive and productive relationships with families.	11. **Families:** Candidate maintains an open, friendly, and cooperative relationship with each child's family, encourages their involvement in the program, and supports the child's relationship with his or her family.
V. To ensure a well-run, purposeful program responsive to participant needs.	12. **Program Management:** Candidate is a manager who uses all available resources to ensure an effective operation. The candidate is a competent organizer, planner, record keeper, communicator, and a cooperative co-worker.
VI. To maintain a commitment to professionalism.	13. **Professionalism:** Candidate makes decisions based on knowledge of early childhood theories and practices. Candidate promotes quality in child care services. Candidate takes advantage of opportunities to improve competence, both for personal and professional growth and for the benefit of children and families.

Source: From Council for Professional Recognition (1996), *The Child Development Associate: Assessment System and Competency Standards* (Washington, DC: Author). Copyright 1996 by the Council for Professional Recognition. Reprinted with permission from The Council for Professional Recognition.

...stic and Cultural Diversity
...s for Effective Early Childhood Education

...ment of the

...ssociation for the Education of Young Children

...pted November 1995

Linguistically and culturally diverse is an educational term used by the U.S. Department of Education to define children enrolled in educational programs who are either non-English-proficient (NEP) or limited-English-proficient (LEP). Educators use this phrase, linguistically and culturally diverse, *to identify children from homes and communities where English is not the primary language of communication (Garciá 1991). For the purposes of this statement, the phrase will be used in a similar manner.*

This document primarily describes linguistically and culturally diverse children who speak languages other than English. However, the recommendations of this position statement can also apply to children who, although they speak only English, are also linguistically and culturally diverse.

Introduction

The children and families served in early childhood programs reflect the ethnic, cultural, and linguistic diversity of the nation. The nation's children all deserve an early childhood education that is responsive to their families, communities, and racial, ethnic, and cultural backgrounds. For young children to develop and learn optimally, the early childhood professional must be prepared to meet their diverse developmental, cultural, linguistic, and educational needs. Early childhood educators face the challenge of how best to respond to these needs.

The acquisition of language is essential to children's cognitive and social development. Regardless of what language children speak, they still develop and learn. Educators recognize that linguistically and culturally diverse children come to early childhood programs with previously acquired knowledge and learning based upon the language used in their home. For young children, the language of the home is the language they have used since birth, the language they use to make and establish meaningful communicative relationships, and the language they use to begin to construct their knowledge and test their learning. The home language is tied to children's culture, and culture and language communicate traditions, values, and attitudes (Chang 1993). Parents should be encouraged to use and develop children's home language; early childhood educators should respect children's linguistic and cultural backgrounds and their diverse learning styles. In so doing, adults will enhance children's learning and development.

Just as children learn and develop at different rates, individual differences exist in how children whose home language is not English acquire English. For example, some children may experience a silent period (of six or more months) while they acquire English; other children may practice their knowledge by mixing or combining languages (for example, "Mi mamá me put on mi coat"); still other children may seem to have acquired English-language skills (appropriate accent, use of vernacular, vocabulary, and grammatical rules) but are not truly proficient; yet some children will quickly acquire English-language proficiency. Each child's way of learning a new language should be viewed as acceptable, logical, and part of the ongoing development and learning of any new language.

Source: From National Association for the Education of Young Children. (1995). *Position Statement: Responding to Linguistic and Cultural Diversity* (Washington, DC: Author). Reprinted by permission.

Defining the Problem

At younger and younger ages, children are negotiating difficult transitions between their home and educational settings, requiring an adaptation to two or more diverse sets of rules, values, expectations, and behaviors. Educational programs and families must *respect* and *reinforce* each other as they work together to achieve the greatest benefit for all children. For some young children, entering any new environment—including early childhood programs—can be intimidating. The lives of many young children today are further complicated by having to communicate and learn in a language that may be unfamiliar. In the past, children entering U.S. schools from families whose home language is not English were expected to immerse themselves in the mainstream of schools, primarily through the use of English (Soto 1991; Wong Fillmore 1991). Sometimes the negative attitudes conveyed or expressed toward certain languages lead children to "give up" their home language. Early childhood professionals must recognize the feeling of loneliness, fear, and abandonment children may feel when they are thrust into settings that isolate them from their home community and language. The loss of children's home language may result *in the disruption of family communication patterns, which may lead to the loss of intergenerational wisdom; damage to individual and community esteem; and children's potential nonmastery of their home language or English.*

NAEYC's Position

NAEYC's goal is to build support for equal access to high-quality educational programs that recognize and promote all aspects of children's development and learning, enabling all children to become competent, successful, and socially responsible adults. Children's educational experiences should afford them the opportunity to learn and to become effective, functioning members of society. Language development is essential for learning, and the development of children's home language does not interfere with their ability to learn English. Because knowing more than one language is a cognitive asset (Hakuta & García 1989), early education programs should encourage the development of children's home language while fostering the acquisition of English.

For the optimal development and learning of all children, educators must *accept* the legitimacy of children's home language, *respect* (hold in high regard) and *value* (esteem, appreciate) the home culture, and *promote* and *encourage* the active involvement and support of all families, including extended and nontraditional family units.

When early childhood educators acknowledge and respect children's home language and culture, ties between the family and programs are strengthened. This atmosphere provides increased opportunity for learning because young children feel supported, nurtured, and connected not only to their home communities and families but also to teachers and the educational setting.

The Challenges

The United States is a nation of great cultural diversity, and our diversity creates opportunities to learn and share both similar and different experiences. There are opportunities to learn about people from different backgrounds; the opportunity to foster a bilingual citizenry with skills necessary to succeed in a global economy; and opportunities to share one's own cherished heritage and traditions with others.

Historically, our nation has tended to regard differences, especially language differences, as cultural handicaps rather than cultural resources (Meier & Cazden 1982). "Although most Americans are reluctant to say it publicly, many are anxious about the changing racial and ethnic composition of the country" (Sharry 1994). As the early childhood profession transforms its thinking,

> The challenge for early childhood educators is to become more knowledgeable about how to relate to children and families whose linguistic or cultural background is different from their own.

Between 1979 and 1989 the number of children in the United States from culturally and linguistically diverse backgrounds increased considerably (NCES 1993), and, according to a report released by the Center for the Study of Social Policy (1992), that diversity is even more pronounced among children younger than age 6. Contrary to popular belief, many of these children are neither foreign born nor immigrants but were born in the United States (Waggoner 1993). Approximately 9.9 million of the estimated 45 million school-age children, more than one in five, live in households in which languages other than English are spoken (Waggoner 1994). In some communities, however, the number of children living in a family in which a language other than English is spoken is likely to be much larger. Head Start reports that the largest number of linguistically and culturally diverse children served through Head Start are Spanish speakers, with other language groups representing smaller but growing percentages (Head Start Bureau 1995).

> *The challenge for teachers is to provide high-quality care and education for the increasing number of children who are likely to be linguistically and culturally diverse.*

Families and communities are faced with increasingly complex responsibilities. Children used to be cared for by parents and family members who typically spoke the home language of their family, be it English or another language. With the increasing need of family members to work, even while children are very young, more and more children are placed in care and educational settings with adults who may not speak the child's home language or share their cultural background. Even so, children will spend an ever-increasing amount of their waking lives with these teachers. What happens in care will have a tremendous impact on the child's social, emotional, and cognitive development. These interactions will influence the child's values, view of the world, perspectives on family, and connections to community. This places a tremendous responsibility in the hands of the early childhood community.

Responding to linguistic and cultural diversity can be challenging. At times the challenges can be complicated further by the specific needs or issues of the child, the family, or the educational program. Solutions may not be evident. Individual circumstances can affect each situation differently. There are no easy answers, and often myths and misinformation may flourish. The challenges may even seem to be too numerous for any one teacher or provider to manage. Nonetheless, despite the complexity, it is the responsibility of all educators to assume the tasks and meet the challenges. Once a situation occurs, the early childhood educator should enter into a dialogue with colleagues, parents, and others in an effort to arrive at

a negotiated agreement that will meet the best interest of the child. For example,

- A mother, father, and primary caregiver each have different cultural and linguistic backgrounds and do not speak English. Should the language of one of these persons be affirmed or respected above the others? How can the teacher affirm and respect the backgrounds of each of these individuals?
- The principal is concerned that all children learn English and, therefore, does not want any language other than English spoken in the early childhood setting. In the interest of the child, how should the educator respond?
- An educator questions whether a child will ever learn English if the home language is used as the primary language in the early childhood setting. How is this concern best addressed?

Solutions exist for each of these linguistic and cultural challenges, just as they do for the many other issues that early childhood educators confront within the early childhood setting. These challenges must be viewed as opportunities for the early childhood educator to reflect, question, and effectively respond to the needs of linguistically and culturally diverse children. Although appropriate responses to every linguistically and culturally diverse situation cannot be addressed through this document, early childhood educators should consider the following recommendations.

Recommendations for a Responsive Learning Environment

Early childhood educators should stop and reflect on the best ways to ensure appropriate educational and developmental experiences for all young children. The unique qualities and characteristics of each individual child must be acknowledged. Just as each child is different, methods and strategies to work with young children must vary.

The issue of home language and its importance to young children is also relevant for children who speak English but come from different cultural backgrounds, for example, speakers of English who have dialects, such as people from Appalachia or other regions having distinct patterns of speech, speakers of

Black English, or second- and third-generation speakers of English who maintain the dominant accent of their heritage language. While this position statement basically responds to children who are from homes in which English is not the dominant language, the recommendations provided may be helpful when working with children who come from diverse cultural backgrounds, even when they only speak English. The overall goal for early childhood professionals, however, is to provide every child, including children who are linguistically and culturally diverse, with a responsive learning environment. The following recommendations help achieve this goal.

A. Recommendations for Working with Children

Recognize that all children are cognitively, linguistically, and emotionally connected to the language and culture of their home.

When program settings acknowledge and support children's home language and culture, ties between the family and school are strengthened. In a supportive atmosphere young children's home language is less likely to atrophy (Chang 1993), a situation that could threaten the children's important ties to family and community.

Acknowledge that children can demonstrate their knowledge and capabilities in many ways.

In response to linguistic and cultural diversity, the goal for early childhood educators should be to make the most of children's potential, strengthening and building upon the skills they bring when they enter programs. Education, as Cummins states, implies "drawing out children's potential and making them more than they were" (1989, vii). Educational programs and practices must recognize the strengths that children possess. Whatever language children speak, they should be able to demonstrate their capabilities and also feel the success of being appreciated and valued. Teachers must build upon children's diversity of gifts and skills and provide young children opportunities to exhibit these skills in early childhood programs.

The learning environment must focus on the learner and allow opportunities for children to express themselves across the curriculum, including art, music, dramatization, and even block building. By using a nondeficit approach (tapping and recognizing children's strengths rather than focusing the child's home environment on skills yet unlearned) in their teaching, teachers should take the time to observe and engage children in a variety of learning activities. Children's strengths should be celebrated, and they should be given numerous ways to express their interests and talents. In doing this, teachers will provide children an opportunity to display their intellect and knowledge that may far exceed the boundaries of language.

Understand that without comprehensible input, second-language learning can be difficult.

It takes time to become linguistically proficient and competent in any language. Linguistically and culturally diverse children may be able to master basic communication skills; however, mastery of the more cognitively complex language skills needed for academic learning (Cummins 1989) is more dependent on the learning environment. Academic learning relies on significant amounts of information presented in decontextualized learning situations. Success in school becomes more and more difficult as children are required to learn, to be tested and evaluated based on ever-increasing amounts of information, consistently presented in a decontextualized manner. Children learn best when they are given a context in which to learn, and the knowledge that children acquire in "their first language can make second-language input much more comprehensible" (Krashen 1992, 37). Young children can gain knowledge more easily when they obtain quality instruction through their first language. Children can acquire the necessary language and cognitive skills required to succeed in school when given an appropriate learning environment, one that is tailored to meet their needs (NAEYC & NAECS/SDE 1991; Bredekamp & Rosegrant 1992).

Although verbal proficiency in a second language can be accomplished within two to three years, the skills necessary to achieve the higher level educational skills of understanding academic content through reading and writing may require four or more years (Cummins 1981; Collier 1989). Young children may seem to be fluent and at ease with English but may not be capable of understanding or expressing themselves as competently as their English-speaking peers. Although children seem to be speaking a second language with ease, *speaking* a language does not equate to being *proficient* in that language. Full proficiency in the first language, including complex uses of the language, contributes to the development of the second language. Children who do not become proficient in their second language after two or three years of regular use probably are not proficient in their first language either.

Young children may seem to be fluent and at ease speaking a second language, but they may not be fully capable of understanding or expressing themselves in the more complex aspects of language and may demonstrate weaknesses in language-learning skills, including vocabulary skills, auditory memory and discrimination skills, simple problem-solving tasks, and the ability to follow sequenced directions. Language difficulties such as these often can result in the linguistically and culturally diverse child being over referred to special education, classified as learning disabled, or perceived as developmentally delayed.

B. Recommendations for Working with Families

Actively involve parents and families in the early learning program and setting.

Parents and families should be actively involved in the learning and development of their children. Teachers should actively seek parental involvement and pursue establishing a partnership with children's families. When possible, teachers should visit the child's community (for example, shops, churches, and playgrounds); read and learn about the community through the use of books, pictures, observations, and conversations with community members; and visit the home and meet with other family members.

Parents and families should be invited to share, participate, and engage in activities with their children. Parent involvement can be accomplished in a number of ways, including asking parents to share stories, songs, drawings, and experiences of their linguistic and cultural background and asking parents to serve as monitors or field trip organizers. Families and parents should be invited to share activities that are developmentally appropriate and meaningful within their culture. These opportunities demonstrate to the parent what their child is learning; increase the knowledge, information, and understanding of all children regarding people of different cultures and linguistic backgrounds; and establish a meaningful relationship with the parent. The early childhood educator should ensure that parents are informed and engaged with their child in meaningful activities that promote linkages between the home and the early care setting.

Encourage and assist all parents in becoming knowledgeable about the cognitive value for children of knowing more than one language, and provide them with strategies to support, maintain, and preserve home-language learning.

In an early childhood setting and atmosphere in which home language is preserved, acknowledged, and respected, all parents can learn the value of home-language development and the strength it provides children as they add to their existing knowledge and understanding. Parents and teachers can learn how to become advocates regarding the long-term benefits that result from bilingualism.

Parents and teachers recognize the acquisition of English as an intellectual accomplishment, an opportunity for economic growth and development, and a means for achieving academic success. There are even times when parents may wish for the ability, or have been mistakenly encouraged, to speak to their children only in English, a language of which the parents themselves may not have command. The educator should understand the effects that speaking only in English can have upon the child, the family, and the child's learning. The teacher must be able to explain that speaking to the child only in English can often result in communications being significantly hindered and verbal interactions being limited and unnatural between the parent and the child. In using limited English, parents may communicate to children using simple phrases and commands (for example, "Sit down" or "Stop"); modeling grammatically incorrect phrases (for example, "We no go store"); or demonstrating other incorrect usages of language that are common when persons acquire a second language. From these limited and incorrect verbal interactions, the amount of language the child is hearing is reduced, and the child's vocabulary growth is restricted, contributing to an overall decrease in verbal expression. When parents do not master the second language yet use the second language to communicate with their child, there is an increased likelihood that the child will not hear complex ideas or abstract thoughts—important skills needed for cognitive and language development. The teacher must explain that language is developed through natural language interactions. These natural interactions occur within the day-to-day setting, through radio and television, when using public transportation, and in play with children whose dominant language is English. The parent and the teacher must work collaboratively to achieve the goal of children's learning English.

Through the home language and culture, families transmit to their children a sense of identity, an understanding of how to relate to other people, and a sense of belonging. When parents and children cannot communicate with one another, family and community destabilization can occur. Children who are proficient in their home language are able to maintain a connectedness to their histories, their stories, and the day-to-day events shared by parents, grandparents, and other family members who may speak only the home language. Without the ability to communicate, parents are not able to socialize their children, share beliefs and value systems, and directly influence, coach, and model with their children.

Recognize that parents and families must rely on caregivers and educators to honor and support their children in the cultural values and norms of the home.

Parents depend on high-quality early childhood programs to assist them with their children's development and learning. Early childhood programs should make provisions to communicate with families in their home language and to provide parent-teacher encounters that both welcome and accommodate families. Partnerships between the home and the early childhood setting must be developed to ensure that practices of the home and expectations of the program are complementary. Linguistic and cultural continuity between the home and the early childhood program supports children's social and emotional development. By working together, parents and teachers have the opportunity to influence the understanding of language and culture and to encourage multicultural learning and acceptance in a positive way.

C. Recommendations for Professional Preparation

Provide early childhood educators with professional preparation and development in the areas of culture, language, and diversity.

Efforts to understand the languages and cultural backgrounds of young children are essential in helping children to learn. Uncertainty can exist when educators are unsure of how to relate to children and families of linguistic and cultural backgrounds different from their own. Early childhood educators need to understand and appreciate their own cultural and linguistic backgrounds. Adults' cultural background affects how they interact with and/or teach young children. The educator's background influences how children are taught, reinforced, and disciplined. The child's background influences how the child constructs knowledge, responds to discipline and praise, and interacts in the early childhood setting.

Preservice and inservice training opportunities in early childhood education programs assist educators in overcoming some of the linguistic and cultural challenges they may face in working with young children. Training institutions and programs can consider providing specific courses in the following topic areas or include these issues in current courses: language acquisition; second-language learning; use of translators; working with diverse families; sociolinguistics; cross-cultural communication; issues pertaining to the politics of race, language, and culture; and community involvement.

Recruit and support early childhood educators who are trained in languages other than English.

Within the field of early childhood education, there is a need for knowledgeable, trained, competent, and sensitive multilingual/multicultural early childhood educators. Early childhood educators who speak more than one language and are culturally knowledgeable are an invaluable resource in the early childhood setting. In some instances the educator may speak multiple languages or may be able to communicate using various linguistic regionalisms or dialects spoken by the child or the family. The educator may have an understanding of sociocultural and economic issues relevant within the local linguistically and culturally diverse community and can help support the family in the use and development of the child's home language and in the acquisition of English. The early childhood teacher who is trained in linguistic and cultural diversity can be a much-needed resource for information about the community and can assist in the inservice cultural orientation and awareness training for the early childhood program. The bilingual educator also can be a strong advocate for family and community members.

Too often, however, bilingual early childhood professionals are called upon to provide numerous other services, some of which they may not be equipped to provide. For example, the bilingual professional, although a fluent speaker, may not have the vocabulary needed to effectively communicate with other adults or, in some instances, may be able to read and write only in English, not in the second language. In addition, bilingual teachers should not be expected to meet the needs of *all* linguistically and culturally diverse children and families in the program, especially those whose language they do not speak. Bilingual providers should not be asked to translate forms, particularly at a moment's notice, nor should they be required to stop their work in order to serve as interpreters. Bilingual teachers should not serve in roles, such as advising or counseling, in which they may lack professional training. These assignments may seem simple but often can be burdensome and must be viewed as added duties placed upon the bilingual teacher.

Preservice and inservice training programs are needed to support bilingual early childhood educators in furthering educators' knowledge and mastery of the language(s) other than English that they speak, and training should also credit content-based courses offered in languages other than English. Professional preparation instructors must urge all teachers to support multilingual/multicultural professionals in their role as advocates for linguistically and culturally diverse children. Early childhood professionals should be trained to work collaboratively with the bilingual early childhood teacher and should be informed of the vital role of the bilingual educator. Additionally, there is a need for continued research in the area of linguistic and cultural diversity of young children.

D. Recommendations for Programs and Practice

Recognize that children can and will acquire the use of English even when their home language is used and respected.

Children should build upon their current skills as they acquire new skills. While children maintain and build upon their home language skills and culture, children can organize and develop proficiency and knowledge in English. Bilingualism has been associated with higher levels of cognitive attainment (Hakuta & García 1989) and does not interfere with either language proficiency or cognitive development. Consistent learning opportunities to read, be read to, and see print messages should be given to linguistically and culturally diverse children. Literacy developed in the home language will transfer to the second language (Krashen 1992). Bilingualism should be viewed as an asset and an educational achievement.

Support and preserve home language usage.

If the early childhood teacher *speaks* the child's home language, then the teacher can comfortably use this language around the child, thereby providing the child with opportunities to hear and use the home language within the early childhood setting. Use of the language should be clearly evident throughout the learning environment (e.g., in meeting charts, tape recordings, the library corner). Educators should develop a parent information board, using a language and reading level appropriate for the parents. Teachers should involve parents and community members in the early childhood program. Parents and community members can assist children in hearing the home language from many different adults, in addition to the teacher who speaks the home language. Parents and community members can assist other parents who may be unable to read, or they can assist the teacher in communicating with families whose home language may not have a written form.

If the early childhood educator *does not speak* the language, he or she should make efforts to provide visible signs of the home language throughout the learning environment through books and other relevant reading material in the child's language and with a parent bulletin board (get a bilingual colleague to help review for accuracy of written messages). The teacher can learn a few selected words in the child's language, thus demonstrating a willingness to take risks similar to the risks asked of children as they learn a second language. This effort by the teacher also helps to validate and affirm the child's language and culture, further demonstrating the teacher's esteem and respect for the child's linguistic and cultural background. The teacher should model appropriate use of English and provide the child with opportunities to use newly acquired vocabulary and language. The teacher also must actively involve the parent and the community in the program.

If the teacher is *faced with many different languages* in the program or classroom, the suggestions listed above are still relevant. Often teachers feel overwhelmed if more than one language is spoken in the program; however, they should remember that the goal is for children to learn, and that learning is made easier when children can build on knowledge in their home language. The teacher should consider grouping together at specific times during the day children who speak the same or similar languages so that the children can construct knowledge with others who speak their home language. The early childhood educator should ensure that these children do not become socially isolated as efforts are made to optimize their learning. Care should be taken to continually create an environment that provides for high learning expectations.

Develop and provide alternative and creative strategies for young children's learning.

Early childhood educators are encouraged to rely on their creative skills in working with children to infuse cultural and linguistic diversity in their programs. They should provide children with multiple opportunities to learn and ways for them to demonstrate their learning, participate in program activities, and work interactively with other children.

To learn more about working with linguistically and culturally diverse children, early childhood educators should collaborate with each other and with colleagues from other professions. To guide the implementation of a developmentally, linguistically, and culturally appropriate program, collaborative parent and teacher workgroups should be developed. These committees should discuss activities and strategies that would be effective for use with linguistically and

culturally diverse children. Such committees promote good practices for children and shared learning between teachers and parents.

Summary

Early childhood educators can best help linguistically and culturally diverse children and their families by acknowledging and responding to the importance of the child's home language and culture. Administrative support for bilingualism as a goal is necessary within the educational setting. Educational practices should focus on educating children toward the "school culture" while preserving and respecting the diversity of the home language and culture that each child brings to the early learning setting. Early childhood professionals and families must work together to achieve high quality care and education for *all* children.

References

Bredekamp, S., & T. Rosegrant, eds. 1992. *Reaching potentials: Appropriate curriculum and assessment for young children.* Vol. 1. Washington, DC: NAEYC.

Center for the Study of Social Policy. 1992. *The challenge of change: What the 1990 census tells us about children.* Washington, DC: Author.

Chang, H. N.-L. 1993. *Affirming children's roots: Cultural and linguistic diversity in early care and education.* San Francisco: California Tomorrow.

Collier, V. 1989. How long: A synthesis of research on academic achievement in second language. *TESOL Quarterly* 23: 509–31.

Cummins, J. 1981. The role of primary language development in promoting educational success for language minority students. In *Schooling and language minority students: A theoretical framework,* eds. M. Ortiz, D. Parker, & F. Tempes. Office of Bilingual Bicultural Education, California State Department of Education. Los Angeles: Evaluation, Dissemination, and Assessment Center, California State University.

Cummins, J. 1989. *Empowering minority students.* Sacramento: California Association for Bilingual Education.

García, E. 1991. *The education of linguistically and culturally diverse students: Effective instructional practices.* Santa Cruz: National Center for Research on Cultural Diversity and Second Language Learning, University of California.

Hakuta, K., & E. García. 1989. Bilingualism and education. *American Psychologist* 44 (2): 374–79.

Head Start Bureau, Administration on Children, Youth, and Families, Department of Health and Human Services. 1995. *Program information report.* Washington, DC: Author.

Krashen, S. 1992. *Fundamentals of language education.* Torrance, CA: Laredo Publishing.

Meier, T. R., & C. B. Cazden. 1982. A focus on oral language and writing from a multicultural perspective. *Language Arts* 59: 504–12.

National Association for the Education of Young Children (NAEYC) and National Association of Early Childhood Specialists in State Departments of Education (NAECS/SDE). 1991. Guidelines for appropriate curriculum content and assessment in programs serving children ages 3 through 8. *Young Children* 46 (3): 21–38.

National Center for Education Statistics (NCES). 1993. *Language characteristics and schooling in the United States, a changing picture: 1979 and 1989.* NCES 93–699. Washington, DC: U.S. Department of Education, Office of Educational Research and Improvement.

Sharry, F. 1994. *The rise of nativism in the United States and how to respond to it.* Washington, DC: National Education Forum.

Soto, L. D. 1991. Understanding bilingual/bicultural children. *Young Children* 46 (2): 30–36.

Waggoner, D., ed. 1993. *Numbers and needs: Ethnic and linguistic minorities in the United States* 3 (6).

Waggoner, D. 1994. Language minority school age population now totals 9.9 million. *NABE News* 18 (1): 1, 24–26.

Wong Fillmore, L. 1991. When learning a second language means losing the first. *Early Childhood Research Quarterly* 6: 323–46.

Resources

Banks, J. 1993. Multicultural education for young children: Racial and ethnic attitudes and their modification. In *Handbook of research on the education of young children,* ed. B. Spodek, 236–51. New York: Macmillan.

Collier, V. 1989. How long: A synthesis of research on academic achievement in second language. *TESOL Quarterly* 23: 509–31.

Collier, V., & C. Twyford. 1988. The effect of age on acquisition of a second language for school. *National Clearinghouse for Bilingual Education* 2 (Winter): 1–12.

Derman-Sparks, L., & the A.B.C. Task Force. 1989. *Antibias curriculum: Tools for empowering young children.* Washington, DC: NAEYC.

McLaughlin, B. 1992. *Myths and misconceptions about second language learning: What every teacher needs to unlearn.* Santa Cruz: National Center for Research on Cultural Diversity and Second Language Learning, University of California.

Neugebauer, B., ed. 1992. *Alike and different: Exploring our humanity with young children.* Redmond, WA: Exchange Press, 1987. Reprint, Washington, DC: NAEYC.

Ogbu, J. U. 1978. *Minority education and caste: The American system in cross cultural perspective.* New York: Academic.

Phillips, C. B. 1988. Nurturing diversity for today's children and tomorrow's leaders. *Young Children* 43 (2): 42–47.

Tharp, R. G. 1989. Psychocultural variables and constants: Effects on teaching and learning in schools. *American Psychologist* 44: 349–59.

absorbent mind Montessori's term used to describe the inquisitive nature of children's intellect

abstract thinking ability to consider theoretical concepts without relying on concrete experiences or examples

accessibility degree to which individuals with disabilities can utilize facilities or services without undue assistance

accommodation according to Piaget, adaptive mental process by which new schemas are constructed when new information or experience is contrary to existing schemas

active learners students who are actively engaged in the learning process

activity centers see learning centers

adaptation dual mental processes that construct or reconstruct new information or experiences to fit with existing knowledge

advisory councils examine information relevant to school policies or plans and offer suggestions about how they think schools should act or respond

advocacy positive social action on behalf of others

advocacy groups include both family members and school personnel who have united for a common cause

affective domain developmental domain that includes aspects of emotional, social, and moral development

age appropriate teaching practices and materials that suit chronological ages of learners

airborne transmission tiny droplets of fluid from the mouth or nose which may contribute to food-borne disease outbreaks

anecdotal record written documentation of single significant behaviors or events

animism mentally attributing lifelike qualities to inanimate objects

antibias curriculum teaching and learning strategies

assessment the process of collecting and documenting evidence of behaviors for interpretation and evaluation

assimilation according to Piaget, adaptive mental process by which new information or experiences are incorporated within existing schemas

associate degree programs two-year college degrees consisting of approximately 60 credit hours

associative play Parten's fourth category of social play, which involves social interactions among children but different play goals

atelier in Reggio Emilia programs, the art studio

atelierista teacher trained in the visual arts in Reggio Emilia programs

at risk children who are more likely to have developmental delays due to environmental issues, genetics, or problems during or at birth

attachment strong positive emotional bonds toward other individuals

attachment in the making Bowlby's second phase of attachment, when infants respond differently to familiar caregivers than to strangers

au pair individual who provides family child care in exchange for room and board and minimal salary

auditory mode learning channel accessed through hearing

authentic assessment attempts to observe and record typical behaviors as they occur without manipulation

autonomous morality stage Piaget's third stage of moral development, when individuals are able to consider the intentions of individuals as well as their misdeeds and believe punishment should be relative to both the misdeed and the intentions

autonomy control over one's own decisions

autonomy versus shame and doubt Erikson's second stage of psychosocial development, when children strive for independence

avoidant attachment pattern of attachment where infants demonstrate distress on departure of familiar caregivers but, conversely, avoid caregivers on their return

axons message sending fibers of neurons

babbling prelinguistic behavior of infants characterized by repetitive consonant/vowel sounds like *da-da* or *ma-ma*

Babinski reflex infants' involuntary movements of the leg toward the body triggered when the sole of the foot is stroked, causing the foot to turn inward and the toes to spread outward

bachelor's degree programs four-year college programs, usually comprised of 120 or more semester credit hours

Bank Street approach see developmental-interaction approach

basic forms stage Kellogg's second stage of drawing, when children make repetitive patterns using shapes and lines

behavior guidance strategies and practices used to help individuals learn and use prosocial behaviors

behaviorist theory constructivist theory that defines learning as a change in behavior

best practice term used to describe the most appropriate teaching methods

bibliotherapy process of using situations in books to stimulate discussions to explore emotions

bilingual ability to speak two or more languages

blinking reflex spontaneous rapid closing and reopening of the eyes when anything is sensed near them

body awareness consciousness of the location of one's body and body parts in relationship to objects and others

career lattice specifies five different levels of education and experience for different staff positions in early care and education settings

categories of attachment classifications of attachment ranging from secure to insecure

categories of temperament clusters of temperament characteristics labeled as easy, difficult, or slow-to-warm-up

center-based child care early care and education that occurs in schools or other settings outside of private homes

center of gravity the midpoint of the distribution of body weight

center time periods when all centers in the classroom are open

centration cognitive tendency to mentally focus on the single, most obvious characteristic

cephalocaudal pattern principle that suggests physical development proceeds from head-to-tail in a top-down sequence

cerebral cortex outer layer of the cerebrum where higher-level mental processes originate

certified personnel individuals who have received certification in a profession

child abuse illegal mistreatment of children by another through actions, such as physical punishment, or lack of action, such as neglect

child care centers see child development center

child-centered teaching builds curriculum in response to children's developmental needs and interests

Child Development Associate Credential (CDA) national credential awarded by the Council for Professional Recognition to candidates who have successfully met educational, experiential, and assessment criteria

child development center facility that provides center-based child care that usually includes both custodial and educational services

child directed situations in which children determine for themselves, within parameters, what they will do and how they will do it

childproofing the needs, abilities, and limitations of infants and toddlers are kept in mind in preparing the environment to be as free as possible from potential safety hazards

child-sized furnishings furniture built to accommodate children's body sizes

choice time periods of the day when children make decisions about where to play, how to play, and with whom to play

choking hazards objects that may become lodged in children's throats

circle time opportunity for large groups of children to participate in singing, music making, and game playing

classification cognitive ability to sort and group objects by one or more attributes

classroom climate overall character of learning environments

clear-cut attachment Bowlby's third stage of attachment, when infants display distress on separation from caregivers

cognitive domain developmental domain that encompasses components of cognition, language, and memory

collaborative dialogues Vygotsky's term for shared conversations

common schools elementary schools in colonial America

communicable diseases infections that can be spread from one person to another community-based volunteer programs arrangements by agencies for volunteers to go to homes or schools to interact with children

community resources public and private agencies at local, state, regional, national, and sometimes global levels that have stepped in to fill the void created by changes in family structure and provide specialized services to children and families

compensate cognitive ability to make mental adjustments for physical changes

competencies statements that identify the skills and behaviors that individuals should be able to do

compulsory education required school attendance

concrete operational stage Piaget's third stage of cognitive development, when children are able to apply logical mental operations such as reversibility and conservation

conflict resolution techniques that scaffold children's attempts to be problem solvers and negotiators and foster attitudes of nonviolence, which boosts their social competence and allows for self-regulation

conservation Piaget's term to describe the cognitive ability to use logical reasoning, rather than perception, to draw conclusions about objects and events

constructive play activity in which children determine what the object does and what they can do with the object, and use the object in some purposeful way

constructivist theory educational theory that individuals construct knowledge as they gain experience through interactions with objects and individuals in their environments

content subject matter of curriculum

conventional moral reasoning Kohlberg's second level of moral reasoning, when individuals make decisions based on the expectations of others (stage 3) or rigid interpretation of rules and laws (stage 4)

cooing prelinguistic behavior of young infants characterized by soft, repetitive vowel sounds like *ooh* and *aah*

cooperative play Parten's highest category of social play, when children participate in play scenarios with common goals

corpus collosum large bundle of neural fibers that act as a bridge between the right and left hemispheres of the brain

co-teachers teachers who equally share teaching responsibilities

Creative Curriculum approach concept of a preschool curriculum framework based on classroom environment

culture collective characteristics of race, ethnicity, language, religion, gender, familiar structures, and value systems common to a group

culturally appropriate one of NAEYC's criteria for developmentally appropriate practice; specifically teaching practices and materials that are sensitive to and celebrate cultural diversity

curriculum a comprehensive course of study including content, methods, and assessment

custodial needs physical needs of children that must be met on a daily basis

daily events periods of the day in which children participate in large-group activities, such as mealtime, story time, rest time, and outdoor play

daily health checks quick visual surveys that focus on appearance of skin, eyes, nose, mouth, and palms to determine if children are exhibiting any symptoms of illness

daily schedule chronological timeline of classroom activities, including learning opportunities, routines, and procedures

dame schools rudimentary schools in colonial America that were usually run by widows (dames)

daycare centers see child development centers

decentrate cognitive ability to focus on more than one aspect of an object or event at a time

deferred imitation ability to imitate behaviors when models are no longer present

dendrites message receiving fibers of neurons

developmental delay comprehensive term used to describe documented special needs for children under age 9

developmental domain broad category representing related areas of growth and maturation

developmental-interaction approach approach to early care and education that encourages active learning and social interaction

developmental milestones significant behaviors or skills that emerge sequentially and thus somewhat predictably

developmental norms statistical age ranges that identify typical emergence of milestone behaviors

developmentally appropriate practice (DAP) NAEYC's term to describe teaching strategies, assessment methods, and materials that are age, individually, and culturally appropriate

didactic learning materials learning materials that focus on a single concept and control for error, usually used in connection with the Montessori method

differentiated crying sounds of crying that vary according to need or purpose

dimensions of temperament distinct traits linked to patterns of emotional response

direct instruction model highly structured method of instruction that relies on formal teaching of curriculum

disabilities atypical development that impedes functioning

discovery learning strategy developed by Jerome Bruner in which self-expression and creativity are encouraged

disequilibrium according to Piaget, a momentary mental imbalance or lack of understanding that triggers adaptive mental processes

DISTAR (Direct Instruction System for Teaching and Re- mediation) formal system designed to accelerate learning through fast-paced, highly structured, teacher-directed lessons that provide immediate corrective feedback

disorganized/disoriented attachment pattern of inse- cure attachment where infants appear confused or disoriented upon return of familiar caregivers

disposition attitude or overall demeanor; collection of stable personality traits that reflect predominant tendencies

documentation physical record of observations, such as written notes, photographs, audio- or video- tapes, and collected samples

dramatic play form of pretend play where individuals assume imaginary roles

early childhood period of human development en- compassing the first eight years of life

early childhood specialist according to NAEYC's career lattice, individuals with high levels of specialized education and experience

Early Head Start federally funded early care and edu- cation program associated with Head Start for eco- nomically disadvantaged children under age 4

echolalia (echo speech) a form of prelinguistic speech characterized by infants' imitative vocalizations of frequently heard words

ecological model systems model of human develop- ment showing ever-expanding spheres of influ- ences over children's development

egocentrism Piaget's term for the cognitive tendency to view objects and events from one's own per- spective and further to assume that others share the same view

emergent curriculum curriculum developed from the observed or expressed interests of learners and their current levels of knowledge about the facts and concepts involved

emergent literacy developmental process whereby children become increasingly aware of the inter- connectedness of listening, speaking, reading, and writing

emotional abuse illegal mistreatment of an individual by another, consisting of verbal comments in- tended to intimidate, threaten, or humiliate

enactive stage Bruner's first stage of cognitive de- velopment from birth to about eighteen months of age in which infants grow cognitively as they explore actions and objects through their senses

equilibrium according to Piaget, a state of mental bal- ance or understanding

equipment durable goods such as furniture, ma- chines, and appliances

experience environmental factors that influence development

expressive vocabulary ability to use spoken language

exosystem individuals and physical settings that do not directly touch children but are linked to chil- dren by their mesosystems

extended families a group of family members that might include parents, children, grandparents, and other relatives

eye-foot coordination perceptual-motor behavior that matches visual input to movement of the feet and toes

eye-hand coordination perceptual-motor behavior that matches visual input to movement of the hands and fingers

facilitators persons implementing the learning by or- ganizing the environment and curriculum

family diverse individuals blended into groups who are emotionally, and usually economically, de- pendent on each other family child care (FCC) child care provided to one or more children in home-based settings; often includes educational experiences

family child care provider individuals who provide home-based care and education to one or more children

family involvement assumes many forms, with varying degrees of participation that give family members a full range of ways to support early care and education efforts of teachers and schools

family-oriented practices family members are recognized as partners and participants in the process or caring for and educating their children

family-teacher conferences planned, scheduled, private meetings organized for the express purpose of having face-to-face meetings with children's parents or primary guardians

fecal-oral transmission germs in fecal matter that are spread to the mouth

field trips groups of children, chaperoned by teachers and family members, that visit selected sites or attend special events sponsored by community organizations

fine motor use of small muscles of the hands and fingers, feet and toes, and face

food allergy production of histamines in the body in reaction to particular foods

Food Guide Pyramid graphic model produced by the United States Department of Agriculture (USDA) that specifies dietary guidelines according to food groups

food intolerance difficulty in digesting particular foods or components of food

formal communication planned forms of communication such as newsletters, handbooks, conferences, meetings, and events

formal operational stage Piaget's fourth and final stage of cognitive development, where individuals utilize abstract thinking

formation of reciprocal relationships Bowlby's fourth stage of attachment, when toddlers learn to negotiate with familiar caregivers and are willing to participate in give-and-take relationships

foundling home antiquated term for orphanages that house children who have been abandoned at birth or during childhood

free appropriate public education (FAPE) one of the mandates from PL 94-142 stipulating that individuals with special needs have the same rights to free public education as their nondisabled peers

free play see self-directed play

frontal lobe region of the brain behind the forehead

functional play children's play made up of repetitive motions as they explore what objects are like and what they can do with objects

games with rules two or more children understand and accept the rules prior to participating in the game

generactivity versus stagnation Erikson's seventh stage of psychosocial development, where adults reflect on their contributions to others, redefine their goals, and make decisions related to those goals

gifts and occupations Froebel's educational toys and materials and activities using them

goals of misbehavior children's misbehavior aimed at obtaining attention, power, revenge, or relief of inadequacies

goodness of fit link between category of temperament and caregiving that relates matching caregiving or parenting practices to complement children's temperament whatever the category

gross motor refers to the use of large muscles in the arms, legs, torso, and neck

guest speakers individuals who share their expertise with others through speeches, discussions, or demonstrations

guided exploration discovery learning experiences in which teachers facilitate exploration

handbooks written polices and guidelines collected and organized into coherent packets of related information

hands-on learning learning supported by varieties of materials and equipment that invite active learning and problem solving

hand-washing techniques effective strategy for cleaning hands in order to reduce the spread of infectious diseases

Head Start comprehensive federal compensatory program that serves children and families who are economically disadvantaged

health appraisals brief review of health status

health histories contain an overview of an individual's general state of health from birth

health screenings administered by certified health personnel and serve as "first-alert systems" to quickly identify children who may need more extensive medical examination to confirm they have certain health conditions that need treatment

hemisphere refers to one side of the brain

heterogeneous groups arrangement of individuals who differ in some way into groups

heteronomous morality stage Piaget's second stage of moral development, when children expect all misdeeds to be punished according to established rules and consequences

hierarchy of needs Maslow's theory identifying ascending levels of human needs from basic survival to self-actualization

High/Scope approach program that advocates for child-initiated activities

holophrases one-word sentences used by toddlers that often convey multiple meanings

home-based child care child care and education in the homes of children or providers

home visitors early childhood educators who visit the homes of students to enhance home-school partnerships

home visits visits to children's homes by teachers

homogeneous groups arrangement of individuals with similar levels of performance into groups

hunger a painful condition associated with the lack of food

hypothetico-deductive reasoning ability to reason about abstract possibilities

iconic stage Bruner's second stage of cognitive development from eighteen months of age to approximately age 6 in which children develop cognitively as they experiment with concrete objects and discover new information

identity Piagetian term to describe the understanding that objects remain the same if nothing is added or removed regardless of their appearance

identity versus role confusion Erikson's fifth stage of psychosocial development, when adolescents seek to better understand their roles

imitation mimicking the behaviors of others while the model is present

immovable features permanently placed structural elements of rooms

immunization medical shots that enable individuals to build resistance to specific diseases

impulses messages that are electrically or chemically transmitted across a gap between neurons

incest sexual activities among members of immediate family; considered a form of sexual molestation when underage individuals are involved

incident report type of written record used to record specific safety-related incidents

inclusion the practice of fully integrating children with special needs into educational programs with typically developing peers

indirect services special assistance for children that do not directly involve teaching and learning

individualized education plan (IEP) special education document mandated by PL 94-142 for children with special needs that targets current level of functioning and future learning goals

individualized family service plan (IFSP) special education document for children under age 3 that identifies current level of functions and future learning goals

individually appropriate teaching practices and materials that consider the needs of specific children as well as children's ages

inductive reasoning associating specific examples with a generalization

industry versus inferiority Erikson's fourth stage of psychosocial development, where children strive to demonstrate their competence

infant-toddler programs early care and education programs for children under age 3

infanticide death of infants due to homicide

infectious diseases see communicable diseases

informal communication occurs spontaneously through unplanned meetings, casual notes, and phone calls

initiative versus guilt Erikson's third stage of psychosocial development, where young children strive to utilize their abilities independently

inservice education job-related training that occurs after one is employed

integrity versus despair individuals often attempt to share their accumulated knowledge and insight with members of newer generations

interdisciplinary curriculum content overlaps traditional subject areas

intergrated curriculum plan of study in which concepts are approached realistically as wholes

interest areas see learning centers

interpersonal dimension aspects of classroom climate that focus on child-to-child, child-to-adult, and adult-to-adult interactions and experiences intimacy versus isolation Erikson stage in which individuals seek stable reciprocal relationships with others

irreversibility inability to mentally reverse a process or series of events

key experiences part of the High/Scope curriculum model representing recommended learning activities in specific developmental areas

kindergarten system of education of children that sought to provide learning environments where they could grow according to their own dispositions and inner development

kinesthetic mode learning channel accessed through movement and touch

knowledge collective understanding of a body of information and related concepts

latchkey program see school-age child care

lateralization specialization of cognitive function to one hemisphere of the brain

learning centers areas of the classroom that contains relevant materials and equipment used to facilitate self-directed activity and play

learning environment physical space in which instruction and learning take place

learning modalities sensory methods individuals use to take in information and to learn

least restrictive environment (LRE) one of the mandates from PL 94–142 stipulating that education should take place in learning environments that do not unduly limit individuals' educational experiences

lending libraries programs that allow teachers to borrow specially developed curriculum materials and resource kits to enrich children's learning and cultural experiences

licensing regulations legal mandates associated with the issuance and maintenance of a license

linguistic speech vocalizations with meaning

literacy center area of the classroom stocked with materials and activities to support emerging skills and abilities of oral and written language

literacy-rich environments classrooms filled with materials and activities that support young children's exploration and experimentation with oral and written language

locomotor skills gross motor behaviors that involve a change in location of the body

logical consequences use of naturally occurring or related consequences for the purpose of behavior guidance

logico-mathematical knowledge Piaget's term to describe awareness of the relationships among objects and events

longitudinal study study reporting that children who participated in child-initiated activities demonstrated higher levels of social responsibilities during adolescence and adulthood than those individuals who attended the direct instruction model

macrosystem represents the larger influence of society including attitudes and values

magical thinking Piaget's term to describe the egocentric assumption that thinking or wishing for an object or event will cause it to happen

malnutrition absence of sufficient quantities of food or the right kinds of foods to obtain all of the nutrients needed for normal growth and development

mandates requirements set forth by state departments of education

mandatory reporters of child abuse adults who interact with children on a regular basis as part of their employment are required by law to report any suspicion of child abuse to proper authorities

manual dexterity specialization and control over the small muscles of the hand and fingers

master teacher effective, experienced teacher with level of education that exceeds minimum requirements

materials consumable goods such as paper, crayons, and small toys

maturation biological sequence of development

meaningful learning instructional content that is relevant to learners

mesosystem system representing the two-way relationships between children and their families and those individuals directly connected to the children on a regular basis

methods instructional strategies associated with curriculum

microsystem children's most immediate environment, such as close family members, their relationships with the children, and physical objects to which children are exposed in their home environments

misbehavior term that describes behaviors that are not considered socially acceptable

mobility degree of movement available between areas of the classroom and access to entrances and exits

modeling term used by social learning theorists to describe actions that others imitate

Montessori method educational technique developed by Montessori that supports individualized learning in prepared environments

moral development component of affective development related to individuals' abilities to reason about right and wrong

morality of caring female form of reasoning based on responsibilities to relationships

morality of justice male form of reasoning based on individual rights and responsibilities

moro reflex involuntary movement where infants arch their backs and quickly fling out their arms in response to loud noises or other unexpected phenomena (also known as the startle reflex)

movable features structures that can be moved such as equipment and furnishings

multilingual ability to speak many different languages

myelination process of sheathing neurons in a layer of fatty protein (myelin)

nanny individual whose primary employment responsibilities are related to the care and education of one or more related children in a home-based setting

nature-nurture controversy ongoing debate about the influences of maturation and/or experience on development

natural environment special education term used to describe the environments children would attend if they were typically developing for the purposes of receiving early intervention

naturalism Rousseau's concept that what is natural is also good

naturalistic observation the process of watching, listening, and recording behaviors as they occur in typical day-to-day settings

neglect adults' illegal failure to provide children with appropriate nourishment, protection, shelter, medical care, or supervision

networking interaction and exchange of ideas, information, and services among professionals

neurons nerve cells of the brain

noncertified personnel teaching staff not associated with public school districts

normal schools historical term for teacher training schools

nuclear families family units composed of parent figures and children

nursery school school that provides for the primary custodial care needs related to health, safety, and nutrition as well as for the educational needs of children under age 7

nutrients food substances that contribute to the healthy operation of the body

nutrition study of foods and how the body processes them

obesity individuals who are 20 percent or more above their normal body weight

object lesson learning that stems from the manipulation of a familiar, concrete (real) object

object permanence limited perception of infants in which there is a lack of awareness that objects continue to exist even when they are not within view or hearing range

objective accurate statements without personal bias

observation the process of watching, listening, and recording behaviors and events

observational learning term used by social learning theorists to describe learned behaviors that occur as a result of modeling

one-way communication strategies for keeping families informed about their children's care and education that have the potential for limiting feedback

onlooker behavior second category of social play, when a child watches another child or group of children play but does not actually participate in the play

open-air nursery school established in England and New York, where the focus was on health in order to prevent the spread of disease

open-ended activities play and learning experiences that allow for a variety of successful outcomes

open-ended questions questions that leave room for discussion

open-framework curriculum options for learning activities that come from collections of learning experiences

outreach programs community resources brought into the school for purposes of special performances or presentations

palmer grasp reflex occuring when something touches the baby's palm and the baby automatically grasps the object by curling the fingers around the object (also known as a grasping reflex)

parallel play third category of play, when a child plays side by side with another child although each child is engaged in a separate play episode

paraprofessionals individuals with some specialized training and education who work in support of a professional

parent education programs to empower family members to continue to be their children's first teacher by providing them with the knowledge and skills they will need to support their children's development, education, and school success

parent educators individuals who provide information and instruction to support parent-child relationships

parent-teacher conferences see family-teacher conferences

parentese when adults speak to newborns using higher-pitched, rhythmic voices

participant observation observation of children's self-directed spontaneous activities

partnership practices actions that focus on ways to make the best use of resources for the benefit of all stakeholders

pedagogy teaching methodology

pedigogista education coordinator

perceptual-motor referring to how muscles coordinate their movements with perceptual input received through the senses

person-first language recommendation from IDEA (Individuals with Disabilities Education Act) to recognize individuals before disabilities

phases of attachment Bowlby's four stages, including preattachment, attachment in the making, clear-cut attachment, and formation of reciprocal relationships

phonemes sounds used to produce language

physical abuse illegal mistreatment of individuals by another through excessive force or restraint such as hitting, shaking, kicking, or other forms of physical punishment

physical dimension concrete aspects of classroom climate that encompass elements of learning environments—safety, health, play, and learning

physical knowledge knowledge of objects and their properties

piazza central open square where children congregate and interact with each other and with adults

pictorial stage the fourth stage of drawing, when children think about what they intend to draw before they begin drawing

pincer grasp when infants use their thumbs and forefingers to hold and pick up objects

placement stage third stage of drawing, where child's deliberate use of shapes and lines to create patterns is extended

plan-do-review three-part process in which children have planning time, work time, and recall time

plasticity malleability of the brain

play activity that is freely chosen and self-satisfying

positive reinforcement social praise or reward tokens used to maintain or increase desired behaviors

postconventional moral reasoning last level of Kohlberg's cognitive stages

pragmatics verbal and nonverbal aspects of language used in social contexts

praise positively acknowledging someone or something

preattachment Bowlby's first phase of attachment, when the infant uses behaviors or signals to get close to the caregiver (birth to six weeks)

precausal reasoning process that prematurely draws cause-and-effect relationships between two or more actions or events that occur close together in proximity or time

preconventional moral reasoning Kohlberg's first level of moral reasoning, when children make decisions about morality based on avoiding punishment (stage 1) or gaining rewards (stage 2)

prekindergarten programs care and education programs for children one or two years prior to kindergarten

prelinguistic speech infant vocalizations without meaning

premoral stage Piaget's first stage of moral development, when children make decisions about right and wrong based only on how it directly affects them rather than considering other perspectives

prenatal period of development from conception to birth

preoperational stage Piaget's second stage of cognitive development, when children demonstrate egocentrism and utilize symbolic representation (approximately ages 2 to 7)

prepared learning environments spaces that include child-sized furnishings and didactic learning materials

preparedness safety and health related term that describes a state of readiness to handle accidents and emergency situations

preschool programs programs that offer less than full-day care and education services to children between ages 2 and 5

pretend play play that involves use of imagination and make-believe elements

preventive safety strategies techniques that seek to anticipate and avoid the potential for harm

primary grades elementary grades 1, 2, and 3; still considered early childhood education

print awareness broadening consciousness of written symbols as well as recognition of the connection between speaking and writing

private speech Vygotsky's term to describe the self-talk behavior often demonstrated by preschool children

problem solving systemic way of figuring things out

professional development the process of acquiring advanced knowledge and skills related to one's career

project approach approach that facilitates children's imaginations, creativity, problem-solving skills, and communication skills as the progress of projects is documented by teachers and family members throughout school with sketches, photos, models, and captions

props various materials and objects that contribute to the expansion of children's play

prosocial behaviors socially acceptable behavior

protective safety strategies measures and techniques used to safeguard individuals

proximodistal pattern how physical development proceeds from the center of the body outward to the extremities ("near" to "far")

psychomotor domain every aspect of physical development including perceptual-motor, fine motor, and gross motor abilities

psychosocial development Erikson's theory that encompasses both emotional and social factors

receptive vocabulary ability to understand spoken language

reciprocal teaching two-way interaction between teacher and learner where each contributes to and benefits by the educational interchange

redirection diverting children's attention to other tasks or objects

reflexes involuntary movements of the muscles

Reggio Emilia approach an approach embracing the contributions of young children to their own learning

resistant attachment another form of insecure attachment, when the infant stays close to the familiar caregiver before departure and displays angry behavior toward the caregiver on return

resource and referral agencies organizations advocating that individuals and organizations take responsibility for improving lives of children and families

reversibility cognitive ability to mentally view a sequence of events in reverse

romancing drawing with no particular intent and then labeling the drawing

room arrangement placement of equipment and materials in relation to the fixed physical features of the environment

rooting reflex a response in infants in which if something strokes the baby's check, it will turn toward the object, open its mouth, and attempt to suck

running record a form of written documentation used to record observed behaviors

scaffolding Vygotsky's term to describe the process of assistance given by a more able individual to help a less able individual perform

schemas existing knowledge or concerns

school-age child care (SACC) care and education provided for children between ages 6 and 12

scribble stage the first stage of drawing, when children make random marks on the paper with little deliberate thought and minimal control over the results

scripted teaching plans plans specifying word-forword what teachers should say and do during the course of a lesson

secure attachment pattern of attachment where the infant is distressed on the departure of a familiar caregiver but is easily comforted on the caregiver's return

self-conscious emotions an understanding that there are expectations or standards that one must meet

self-help skills physical behaviors that enable children to attend to some of their own needs for eating, dressing, toileting, and grooming self-propelled thinkers learners who are self-motivated to learn about something through discovery

semantics meanings associated with the sounds and words of a language

sensitive periods time of intense change when children are more receptive to stimulation followed by slower-paced intervals of less receptiveness

sensorimotor stage Piaget's first stage of cognitive development, when children respond to their environment through sensory and motor behaviors (birth to approximately age 2)

sensory exploration process of using the senses to examine objects

service delivery systems developed by organizations to cut through some of the bureaucratic red tape so that individuals who qualify can receive services in a more timely manner

service projects children receive firsthand experiences at supporting their communities even as communities support them and their families

service providers individuals who provide specialized services to others

sexual abuse illegal mistreatment of individuals by another through physical or emotional actions that have sexual overtones

skills collection of abilities specific to an occupation

social competence the ability to effectively engage in appropriate social behaviors and maintain interpersonal relationships

social referencing infant may seek out the trusted adult and base response on the reactions exhibited by the adult

social smile emotional expressions of joy and interest

sociocentric Vygotsky's term describing the socially centered view of understanding

socioconventional knowledge knowledge of customs, laws, values, and language systems of social or cultural groups

sociocultural theory Vygotsky's theory that suggests language and culture affect learning

sociodramatic play dramatic play involving two or more children

soft-wired preliminary wiring of the brain

solitary play first category of social play, when the child plays alone without regard to the play activities of others

spatial awareness consciousness of the location of objects in relationship to the other objects

special needs any type of differences in learning abilities or styles that require significant adaptation of learning situations

spiral curriculum sequence of study where current content overlaps prior and subsequent learning content

standards the quality, and in some cases the minimum acceptable level of quality, judged appropriate by experts in the field

static reasoning thought process that focuses on the outcome of the transformation rather than the process of the transformation

stranger anxiety the infant expresses fear at the appearance of unfamiliar people

subjective statements of opinion or assumption

sucking reflex involuntary muscular response triggered when an object is placed in the infant's mouth

supervision direct observation and alert attention to nearby individuals, objects, and events

symbolic representation representing objects, actions, and ideas with symbols; using objects or actions to represent other objects or actions

symbolic stage Burner's third stage from ages 6 to 7 and onward in which individuals draw meaning from abstract concepts through the use of logic and problem solving

synapse a gap between neurons across which messages are sent

syntax sentence structure or language

tabula rasa Locke's view that children's minds are neither evil nor pure but rather "blank slates"

tactile experiences involving the sense of touch

task forces formed for a single purpose; members can be volunteers or appointees and frequently include school personnel as well

teachable moments informal teaching opportunities for helping children learn and practice appropriate safety, health, and nutrition behaviors

teacher-centered model that uses predetermined curriculum content that is sequenced by level of complexity, without direct involvement of the learners

teacher-centered curriculum curriculum that is designed according to predetermined criteria set by teachers or other entities

teacher certification license to teach issued by state departments of education to individuals after successful completion of predetermined standards telegraphic sentence truncated sentence of two or three key words but lacking less important details; frequently used by young children

temperament inborn, stable pattern of emotional response

temper tantrum utilizing emotional responses and behavior to achieve desired results

temporal dimension aspects of classroom climate related to time, such as daily schedules, routines, and transitions

thematic curriculum integrated exploration of general topics

thematic curriculum web graphic organizer used to visually construct the connections between various aspects of the theme

theory of psychosocial development Erikson's theory that describes a series of emotional-social crises, or conflicts, that must be resolved by the individual (Eight Ages of Man)

transformation change in the physical nature of objects

transitions periods of adjustment or change between activities or events

trust versus mistrust Erikson's first stage of psychosocial development, when the child faces the crisis of trust versus mistrust

tuberculosis skin tests state required test for children and adults who work in schools, hospitals, or restaurants used to detect tuberculosis

two-way communication interactions that result in the exchange of information

typical daily schedules usual temporal structure and sequence of the day

undernutrition see malnutrition

undifferentiated crying infant crying that sounds alike no matter what the cause

universal education the ideal of equitable education of both boys and girls

universal precautions the process of preventing and controlling infection by use of prescribed sanitary measures such as hand washing and wearing disposable gloves

unoccupied behavior Parten's term for children's noninvolvement in play accompanied with direct observation of the play of others

verbal mediation ability to attach names, or labels, to objects and processes

vernacular schools where individuals are taught in their native language

visual acuity sharp vision

visual discrimination ability to differentiate between symbols and patterns

visual memory images that have been processed by the brain

visual mode learning channel accessed through vision

visual-motor coordination the ability to match muscular responses and movements to visual input

visual tracking ability to follow moving objects with the eyes

Waldorf approach educational system developed by Rudolf Steiner

whole child phrase representing the view that children's development across the domains is both simultaneous and overlapping

zone of proximal development (ZPD) Vygotsky's term to describe the area of performance that is beyond an individual's ability if attempted alone but achievable if assisted by a more able individual

Index

Note: f indicates a figure, and *t* indicates a table.

Natural environment, 13, 308
Naturalism, 130, 308
Naturalistic observation, 187, 308
Nature-nurture controversy, 4–5, 48–49, 308
Needs
custodial, 224, 303
economic, 281–282
educational, 283–285
emotional, 180–181
hierarchy of, 180, 181*f*, 306
physical, 180, 224
safety, 179–181
social, 282
special, 12, 311 (*See also* Children with special needs)
Neglect, 87–88, 308
Networking, 308
Neural networks, 43–44, 45*f*, 47
Neurons, 43–44, 46*f*, 47, 308
No Child Left Behind Act, 114
Noise level, in classrooms, 230
Noncertified personnel, 111, 308
Normal school, 132, 308
Norms, developmental, 303
Nuclear families, 264, 308
Nursery school, 308
historical development of, 135–138
open-air, 136, 308
Nurturers, teachers as, 179–184
Nutrients, 251, 308
Nutrition, 251–255, 308

Obedience-and-punishment orientation, of moral reasoning, 91, 91*t*
Obesity, 251, 308
Object lesson, 132, 308
Object permanence, 54–55, 308
Objectivity, 189, 308
Observation, 186–192, 202, 308
documentation of, 188–192, 191*f*
in High/Scope approach, 163
in Montessori method, 150
naturalistic, 187, 308
participant, 309
Observational learning, 218, 308
Occipital lobe, 45*f*
One-way communication, 268–269, 268*t*, 308
Onlooker behavior, 6–7, 6*t*, 308
Open-air nursery school, 136, 308
Open-ended activities, 12, 184–185, 308
Open-ended questions, 162, 308
Open-framework curriculum, 164, 308
Oral language, 203–204
Orbis Pictus (Comenius), 129
Orphanages, 125
Outdoor activities
and psychomotor domain development, 37–38
safety of, 244, 245*f*
Outdoor play areas, 231
Outreach programs, 285–286, 308
Outside time, in High/Scope approach, 163

Palmar grasp reflex, 24, 308
Parallel play, 6*t*, 7, 309
Paraprofessionals, 117, 309
Parent(s). *See* Families
Parent education programs, 271, 309
Parent educators, 118, 309
Parent-teacher conferences. *See* Family-teacher conferences
Parentese, 23, 309
Parents-as-teachers (PAT) programs, 118, 283
Parietal lobe, 45*f*
Parten, Mildred, 6–7
Participant observation, 150, 309
Partnership practices, 284, 309
Pattern recognition, by infants, 22–23
Peabody, Elizabeth Palmer, 134
Pearson, Elizabeth Winsor, 137
Pedagogy, 309
Pedigogista, in Reggio Emilia approach, 158, 309
Peer play, competent forms of, 7–8
Peers
and social development, 89
in sociocultural theory, 62–63
Perceptual-motor development, 21, 35–36, 309
Perry Preschool Project, 159–161
Persistence -withdrawal, and temperament, 76*t*
Person-first language, 12, 309
Personality. *See* Affective domain
Personnel. *See also* Teacher(s)
certified, 111, 302
noncertified, 111, 308
Pestalozzi, Johann Heinrich, 130–132
Phases of attachment, 81, 81*t*, 309
Phonemes, 66, 309
Physical abuse, 87–88, 309
Physical dimensions, of classroom, 225–234, 309
Physical knowledge, 52, 309
Physical needs, 180, 224
Piaget, Jean
categories of knowledge of, 51–52
cognitive development theory of, 49–61, 50*f*, 53*t*, 63, 201
moral development stages of, 90–91
Piazzas, in Reggio Emilia approach, 158, 309
Pictorial stage, of drawing, 33–34, 33*t*, 309
Pilgrims, 126
Pincer grasp, 26, 309
Placement stage, of drawing, 33, 33*t*, 309
Plan-do-review process, 162, 309
Plasticity, of brain, 43, 309
Plato, 124
Play, 5–12, 201, 203, 309
associative, 6*t*, 7, 301
cognitive, 68–70, 70*t*
competent forms of, 7–8
constructive, 68–69, 70*t*, 303
cooperative, 6*t*, 7–8, 303
dramatic, 8–9, 69, 70*t*, 304
free (*See* Self-directed play)
functional, 68, 70*t*, 305

in High/Scope approach, 162
parallel, 6*t*, 7, 309
pretend, 8–12, 69, 203, 204, 310
self-directed, 6–7
social, 5–8, 6*t*
sociodramatic, 8, 69–70, 311
solitary, 6, 6*t*, 311
Playgrounds, safety of, 244, 245*f*
Pons, 45*f*
Positive guidance, 213–217
Positive reinforcement, 164–165, 309
Postconventional level, of moral reasoning, 91*t*, 94, 309
Power struggle, misbehavior and, 214–215
Practical life area, in Montessori method, 151
Pragmatics, 66, 309
Praise, 217, 309
Pratt, Caroline, 137
Preattachment, 81, 81*t*, 309
Precausal reasoning, 57, 309
Preconventional level, of moral reasoning, 91–92, 91*t*, 309
Prekindergarten programs, 114, 309
Prelinguistic speech, 63, 64*t*, 309
Premoral stage, of moral development, 90, 309
Prenatal, 309
Prenatal environment
brain development in, 43, 44*f*
gross motor development in, 25, 25*f*
physical development in, 26, 27*f*
sensory abilities in, 21
Preoperational stage, of cognitive development, 53*t*, 55–58, 309
Prepared learning environments, 149–150, 310
Preparedness, for emergencies, 244–246, 310
Preschool, 113, 114, 310
in Creative Curriculum approach, 167–171
in direct instruction method, 165
Perry Preschool Project, 159–161
Preschool-age children
classrooms for, 227
and gross motor development, 28
supervision of, 242–243
Preschool Curriculum Comparison Study, 160, 166
Preservice teachers, 104, 108–109
Pretend play, 8–12, 69, 203, 204, 310
Preventive safety strategies, 242–243, 310
Prewriting, 206*f*
Primary motor cortex, 45*f*
Primary school, 117, 310
Primary somatosensory cortex, 45*f*
Print awareness, 204, 310
Private speech, 62, 310
Problem solving, 212, 214–215, 310
Professional development, 193–194, 310
Professional organizations, 194
Professionals, teachers as, 192–194
Progressive movement, 139